Artificial Intelligence in Software Engineering

Artificial Intelligence in Software Engineering

Guest Editors

Linda Vickovic
Maja Braović

MDPI

Basel • Beijing • Wuhan • Barcelona • Belgrade • Novi Sad • Cluj • Manchester

Guest Editors
Linda Vickovic
Faculty of Electrical Engineering
Mechanical Engineering and
Naval Architecture
University of Split
Split
Croatia

Maja Braović
Faculty of Electrical Engineering
Mechanical Engineering and
Naval Architecture
University of Split
Split
Croatia

Editorial Office
MDPI AG
Grosspeteranlage 5
4052 Basel, Switzerland

This is a reprint of the Special Issue, published open access by the journal *Applied Sciences* (ISSN 2076-3417), freely accessible at: https://www.mdpi.com/journal/applsci/special_issues/87UDOZAV6Z.

For citation purposes, cite each article independently as indicated on the article page online and as indicated below:

Lastname, A.A.; Lastname, B.B. Article Title. *Journal Name* **Year**, *Volume Number*, Page Range.

ISBN 978-3-7258-7721-8 (Hbk)
ISBN 978-3-7258-7722-5 (PDF)
https://doi.org/10.3390/books978-3-7258-7722-5

Contents

About the Editors

Linda Vicković

Linda Vicković is a Full Professor in Computing Science at the Faculty of Electrical Engineering, Mechanical Engineering and Naval Architecture (FESB) at the University of Split, Croatia. Her primary research interests encompass software engineering, data mining, deep learning, convolutional neural networks, image processing, and discrete event simulation. In terms of ongoing projects and major collaborations, she has been an active member of the ALICE Collaboration at the European Organization for Nuclear Research (CERN) since 2004, where she originally conducted her doctoral research with the ALICE DAQ group.

Maja Braović

Maja Braović is an associate professor at the Faculty of Electrical Engineering, Mechanical Engineering, and Naval Architecture, University of Split, Croatia. Her research interests include artificial intelligence, natural language processing, computational linguistics, and C4ISR systems. She currently focuses on AI applications in civil protection and dual-use technologies. She has participated in numerous projects, including the European Network on Extreme Fire Behavior (NERO), National Competence Centres in the framework of EuroHPC (Phase 1 and 2), and FirEURisk—Developing a Holistic, Risk-Wise Strategy for European Wildfire Management.

Preface

Welcome to this Special Issue on Artificial Intelligence in Software Engineering. We find ourselves at a pivotal moment in the history of technology. The rapid and relentless advancement of Artificial Intelligence (AI) is no longer a distant promise; it is an active force profoundly reshaping the industrial landscape. Within this revolution, Software Engineering (SE) stands out as a domain on the cusp of an unprecedented and exciting transformation. As the digital backbone of our modern world expands, software systems are growing exponentially in scale and complexity. Traditional engineering methodologies, while foundational, are being increasingly challenged to meet the modern demand for uncompromising reliability, speed, adaptability, and quality. It is here that AI steps in—not merely as an automated tool, but as a paradigm-shifting partner in the development lifecycle.

This Special Issue was conceived to explore and document this critical intersection. Our goal is to bring together high-quality, cutting-edge research that illuminates how AI technologies—encompassing machine learning, natural language processing, knowledge-based systems, and intelligent decision-making algorithms—can revolutionize the entire spectrum of software engineering processes.

The contributions and topics curated for this collection span the complete software development lifecycle, including:

1. Requirements and Planning: Leveraging semantic analysis and NLP to untangle complex stakeholder needs and refine system requirements.
2. Design and Implementation: Utilizing AI models to automate coding tasks, suggest architectural improvements, and accelerate development.
3. Quality Assurance and Testing: Showcasing how machine learning can predict vulnerabilities, identify anomalies, and optimize automated regression testing.
4. Deployment and Maintenance: Exploring AI-driven CI/CD pipelines, predictive analytics for resource management, and self-healing mechanisms for autonomous software maintenance.

Beyond mere automation, the research highlighted here emphasizes AI's role in enhancing data-driven decision-making and personalizing user experiences. By bridging the gap between theoretical AI research and practical software engineering applications, we aim to provide a vital platform for emerging insights, novel frameworks, and empirical evaluations.

We invite you to explore the studies presented in this issue. It is our sincere hope that this collection will foster interdisciplinary collaboration and deepen our collective understanding of how AI-driven innovation is redefining the principles, processes, and ultimate outcomes of software engineering for the next generation of intelligent systems.

Linda Vickovic and Maja Braović
Guest Editors

applied sciences

MDPI

Article

Combining Model-Based Systems Engineering and Knowledge-Centric Systems Engineering to Design Reliable Systems in Practice

Juan Manuel Morote [1], Jose Luis de la Vara [2,*], Giovanni Giachetti [3,4], Clara Ayora [2] and Luis Alonso [5]

1 Independent Researcher, 02003 Albacete, Spain
2 Departamento de Sistemas Informáticos, Universidad de Castilla-La Mancha, Avda. España s/n, 02071 Albacete, Spain; clara.ayora@uclm.es
3 Facultad de Ingeniería, Universidad Andrés Bello, Antonio Varas 880, Providencia, Santiago 7591538, Chile; giovanni.giachetti@unab.cl
4 Valencian Research Institute for Artificial Intelligence (VRAIN), Universitat Politècnica de València, Camí de Vera, s/n, 46022 Valencia, Spain
5 The REUSE Company, C/ Margarita Salas 16, 28919 Madrid, Spain; luis.alonso@reusecompany.com
* Correspondence: joseluis.delavara@uclm.es

Abstract

The use and importance of complex software-intensive systems are growing. As they are used in a wider range of situations in which dependability must be ensured, the reliability of the systems and of their components needs to be addressed throughout their lifecycle, including at early development stages. In addition, the means used to deal with reliability need to be linked to and integrated into the overall systems engineering practices and processes. Within this context, we present an approach to design reliable systems in practice in the scope of model-based systems engineering (MBSE) and knowledge-centric systems engineering (KCSE), two systems engineering perspectives whose adoption is increasing. While MBSE relies on explicit system models, KCSE places artificial intelligence at its core to capture, formalise, and reason over system knowledge. Both perspectives are combined to model systems and analyse whether their design addresses the expected system reliability properties, leveraging knowledge representation, natural language processing, and inference mechanisms. The approach links the processes and tools of Arcadia/Capella for MBSE and of SES Engineering Studio for KCSE. A joint application process has been defined for system modelling, ontology development, structured textual requirements specification, traceability management, and model quality analysis, all of which are targeted at system reliability. For validation, the approach has been applied on eight systems that cover five different application domains, considering tens of diagrams, of knowledge elements, of reliability properties, and of analysis possibilities. Based on the validation results, we argue that the approach is a feasible means to design reliable systems. The approach is also the first one that effectively combines MBSE with Arcadia/Capella and KCSE with SES to design reliable systems in practice.

Keywords: model-based systems engineering; knowledge-centric systems engineering; reliability; system design; artificial intelligence; Arcadia; Capella; SES Engineering Studio

1. Introduction

Software-intensive systems pervade society nowadays. For example, cyber-physical systems, automated systems, autonomous systems, and software-intensive electronic sys-

https://doi.org/10.3390/app16052179

tems and components play a major role in communications, Industry 4.0, healthcare, and transport, making our lives easier and better. The range of functions and applications of the systems is increasing, leading to a larger set of usages in which dependability must be ensured [1]. For many systems, it is not acceptable that they fail or that their failure can pose an unreasonable risk. In critical domains, dependability is addressed in accordance with industrially agreed best practices presented in engineering and assurance standards [2], e.g., DO-178C [3] in aerospace, ISO 26262 [4] in automotive, and EN 50128 [5] in railway. The quality of the systems needs to be guaranteed so that they can be deemed dependable, including their reliability, and so that they are allowed to operate.

Reliability can be defined as the ability of systems and components to perform their required functions under stated conditions for a specified period of time [6]. In essence, reliability relates to the extent to which a system behaves well and without failure. Reliability needs to be considered during the whole system lifecycle, from inception until decommission. For example, systems can be monitored during operation to analyse if their behaviour is as defined. At early development stages, reliability must be addressed when a system is envisioned, specified, and designed, i.e., when engineers make decisions about how the system will be. It is at these stages that the expected functionality and operation conditions of a system are defined, as well as how they will be satisfied. Means to characterise and analyse system reliability according to the decisions made must be used.

The means used to characterise and analyse system reliability must also be linked to and integrated into the overall systems engineering practices and processes. We focus on two perspectives currently used in industry, whose adoption is growing, and that can be used together: model-based systems engineering (MBSE) [7] and knowledge-centric systems engineering (KCSE) [8]. In MBSE, models that represent systems and their elements (e.g., in diagrams) are used to specify, analyse, realise, and manage system artefacts. MBSE is commonly applied for complex systems in a wide range of application domains, such as aerospace, automotive, defence, and railway. KCSE specialises in MBSE from the main principle that systems and software engineering processes can exploit knowledge bases about systems and their lifecycles. These knowledge bases, which are traditional artificial intelligence (AI) means [9], can correspond to ontologies that characterise system domains and consider different types of knowledge elements and of semantic aspects. The growing complexity of system architectures and the need for sound knowledge require approaches that can capture, structure, and reason over diverse engineering knowledge. KCSE meets this requirement by using AI techniques such as ontologies and automated reasoning to facilitate systematic analysis, traceability, and decision-making. These capabilities are particularly relevant in the field of reliability engineering, where implicit expert knowledge, cross-domain dependencies, and early-stage uncertainty must be managed explicitly. The ontologies can be employed for, e.g., system specification and analysis. KCSE also usually exploits other traditional AI techniques, e.g., natural language processing (NLP). The use of AI for different tasks is positioned as a key aspect for current and future systems and software engineering (see e.g., [10–13]).

We present an approach that combines MBSE and KCSE to design reliable systems in practice. The approach integrates (a) the Arcadia method and the Capella tool for MBSE [14] and (b) SES Engineering Studio [15] (hereafter referred to as SES) for KCSE. Arcadia is an MBSE method for systems, hardware, and software architectural design developed by Thales, and Capella is the tool that implements and supports Arcadia, providing methodological guidance and intuitive model edition features. SES is a tool to orchestrate the development of all kinds of systems (hardware, software, hybrid…), supporting interoperability between an unlimited number of existing systems engineering tools. SES integrates several (sub-)tools for specific KCSE tasks, e.g., ontology management and system artefact

https://doi.org/10.3390/app16052179

quality analysis. Many companies from different application domains use and support Arcadia/Capella and SES in the industry, most often companies that develop critical systems. Nonetheless, a reliability-oriented joint application of Arcadia/Capella and SES has not been defined. Our approach has been developed in the scope of two large-scale industry-academia European projects: iRel40 (intelligent Reliability 4.0) [16] and VALU3S (Verification and Validation—V&V—of Automated Systems' Safety and Security) [17]. The projects dealt with how to increase the reliability of modern systems and applications and with how to improve the way suitability and quality of safety- and security-critical systems are confirmed, respectively. Industrial partners from the projects expressed the need for and their interest in combining Arcadia/Capella and SES.

The approach defines how Arcadia/Capella and SES can be combined for the design of reliable systems in practice. It also considers compliance with standards. The approach consists of five activities: (1) System modelling, (2) Ontology development, (3) Structured textual requirements specification, (4) Traceability management, and (5) Model quality analysis. The activities address different reliability needs and use Arcadia/Capella, SES, or both, as well as AI. For validation, the use of the approach on eight systems has been studied, covering five different application domains and tens of diagrams of knowledge elements, of reliability properties, and of analysis possibilities.

The main contribution of our work is the development and application of an approach that effectively combines MBSE with Arcadia/Capella and KCSE with SES to design reliable systems in practice. To the best of our knowledge, other researchers have not presented such results. Practitioners and researchers interested in or working with MBSE and KCSE can benefit from the approach, and they can now know more precisely how to use Arcadia/Capella and SES together for reliable-system design, as well as how this joint use has been enacted for specific systems. Beyond the contributions on tool interoperability, the approach sets principles on how to specify reliability data in Arcadia/Capella diagrams and how to use reliability-related information in different KCSE tasks, with the ultimate goal of designing reliable systems.

In addition, we extend our prior work. First, we outlined our vision to link Arcadia/Capella and SES for model-based reliability-oriented system design [18], introducing possibilities and alternatives. Later, we presented the possibilities and alternatives selected and their initial application [19]. The main extensions in this paper from these prior publications are: (a) the update of the approach according to the latest versions of Arcadia/Capella and of SES; (b) a revised, more thorough description of the activities of the approach, including major details not presented yet such as all the reliability characteristics that can be specified in Arcadia/Capella diagrams and the existing SES quality analyses that can be used, and; (c) a full validation considering different systems in depth and covering all the activities of the approach. This results in an updated, complete, and validated description of the approach, which facilitates its application and provides evidence of its effectiveness.

The next sections present the background of our work (Section 2), the approach (Section 3), its validation (Section 4), and our main conclusions (Section 5).

2. Background

The background is divided into Arcadia/Capella, SES, and related work.

2.1. Arcadia/Capella

Arcadia/Capella [14] is an Eclipse-based open-source MBSE solution. While Arcadia serves as a methodology for architecture engineering of systems, software, and hardware, Capella (Figure 1) functions as the implementation tool for Arcadia. Major companies,

https://doi.org/10.3390/app16052179

including Thales, GMV, and Siemens, are among those that utilise Arcadia/Capella in their operations.

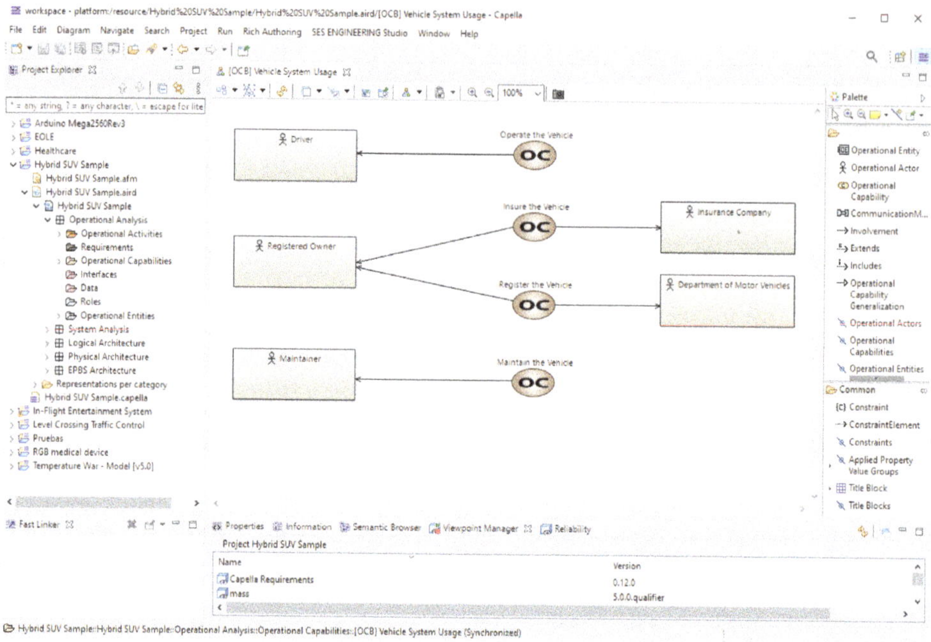

Figure 1. Capella screenshot.

Capella implements specific functionalities to follow the Arcadia method, such as the method explorer and a wide range of modelling accelerators and aids, so that systems engineers can focus on design instead of on model maintenance. Capella is a modelling tool that provides a wide range of diagram types organised into the five engineering steps defined in Arcadia, and whose use can be tailored to project- and system-specific needs and characteristics:

1. Operational Analysis captures the goals and conditions that system users need to meet in their work or mission, without consideration of any particular solution or system to accomplish these goals. The main diagrams of this step are the Operational Capabilities diagram, Operational Activity Interaction diagram, Operational Activity Breakdown diagram, and Operational Architecture diagram.
2. System Analysis specifies how the system is expected to meet the users' needs, as outlined in the prior Operational Analysis or in the form of requirements provided by a client. The main diagrams of this step are the System Functional Dataflow diagram, System Functional Breakdown diagram, System Architecture diagram, Functional Scenario diagram, and Exchange Scenario diagram.
3. Logical Architecture represents the initial design decisions of a solution's architecture. The main diagrams of this step are the Logical Functional Breakdown diagram, Logical Functional Dataflow diagram, Logical Component Breakdown diagram, and Logical Architecture diagram.
4. Physical Architecture provides a detailed specification of all the subsystems or components to be developed or acquired. It also defines the system integration, verification, and validation phases. The main diagrams of this step are the Physical Functional

https://doi.org/10.3390/app16052179

Breakdown diagram, Physical Functional Dataflow diagram, Physical Component Breakdown diagram, and Physical Architecture diagram.

5. End-Product Breakdown Structure (EPBS) establishes the expectations for each system component and specifies the conditions for their integration, leading up to product V&V. The main diagrams in this step are the Configuration Items Breakdown diagram and EPBS Architecture diagram.

Capella offers extension and integration mechanisms, e.g., viewpoints to extend and enhance system specification. Expert knowledge is required to define viewpoints for specific domains, which are implemented using Capella Studio [20]. Viewpoints define extensions that are specific to the model elements managed by Capella, define additional properties to the elements, and can add a new group of commands to the palette of the diagram editor.

2.2. SES Engineering Studio

SES [15] is a commercial environment for KCSE that different large companies use in their systems and software engineering processes, e.g., Airbus, Toyota, and Ariane, among others. It is a software solution specifically created to coordinate the development of diverse system types, including hardware, software, and hybrid systems. SES facilitates seamless interaction between many existing systems engineering tools, such as tools for requirements management, MBSE, simulation, risk management, RAMS (reliability, availability, maintainability, and safety) management, and MS Office.

SES integrates various (sub-)tools to support key KCSE activities, most notably:

- RQA—Quality Studio (hereafter referred to as RQA) for system artefact quality analysis. It allows users to define, calculate, manage, and report quality for any engineering item that can be accessed through any available connection in SES.
- V&V Studio for V&V management. V&V is connected to the notion of quality assurance and management. V&V Studio merges the three concepts, managing the V&V actions necessary for quality assessment processes.
- RAT—Authoring tools (hereafter referred to as RAT) for text-based system specification. It is a tool for system analysts and engineers during the writing or model creation process.
- Traceability Studio for traceability management. It provides support to manage and specify traces between elements of system artefacts and automatically identify potentially missing traces.
- Knowledge Manager for ontology management. It supports the development and maintenance of knowledge bases from a systems engineering standpoint, enabling the storage of valuable system information in a shared system knowledge repository.

When entering SES, the user can select the different artefacts that they want to manage for KCSE, considering the different functionality provided by the (sub-)tools. Connections are established with the artefact sources, e.g., Excel spreadsheets and Capella projects. All in all, SES can be regarded as an expert, rule-based system for systems and software engineering that exploits semantic information about a domain and that uses AI techniques such as NLP and machine learning.

SES exploits ontologies that consist of five distinct parts [21]:

1. Terminology, which includes the terms used in a specific domain and their syntactic information. For instance, the word 'car' is a noun.
2. Conceptual Model, which focuses on semantics and relationships. For instance, the semantics of 'car' can be 'system' and it specialises 'vehicle'.
3. Patterns, which are templates (aka boilerplates) used for structured system information specification and analysis.

https://doi.org/10.3390/app16052179

4. Formalisation, which involves the semantic representation of system information according to patterns.
5. Inference Rules, which are procedures utilised to derive information, such as determining the correctness of specifications based on the structure and content of textual requirements and model elements.

Each part of an ontology uses elements of the previous ones. The elements of the different parts are employed for quality analysis, structured textual specification, and traceability management.

2.3. Related Work

Related work can be divided into general work that has dealt with, e.g., reliability aspects in MBSE or ontology-based systems and software engineering, work with Arcadia/Capella, and work with SES.

As the work on and interest in MBSE has increased, it has become easier to find general work on, e.g., model-based safety analysis [22], V&V [23], risk management [24], and traceability [25]. Pieces of work on system modelling and reliability can be found for specific languages and tools such as AADL [26], Papyrus [27], Rhapsody [28], and SysML [29], but not integrated with KCSE. It has also become easier to find publications on the use of ontologies to support different systems and software engineering activities, e.g., safety, security, and dependability risk assessment [30], requirements engineering [31], and software reliability modelling [32].

Closer to this paper, some publications have used both models and ontologies for systems and software engineering. The goals of these publications include the definition and usage of ontologies for software [33] and V&V [34] processes in general, as well as more specific purposes. For instance, Dong et al. [35] proposed an ontology and semantic rules for traceability management in MBSE, Jinzhi et al. [36] explored the concept of cognitive digital twin, and Peugeot [37] presented the GONG environment for ontology-based MBSE with UML class diagrams. Visions and initiatives have also been reported in the context of ESA [38] and NASA [39]. Nonetheless, the structure and content of the ontologies used in prior general work are different to those exploited by SES, which consist of further element types, are based on KCSE industrial needs and practices in several domains and enable a more detailed and broader system specification and analysis possibilities. In addition, to the best of our knowledge, the publications that have combined models and ontologies for systems and software engineering have not focused on the design of reliable systems in compliance with standards.

Different publications have presented work with Arcadia/Capella, addressing aspects areas such as cybersecurity risk assessment [40] and integration, verification, and validation [41], also considering safety [42], safety-security [43], and reliability aspects [44]. Some authors have addressed solutions and usages more specific than only the application of Arcadia/Capella in a given case. For instance, Brau et al. [45] proposed a solution for satellite system availability evaluation on the basis of its physical architecture, and Brunel et al. [46] defined a viewpoint for formal safety and security assessment of system architectures with Alloy. It has been mentioned that there is an interest in an ontology-driven framework for simulation model development connected with Arcadia/Capella [47], but such a solution does not appear to have been created.

The joint use of Arcadia/Capella with other engineering methods and tools has also been presented, e.g., with Cyber Architect [43], STPA (System-Theoretic Process Analysis) [48], and Valispace [49]. These pieces of work aim to provide broader, more suitable solutions that mitigate the limitations of the different individual methods and tools. This is in line with our integration with SES, which aims for Arcadia/Capella and

https://doi.org/10.3390/app16052179

SES to benefit each other to design reliable systems. Regarding commercial tools, some (e.g., ATICA [50]) support model-based safety analysis with Capella, covering analyses for faults, failures, and reliability in general. As indicated below in Section 3, these kinds of tools complement our work. In essence, they can provide input about reliability data and needs to consider for, e.g., system architecture design. Although the work on and interest in Arcadia/Capella is growing both in academia and in industry, we are not aware of any publication by other authors that has reported in detail the link of Arcadia/Capella with KCSE.

In relation to work with SES, integration of SES and system modelling has been reported or referred to in the past. Historically, structured textual requirements specification with RAT and requirements quality analysis with RQA have been proposed as possible parts of MBSE processes (e.g., [51]), although not integrated as such. For instance, requirements specification on diagrams was not possible. Nonetheless, SES sub-tools have evolved during the last few years to enable full integration.

In the scope of the AMASS project (Architecture-driven, Multi-concern and Seamless Assurance and Certification of Cyber-Physical Systems) [52], we worked on different aspects of the integration of KCSE with SES and MBSE. For assurance and certification purposes, RQA was integrated with a method and tool for model-based assurance evidence management [53] and was used for quality analysis of safety cases [54]. The use of SES features for traceability and for semantic information search was also studied [55]. For artefact quality analysis [8], progress was made in relation to requirements metrics (e.g., based on the Conceptual Model part of an ontology), model metrics for Simulink, SysML, and UML diagrams, and the use of checklists for manual artefact analysis, in addition to analysis of artefact quality evolution [56]. We also worked on ontology development in the context of compliance with standards [57], but not considering the combination of MBSE and KCSE.

Attention has been paid to facilitate model reuse with SES for different system modelling languages, e.g., SysML [58]. This is based on the more effective semantics-based searches that SES can enable when compared to other MBSE tools such as Rhapsody and Papyrus. Tool interoperability [59] and trace discovery [60] have been and are a major concern for SES, including interoperability with MBSE tools and model element traceability.

As can be observed, progress has been made towards the integration of system modelling and SES, especially recently. However, in-depth work on the link of Arcadia/Capella and SES to design a reliable system has only been presented in our prior publications, which present the previous, reduced versions of our approach.

3. Approach Description

Our approach to designing reliable systems in practice combines (a) MBSE with Arcadia/Capella and (b) KCSE with SES. It mainly exploits available means in these solutions, including AI-based SES capabilities. The approach adapts how the means are used to the specific needs of reliable-system design and provides an integrated process that combines MBSE and KCSE. The approach is also aligned with how practitioners use Arcadia/Capella [61] and SES [62].

As shown in Figure 2, the approach has been divided into five activities for System modelling, Ontology development, Structured textual requirements specification, Traceability management, and Model quality analysis, all of which are targeted at system reliability. Structured textual requirements specification, Traceability management, and Model quality analysis use the results from System modelling and Ontology development. It must be noted that SES is a proprietary solution; thus, all the tool support that the approach

https://doi.org/10.3390/app16052179

exploits cannot be shared via, e.g., an open-source repository, and full disclosure of SES implementation details is not possible.

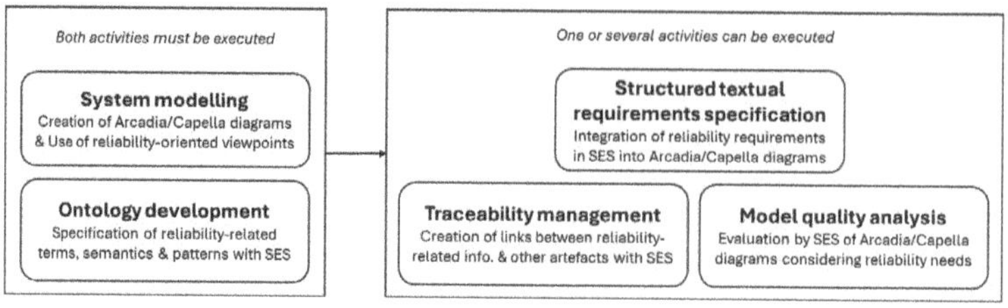

Figure 2. Overview of the approach.

The following sub-sections describe the approach activities, using an in-flight entertainment (IFE) system as a running example. IFE refers to the entertainment available to aircraft passengers during a flight, which must be reliable and safe. With the sometimes miles of wiring involved, voltage leaks and arcing can become a problem. For instance, an IFE system was implicated in the crash of Swissair Flight 111 in 1998 [63]. To address possible issues, IFE systems are typically isolated from the main systems of an aircraft. There exist public examples of IFE models [14] and of reference requirements [64].

3.1. System Modelling

The initial step of the approach involves creating Arcadia/Capella diagrams. The selection of Arcadia/Capella steps and diagram types will vary depending on the goal and extent of the modelling project. For instance, if the requirements are managed in DOORS, there might not be a need to model requirements in Arcadia/Capella diagrams. For the IFE system, a Physical Architecture diagram contains different physical components such as the passenger remote control, video server unit, and private video display unit (Figure 3). Arcadia/Capella diagrams could be part of the Software Requirements Data and the Design Description that DO-178C requires.

An important feature of our approach is the extension of Capella, allowing the specification of reliability information for diagram elements (Figure 3; Reliability Attributes below). We have created viewpoints with the Capella Studio development environment (Figure 4) that can be used for different systems. Certain diagrams may contain information regarding anticipated reliability features, while other diagrams may depict actual features. Such actual features are represented in physical architecture diagrams. The determination of reliability information will follow the specification, decomposition, and refinement steps of Arcadia, from high-level characteristics in logical diagrams to lower-level characteristics in physical diagrams.

For the development of the viewpoints, first, we studied which diagrams could be correctly extended in Capella Studio. Once this was confirmed, we examined for which elements of the diagram it made sense to add reliability information. We then chose what viewpoints would be developed and the information to be included using them. After the implementation, the behaviour of the viewpoints was tested within Capella Studio. Finally, the viewpoints were installed in Capella and activated in the corresponding diagrams.

The Arcadia/Capella diagrams and their respective elements to which reliability information can be added using the developed viewpoints are as follows:

- Logical Architecture diagram: Logical Components and Logical Actors.
- Physical Architecture diagram: Physical Components and Physical Actors.
- EPBS Architecture: Configuration Items.
- System Functional Dataflow diagram: System Functions.

https://doi.org/10.3390/app16052179

- Logical Functional Dataflow diagram: Logical Functions.
- Physical Functional Dataflow diagram: Physical Functions.

Two different viewpoints have been developed: one with reliability and environment information for the Logical Architecture, Physical Architecture, and EPBS Architecture diagrams, and another for the functions in the System Functional Dataflow, Logical Functional Dataflow, and System Functional Dataflow diagrams. The first viewpoint consists of two parts. The first part contains general attributes of reliability, while the second part contains attributes on environmental aspects. The attributes have been selected from existing sources, e.g., [65–68]. The information to be added to the viewpoint can be adapted to the types of elements or systems under development. Appendix A lists the complete set of reliability attributes (e.g., Mean Time Between Failure and Failures in Time) and of environmental aspect attributes (e.g., Temperature and Humidity) considered. The second viewpoint applies to the system functions, logical functions, or physical functions of dataflow diagrams. It adds the attribute "response time" to those functions.

As an example, the IFE system requires voltage considerations for its elements [64], which can be specified in Capella using the viewpoint. The value of viewpoint attributes related to failure rates may vary depending on the assurance level of the system.

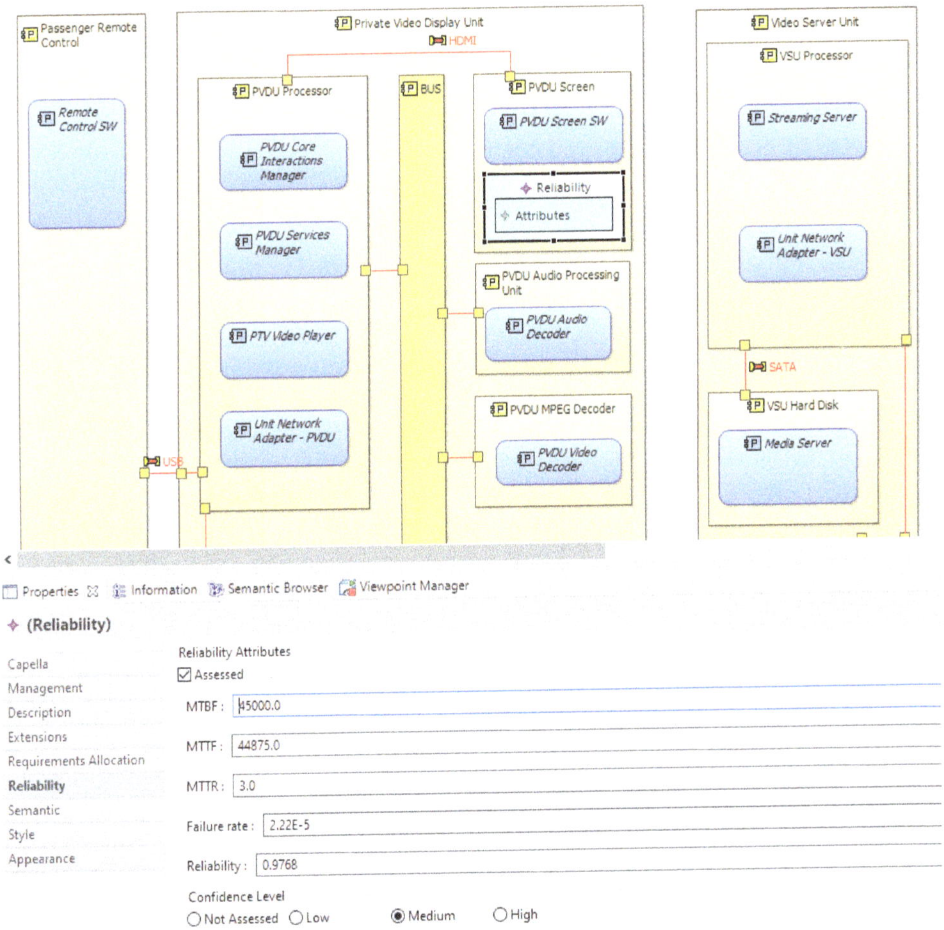

Figure 3. Arcadia/Capella diagram and reliability viewpoint.

https://doi.org/10.3390/app16052179

It is important to note that our approach does not involve conducting analyses to obtain system reliability data, such as fault tree analysis. It is assumed that the required information, including the specifications of existing components that will be part of a system, is available or has been obtained. Arcadia/Capella diagrams have been integrated with various reliability and safety analysis methods and tools, e.g., ATICA [50]. These methods and tools, and others, can be utilised prior to conducting the System Modelling activity, and their outcomes can be used as inputs for the activity.

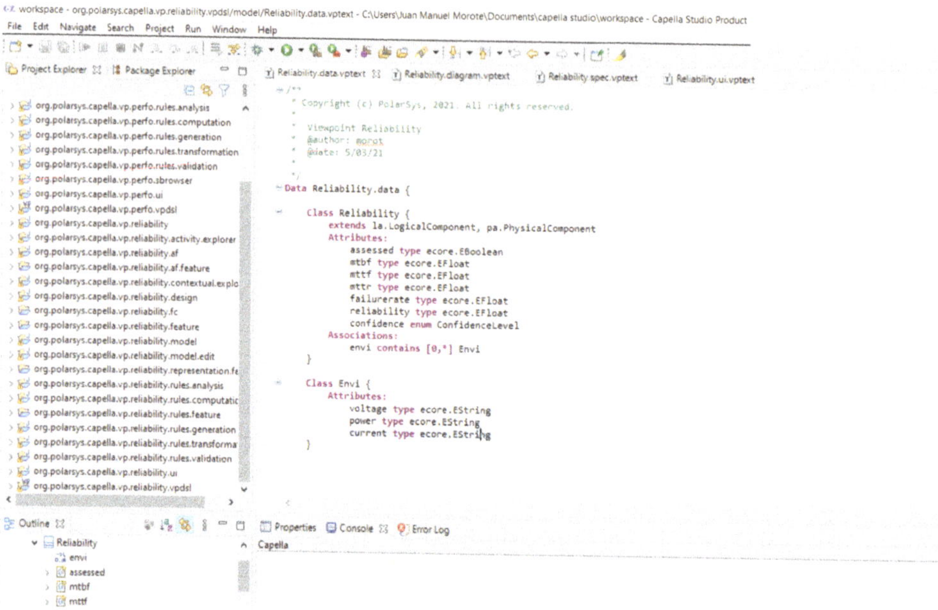

Figure 4. Capella Studio: definition of attributes of a viewpoint.

3.2. Ontology Development

In modern organisations, knowledge has become one of the most valuable assets. Effective management of this asset is crucial for success. This involves gathering knowledge from various sources and storing it in repositories. This knowledge can then be reused as a key asset in systems and software projects. Knowledge Manager supports these needs via storage of knowledge by means of ontologies in well-structured repositories, ensuring easy access and maintenance. The knowledge stored is organised within a System Knowledge Repository and is used by other SES tools.

Ontologies are necessary to apply KCSE with SES, including for AI-based capabilities. Default ontologies are provided by SES for various languages, containing predefined terms, semantic categories, and patterns, among other elements. These ontologies must be customised and expanded to meet the specific needs of system domains and reliability analysis.

Our approach does not define specific needs for the Formalisation and Inference Rules parts of the ontologies used by SES, but only reutilizes their existing elements for purposes such as quality analysis. The rest of the parts must include specific elements:

1. In the Terminology part, the user defines terms related to the domain, such as those pertaining to reliability, as well as those from relevant engineering and assurance standards. System-specific terms can be automatically imported from Arcadia/Capella diagrams.

https://doi.org/10.3390/app16052179

2. In the Conceptual Model part, the user specifies the semantic categories for terms, such as those related to standards, and specifies the relationship types between system artefacts. All the ontologies created for standards have two clusters, one for the glossary of terms and another for the acronyms (Figure 5).
3. In the Patterns part, the user can add, edit, or delete system specification patterns. The approach focuses on patterns for reliability and safety requirements. A total of 26 sentence patterns have been specified from the literature [69–71]. An example of the patterns is the following: When detecting <failure modes> <within-before-after-exactly at-no later than-every>, <Logical component> should <alarm> <for relevant persona>.

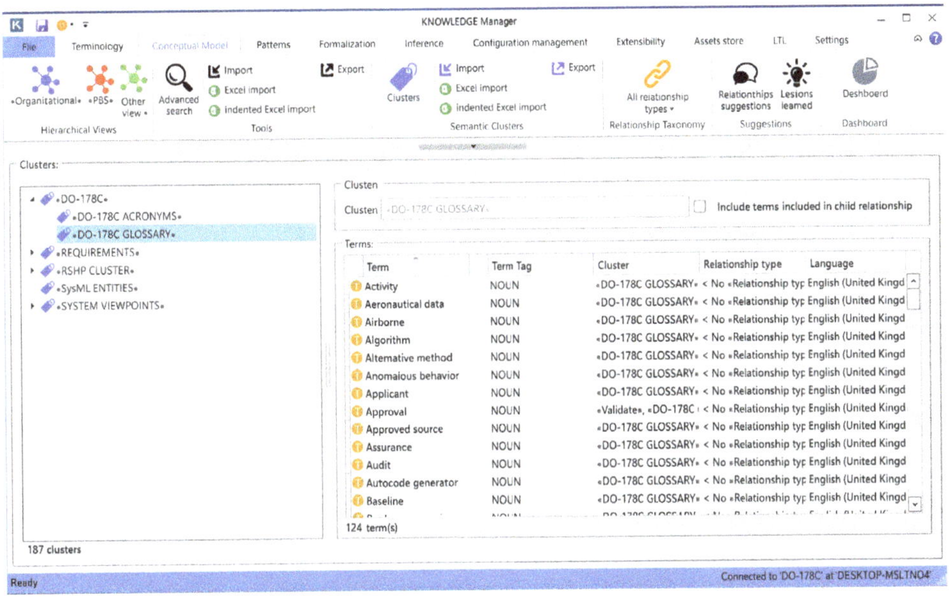

Figure 5. Ontology for the DO-178C standard in Knowledge Manager.

These elements are used in other activities of the approach, e.g., for NLP and reasoning. NLP exploits terms and their syntactic information from the Terminology part, their relationships and semantic information from the Conceptual Model part, and references to terms, to syntactic information, and to semantic information from the Patterns part. Reasoning (Inference Rules part) is mainly based on elements of the other parts of an ontology via procedures that consider these elements.

The ontologies are tailored to specific scopes, such as reliability considerations, system domains, and engineering and assurance standards. SES also provides ontology management functionality [21], including copy and merge, enabling users to jointly utilise content from multiple base ontologies while also managing ontology versions. This functionality also considers possible semantic conflicts when merging ontologies from different domains or overlapping standards, warning users and guiding them in their resolution.

Regarding the IFE system:

1. The DO-178C standard incorporates relevant terms such as 'configuration item', 'high-level requirement', 'memory device', and 'safety monitoring', 'video monitor' is a term from the Arcadia/Capella diagrams of the system, and failure is a reliability-related term (in addition to a DO-178C one).

2. The 'video monitor' term is classified as a 'component' based on its semantics.
3. The pattern 'The <component characteristic> of the <component> shall be between NUMBER and NUMBER <unit>' can be applied to specify certain characteristics of a component, such as stating that 'The touch temperature of the video monitor shall be between 0 and 49 Celsius degrees'.

3.3. Structured Textual Requirements Specification

Using the RAT tool as a plug-in (Figure 6), an engineer can specify textual requirements on Arcadia/Capella diagrams based on SES ontologies and using NLP. These requirements are linked to diagram elements such as functions of a System Functional Breakdown diagram or components of a Logical Architecture diagram. NLP features analyse the content of textual requirements to determine, e.g., whether they match an established, recommended specification pattern.

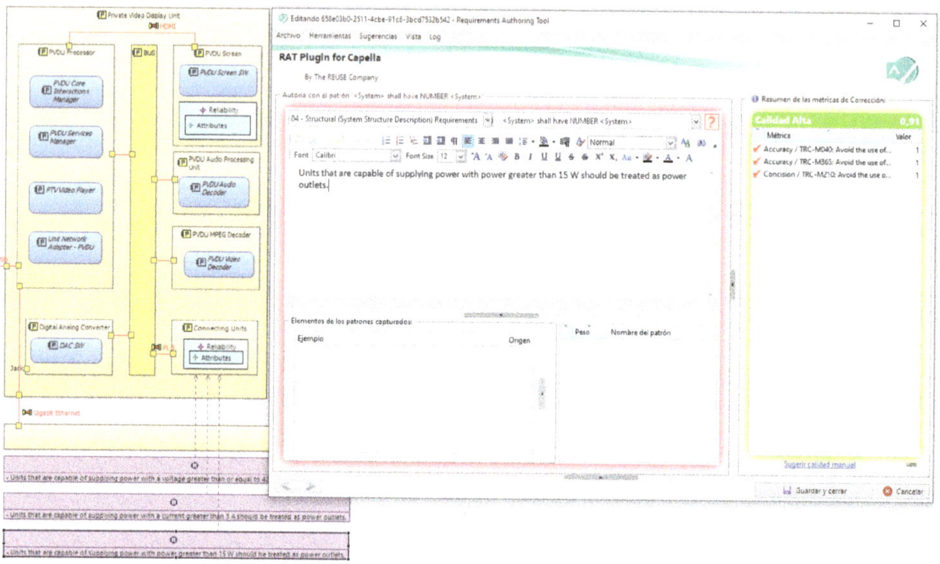

Figure 6. Requirement specification on Capella with RAT.

Writing requirements can be a challenging task that requires familiarity with, e.g., the appropriate vocabulary, specification structures, and measurement units determined for a project, and with quality standards or regulations to conform to. As a solution, RAT is a valuable tool that can assist in creating requirements specifications. By offering a collection of best practices, RAT guides engineers in selecting the most suitable content and ensuring proper grammar for their requirements, according to the Terminology, Conceptual Model, and Patterns of an ontology. Additionally, RAT generates real-time quality reports (based on the Inference Rules part) that identify possible issues in the requirements, reducing the need for time-consuming V&V, peer-review, and double-checking.

The patterns that RAT exploits can be easily tailored and managed through integration with Knowledge Manager, including those patterns defined for reliability and safety requirements during Ontology development. If new patterns are generated and transferred to the production environment, RAT can detect them, allowing authors to use them immediately. Furthermore, RAT can suggest new patterns or modifications to existing ones, alerting knowledge architects who can either approve or reject these suggestions. These features exploit NLP.

https://doi.org/10.3390/app16052179

By utilising RAT for requirements specification, a structured specification can be developed and aligned with the content of ontologies. This helps to ensure that, e.g., the reliability requirements associated with diagram elements are of high quality. RAT can use off-the-shelf quality metrics (Inference Rules) provided by RQA to perform on-the-fly analysis, e.g., about possible ambiguities, imprecisions, or inconsistencies in a requirement, as a rule-based intelligent system. The metrics can be enabled or disabled as needed, depending on the Capella elements where RAT is being used. Additionally, the use of RAT may lead to the refinement of ontologies, as requirement authors can identify elements that are missing in an ontology, potentially causing quality issues such as the absence of domain concepts. More details about the definition and usage of RQA requirements quality metrics can be found in other publications, e.g., [72].

Reliability-related information can be added through requirements using RAT to the following Arcadia/Capella diagrams and elements:

- Operational Capabilities diagram: Operational Capabilities.
- Operational Activity Interaction diagram: Operational Activities, Interactions.
- Operational Activity Breakdown diagram: Operational Activities.
- Operational Architecture diagram: Operational Activities, Operational Entities, Interactions
- Class diagram: Classes, Associations.
- System Functional Breakdown diagram: System Functions.
- System Architecture diagram: System Functions, System Components, Component Exchanges.
- Logical Functional Breakdown diagram: Logical Functions.
- Logical Component Breakdown diagram: Logical Components.

For the IFE system, RAT can be used to specify requirements for the power, voltage, and current of Connecting Units (physical component), and to associate the requirements with diagram elements. These requirements can be found in rules related to airworthiness of products, parts, and appliances [64]. In addition, according to DO-178C, the requirements should be analysed for ambiguities, inconsistencies, and undefined conditions. RAT can be used for such an analysis.

3.4. Traceability Management

For Traceability management, it may be necessary to handle connections between (a) Arcadia/Capella diagrams or their individual components and (b) other system artefacts of different types (such as requirements or design artefacts) and in various formats (such as models, documents and spreadsheets produced with other tools), as well as between elements of Arcadia/Capella diagrams. This includes traceability management for reliability-related information. The types of relationships can be defined within an ontology's Conceptual Model. Artefact semantics is also considered for traceability purposes.

Traceability Studio enables system engineers to manage various types of system artefacts, ranging from high-level goals and requirements to system or subsystem requirements, risks, and verification actions. In addition, through its connectivity capabilities and based on the Formalisation part of its ontologies, SES can import data from external tools and artefacts, including SysML/UML models, simulation models, MS Excel worksheets, MS Word documents, and requirements managed in various types of repositories (DOORS, Teamcenter, Polarion...) [15]. NLP is used when importing text, e.g., to transform it into SES data format according to patterns. As a result, textual artefacts will be represented in a semantically rich format that does not consider non-meaningful details of the artefacts, such as articles.

Given the large number of different sources involved in a complex systems engineering project, maintaining traceability among all the elements is crucial for project success and often required by standards, guidelines, best practices, or recommendations. Therefore,

SES provides mechanisms to specify all the system artefacts of a project, including models, physical documents, and other types of containers of engineering work products, and to define the different semantics of the traces to be created between the items contained in those elements. This can be accomplished without opening the source tool used to create and manage the items involved. Traceability Studio offers the possibility to create a Module Map, which is a graphical representation of the structure of a traceability project. Traceability Studio also has the capability to suggest new traces by analysing system artefacts (based on the Inference Rules part of an ontology) and allows users to generate an Impact Analysis. The suggestions can consider the terminological, semantic, and structural similarity of the artefacts according to the content of an ontology, among other characteristics. Thresholds can be specified to determine how similar two artefacts must be to suggest that a relationship could exist between them. Trace suggestion is part of the SES inference mechanisms.

As an example, 'realizes' is a relationship type for the IFE system (Figure 7) that can be employed to establish links between Arcadia/Capella diagram elements and reference requirements [64] in an Excel file. These reference requirements may include reliability ones, e.g., "If a component of the IFE system is designed to transmit the necessary safety information (e.g., the passenger briefing), any replacement system should also fulfil the safety objectives mandated for that function." Specific relationship types to consider for compliance with DO-178C include those between system requirements allocated to software and high-level requirements, high-level requirements and low-level requirements, low-level requirements and source code, and software requirements and test cases.

3.5. Model Quality Analysis

Low-quality system artefacts during the concept and design stages of a project can result in rework, additional expenses, delays, and potentially significant consequences if not detected, in addition to system reliability issues. To avoid these problems, RQA is a rule-based intelligent system that automates the process of inspecting and analysing different types of system artefacts, reducing the effort of quality reviews.

To analyse the quality of Arcadia/Capella diagrams in SES, diagram data, including reliability data, can be imported (Formalisation part of an ontology). First, a connection must be established between SES and an ontology that serves as the basis for the analysis. Second, it is necessary to connect Capella and SES. RQA can then utilise data from Arcadia/Capella diagrams (Figure 8) to automate the process of inspecting and evaluating diagram quality. After importing the data, a quantitative analysis of the quality can be performed using various existing metrics and measurement procedures in RQA (Inference Rules part of a SES ontology, based on elements of other parts of the ontology). The content of the Terminology, Conceptual Model, and Patterns of an ontology is also used, as well as NLP, when analysing textual artefacts. NLP functionality can distinguish the different elements of textual artefacts, classify the elements according to their semantics, disregard those elements that do not contribute to establishing semantics (e.g., articles), match the artefacts with patterns, and reason from all these aspects to evaluate artefact quality, among other features.

The evaluations with RQA primarily involve text analysis based on ontology content, such as identifying the use of certain terms and patterns, according to industrial recommendations and best practices. Appendix B lists all the characteristics (30) that are already covered by default in RQA and can be checked for quality analysis of Arcadia/Capella diagrams, such as Ambiguous universal keywords (e.g., "all", "any", or "both"), escape clauses (e.g., "when possible", "if necessary", and "and so on", whose use is an indicator of imprecision, ambiguity, and non-verifiability) and passive voice (as an indicator of

https://doi.org/10.3390/app16052179

imprecision and ambiguity). Early identification of the associated issues is essential for system reliability. Missing them might result in incorrect or incomplete implementation of required functions, e.g., as a consequence of an ambiguous system specification.

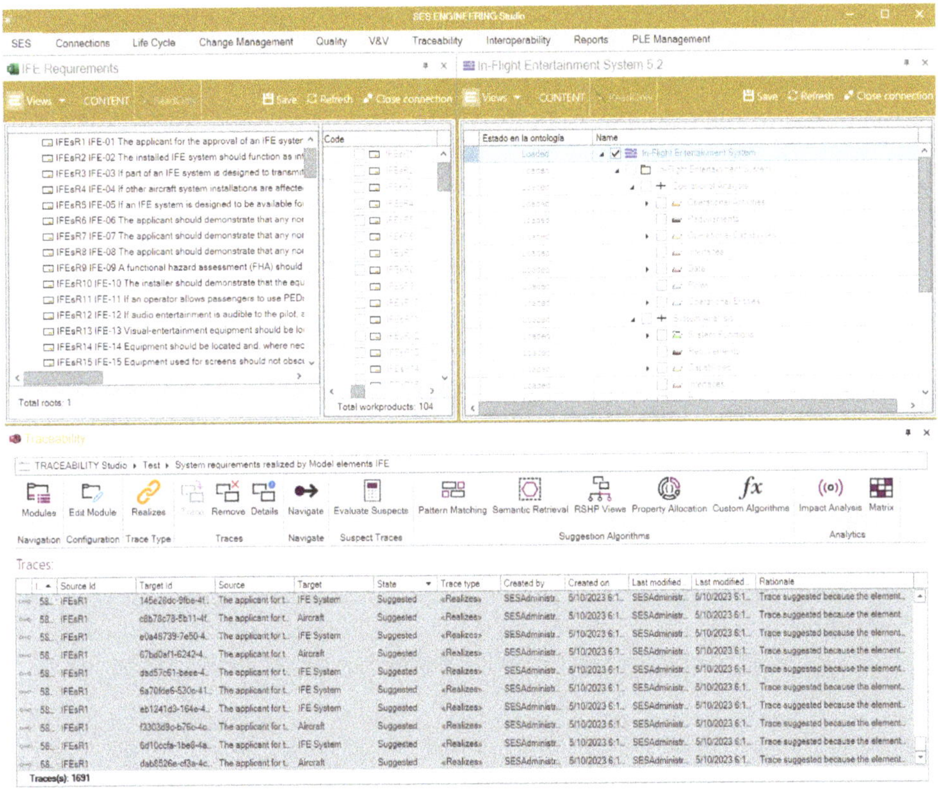

Figure 7. Traceability Studio screenshot.

The information included in the viewpoints can also be analysed to check its consistency, e.g., between the reliability information of a component and the reliability information of its sub-components. To this end, a property consistency metric can be created in RQA to compare the values of (reliability) properties extracted from the elements of Arcadia/Capella diagrams. For example, it must be ensured that the expected failure rate or mean time between failure of a sub-component ensures that the expected failure rate or mean time between failure of its parent component can be achieved.

Users can enable or disable metrics for element types whose quality needs to be evaluated. For instance, when evaluating the quality of an operational capability, it might be necessary to enable metrics that detect the use of passive voice or vague verbs. But if the user wants to measure the quality of a logical or physical component, these metrics will most likely not be useful because of how they are usually named (without verbs). In this case, metrics that, e.g., evaluate readability or check the text length might be enabled.

https://doi.org/10.3390/app16052179

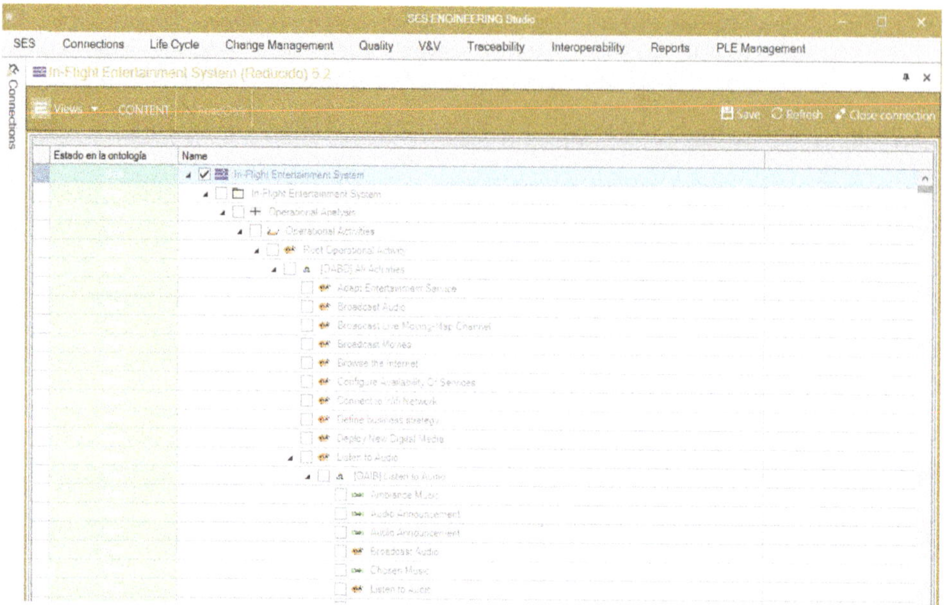

Figure 8. Data from Arcadia/Capella diagrams imported into SES.

For further quality analysis, V&V Studio supports manual assessment by allowing engineers to create and perform other specific V&V actions via various means, e.g., checklists with items related to Arcadia/Capella projects and diagrams. This feature can also be used to create checklists for assessing compliance against engineering and assurance standards, which can serve as assurance evidence [53].

As an example, it is possible to evaluate for the IFE system whether its operational capabilities follow the pattern verb-object, such as 'Provide Video Gaming Services'. For a DO-178C checklist, items to consider may include checking whether interface, performance, and reliability requirements have been specified, among other criteria. Figure 9 shows an overview of quality analysis results for the individual elements of the Arcadia/Capella diagrams of the IFE system. RQA qualitatively rates the quality as low, medium, or high, representing this with one, two, or three stars, respectively. Quality (thus star) rating is based on quantitative quality scores that RQA provides. We use RQA default criteria on what low, medium, and high quality are, e.g., based on the weight assigned to different quality metrics, but users can tailor them. These analyses can contribute to confirming characteristics that DO-178C requires for requirements and architecture artefacts, such as accuracy, consistency, verifiability, and conformance to standards.

Finally, it is important to mention that model quality analysis with RQA complements Capella Validation Rules. Capella provides a diagram validation feature that executes a set of rules to analyse certain characteristics of Arcadia/Capella diagrams, e.g., that the elements have a name, that the names of the elements are not repeated in the same scope, that the elements are associated with others, and the consistency between some elements of the different Arcadia steps. The set of rules to execute can be customised.

https://doi.org/10.3390/app16052179

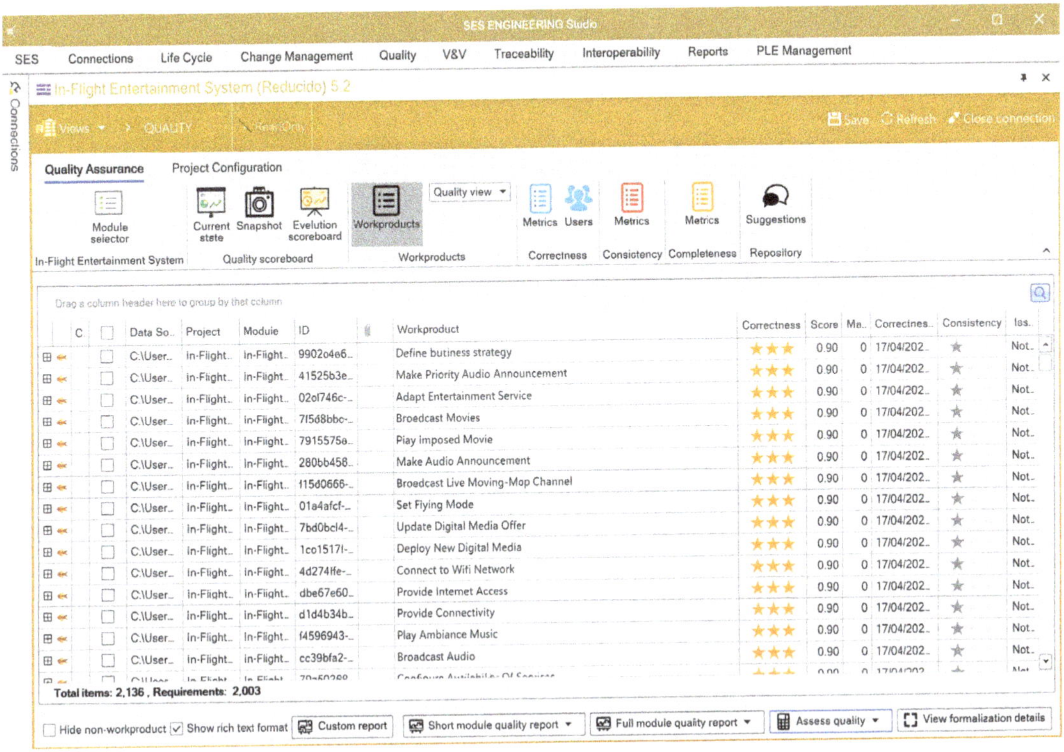

Figure 9. Arcadia/Capella diagram quality analysis with RQA: overall results.

4. Approach Validation

This section presents how we have validated the approach that combines MBSE and KCSE to design reliable systems in practice. We have applied the approach to different existing systems, considering system modelling with Arcadia/Capella and system information management with SES (including AI-based features), and taking into account system, software, and hardware aspects. Such validation can be regarded as case study research [73]. This type of research aims to investigate contemporary phenomena within their real-life context, especially when the boundary between the phenomena and the context cannot be clearly specified. Case study research is typically exploratory and flexible and uses qualitative data as the primary source.

The goal of the validation was to evaluate the effectiveness of the approach that combines MBSE and KCSE to design reliable systems. Two research questions were formulated:

- RQ1: How can the approach be applied to design specific systems?
- RQ2: Can the approach be a feasible means to design reliable systems?

The next sections present the design, the results, and a discussion of the validation.

4.1. Design

The design used to answer the research questions consisted of three elements: (1) selection of relevant and representative systems as MBSE case studies; (2) combination of MBSE and KCSE in the case studies to design reliable systems, and; (3) collection of feedback from practitioners about the combination.

We applied the approach to the following systems:

https://doi.org/10.3390/app16052179

1. The IFE system (introduced in Section 3).
2. Level Crossing Traffic Control [14]: A level crossing is an intersection where a railway line crosses a road or path, or in rare situations an airport runway, at the same level, as opposed to the railway line crossing over or under using an overpass or tunnel. Level crossings account for many of the catastrophic train accident risks on railways. The reliable and safe design, management, and operation of level crossings can reduce the risks, have a positive effect on user behaviour, and so reduce the number of fatal and serious incidents.
3. Environment Observation Link to Earth (EOLE) [74]: EOLE is a sounding weather balloon system, whose main goal is to provide meteorological data for various scientific users. The EOLE system missions are: (a) to collect weather data (atmospheric pressure, temperature, humidity...) on demand, or according to a predefined schedule; (b) to capture aerial images; (c) to transmit the captured data to a ground station in real-time, and; (d) to propose a subscription mechanism for weather operators.
4. Nutrition Care System [75]: Patients with chronic disease processes are often malnourished on admission to hospital or healthcare facilities. The system deals with the interaction between the patient and various healthcare entities and the definition of patient nutrition care objectives.
5. Arduino Mega2560Rev3 Microcontroller board [76]: It is a microcontroller board with 54 digital input/output pins, 16 analogue inputs, 4 hardware serial ports, a USB connection, a power jack, and a reset button, among other characteristics. The board contains everything needed to support the microcontroller. It can be simply connected to a computer with a USB cable or powered with an AC-to-DC adapter or battery to get started.
6. Hybrid Sports Utility Vehicle (SUV) [76]: A Hybrid SUV car consists of different structural components, such as the engine, body, suspension, gearbox, etc. Its structure, subcomponents, and functions to be performed can be modelled, e.g., the acceleration function, the braking function, the vehicle traction, or how the wheels are assembled.
7. Temperature War [77]: The Temperature War project aims to define, specify, design, build, and run a hardware/software system capable of managing the ambient temperature around itself. The system will operate in the same physical space as other similar systems. The objective of the Temperature War project is the development of a system capable of maintaining its surrounding environment between previously defined thresholds, assuming that the temperature can be affected by the operation of similar systems within its proximity, or by the activity of controlled external agents. It is a system that The REUSE Company (SES developer) uses for testing and product demonstration purposes.
8. Neuromuscular Transmission (NMT) controller [17]: An intelligent infusion controller for vital signs is a medical device that monitors specific vital signs parameters (e.g., blood pressure or NMT) to be regulated. It also infuses, at regular intervals, an updated drug dose value in order to achieve a specific target value for the physiological value under control. This device aims to use a very innovative technology to support the anaesthesiologist in measuring muscle relaxation during an operating room intervention. It corresponds to an industrial use case of the VALU3S project.

The criteria for system selection were availability of diagrams and information, coverage of system, hardware, and software aspects, and coverage of different application domains.

In addition, we considered these standards applicable to the selected systems:

- Automotive: ISO 26262 [4] (Functional safety of road vehicles).

https://doi.org/10.3390/app16052179

- Avionics: ARP 4754 [78] (Development of civil aircraft and systems), DO-178C [3] (Software of airborne systems and equipment), and DO-254 [79] (Airborne electronic hardware).
- Healthcare: IEC 62304 [80] (Medical device software), ISO 13485 [81] (Quality management systems of medical devices), and ISO 14971 [82] (Application of risk management to medical devices).
- Railway: EN 50126 [83] (Reliability, availability, maintainability, and safety of railway applications), EN 50128 [5] (Software for railway control and protection systems), and EN 50129 [84] (Safety-related railway electronic systems for signalling, communication, signalling, and processing systems).
- The generic IEC 61508 standard [85] (Functional safety of electrical/electronic/programmable electronic safety-related systems).

Finally, we presented the approach and its application to the staff of The REUSE Company, SES users, iRel40 industrial partners, and VALU3S industrial partners.

4.2. Results

Table 1 summarises the application of the approach and its results for the different systems addressed. System modelling, Ontology development, and Model quality analysis were performed for all the systems, whereas Structured textual requirements specification and traceability management were performed for three systems. Different standards have been considered for each system, according to its application domain. The next paragraphs outline the results for each approach activity.

Table 1. Summary of the application of the approach.

	System Modelling	Ontology Dev.	Structured Textual Reqs. Spec.	Traceability Management	Model Quality Analysis	Standards
IFE system	111 diagrams (Viewpoints applicable to 42)	Yes	Yes (applicable to 16 diagrams)	Yes (diagrams and 103 requirements)	Yes	ARP 4754, DO-178C, DO-254,
Level Crossing Traffic Control	102 diagrams (Viewpoints applicable to 46)	Yes	No	No	Yes	EN 50126, EN 50128, EN 50129
EOLE system	29 diagrams (Viewpoints applicable to 12)	Yes	No	No	Yes	ARP 4754, DO-178C, DO-254
Nutrition Care System	13 diagrams (Viewpoints applicable to 5)	Yes	No	No	Yes	ISO 13485, IEC 62304, ISO 14971
Arduino board	21 diagrams (Viewpoints applicable to 20)	Yes	No	No	Yes	IEC 61508
Hybrid SUV	17 diagrams (Viewpoints applicable to 7)	Yes	No	No	Yes	ISO 26262

https://doi.org/10.3390/app16052179

Table 1. *Cont.*

	System Modelling	Ontology Dev.	Structured Textual Reqs. Spec.	Traceability Management	Model Quality Analysis	Standards
Temperature War	9 diagrams (Viewpoints applicable to 2)	Yes	Yes (applicable to 3 diagrams)	Yes (diagrams and 484 requirements)	Yes	IEC 61508
NMT controller	7 diagrams (Viewpoints applicable to 4)	Yes	Yes (applicable to 3 diagrams)	Yes (diagrams and 42 requirements)	Yes	ISO 13485, IEC 62304, ISO 14971

For System modelling, we considered Arcadia/Capella diagrams and how the viewpoints could be used:

- The diagrams of the IFE system and Level Crossing Traffic Control are publicly available for download [14].
- The diagrams of EOLE and the Nutrition Care systems were reproduced from their main sources ([74] and [75], respectively).
- The diagrams of Arduino and Hybrid SUV were created from available SysML ones [76].
- The diagrams of Temperature War were provided by The REUSE Company.
- The diagrams of the NMT controller were created as a part of the work for the industrial use case of the VALU3S project.

Appendix C lists all the diagrams of the systems. All the Arcadia steps and main diagram types (Section 2.1) were considered, as well as some additional diagram types. For the data in the viewpoints, we either used data from existing component specifications (e.g., [86,87]) or decided upon values that would be representative. Figure 10 shows a Physical Architecture diagram for the Arduino board, including viewpoint data.

In Ontology development, we developed ontologies with the terms, acronyms, and relationship types of the standards taken into account for each system. For example, for the Hybrid SUV, we created an ontology of ISO 26262 with 185 terms, 105 acronyms, a PBS structure (in the Conceptual Model part), and 10 relationship types.

Structured textual requirements specification was addressed for the IFE system (see example in Section 3.3), Temperature War (Figure 11), and NMT controller. We used sets of available system requirements for their specification, analysis, and improvement with RAT, considering specification patterns (available in SES and added) and requirements quality metrics (e.g., about the use of will, must, or shall in the text of the requirements and the use of vague terms).

Similar to the previous activity, traceability management dealt with Arcadia/Capella diagrams and textual requirements (in Excel) of the IFE system, Temperature War, and NMT controller (Figure 12). We specified traces for them, considering the trace types (relationship types in Knowledge Manager) indicated in the standards. In addition, we used Traceability Studio functionality for automated trace discovery and for change impact analysis.

The Arcadia/Capella diagrams of the systems were imported into SES for Model quality analysis. The results from the analysis with existing RQA metrics indicated that the overall quality of the diagrams was high. Nonetheless, a few possible issues were detected, e.g.:

https://doi.org/10.3390/app16052179

- The length of the description of most of the diagram elements was not adequate (no description).
- In Level Crossing Traffic Control, the comment "A train leaving should not be delayed more than 5 mn" uses "should" (imprecise modal verb), "not" (ambiguous), passive voice (imprecise indication), and "mn" (not in the ontology as a measurement unit).
- In Temperature War, the operational capability "Temperature Regulation" does not follow the pattern verb + object.

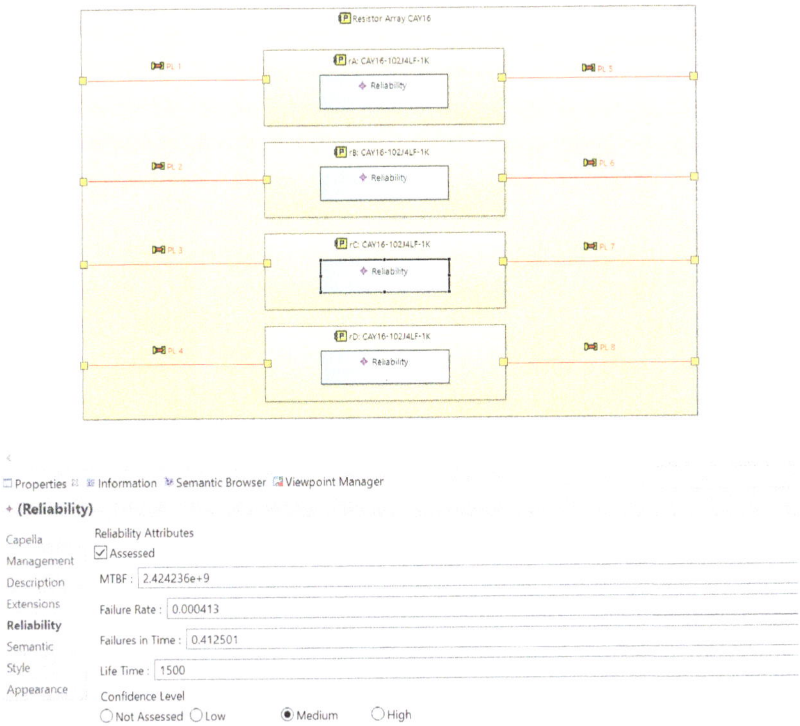

Figure 10. Physical Architecture diagram and viewpoint data for the Arduino board.

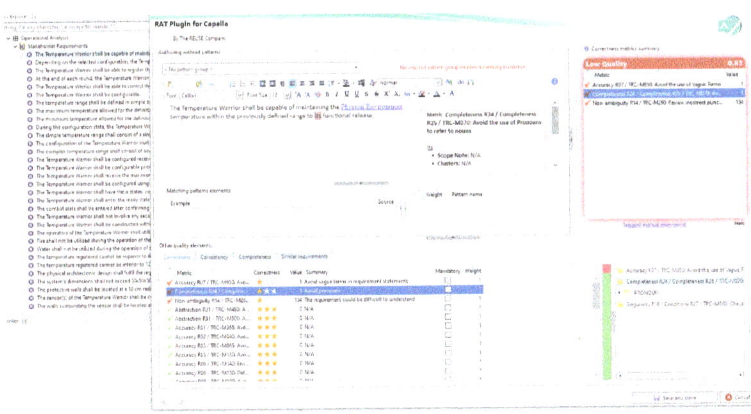

Figure 11. Requirements specification with RAT for Temperature War.

https://doi.org/10.3390/app16052179

Regarding the checklists, we analysed the coverage of the items identified in the standards related to the requirements and design system lifecycle phases, including requirements and design verification.

Finally, for feedback collection, the approach and its application were presented to tens of practitioners at different events and meetings. Staff of The REUSE Company, SES users, and iRel40 and VALU3S industrial partners provided positive feedback on the feasibility of the approach. Consultants and users of Arcadia/Capella and of SES confirmed the alignment of the approach with how the solutions were used, acknowledging that their combination could be beneficial to design reliable systems. In addition, the practitioners showed particular interest in how Capella had been extended, as well as in the integration and execution of the different activities of the approach in SES. They also asked about how the approach could be adapted to specific project needs and settings, such as the execution of some systems engineering or compliance management tasks with other tools.

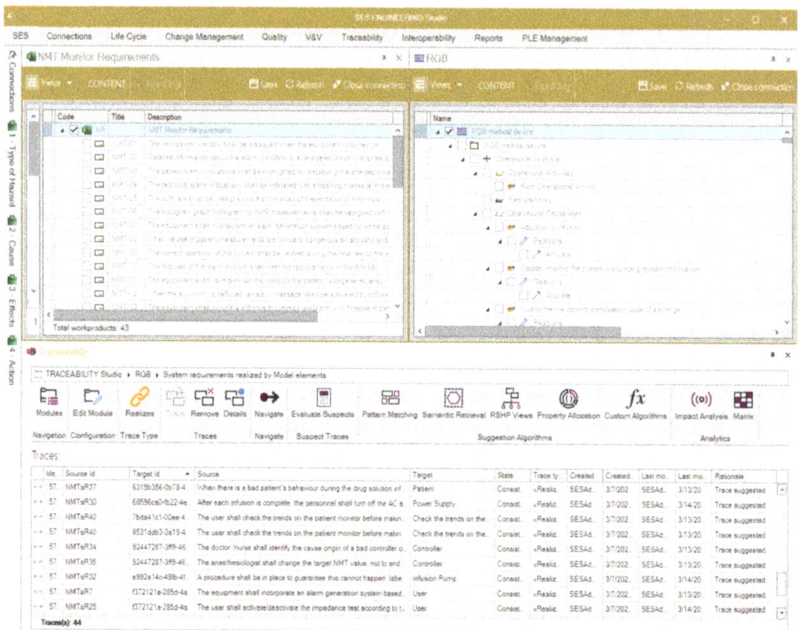

Figure 12. Traceability management with Traceability Studio for the NMT controller.

4.3. Discussion

This section discusses the answers to the research questions formulated, the validity of the approach, and how it has been applied.

4.3.1. Application of the Approach (RQ1)

We have successfully applied the approach on eight systems that cover five different application domains (aerospace, automotive, healthcare, railway, and generic system) and 11 standards, considering tens of diagrams, of knowledge elements, of reliability properties, and of analysis possibilities. System, software, and hardware reliability aspects have been taken into account. Based on the data available about the systems, some activities of the approach have been performed for all the systems, and others only for a few. The systems and their components have been modelled with Capella, and reliability information has been specified via viewpoints. Ontologies have been developed with Knowledge Manager from the knowledge available in standards. Structured textual requirements have been added to Arcadia/Capella diagrams with RAT. Traceability between Arcadia/Capella diagrams and requirements in spreadsheets has been managed with Traceability Studio. Finally, the quality of Arcadia/Capella diagrams has been analysed, and possible quality issues have been identified with RQA and V&V Studio.

For the application of the approach, it is important to note that it might vary among systems and projects. Some activities of the approach might be executed in a different way or not executed. For example, depending on the needs of the systems and projects, compliance with standards might not be required. This affects Ontology development, Traceability management, and Model quality analysis, which use or can use knowledge from standards. Depending on the settings of the systems or projects, other tools might be used for, e.g., textual requirements specification or traceability management (DOORS, Polarion, PTC Integrity, Reqtify...). Such variations and adaptations are common needs and have been discussed for systems engineering toolchains (e.g., [2]).

4.3.2. Feasibility of the Approach (RQ2)

We argue that the approach can be a feasible means to design reliable systems. As discussed above, we have been able to apply it to different systems, considering their reliability characteristics. In addition, practitioners' feedback has been positive in relation to approach feasibility and to its link with their MBSE or KCSE practices. These practitioners came from different sources, e.g., The REUSE Company and the VALU3S and iRel40 projects.

Nonetheless, some aspects of the feasibility of the approach deserve some further discussion. There are important dependencies with the knowledge about and expertise in MBSE with Arcadia/Capella and KCSE with SES. For example, effective quality analysis with RQA might not be straightforward for novice users because of the background that it requires about ontology development and usage, and about quality analysis configuration. These aspects need to be considered so that the approach is actually feasible. In addition, the actual reliability of the systems would need to be confirmed at operation time. The approach supports the execution of specification and analysis actions at early development stages to ensure that a system will be reliable. Regarding effort and costs in applying the approach, SES usage requires an additional engineering effort when compared to other tools, as well as specific training. Nonetheless, such aspects are expected and even required when engineering, e.g., safety-critical systems, for which ensuring the quality of the systems (including their reliability) and of system specifications is a must. This is necessary for compliance with engineering and assurance standards. Overall, the approach and its application are aligned with what practitioners in general and users of Arcadia/Capella and of SES in particular regard as cost-effective practices.

Last but not least, when comparing the approach and its application with existing solutions, quantitative differences exist. Among them, it can be highlighted that such solutions have not considered:

1. A large set of reliability and environment aspect attributes when modelling systems (24 in our approach).
2. The extent to which various system-, reliability-, and standard-specific terms, semantic aspects, and patterns must be considered in ontology development for reliable-system design (tens of elements when applying our approach).
3. How many types of Arcadia/Capella diagrams and elements can benefit from their integration with RAT for reliability requirement specification (nine diagrams and 15 diagram elements in our approach)?

https://doi.org/10.3390/app16052179

4. Different artefact types that can be used for advanced traceability management towards system reliability (tens of types in our approach, including all the types of Arcadia/Capella diagrams and elements).
5. The identification of specific metrics for reliability-oriented model quality analysis (30 in our approach).

Therefore, we consider that our approach is a more feasible means than prior work in order to design reliable systems in practice in the context of MBSE and KCSE, and more specifically, combining Arcadia/Capella and SES.

4.3.3. Validity

We discuss validity according to the aspects proposed by Runeson et al. for case study research [73].

We consider that construct validity is largely ensured because of the adequacy of the systems on which the approach that combines MBSE and KCSE to design reliable systems was applied. They correspond to real and representative systems whose reliability must be ensured. The standards considered are also relevant in industry. The threat of mono-method bias could be addressed in the future by conducting experiments that study the use and benefits of the approach, e.g., more accurate requirements specification and diagram quality analysis.

An aspect that affects internal validity is that we, the researchers, were mainly responsible for approach application. We have background on MBSE and KCSE, which impacts the results. They would most likely be different for novice users, who would need extensive training on MBSE, KCSE, Arcadia/Capella, and SES to reach our level of expertise. A key aspect to effectively use SES is to understand how ontologies are developed (e.g., considering different parts) and later used for different KCSE tasks. Another threat is the existence of a relationship with the practitioners who provided feedback on the approach, which can result in a more positive (or more negative) opinion about the approach based on their knowledge about and experience with our work. The opinions might also be different from practitioners who apply the approach as a whole, instead of, e.g., practitioners with great experience, mostly with some parts, such as system modelling with Arcadia/Capella or KCSE with SES.

In general, case study research does not aim to broadly generalise its findings, which impacts external validity. However, our findings are expected to be applicable to system design in situations similar to those in the systems considered, e.g., for systems with similar characteristics and from the same application domains. We also argue that the broad scope of the application of the approach, considering different systems, standards, and application domains, contributes to external validity. It is not common for papers report the validation of some technology with eight systems. Another aspect that contributes to external validity is the fact that Arcadia/Capella and SES have been and are used in different projects, systems, and application domains.

Regarding reliability, our involvement in the approach application affects it. Other people might obtain different results, e.g., when modelling the systems. Nonetheless, we also consider that the degree of detail provided when describing the approach and its application contributes to reproducibility. The lack of a more structured way for feedback collection, e.g., through a predefined questionnaire, affects reliability. Higher priority was assigned to ease feedback provision by practitioners with less formal means, e.g., at meetings of the VALU3S and iRel40 projects with all the partners.

https://doi.org/10.3390/app16052179

5. Conclusions

It is a must nowadays in many application domains to ensure the reliability of software-intensive systems and to start addressing it at early system lifecycle phases. As support, we have described an approach that combines two industrial practices: MBSE with Arcadia/Capella and KCSE with SES. The approach further exploits AI via knowledge management, NLP, and reasoning capabilities, enabling ontology-driven representation of system and reliability knowledge, automated inference, and semantic traceability analysis.

The approach consists of five activities: (1) System modelling with Arcadia/Capella; (2) ontology development with SES; (3) structured textual requirements specification on Capella with SES; (4) traceability management with SES (including traceability of Arcadia/Capella elements), and; (5) model quality analysis for Arcadia/Capella diagrams with SES. The activities take different pieces of reliability information into account, enabling and supporting the specification and analysis of this information and its association with different elements. Specifically, engineers can (1) use two new viewpoints to specify reliability data in Arcadia/Capella diagrams, (2) include reliability-related concepts and relationships in ontologies, (3) specify textual reliability requirements in a structured way and integrate them into Arcadia/Capella diagrams, (4) create links between reliability-related information and other system artefacts, and (5) conduct model quality analyses that consider reliability aspects. This can be regarded as new reliable system design principles. The approach also addresses compliance with standards, mostly from the development of ontologies that include knowledge from the standards.

We have validated the approach with eight systems from different application domains. We have also presented the approach and its application to tens of practitioners and collected their feedback, which has been positive. These actions have allowed us to show how the proposed combination of MBSE with Arcadia/Capella and KCSE with SES can be used to design specific systems and that the combination can be a feasible means to design reliable systems in practice.

Thanks to the approach, MBSE with Arcadia/Capella and KCSE with SES can benefit from each other, and specifically for reliable-system design. Arcadia/Capella can benefit from new viewpoints, from ontologies, and from AI features in different systems engineering tasks, whereas SES can benefit from the integration with a model-based means whose adoption is growing and whose diagrams and diagram elements can be used in different KCSE tasks. Arcadia/Capella and SES are generic engineering environments applicable to different purposes, such as security-critical system engineering. The approach enacts a feasible combined use of MBSE and KCSE to design reliable systems in practice. This is arguably the main outcome of our work, in addition to the validation results and the corresponding evidence of the effectiveness of the approach. No prior work has effectively combined Arcadia/Capella and SES for reliable-system design, has addressed specification and analysis of reliability needs with MBSE and KCSE to such a large extent, or has validated its results with so many different systems. This includes validation with both well-known, reference industrial systems (e.g., IFE systems) and real ones (e.g., the NMT controller). The approach further builds on mature industrial solutions and provides new means aligned with how the solutions are already used for large, complex critical systems.

In the future, it would be useful to define new, specific quality metrics for Arcadia/Capella diagrams and to implement them in SES. It would also be interesting to study the application of the approach on further systems, especially in collaboration with Capella users and SES users, and considering third-party feedback or independent user studies. The design and execution of experiments that provide further evidence of the benefits of the approach, e.g., for reliability issue detection with RQA vs. via traditional manual reviews, would be valuable as well. Other recommendations for future research include the application of different AI techniques (e.g., generative AI or agents) in the combination of MBSE and KCSE and the extension of the approach towards solutions that address and analyse reliability in other lifecycle stages (e.g., at runtime) and with further means (e.g., digital twins).

Author Contributions: Conceptualization, J.M.M., J.L.d.l.V., G.G., C.A. and L.A.; Methodology, J.M.M., J.L.d.l.V., G.G., C.A. and L.A.; Software, J.M.M., J.L.d.l.V. and L.A.; Validation, J.M.M., J.L.d.l.V., G.G., C.A. and L.A.; Formal Analysis, J.M.M., J.L.d.l.V., G.G., C.A. and L.A.; Investigation, J.M.M., J.L.d.l.V., G.G., C.A. and L.A.; Resources, J.M.M., J.L.d.l.V., G.G., C.A. and L.A.; Data Curation, J.M.M., J.L.d.l.V. and L.A.; Writing—Original Draft Preparation, J.M.M. and J.L.d.l.V.; Writing—Review and Editing, J.M.M., J.L.d.l.V., G.G., C.A. and L.A.; Visualisation, J.M.M., J.L.d.l.V., G.G., C.A. and L.A.; Supervision, J.L.d.l.V. and L.A.; Project Administration, J.M.M., J.L.d.l.V., G.G., C.A. and L.A.; Funding Acquisition, J.L.d.l.V. All authors have read and agreed to the published version of the manuscript.

Funding: The work leading to this paper has received funding from the following projects: iRel40 (H2020-ECSEL ref. 876659; MCIN/AEI/10.13039/501100011033 ref. PCI2020-112240; NextGenerationEU/PRTR), VALU3S (H2020-ECSEL ref. 876852; MCIN/AEI/10.13039/501100011033 ref. PCI2020-112001; NextGenerationEU/PRTR), REBECCA (HORIZON-KDT ref. 101097224; MICINN/AEI/10.13039/501100011033 ref. PCI2022-135043-2; NextGenerationEU/PRTR), Music360 (Horizon Europe ref. 101094872), AETERNAL (MCIN/AEI/10.13039/501100011033 ref. PID2023-149753OB-C21; ERDF), FDT4S (JCCM ref. SBPLY/24/180225/000020; ERDF), CoMoDiD (Generalitat Valenciana CIPROM/2021/023), and "Una propuesta integral para el desarrollo independiente de dominio de gemelos digitales" (UCLM ref. 2025-GRIN-38441; ERDF). The Ramon y Cajal Program (MCIN/AEI/10.13039/501100011033 ref. RYC-2017-22836; ESF) has also funded the work.

Data Availability Statement: All the research data is not publicly available due to intellectual property reasons.

Acknowledgments: We are grateful to the staff of The REUSE Company, SES users, and iRel40 and VALU3S industrial partners who provided input for and feedback on the approach.

Conflicts of Interest: Author Luis Alonso was employed by the REUSE Company. The remaining authors declare that the research was conducted in the absence of any commercial or financial relationships that could be construed as a potential conflict of interest.

Appendix A. Reliability Attributes and Environmental Aspect Attributes for System Modelling

Reliability attributes considered:

- Reliability: probability of success at time t, which is denoted R(t).
- MTBF: Mean Time Between Failure.
- MTTF: Mean Time to Failure.
- MTTR: Mean Time to Repair.
- FIT: Failures in Time.
- Failure Rate: failure/t.
- MTBMA: Mean Time Between Maintenance Actions.
- MTBUR: Mean Time Between Unscheduled Removal.
- Availability: probability that the system is applicable for use at a given time.
- Maintainability: probability that a system or system element can be repaired in a defined environment within a specified period of time.
- ROCOF: Rate of occurrence of failure. The number of unexpected events over a specific time of operation.
- POFOD: Probability of Failure on Demand. Possibility that the system will fail when a service request is made.

https://doi.org/10.3390/app16052179

- PPC: Planned Maintenance Percentage. Percentage of time spent on planned maintenance in contrast to unplanned maintenance tasks. PPC = (Planned maintenance time/Total maintenance time) × 100.
- Probability of survival, for a specific period of time t.
- Probability of success, independent of time.
- Life Time.

Environmental aspect attributes considered:

- Temperature
- Humidity
- Voltage
- Vibration
- Weather (wind, rain, snow)
- Pressure
- Ambient Light
- Operator Skills

Appendix B. Quality Analysis Characteristics

Characteristics that can be checked for quality analysis of Arcadia/Capella diagrams:

- Ambiguous universal keywords, e.g., "all", "any", or "both".
- Combinators out of the condition block, because the use of, e.g., "and", "or", "unless", and "but also" can be ambiguous and show lack to atomicity.
- Convention for logical expression forms, because the use of "and/or" is ambiguous.
- Element description length, for clarity and understandability.
- Element name length, for clarity and understandability.
- Escape clauses, such as "when possible", "if necessary", and "and so on", whose use is an indicator of imprecision, ambiguity, and non-verifiability.
- Flow sentences, because terms such as "although", "as well as", "except", and "unless" should be avoided to ensure the consistency of a specification.
- Imprecise modal verbs, because the use of "should", "might", and "may" might result in imprecise and ambiguous sentences.
- Imprecise quantifiers, such as "a lot of", "hundreds of", "portions of", and "plenty of".
- Inadequate unit for a characteristic, because otherwise a specification would be inaccurate.
- Incorrect punctuation, for non-ambiguity.
- Incorrect spelling, for non-ambiguity.
- Indefinite articles in front of an agent, because "a" and "an" should not be used for accuracy.
- Mixing up different measurement systems, which indicate imprecision and inconsistency.
- Multiple verbs, which show lack of atomicity.
- 'Not' and other negative expressions, because they can result in confusion.
- Numbers followed by units or noun qualifications, for accuracy.
- Open-ended clauses, e.g., "TBD", "etc.", and "including but not limited to", which are imprecise, ambiguous, and non-verifiable.
- Parentheses, as an indicator of imprecision and ambiguity.
- Passive voice, as an indicator of imprecision and ambiguity.
- Pattern matching metric for Noun structure, to ensure the use of suitable name structures for certain Arcadia/Capella diagram elements.
- Pattern matching metric for Verb + Object, to ensure the use of suitable name structures for certain Arcadia/Capella diagram elements.
- Phrases that indicate the purpose, such as "in order to", "so that", and "thus allowing", which can be confusing.

https://doi.org/10.3390/app16052179

- Pronouns to refer to nouns, which can indicate ambiguity and be inconsistent.
- Readability, as an indicator of ambiguity.
- Superfluous infinitives, e.g., "be capable of" and "be designed to", as an indicator of possible issues in clarity and understandability.
- Synonyms, because the use of the main term instead of synonyms contributes to precision and consistency.
- Temporal indefinite keywords out of the condition part, because terms such as "finally", "almost always", "in the end", or "ultimately" can cause confusion or unintended meaning.
- Unachievable absolutes expressions, i.e., unrealistic, absolute, and non-verifiable expressions such as "100% availability", "always", and "never".
- Vague terms, including adjectives (e.g., "small", "typical", "appropriate", and "common"), adverbs (e.g., "usually", "approximately", and "sufficiently"), and verbs (e.g., "assist", "facilitate", and "manage") whose use can lead to imprecision, ambiguity, and non-verifiability.

Appendix C. Diagrams for Approach Validation

IFE System (111 diagrams)

- Operational Analysis
    - 1 Operational Entity Breakdown diagram
    - 1 Operational Capabilities diagram
    - 1 Operational Activity Breakdown diagram
    - 3 Operational Activity Interaction diagrams
    - 2 Operational Process Description diagrams
    - 2 Operational Architecture diagrams
    - 1 Operational Entity Scenario diagram
- System Analysis
    - 5 Model State Machine diagrams
    - 1 Contextual System Actors diagram
    - 2 System Functional Breakdown diagrams
    - 9 System Functional Dataflow diagrams
    - 5 System Functional Chain Descriptions
    - 6 Functional Scenario diagrams
    - 2 System Architecture diagrams
    - 6 Exchange Scenario diagrams
    - 1 Missions Capabilities diagram
    - 1 Contextual Detailed Interfaces diagram
    - 3 Class diagrams
    - 2 Contextual Capability diagrams
    - 2 Contextual Mission diagrams
- Logical Architecture
    - 1 Logical Functional Breakdown diagram
    - 10 Logical Functional Dataflow diagrams
    - 5 Logical Functional Chain Description diagrams
    - 1 Logical Component Breakdown diagram
    - 6 Logical Architecture diagrams
- Physical Architecture
    - 1 Physical Functional Breakdown diagram

https://doi.org/10.3390/app16052179

  - 11 Physical Functional Dataflow diagrams
  - 6 Physical Functional Chain Description diagrams
  - 1 Physical Path Description diagram
  - 2 Physical Component Breakdown diagrams
  - 10 Physical Architecture diagrams
- End-Product Breakdown Structure
  - 1 EPBS Architecture diagram

Level Crossing Traffic Control (102 diagrams)

- Operational Analysis
  - 1 Operational Entity Breakdown diagram
  - 1 Operational Capabilities diagram
  - 3 Operational Process Description diagrams
  - 4 Operational Architecture diagrams
  - 5 Operational Entity Scenario diagrams
  - 1 Capability Realisation diagram
- System Analysis
  - 5 Model State Machine diagrams
  - 2 System Functional Breakdown diagrams
  - 9 System Functional Dataflow diagrams
  - 9 System Functional Chain Description diagrams
  - 1 Functional Scenario diagram
  - 9 System Architecture diagrams
  - 3 Exchange Scenario diagrams
  - 1 Missions Capabilities diagram
  - 1 Contextual External Interface diagram
  - 9 Class diagrams
- Logical Architecture
  - 2 Logical Functional Breakdown diagrams
  - 5 Logical Functional Dataflow diagrams
  - 1 Logical Functional Chain Description diagram
  - 8 Logical Architecture diagrams
- Physical Architecture
  - 1 Physical Functional Breakdown diagram
  - 2 Physical Functional Dataflow diagrams
  - 18 Physical Architecture diagrams
- End-Product Breakdown Structure
  - 1 Configuration Items Breakdown diagram

EOLE system (29 diagrams)

- Operational Analysis
  - 1 Operational Entity Breakdown diagram
  - 1 Operational Capabilities diagram
  - 3 Operational Activity Interaction diagrams
  - 1 Operational Architecture diagram
  - 1 Operational Entity Scenario diagram
- System Analysis
  - 1 System Functional Breakdown diagram

https://doi.org/10.3390/app16052179

- 3 System Functional Dataflow diagrams
- 2 System Functional Chain Description diagrams
- 1 Functional Scenario diagram
- 2 System Architecture diagrams
- 1 Exchange Scenario diagram
- 1 Contextual Detailed Interfaces diagram
- 1 Contextual External Interface diagram
- 1 Class diagram
- 1 Model State Machine diagram

- Logical Architecture
  - 1 Logical Architecture diagram
- Physical Architecture
  - 1 Physical Functional Breakdown diagram
  - 1 Physical Functional Dataflow diagram
  - 1 Physical Functional Chain Description diagram
  - 1 Physical Path Description diagram
  - 1 Physical Architecture diagram
- End-Product Breakdown Structure
  - 1 Configuration Items Breakdown diagram
  - 1 EPBS Architecture diagram

Nutrition Care System (13 diagrams)

- Operational Analysis
  - 1 Operational Entity Breakdown diagram
  - 2 Operational Capabilities diagrams
  - 2 Operational Activity Interaction diagrams
  - 2 Operational Process Description diagrams
  - 1 Operational Architecture diagram
- System Analysis
  - 1 Model State Machine diagram
  - 1 System Functional Dataflow diagram
  - 1 System Architecture diagram
  - 1 Missions Capabilities diagram
- Logical Architecture
  - 1 Logical Architecture diagram

Arduino Mega2560Rev3 Microcontroller board (21 diagrams)

- Logical Architecture
  - 1 Logical Component Breakdown diagram
  - 3 Logical Architecture diagrams
- Physical Architecture
  - 17 Physical Architecture diagrams

Hybrid Sports Utility Vehicle (17 diagrams)

- Operational Analysis
  - 2 Operational Capabilities diagrams
  - 2 Operational Activity Interaction diagrams
- System Analysis

https://doi.org/10.3390/app16052179

- 7 Model State Machine diagrams
- 1 Logical Component Breakdown diagram
- 5 Logical Architecture diagrams

Temperature War (9 diagrams)

- Operational Analysis
  - 1 Operational Entity Breakdown diagram
  - 1 Operational Capabilities diagram
- System Analysis
  - 1 Contextual System Actors diagram
  - 1 System Functional Breakdown diagram
  - 1 Missions Capabilities diagram
  - 1 Model State Machine diagram
- Logical Architecture
  - 1 Logical Component Breakdown diagram
  - 1 Logical Architecture diagram
- Physical Architecture
  - 1 Physical Architecture diagram

NMT controller (7 diagrams)

- Operational Analysis
  - 1 Operational Capabilities diagram
- System Analysis
  - 1 System Architecture diagram
  - 1 Model State Machine diagram
- Logical Architecture
  - 1 Logical Component Breakdown diagram
  - 3 Logical Architecture diagrams

References

1. de la Vara, J.L.; Bauer, T.; Fischer, B.; Karaca, M.; Madeira, H.; Matschnig, M.; Mazzini, S.; Nandi, G.S.; Patrone, F.; Pereira, D.; et al. A Proposal for the Classification of Methods for Verification and Validation of Safety, Cybersecurity, and Privacy of Automated Systems. In Proceedings of the 14th International Conference on the Quality of Information and Communications Technology (QUATIC 2021), Algarve, Portugal, 8–11 September 2021.
2. de la Vara, J.L.; Ruiz, A.; Blondelle, G. Assurance and Certification of Cyber-Physical Systems: The AMASS Open Source Ecosystem. *J. Syst. Softw.* **2021**, *171*, 110812. [CrossRef]
3. *DO-178C*; Software Considerations in Airborne Systems and Equipment Certification. RTCA: Washington, DC, USA, 2012.
4. *ISO 26262*; Road Vehicles—Functional Safety. 2nd ed. ISO: Geneva, Switzerland, 2018.
5. *EN 50128*; Railway Applications—Communications, Signalling and Processing Systems—Software for Railway Control and Protection Systems. 2nd ed. CENELEC: Brussels, Belgium, 2011.
6. *ISO/IEC/IEEE 24765*; Systems and Software Engineering—Vocabulary. 2nd ed. ISO: Geneva, Switzerland, 2017.
7. Holt, J.; Perry, S.; Brownsword, M. *Foundations for Model-Based Systems Engineering: From Patterns to Models*; IET: Stevenage, UK, 2016.
8. Parra, E.; Alonso, L.; Mendieta, R.; de la Vara, J.L. Advances in Artefact Quality Analysis for Safety-Critical Systems. In Proceedings of the 30th International Symposium on Software Reliability Engineering (ISSRE 2019), Berlin, Germany, 27–30 October 2019.
9. Russel, S.; Norvig, P. *Artificial Intelligence: A Modern Approach*, 4th ed.; Pearson: Harlow, UK, 2021.
10. Al-Sharif, Z.A.; Jeffery, C.L. AbstractTrace: The Use of Execution Traces to Cluster, Classify, Prioritize, and Optimize a Bloated Test Suite. *Appl. Sci.* **2024**, *14*, 11168. [CrossRef]

https://doi.org/10.3390/app16052179

11. Maru, G.G.; Lee, S.; Ji, S.; Ko, S.K.; Im, H. Neural Methods for Programming: A Comprehensive Survey and Future Directions. *Appl. Sci.* **2025**, *15*, 12150. [CrossRef]
12. Sultan, B.; Apvrille, L. AI-Driven Consistency of SysML Diagrams. In Proceedings of the ACM/IEEE 27th International Conference on Model Driven Engineering Languages and Systems (MODELS 2024), Linz, Austria, 22–27 September 2024.
13. Yadav, P.S.; Rao, R.S.; Mishra, A.; Gupta, M. Machine Learning-Based Methods for Code Smell Detection: A Survey. *Appl. Sci.* **2024**, *14*, 6149. [CrossRef]
14. Eclipse. Capella. Available online: https://mbse-capella.org/ (accessed on 9 January 2026).
15. The REUSE Company. Systems Engineering Suite. Available online: https://www.reusecompany.com/systems-engineering-suite (accessed on 9 January 2026).
16. iRel40 Project. Available online: https://www.irel40.eu/ (accessed on 9 January 2026).
17. VALU3S Project. Available online: https://valu3s.eu/ (accessed on 9 January 2026).
18. de la Vara, J.L.; Morote, J.M. A Proposal for Model-Based Reliability-Oriented System Design in Industry. In Proceedings of the 21st IEEE International Conference on Software Quality, Reliability, and Security (QRS 2021), Hainan, China, 6–10 December 2021.
19. Morote, J.; de la Vara, J.L.; Giachetti, G.; Ayora, C.; Alonso, L. An Industrial Approach for Model-Based Reliability-Oriented System Design. In Proceedings of the 27th IEEE Pacific Rim International Symposium on Dependable Computing (PRDC 2022), Beijing, China, 28 November–1 December 2022.
20. Eclipse. Capella Studio. Available online: https://github.com/eclipse-capella/capella-studio (accessed on 9 January 2026).
21. Lopez, B.; Álvarez-Rodríguez, J.M.; Parra, E.; de la Vara, J.L. Ontology Configuration Management for Knowledge-Centric Systems Engineering in Industry. In Proceedings of the 50th IEEE/IFIP International Conference on Dependable Systems and Networks (DSN 2020), Valencia, Spain, 29 June–2 July 2020.
22. Rauzy, A.B.; Haskins, C. Foundations for model-based systems engineering and model-based safety assessment. *Syst. Eng.* **2019**, *22*, 146–155. [CrossRef]
23. Ticona Coaquira, F.J.; Wang, X.; Vidaurre Torrez, K.W.; Mamani Quiroga, M.J.; Silva Plata, M.A.; Luna Verdueta, G.A.; Murillo Quispe, S.E.; Auza Banegas, G.J.; Antezana Lopez, F.P.; Rojas, A. Model-Based Design and Testbed for CubeSat Attitude Determination and Control System with Magnetic Actuation. *Appl. Sci.* **2024**, *14*, 6065. [CrossRef]
24. Uludağ, Y.; Evin, E.; Gürbüz, N.G. Integration of systems design and risk management through model-based systems development. *Syst. Eng.* **2023**, *26*, 48–70. [CrossRef]
25. Valdivia-Dabringer, M.L.; Dybov, A.; Fresemann, C.; Stark, R. Towards Integrated Safety Analysis as Part of Traceable Model-Based Systems Engineering. *Proc. Des. Soc.* **2022**, *2*, 2005–2014. [CrossRef]
26. Zhang, Q.; Wang, S.; Liu, B. Approach for integrated modular avionics reconfiguration modelling and reliability analysis based on AADL. *IET Softw.* **2016**, *10*, 18–25. [CrossRef]
27. Rapin, N.; Bannour, B.; Adedjouma, M. Model-Based Generation and Analysis Toolset of Fault Trees with Heterogeneous Failure Events. In Proceedings of the 27th Pacific Rim International Symposium on Dependable Computing (PRDC 2022), Beijing, China, 28 November–1 December 2022.
28. Brusa, E. Digital Twin: Toward the Integration Between System Design and RAMS Assessment Through the Model-Based Systems Engineering. *IEEE Syst. J.* **2020**, *15*, 3549–3560. [CrossRef]
29. Vaicenavičius, J.; Wiklund, T.; Kavolis, D.; Draukšas, S.; Kalkauskas, A.; Vaicenavičius, R. SysIDE: SysML v2 textual editing and analysis system: Overview and applications. *CEAS Space J.* **2025**. [CrossRef]
30. Alanen, J.; Linnosmaa, J.; Malm, T.; Papakonstantinou, N.; Ahonen, T.; Heikkilä, E.; Tiusanen, R. Hybrid ontology for safety, security, and dependability risk assessments and Security Threat Analysis (STA) method for industrial control systems. *Reliab. Eng. Syst. Saf.* **2022**, *220*, 108270. [CrossRef]
31. Chen, R.; Chen, C.H.; Liu, Y.; Ye, X. Ontology-based requirement verification for complex systems. *Adv. Eng. Inform.* **2020**, *46*, 101148. [CrossRef]
32. Zhou, J.; Niemelä, E.; Evesti, A. Ontology-based software reliability modelling. In Proceedings of the Software and Services Variability Management Workshop—Concepts, Models, and Tools (SVM 2007), Helsinki, Finland, 24 April 2007.
33. Giachetti, G.; de la Vara, J.L.; Marín, B. Mastering Agile Practice Adoption through a Model-Driven Approach for the Combination of Development Methods. *Bus. Inf. Syst. Eng.* **2023**, *65*, 103–125. [CrossRef]
34. Delabeye, R.; Penas, O.; Plateaux, R. Scalable ontology-based V&V process for heterogeneous systems and applications. In Proceedings of the 14th System Analysis and Modelling Conference (SAM 2022), Montreal, QC, Canada, 23–28 October 2022.
35. Dong, M.; Wang, G.; Lu, J.; Wu, S.; Ma, J. Ontology formalism and semantic rules supporting traceability management in model-based systems engineering. *J. Eng. Des.* **2025**, 1–26. [CrossRef]
36. Jinzhi, L.; Zhaorui, Y.; Xiaochen, Z.; Jian, W.; Dimitris, K. Exploring the concept of Cognitive Digital Twin from model-based systems engineering perspective. *Int. J. Adv. Manuf. Technol.* **2022**, *121*, 5835–5854. [CrossRef]
37. Peugeot, T. GONG: An open source Ontology Based System Engineering toolset. In Proceedings of the 8th International Symposium on Systems Engineering (ISSE 2022), Vienna, Austria, 24–26 October 2022.

https://doi.org/10.3390/app16052179

38. Maleki, E.; Fernandez, A.G.; Fischer, N.; Wijnands, Q.; Christofi, N. Semantic-based systems engineering for digitalization of space mission design. *Front. Ind. Eng.* **2024**, *2*, 1426074. [CrossRef]
39. Elaasar, M.; Rouquette, N.; Wagner, D.; Oakes, B.J.; Hamou-Lhadj, A.; Hamdaqa, M. openCAESAR: Balancing Agility and Rigor in Model-Based Systems Engineering. In Proceedings of the 15th System Analysis and Modelling Conference (SAM 2023), Västerås, Sweden, 1–6 October 2023.
40. Naouar, D.; El Hachem, J.; Voirin, J.L.; Foisil, J.; Kermarrec, Y. Towards the Integration of Cybersecurity Risk Assessment into Model-based Requirements Engineering. In Proceedings of the 29th IEEE International Requirements Engineering Conference (RE 2021), Notre Dame, IN, USA, 20–24 September 2021.
41. Voirin, J.L.; Bonnet, S.; Normand, V.; Exertier, D. Model-Driven IVV Management with Arcadia and Capella. In Proceedings of the 6th International Conference on Complex Systems Design & Management (CSDM 2015), Paris, France, 23–25 November 2015.
42. Sango, M.; Vallée, F.; Vié, A.C.; Voirin, J.L.; Leroux, X.; Normand, V. MBSE and MBSA with Capella and Safety Architect Tools. In Proceedings of the 7th International Conference on Complex Systems Design & Management (CSDM 2016), Paris, France, 13–14 December 2016.
43. Sango, M.; Godot, J.; Gonzalez, A.; Ruiz-Nolasco, R. Model-based system, safety and security co-engineering method and toolchain for medical devices design. In Proceedings of the 2019 Design of Medical Devices Conference (DMD 2019), Minneapolis, MN, USA, 15–18 April 2019.
44. Bitetti, L.; De Ferluc, R.; Mailland, D.; Gregoris, G.; Capogna, F. Model Based Approach for RAMS Analyses in the Space Domain with Capella Open-Source Tool. In Proceedings of the 6th International Symposium on Model Based Safety and Assessment (IMBSA 2019), Thessaloniki, Greece, 16–18 October 2019.
45. Brau, G.; Jenn, E.; Radu, S. A Capella-Based Tool for the Early Assessment of Nano/Micro Satellites Availability. In Proceedings of the 9th International Symposium on Model Based Safety and Assessment (IMBSA 2022), Munich, Germany, 5–7 September 2022.
46. Brunel, J.; Chemouil, D.; Rioux, L.; Bakkali, M.; Vallée, F. A Viewpoint-Based Approach for Formal Safety & Security Assessment of System Architectures. In Proceedings of the 11th Workshop on Model-Driven Engineering, Verification and Validation (MoDeVVA 2014), Valencia, Spain, 30 September 2014.
47. Ponnusamy, S.S.; Thebault, P.; Albert, V. Towards an Ontology-Driven Framework for Simulation Model Development. In Proceedings of the 8th European Congress on Embedded Real Time Software and Systems (ERTS 2016), Toulouse, France, 27–29 January 2016.
48. Hetherington, D.; Roques, P. STPA Analysis of Automotive Safety Using Arcadia and Capella. In Proceedings of the 11th European Congress on Embedded Real Time Systems (ERTS 2022), Toulouse, France, 1–2 June 2022.
49. Minacapilli, P.; Criado, F.; Campo, S.; Rodríguez, A.; Escudero, D. Small satellites mission design enhancement through MBSE and DDSE toolchain. In Proceedings of the Model Based Space Systems and Software Engineering (MBSE2022), Toulouse, France, 22–24 November 2022.
50. Anzen Engineering. Atica4Capella. Available online: https://www.anzenengineering.com/anzen-wiki/atica4capella/ (accessed on 9 January 2026).
51. Bogusch, R.; Ehrich, S.; Scherer, R.; Sorg, T.; Wöhler, R. A Lean Systems Engineering Approach for the Development of Safety-critical Avionic Systems. In Proceedings of the 8th European Congress on Embedded Real Time Software and Systems (ERTS 2016), Toulouse, France, 27–29 January 2016.
52. de la Vara, J.L.; Parra, E.; Ruiz, A.; Gallina, B. AMASS: A Large-Scale European Project to Improve the Assurance and Certification of Cyber-Physical Systems. In Proceedings of the 20th International Conference Product-Focused Software Process Improvement (PROFES 2019), Barcelona, Spain, 27–29 November 2019.
53. de la Vara, J.L.; García, A.; Valero, J.; Ayora, C. Model-Based Assurance Evidence Management for Safety-Critical Systems. *Softw. Syst. Model.* **2022**, *21*, 2329–2365. [CrossRef]
54. de la Vara, J.L.; Jiménez, G.; Mendieta, R.; Parra, E. Assessment of the Quality of Safety Cases: A Research Preview. In Proceedings of the 25th International Working Conference Requirements Engineering: Foundation for Software Quality (REFSQ 2019), Essen, Germany, 18–21 March 2019.
55. de la Vara, J.L.; Parra, E.; Alonso, L.; López, B.; Álvarez-Rodríguez, J.M. Integration of Tool Support for Assurance and Certification and for Knowledge-Centric Systems Engineering. In Proceedings of the 9th IEEE International Workshop on Software Certification (WoSoCer 2019), Berlin, Germany, 27–30 October 2019.
56. Parra, E.; de la Vara, J.L.; Alonso, L. Analysis of Requirements Quality Evolution. In Proceedings of the 40th International Conference on Software Engineering (ICSE 2018), Gothenburg, Sweden, 27 May–3 June 2018.
57. de la Vara, J.L.; Bahamonde, H.; Ayora, C. Assessment of the Quality of the Text of Safety Standards with Industrial Semantic Technologies. *Comput. Stand. Interfaces* **2024**, *88*, 103803. [CrossRef]
58. Mendieta, R.; de la Vara, J.L.; Llorens, J.; Álvarez-Rodríguez, J.M. Towards Effective SysML Model Reuse. In Proceedings of the 5th International Conference on Model-Driven Engineering and Software Development (MODELSWARD 2017), Porto, Portugal, 19–21 February 2017.

https://doi.org/10.3390/app16052179

59. de la Vara, J.L.; Howard, P.; Ayora, C. An Ontology Metamodel for Knowledge-Centric Systems Engineering in Practice. In Proceedings of the 44th International Conference on Conceptual Modeling (ER 2025), Poitiers, France, 20–23 October 2025.
60. de la Vara, J.L.; Morote, J.M.; Ayora, C.; Giachetti, G.; Alonso, L.; Mendieta, R.; Muñoz, D.; Ruiz-Nolasco, R.; González, A. Early V&V in Knowledge-Centric Systems Engineering: Advances and Benefits in Practice. In Proceedings of the 18th IEEE International Conference on Software Testing, Verification and Validation (ICST 2025), Napoli, Italy, 31 March–4 April 2025.
61. Eclipse. Capella Days. Available online: https://mbse-capella.org/capella_days.html (accessed on 9 January 2026).
62. The REUSE Company. TRC Forum. Available online: https://www.reusecompany.com/trc-forums (accessed on 9 January 2026).
63. Transportation Safety Board of Canada. Swissair 111 Investigation Report—Executive Summary. Available online: https://www.tsb.gc.ca/eng/medias-media/fiches-facts/a98h0003/sum_a98h0003.html (accessed on 9 January 2026).
64. EASA. *Easy Access Rules for Acceptable Means of Compliance for Airworthiness of Products, Parts and Appliances (AMC-20)*; Amendment 19; European Union Aviation Safety Agency (EASA): Cologne, Germany, 2021.
65. Birolini, A. *Reliability Engineering: Theory and Practice*, 6th ed.; Springer: Berlin/Heidelberg, Germany, 2010.
66. Lazzaroni, M.; Cristaldi, L.; Peretto, L.; Rinaldi, P.; Catelan, M. *Reliability Engineering: Basic Concepts and Applications in ICT*; Springer: Berlin/Heidelberg, Germany, 2011.
67. O'Connor, P.D.T.; Kleyner, A.V. *Practical Reliability Engineering*; John Wiley & Sons: Hoboken, NJ, USA, 2012.
68. Stapelberg, R.F. *Handbook of Reliability, Availability, Maintainability and Safety in Engineering Design*; Springer: London, UK, 2009.
69. Antonino, P.O.; Trapp, M.; Barbosa, P.; Sousa, L. The Parameterized Safety Requirements Templates. In Proceedings of the 8th IEEE/ACM International Symposium on Software and Systems Traceability (SST 2015), Florence, Italy, 17 May 2015.
70. Fu, R.; Bao, X.; Zhao, T. Generic Safety Requirements Description Templates for the Embedded Software. In Proceedings of the 9th IEEE International Conference on Communication Software and Networks (ICSSN 2017), Guangzhou, China, 6–8 May 2017.
71. Westfall, L. *The Certified Software Quality Engineer Handbook*, 2nd ed.; ASQ Quality Press: Milwaukee, WI, USA, 2016.
72. Gallego, E.; Chalé-Góngora, H.-G.; Llorens, J.; Fuentes, J.; Álvarez, J.; Génova, G.; Fraga, A. Requirements Quality Analysis: A Successful Case Study in the Industry. In Proceedings of the Seventh International Conference on Complex Systems Design & Management (CSD&M 2016), Paris, France, 13–14 December 2016.
73. Runeson, P.; Höst, M.; Rainer, A.; Regnell, B. *Case Study Research in Software Engineering—Guidelines and Examples*; John Wiley & Sons: Hoboken, NJ, USA, 2012.
74. Roques, P. *Systems Architecture Modeling with the Arcadia Method: A Practical Guide to Capella*; ISTE Press: London, UK; Elsevier: Oxford, UK, 2017.
75. Lacrampe, S.; Thukral, V. Healthcare Use Case—Application of MBSE in managing patient care in patients suffering from malnutrition. In Proceedings of the 6th Annual Systems Engineering in Healthcare Conference (HWG 2020), Minneapolis, MN, USA, 28–30 April 2020.
76. Webel IT Australia. Examples of Applications of Systems Modelling Language (SysML) and Model-Based Systems Engineering (MBSE). Available online: https://www.webel.com.au/node/3517 (accessed on 9 January 2026).
77. The REUSE Company. From Zero to Hero: The Temperature War. Available online: https://www.reusecompany.com/webinars/from-zero-to-hero-the-temperature-war (accessed on 9 January 2026).
78. *ARP4754A*; Guidelines for Development of Civil Aircraft and Systems. SAE International: Warrendale, PA, USA, 2010.
79. *DO-254*; Design Assurance Guidance for Airborne Electronic Hardware. RTCA: Washington, DC, USA, 2000.
80. *IEC 62304*; Medical Device Software—Software Life Cycle Processes. IEC: Geneva, Switzerland, 2006.
81. *ISO 13485*; Medical Devices—Quality Management Systems—Requirements for Regulatory Purposes. ISO: Geneva, Switzerland, 2016.
82. *ISO 14971*; Medical Devices—Application of Risk Management to Medical Devices. 3rd ed. ISO: Geneva, Switzerland, 2019.
83. *EN 50126*; Railway Applications—The Specification and Demonstration of Reliability, Availability, Maintainability and Safety (RAMS). 2nd ed. CENELEC: Brussels, Belgium, 2017.
84. *EN 50129*; Railway Applications—Communication, Signalling and Processing Systems—Safety Related Electronic Systems for Signalling. 2nd ed. CENELEC: Brussels, Belgium, 2018.
85. *IEC 61508*; Functional Safety of Electrical/Electronic/Programmable Electronic Safety-Related Systems. 2nd ed. IEC: Geneva, Switzerland, 2010.
86. Arduino. Arduino Mega 2560 Rev3. Available online: https://store.arduino.cc/products/arduino-mega-2560-rev3 (accessed on 9 January 2026).
87. Bourns. CAT 16. Available online: https://www.bourns.com/products/resistors/chip-resistor-arrays/product/CAT16 (accessed on 9 January 2026).

https://doi.org/10.3390/app16052179

applied sciences

MDPI

Article

Context-Aware Code Review Automation: A Retrieval-Augmented Approach

Büşra İçöz [1,2,*] and Göksel Biricik [1]

1 Department of Computer Engineering, Yildiz Technical University, 34220 Istanbul, Turkey; gbiricik@yildiz.edu.tr
2 ING Netherlands, 1102 CT Amsterdam, The Netherlands
* Correspondence: busra.icoz@std.yildiz.edu.tr

Abstract

Manual code review is essential for software quality, but often slows down development cycles due to the high time demands on developers. In this study, we propose an automated solution for Python (version 3.13) projects that generates code review comments by combining Large Language Models (LLMs) with Retrieval-Augmented Generation (RAG). To achieve this, we first curated a dataset from GitHub pull requests (PRs) using the GitHub REST Application Programming Interface (API) (version 2022-11-28) and classified comments into semantic categories using a semi-supervised Support Vector Machine (SVM) model. During the review process, our system uses a vector database to retrieve the top-k most relevant historical comments, providing context for a diverse spectrum of open-weights LLMs, including DeepSeek-Coder-33B, Qwen2.5-Coder-32B, Codestral-22B, CodeLlama-13B, Mistral-Instruct-7B, and Phi-3-Mini. We evaluated the system using a multi-step validation that combined standard metrics (BLEU-4, ROUGE-L, cosine similarity) with an LLM-as-a-Judge approach, and verified the results through targeted human review to ensure consistency with expert standards. The findings show that retrieval augmentation improves feedback relevance for larger models, with DeepSeek-Coder's alignment score increasing by 17.9% at a retrieval depth of $k = 3$. In contrast, smaller models such as Phi-3-Mini suffered from context collapse, where too much context reduced accuracy. To manage this trade-off, we built a hybrid expert system that routes each task to the most suitable model. Our results indicate that the proposed approach improved performance by 13.2% compared to the zero-shot baseline ($k = 0$). In addition, our proposed system reduces hallucinations and generates comments that closely align with the standards expected from the experts.

Keywords: code review; code review automation; Large Language Models (LLMs); Retrieval-Augmented Generation (RAG); software automation; semi-supervised learning

1. Introduction

Modern software engineering relies heavily on code review, not only to catch defects early, but also to enforce coding standards and prevent security issues from reaching production [1]. Empirical studies on Modern Code Review (MCR) in major technology companies, such as Google, identify rigorous peer review as the main driver for maintaining long-term software quality [2].

Despite its critical importance, the manual nature of this process creates a significant bottleneck. As codebases expand, the cognitive load on developers also increases. Research indicates that engineers dedicate approximately six hours per week exclusively to code review, wasting valuable time on feature development [3]. Human reviews are subjective; the quality of feedback depends on the expertise of the engineer making the review, and this can often lead to minor logical errors that are overlooked in inconsistent assessments [4].

Although the industry has adopted static analysis tools (SAST) such as SonarQube or ESLint to mitigate these issues, their impact is limited. They are effective at catching syntax violations, but these rule-based systems lack a semantic understanding of business logic and cannot offer context-sensitive suggestions [5]. The recent emergence of Large Language Models (LLMs) offers a promising alternative that demonstrates advanced capabilities in code summarization and generation [6]. However, deploying standard LLMs for code review remains problematic. Without access to a project's specific history or conventions, these models frequently generate generic feedback or hallucinations—reasonable but incorrect recommendations that fail to align with project requirements [7].

In this study, we introduce a Python code review automation framework implemented via Retrieval Augmented Generation (RAG). Unlike generic retrieval approaches that treat all code changes uniformly, our system employs a two-stage process. First, it classifies the pull request into a semantic category (e.g., Functional, Refactoring) to determine the reviewer's intent. Crucially, we implement a dynamic model routing strategy: based on this classification, the system directs the prompt and retrieved context to the specific open-weight LLM architecture (e.g., Qwen2.5-Coder:32B for functional defects, Mistral-Instruct:7B for documentation) that is empirically optimized for that type of category. This structured context and specialized routing enable the selected expert LLM to generate precise, consistent, and actionable feedback. Specifically, this study addresses the following Research Questions (RQs):

- RQ1: To what extent does Retrieval-Augmented Generation (RAG) improve the specificity and accuracy of automated code reviews compared to baseline Large Language Models?
- RQ2: What is the optimal retrieval depth (k) to balance context availability with cognitive load, and at what point does information overload occur?
- RQ3: Do specific LLM architectures demonstrate specialized capabilities across different semantic categories, such as detecting functional bugs versus suggesting refactoring?
- RQ4: To what extent does a dynamic Expert Routing mechanism that assigns tasks to specialized architectures based on semantic category enhance the overall technical accuracy of automated code reviews compared to zero-shot baselines?
- RQ5: How do traditional n-gram metrics (e.g., BLEU, ROUGE) compare to semantic verification methods (such as LLM-as-a-Judge) in accurately assessing the quality of automated code reviews?

Motivated by these questions, our primary contributions to this study are as follows:

- We constructed a specialized dataset of Python code reviews and classified them into semantic categories: Functional, Refactoring, Documentation, and Discussion, based on the taxonomy established by Turzo et al. [8], using a semi-supervised SVM approach.
- We developed a RAG-based pipeline that uses top-k retrieval to guide the LLM, significantly suppressing hallucinations compared to zero-shot baselines.
- We benchmarked our system against human-written ground truth using both traditional metrics and a semantic judge, demonstrating that retrieval-augmented models produce comments with significantly higher relevance and specificity.

The remainder of this paper is organized as follows. Section 2 reviews the literature on MCR and LLM-based automation. Section 3 details our data curation process, classification

https://doi.org/10.3390/app16041875

strategy, and RAG architecture. Section 4 outlines the experimental setup, including the models and metrics used. Section 5 presents a comprehensive analysis of the results. Finally, Section 6 discusses threats to validity, and Section 7 concludes the study with directions for future work.

2. Related Work

In this section, we summarize the evolution of code review research from manual methods to automated systems. We divide our review into three main parts: the evolution of automated code review, the application of Large Language Models (LLMs) in software engineering, and the integration of Retrieval-Augmented Generation (RAG) for these tasks.

2.1. The Evolution of Code Review Automation

We first examine the origins of code review. This process began with Fagan's code inspection, which established peer review as a critical method for identifying defects [9]. While manual review is effective, we note that it is labor-intensive and often causes delays due to the limited availability of developers.

To address these bottlenecks, the industry first adopted Static Analysis Tools (SAST). These tools automatically detect syntax errors. However, as Johnson et al. pointed out, these systems often generate false alarms and lack a semantic understanding of the code's business logic [5].

Following this, researchers developed Context-Aware Recommender Systems (CARS). We observe that these systems focus on optimizing the process rather than the content. Mateos and Bellogín note that including spatial and temporal context improves the precision of recommendations [10]. Similarly, Sadman et al. introduced the ADCR tool to assign reviewers based on expertise, while Strand et al. confirmed that such context-aware assignments reduce review turnaround times in industrial settings [11].

Eventually, research shifted toward fully Automated Code Review (ACR). Tufano et al. treated code review as a translation task, training models to "translate" buggy code into fixed code [12]. Building on this, Li et al. introduced CodeReviewer, a model designed to understand code changes [13]. We also highlight Lin et al., who argued that automated systems perform better when trained on data filtered for reviewer expertise [14].

Although these models were effective, the rise of Large Language Models (LLMs) offered a more powerful and general solution. This research laid the foundation for using LLMs in code review, which we discuss in the next section.

2.2. Large Language Models for Software Engineering

Large Language Models have significantly improved the automation capabilities of software engineering processes. Unlike previous deep learning models, LLMs can interpret complex logic and provide explanations in natural language. Rasheed et al. showed that LLM-based tools can detect code smells and vulnerabilities that traditional tools do not detect [15]. In addition, Rybalchenko and Al-Turany proposed Pearbot, which uses a multi-agent architecture to simulate collaborative reviews and identify issues that single models might overlook [16].

However, we identify a critical limitation: LLMs often lack project-specific context. Li et al. attempted to solve this by using "code slicing" to provide relevant variable definitions [13]. Haroon et al. also emphasized the need to verify whether LLMs truly understand the code or are just hallucinating [17]. These challenges motivate the need for retrieval-based approaches, which we discuss next.

https://doi.org/10.3390/app16041875

2.3. RAG for Code Review Tasks

Finally, we examine Retrieval-Augmented Generation (RAG). Lewis et al. define RAG as a framework that retrieves external data to ground the responses of the model, thus reducing hallucinations [18].

In the context of code review, Hong and Baik developed RAG-Reviewer. They used retrieval to find similar historical reviews, which helped the model predict rare, domain-specific technical terms [19]. RAG mitigates the knowledge gap by retrieving external data to ground the model's responses. Wang et al. demonstrated in the CODERAG-BENCH study that RAG significantly boosts performance in code generation tasks by providing the necessary context [20].

2.4. Summary and Research Gap

In summary, while prior studies have successfully applied LLMs to code review, we observe that they mostly rely on generic models or static retrieval methods. Current systems, such as RAG-Reviewer [19], treat all code changes uniformly. They lack the flexibility to adapt to the specific intent of a modification, such as distinguishing between a complex bug fix and a documentation update. In this study, we address this limitation by introducing a dynamic routing strategy. Unlike previous approaches, we first categorize the code change and then route it to the most suitable expert model, ensuring that the retrieval process is optimized for the specific task type.

3. Methodology

We propose a framework to automate code review by augmenting LLMs with domain-specific context. The architecture (Figure 1) operates as an event-driven pipeline from a developer's Pull Request (PR) to the generated review comments. We also constructed a dataset derived from high-quality open-source repositories (Figure 2).

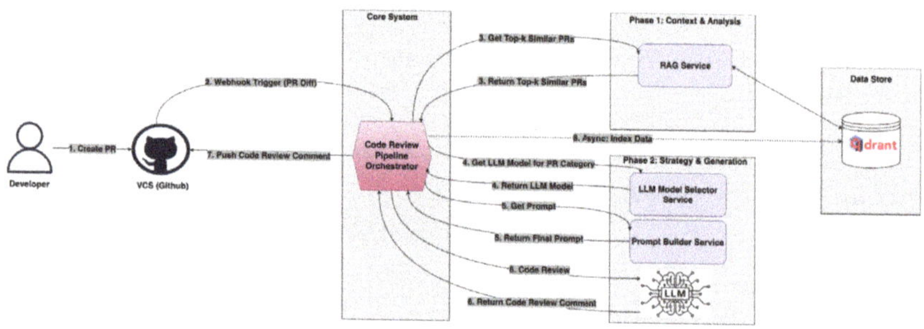

Figure 1. System architecture of the proposed Code Review Pipeline Orchestrator. The orchestrator bridges the developer's VCS (GitHub) and LLMs. Qdrant [21] serves as the vector store for RAG, enabling categorized and strategy-driven code reviews.

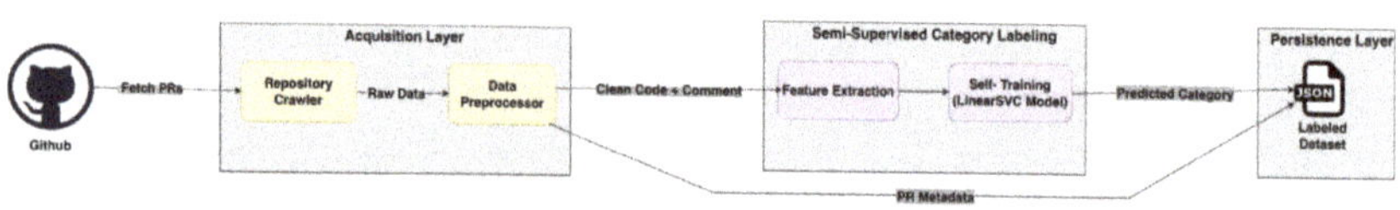

Figure 2. The end-to-end data collection and processing pipeline. The system ingests raw data from GitHub, filters for quality, and applies semi-supervised labeling before indexing.

3.1. System Architecture

Our proposed system works as a middleware layer between the developer's version control system (VCS) and the LLMs, organized into a core workflow plus two phases: Phase 1 (Context & Analysis) and Phase 2 (Strategy & Generation).

https://doi.org/10.3390/app16041875

3.1.1. The Core Workflow

The process begins when a developer creates a Pull Request (PR), which triggers a webhook event (Steps 1–2). The Code Review Pipeline Orchestrator captures this payload, extracting the code diff, file paths, and metadata. This central component acts as a state manager, routing data between the vector store and the inference engine.

3.1.2. Phase 1: Contextual Retrieval and Semantic Analysis

Standard LLMs often struggle with hallucinations when generating code reviews due to a lack of repository-specific context [22]. To mitigate this, we employ a Retrieval-Augmented Generation (RAG) approach powered by Qdrant [21].

- **Vector Space Modeling:** We embed each code snippet (or diff) using the `sentence-transformers/all-MiniLM-L6-v2` encoder, which generates a 384-dimensional vector representation ($n = 384$) [23]. To measure semantic relatedness between an incoming query vector $\mathbf{A}$ and a stored review vector $\mathbf{B}$, we use cosine similarity, i.e., the cosine of the angle between the two vectors [24,25]:

$$\cos(\mathbf{A}, \mathbf{B}) = \frac{\mathbf{A} \cdot \mathbf{B}}{||\mathbf{A}||\,||\mathbf{B}||}. \tag{1}$$

- **Retrieval-Informed Categorization:** For every incoming PR, the system retrieves the top-k most similar historical examples (Step 3). In this study, we use the term "neighbors" to refer to the vectors in the 384-dimensional embedding space [23] that have the highest cosine similarity to the query vector [24,25]. The system then uses the metadata of these semantic neighbors to infer the category of the new change. For instance, if the majority of the retrieved neighbors are labeled as "Refactoring", the system uses this as a strong prior for the new Pull Request (PR).
  To clearly distinguish the role of categorization in our pipeline: The LinearSVC model (Section 3.4) is employed strictly in the Offline Training Phase to label and expand the historical training dataset. In contrast, during the Online Inference Phase for PR code review, the system utilizes a Retrieval-Informed Categorization strategy. As defined in Equation (1), the semantic category of a new PR is inferred via majority voting from the metadata of the retrieved top-k neighbors ($n = 384$). This ensures that the routing decision is dynamically driven by the most relevant context.

3.1.3. Phase 2: Strategy and Generation

Once the relevant context and inferred category are established, our pipeline moves to the generation phase.

- **Prompt Construction:** The Prompt Builder Service synthesizes a composite prompt (Step 5). This prompt includes the new code diff, the retrieved top-k examples, the inferred category, and subcategory as a strong prior; the complete system prompt template is provided in Appendix A.
- **Guided Generation:** The constructed prompt is sent to the expert LLM (our chosen generator model; details in Section 5). Since the prompt explicitly contains similar historical examples along with their categories, the LLM performs Few-Shot Learning [26]. Using the retrieved examples as a template, it generates a review comment that mimics the style, tone, and technical depth of the retrieved "gold standard" reviews (Step 6).

Finally, the generated review comments are pushed back to the VCS (Step 7).

https://doi.org/10.3390/app16041875

3.1.4. Continuous Feedback Loop (Async Indexing)

To ensure that the system stays in the loop with the project's evolution, we implemented an Asynchronous Indexing Worker (Step 8 in Figure 1). This component runs as a background process to avoid slowing down the main review workflow. Once a PR is successfully merged, this worker captures the final approved code and the reviewer's comments. Then it vectorizes these pairs using the encoder described in Section 3.1.2 and updates the Qdrant index [21]. This decoupling ensures that our knowledge base is continuously refreshed with new "gold standard" (i.e., approved and merged) examples without adding latency to the active pipeline.

3.2. *Data Collection and Processing Pipeline*

To support the architecture described in the previous section, we developed a robust data pipeline designed for continuous ingestion and automated categorization. The framework consists of three primary layers: Acquisition, Semi-Supervised Labeling, and Persistence, as illustrated in Figure 2.

3.2.1. Dynamic Data Acquisition Strategy

Static datasets in software engineering often become outdated as coding standards and libraries evolve, a challenge highlighted in recent studies on software repository mining [27]. To address this limitation, we designed a Dynamic Data Acquisition Pipeline that autonomously ingests real-world development data via a scheduled crawler. This approach ensures that our retrieval base remains aligned with current Python practices. The dataset is open-source and continuously updated: https://github.com/busraicoz/crc-py-dataset (accessed on 26 December 2025).

3.2.2. Continuous Ingestion Heuristics and Temporal Isolation

The crawler employs a Daily Trending Heuristic that queries the GitHub Application Programming Interface (API) every 24 h, targeting the top 10 trending Python repositories in the English language. To ensure the integrity of our evaluation, we apply a strict filtering process:

1. **Temporal Cutoff (Anti-Leakage):** To prevent data contamination, we enforced a strict Temporal Cutoff. We only selected PRs created after 1 June 2024. This date post-dates the knowledge cutoff of the evaluated models, ensuring that the test set consists of unseen data that could not have been memorized during the models' pre-training phase. By targeting only recent contributions that post-date the training cutoffs of the evaluated models, we ensure that our benchmark measures true generalization capability rather than recall.
2. **PR Status:** We only ingest "closed" or "merged" Pull Requests (PRs) to ensure the review cycle is complete, and the code changes are verified.
3. **Comment Selection:** We prioritize the first technical comment in a review thread because subsequent replies often contain conversational text (e.g., "Thanks", "Will fix") rather than independent technical feedback, and filtering these out ensures that the model trains on the primary review instruction.
4. **Data Sanitization:** We filtered the dataset to remove non-informative content. This process excluded automated bot messages and trivial conversational replies (e.g., "Thanks", "Ok") that lack technical substance, adhering to standard data preparation protocols.

https://doi.org/10.3390/app16041875

3.3. Taxonomy and Semi-Supervised Categorization

We adopted the hierarchical taxonomy established by Turzo and Bosu [8], condensing their 17 subcategories into five high-level intents suitable for retrieval tasks (Table 1). To manage the trade-off between detail and data availability, we employ a hybrid strategy: we use the 17 specific subcategories from the original taxonomy (e.g., "Variable Naming") to provide detailed context in the system prompt detailed in Section 3.1.3. However, for the routing mechanism detailed in Section 5.4, we aggregate these into 5 high-level categories, which allows for the model to access specific semantic labels without causing data sparsity issues in the routing layer.

Table 1. Code Review Categorization Taxonomy. The high-level categories are optimized to guide the RAG retrieval process.

Category	Description	Mapped Subcategories
Functional	Issues affecting correctness, logic, runtime behavior, or resource management.	Logical errors; Resource handling; Timing; Interface mismatches.
Refactoring	Improvements to code structure, readability, or maintainability.	Variable naming; Code organization; Validation cleanup; Alternate output.
Documentation	Updates to docstrings, inline comments, or external docs.	Documentation.
Discussion	Interactions involving clarification requests or design debates.	Design discussions; Questions; Praise.
False Positive	Invalid concerns or comments explicitly refuted by the author.	False Positive.

3.4. Model Selection and Benchmarking

To automate the labeling of the incoming data category, we benchmarked three different approaches: (1) Zero-Shot classification using GPT-3.5 [26], (2) Logistic Regression with TF–IDF vectors [28], and (3) Linear Support Vector Classification (LinearSVC) with TF–IDF vectors [29].

As presented in Table 2, the LinearSVC approach achieved the highest accuracy (0.622), significantly outperforming the Zero-Shot LLM baseline. Consequently, we selected LinearSVC as the core classifier for our semi-supervised framework.

Table 2. Performance Comparison of Categorization Models. Note: We implemented and evaluated the Zero-Shot LLM [26] and TF-IDF + LogReg [28] baselines specifically for this study to provide a comparative benchmark for our TF-IDF + LinearSVC [29] approach.

Method	Accuracy	F1 Macro	F1 Weighted
Zero-Shot LLM	0.494	0.289	0.479
TF-IDF + LogReg	0.589	**0.414**	0.609
TF-IDF + LinearSVC	**0.622**	0.398	**0.627**

Bold values indicate the best performance in each column.

3.5. Self-Training Algorithm

Using the LinearSVC model, we implemented a self-training loop, as detailed in Algorithm 1, to expand our dataset, a technique proven effective for labeling tasks with limited seed data [30]. The process begins with a manually labeled seed set of 1273 PRs and iteratively labels high-confidence samples from the unlabeled stream.

However, since standard Support Vector Machines (SVMs) output a signed distance rather than a probability, we wrapped the model within a `CalibratedClassifierCV`. This step transforms the raw distance into a calibrated probability distribution (confidence

https://doi.org/10.3390/app16041875

score). Enabling probability output is essential for our self-training loop [30], as it allows us to strictly apply the confidence threshold ($\tau = 0.7$). Predictions falling below this threshold are discarded to prevent noisy labels from entering the training set.

Algorithm 1 Semi-Supervised Categorization Loop

Require: L: Manually labeled seed set ($N = 1273$)
Require: U: Incoming unlabeled stream from crawler
Require: τ: Confidence threshold (0.7)
Ensure: C: Robust Classifier

1. Dual-Branch Feature Extraction
$V_{\text{text}} \leftarrow \text{TF-IDF}(\textit{text}, \text{ngram} = (1,2))$
$V_{\text{code}} \leftarrow \text{TF-IDF}(\textit{code}, \text{char\_ngram} = (3,5))$
$X \leftarrow \text{Concat}(V_{\text{text}}, V_{\text{code}})$
2. Training & Calibration
$C \leftarrow \text{LinearSVC}(\text{class\_weight} =' \textit{balanced}')$ ▷ Handle class imbalance
$C_{\text{cal}} \leftarrow \text{CalibratedClassifierCV}(C)$ ▷ Enable probability output
$C_{\text{cal}}.\text{fit}(X_L, Y_L)$
3. Pseudo-Labeling & Expansion
for $x_j \in U$ **do**
  $\textit{probs} \leftarrow C_{\text{cal}}.\text{predict\_proba}(x_j)$
  if $\max(\textit{probs}) > \tau$ **then**
    $y_{\text{pred}} \leftarrow \text{argmax}(\textit{probs})$
    $L \leftarrow L \cup \{(x_j, y_{\text{pred}})\}$
  end if
end for
return C_{cal}

3.6. Data Persistence and Schema Design

To ensure consistent processing across the RAG pipeline, all collected and labeled data are serialized into a standardized JSON format. This schema was designed to preserve critical metadata—such as the repository (repo) origin and the timestamp (created_at)—which provides temporal and project-specific context during the retrieval phase.

As shown in Figure 3, each entry encapsulates the code diff, the reviewer's comment, and the inferred semantic labels. This structured representation facilitates efficient parsing using the embedding models described in Section 3.


```
{
  "code": "@@ -35.11 +35.11 @@\n
          -    except TypeError as te:\n
          +    except TypeError as te: # codespell...",
  "comment": "you can just use ‘e‘ for these, no need\n
              to clutter with codespell...",
  "file_path": "reflex/base.py",
  "category": "functional",
  "subcategory": "solution approach",
  "repo": "reflex-dev/reflex",
  "pr_number": 4831,
  "created_at": "2025-02-18T20:50:42Z"
}
```


(a)


```
{
  "code": "@@ -1126.7 +1126.12 @@\n
            -        assert_(sys.getrefcount(ob) ==
            -        ...\n
            +        if sys.version_info < (3.14):
            +        \n assert_(newrc == rc - 1)",
  "comment": "I don’t understand why this changed
              -\n maybe @seberg or @mhvk might have
              ...",
  "file_path": "numpy/_core/tests/test_nditer.py",
  "category": "discussion",
  "subcategory": "question",
  "repo": "numpy/numpy",
  "pr_number": 28748,
  "created_at": "2025-04-17T15:54:27Z"
}
```


(b)

Figure 3. Representative JSON entries from the `crc-py-dataset`. The schema standardizes unstructured code reviews into a machine-readable format optimized for vector embedding. (**a**) Sample A: Functional Category. A variable naming suggestion in the `reflex` repository. (**b**) Sample B: Discussion Category. An inquiry regarding version-specific behavior in `numpy`.

https://doi.org/10.3390/app16041875

4. Experimental Design and Evaluation

To validate the efficiency of our proposed framework, we conducted a large-scale comparative study aligned with the defined Research Questions (RQ) in Section 1. Unlike synthetic benchmarks, our experimental setup simulates a real-world enterprise software environment using the Home Assistant project [31] as a test set. This approach allows us to assess model performance within a complex and actively maintained software project, thus replicating the dynamics of real-world collaborative development.

4.1. Dataset Characteristics and Knowledge Base Construction

We focus our evaluation on *Home Assistant Core* (`home-assistant/core`), a modular Python codebase that presents a heterogeneous contribution surface suitable for project-based code review experiments [32].

To simulate a robust Context-Aware AI agent, we built a Composite Knowledge Base designed to capture both project-specific data and general coding best practices. Our retrieval corpus consists of two distinct layers:

1. **Target Project History (Primary Source):** We extracted 3739 historical review pairs directly from the *Home Assistant Core* repository. These samples represent the specific coding style, architectural patterns, and conventions unique to the target project.
2. **crc-py-dataset (Secondary Source):** To address the "cold start" problem—where specific patterns may not yet exist in the project history—we augmented the vector store with our *crc-py-dataset* dataset. This corpus contains high-quality review samples from diverse top-tier open-source repositories to ensure that the model has a fundamental understanding of general software engineering principles.

Retrieval Strategy: We utilize a unified vector space for both data sources. During the inference phase, the retrieval mechanism performs a semantic search across this composite index, establishing an implicit fallback mechanism:

- If the code difference is semantically close to the previous *Home Assistant Core* PR, the system prioritizes retrieving project-specific context, ensuring style alignment.
- If no high-confidence match is found within the project history, the retrieval system naturally falls back to relevant examples from the *crc-py-dataset* dataset.

Data Splitting: The test set remains strictly isolated to prevent data leakage. We enforced a strict chronological split:

- **Knowledge Base (Project Memory):** The training split ($N = 3739$) populates the RAG Vector Store with historically observed review patterns.
- **Test Set (Unseen Contributions):** The test split ($N = 1625$) contains contributions strictly after the cutoff date, emulating deployment on unseen changes [33].

Semantic Distribution Analysis

To understand the complexity of the review task, we analyzed the semantic distribution of the dataset (Figure 4).

As shown in Figure 4, the dataset is oriented mainly toward constructive feedback types (>67% Solution Approach and Question). This distribution justifies our preference for using reasoning-based models such as DeepSeek-Coder-33B and Qwen2.5-Coder-32B. To avoid distorting the assessment, we layered the test set (Table 3) to ensure adequate representation of minority classes such as "False Positive" ($N = 15$).

https://doi.org/10.3390/app16041875

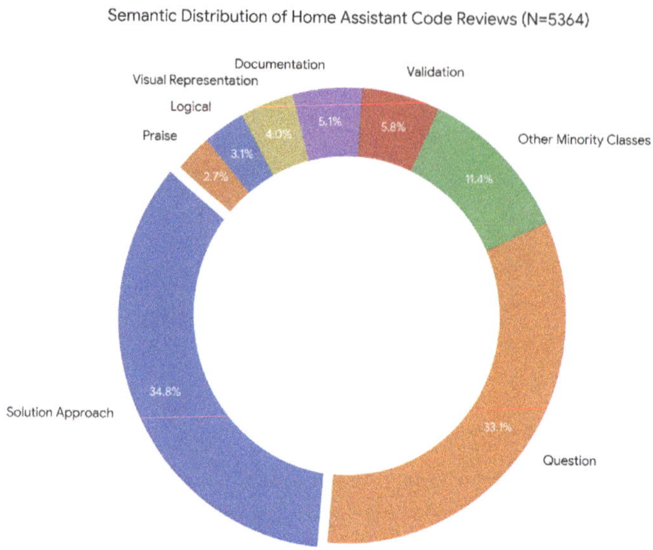

Figure 4. Semantic distribution of the Home Assistant dataset ($N = 5364$). The dominance of "Solution Approach" (34.8%) and "Question" (33.1%) categories shows that models are evaluated on their ability to provide actionable feedback rather than simple validation.

Table 3. Composition of the Evaluation Dataset (test set). We enforced a minimum constraint ($N \geq 15$) for minority classes to ensure rigorous testing of edge cases.

Subcategory	Total Available	Test Set (N)	Test Ratio (%)
Alternate Output	84	40	47.6%
Code Organization	70	25	35.7%
Design Discussion	54	25	46.3%
Documentation	276	75	27.2%
False Positive	17	15	88.2%
Functional	65	25	38.5%
Interface	77	35	42.5%
Logical	166	65	39.2%
Praise	146	65	44.5%
Question	1776	435	24.5%
Resource	20	15	75.0%
Solution Approach	1867	530	28.4%
Support Issues	77	25	45.5%
Timing	105	45	42.9%
Validation	311	115	37.0%
Variable Naming	41	15	36.6%
Visual Representation	212	75	35.4%
Total	5364	1625	30.3%

4.2. Subject Models

To answer RQ1, we selected six state-of-the-art open-weight LLMs (presented in Table 4) based on their rankings on the Hugging Face Open LLM Leaderboard [34] and architectural diversity.

https://doi.org/10.3390/app16041875

Table 4. Subject Models utilized in the experiment. All models were executed locally via the Ollama framework [35] to ensure reproducibility.

Model	Params	Context	Selection Rationale
DeepSeek-Coder	33B	16k	SOTA Open Code Model [36]
Qwen2.5-Coder	32B	32k	Advanced Reasoning Logic [37]
Codestral	22B	32k	Optimized for Code Completion [38]
CodeLlama	13B	16k	Industry Standard Baseline [39]
Mistral-Instruct	7B	8k	General Purpose Reasoning [40]
Phi-3-Mini	3.8B	4k	Efficiency Benchmark (SLM) [41]

4.3. Experimental Configuration

We manipulate the retrieval strategy as the primary independent variable. We tested four distinct configurations for each subject model:

1. **Baseline ($k = 0$):** The model reviews the code solely based on its pre-trained parametric knowledge (Zero-Shot).
2. **Project-Aware RAG ($k \in \{1, 3, 5\}$):** The model is augmented with the top-k most similar historical reviews, retrieved exclusively from the knowledge base.

To ensure that the observed improvements were due to the RAG mechanism rather than random variance, we fixed the generation temperature to $\tau = 0.1$ and standardized the context window to 4096 tokens across all models.

4.4. Evaluation Methodology

Given the linguistic variability of code reviews, we employed a multifaceted evaluation protocol involving automated metrics, large-scale LLM scoring, and targeted human verification.

4.4.1. Automated Text Similarity Metrics

We use three automatic metrics to compare each generated review comment with its human-written reference. BLEU-4 and ROUGE-L capture surface overlap in different ways, while an embedding-based cosine score provides a coarse semantic signal when multiple phrasings are reasonable [25,42,43]. Because BLEU scores can vary with tokenization and other evaluation settings, we keep the implementation of the metric fixed across all experiments and document the configuration for reproducibility [44].

BLEU-4 is computed as the geometric mean of modified n-gram precisions up to $n = 4$, with a brevity penalty (BP) applied at the corpus level [42]. With uniform weights $w_n = \frac{1}{4}$,

$$\text{BLEU-4} = \text{BP} \cdot \exp\left(\sum_{n=1}^{4} w_n \log p_n\right). \tag{2}$$

We use the original definition of the brevity penalty with candidate length c and effective reference length r [42]:

$$\text{BP} = \begin{cases} 1, & c > r, \\ \exp\left(1 - \frac{r}{c}\right), & c \leq r. \end{cases} \tag{3}$$

To make BLEU results comparable between runs, we standardized our configuration following the established guidance on BLEU reporting [44].

ROUGE-L is based on the Longest Common Subsequence (LCS), which rewards in-order overlap without requiring contiguous matches [43]. For reference X (length m) and

https://doi.org/10.3390/app16041875

hypothesis Y (length n), let $\text{LCS}(X,Y)$ denote the LCS *length*. We compute LCS-based recall and precision [43]:

$$R_{\text{LCS}} = \frac{\text{LCS}(X,Y)}{m}, \qquad P_{\text{LCS}} = \frac{\text{LCS}(X,Y)}{n}. \tag{4}$$

We report sentence-level ROUGE-L F_1 with $\beta = 1$ (precision and recall weighted equally), following Lin (2004) [43]:

$$F_{\text{LCS}} = \frac{(1+\beta^2)\, P_{\text{LCS}} R_{\text{LCS}}}{R_{\text{LCS}} + \beta^2 P_{\text{LCS}}}. \tag{5}$$

We also compute cosine similarity between sentence embeddings as a simple semantic proximity measure [24,25]:

$$\cos(\mathbf{u},\mathbf{v}) = \frac{\mathbf{u}^\top \mathbf{v}}{\|\mathbf{u}\|_2\, \|\mathbf{v}\|_2}. \tag{6}$$

We obtain embeddings using `sentence-transformers/all-MiniLM-L6-v2` (384 dimensions) [23]. We use this score as a supplement to lexical metrics; it is not intended to verify technical correctness on its own.

4.4.2. Large-Scale Semantic Evaluation (LLM-as-a-Judge)

To assess technical precision in our extensive test set ($N = 1625$), we implemented a scalable "LLM-as-a-Judge" protocol [45]. We deployed Llama-3-70B-Instruct [46] as the evaluator to efficiently handle the >39,000 inference steps. The judge evaluates each review on a 10-point scale (Table 5).

Table 5. Scoring rubric for the LLM-as-a-Judge protocol, adapted from the MT-Bench methodology [45].

Score	Criteria Definition
10	Perfect: Identifies exact issue and suggests correct fix.
8–9	High Quality: Technically correct, minor tone issues.
5–7	Partial: Identifies topic but solution is incomplete.
1–4	Failure: Misses core issue or hallucinates.
0	Invalid: Factually incorrect or empty.

4.4.3. Human Evaluation and Calibration

To mitigate the inherent bias of automated judge models, we conducted a targeted human verification study. A team of three senior backend engineers, each with over nine years of experience, conducted a manual evaluation of randomly selected samples from the dataset.

Sampling Strategy: We selected at least 5 distinct examples for each of the 17 subcategories listed in Table 3, resulting in a high-quality validation set of 105 samples.

Calibration Protocol: The human reviewer scored the sampled instances using the rubric in Table 5, while remaining blind to the LLM-as-a-Judge outputs. We then quantified the agreement between the human and judge scores. This calibration step was used to assess whether automated ratings reflect human perceptions of review quality, with particular attention to more subjective categories such as "Design Discussion" and "Code Organization".

5. Experimental Results and Discussion

In this section, we critically evaluated the experimental findings to address the five Research Questions (RQs) proposed in Section 1. We examine the interaction among

https://doi.org/10.3390/app16041875

retrieval strategies, model architectures, and evaluation metrics, and interpret the findings through the concepts of Information Overload and Semantic Alignment.

5.1. RQ1: Baseline Capabilities and the "Reasoning Gap"

RQ1: To what extent does Retrieval-Augmented Generation (RAG) improve the specificity and accuracy of automated code reviews compared to baseline Large Language Models?

To better understand how each architecture performs without the influence of retrieval, we start by looking at the zero-shot performance ($k = 0$). This baseline shows the knowledge that the model has built up during pre-training. As seen in Table 6, the results highlight a clear ranking in performance, which is driven more by how well the model specializes in the domain rather than just the size of the parameters.

Table 6. Performance comparison across varying retrieval depths (k). We report BLEU-4 and ROUGE-L for lexical overlap, alongside Semantic Similarity, Judge Score (0–10), and Human Evaluation (0–10). Note: All results presented in this table are derived from our experimental evaluation on the Home Assistant Core test set [31,32] as defined in Section 4.1. The models were executed locally using the Ollama framework [35].

Model	k	BLEU-4	ROUGE-L	Sem. Sim	Judge Score	Human Eval.
CodeLlama-13B	0	0.009	**0.111**	**0.318**	3.54	3.80
	1	0.007	0.099	0.233	3.60	4.20
	3	0.008	0.104	0.263	**3.87**	**4.80**
	5	**0.010**	0.100	0.245	3.77	4.20
Codestral-22B	0	0.011	0.133	0.397	5.06	6.00
	1	0.014	0.134	0.398	5.47	6.40
	3	0.018	0.141	**0.418**	**5.67**	**7.20**
	5	**0.021**	**0.144**	0.416	5.42	6.20
DeepSeek-Coder-33B	0	0.011	**0.127**	0.329	4.45	5.20
	1	0.011	0.117	0.356	4.67	5.60
	3	**0.013**	0.123	**0.361**	**5.24**	**6.40**
	5	0.012	0.121	0.358	5.02	6.00
Mistral-Instruct-7B	0	0.012	0.126	**0.416**	**6.01**	**6.00**
	1	0.016	0.129	0.386	5.62	5.80
	3	0.015	0.131	0.388	5.63	5.80
	5	**0.017**	**0.133**	0.386	5.46	5.20
Phi-3-Mini (3.8B)	0	0.009	**0.123**	**0.384**	**5.52**	**6.00**
	1	0.009	0.121	0.359	5.28	5.60
	3	0.010	0.116	0.336	5.23	5.80
	5	**0.013**	0.112	0.311	4.74	5.00
Qwen2.5-Coder-32B	0	0.020	0.153	0.447	6.34	7.00
	1	**0.031**	0.161	0.472	6.68	7.40
	3	0.028	**0.165**	**0.478**	**6.76**	**7.60**
	5	0.028	0.164	0.467	6.54	7.40

Bold indicates the highest score within each model's group.

Analysis: The strong performance of Qwen2.5-Coder-32B (6.34) demonstrates the effectiveness of zero-shot learning. Unlike general-purpose models, Qwen2.5-Coder-32B has a natural "code intuition" that allows it to identify functional problems without needing external context [39].

Interestingly, there is a gap between lexical fluency and functional accuracy in general models such as Mistral-Instruct-7B. Although Mistral-Instruct-7B scores high in Semantic Similarity (0.416), its technical precision drops when using RAG (6.01 $\rightarrow$ 5.46). We can call this Surface-Level Semantic Alignment: the model may sound like it is providing a solid code review, but it loses its technical accuracy when the context becomes too complex. This

https://doi.org/10.3390/app16041875

suggests that tuning models for general dialog could unintentionally weaken their ability to maintain technical precision in specialized tasks [47].

5.2. RQ2: Context Saturation and the "Attention Bottleneck"

RQ2: What is the optimal retrieval depth (k) to balance context availability with cognitive load, and at what point does information overload occur?

Our sensitivity analysis, visualized in Figure 5, uncovers two divergent behaviors governed by model scale, confirming the hypothesis that RAG is not a "free lunch" for all architectures [48].

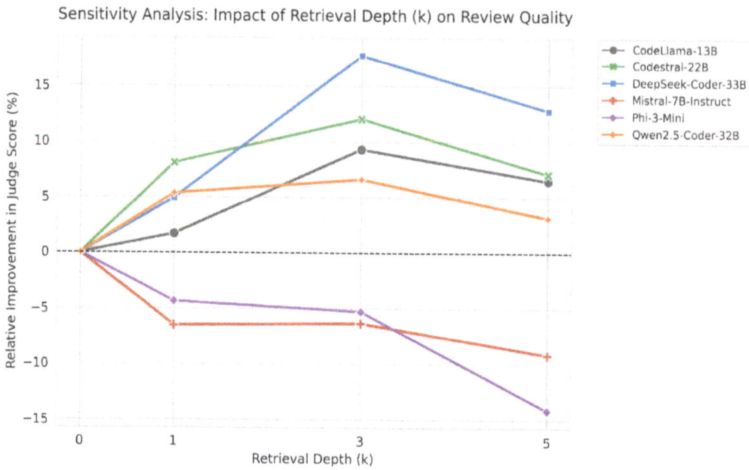

Figure 5. Sensitivity Analysis: Impact of Retrieval Depth (k) on Technical Accuracy. Note the sharp divergence: specialized models (DeepSeek-Coder-33B, Qwen2.5-Coder-32B) benefit from context, whereas smaller models (Phi-3-Mini, Mistral-Instruct-7B) suffer from "Context Collapse" at $k = 5$.

5.2.1. Latent Knowledge Activation

Specialized code models such as DeepSeek-Coder-33B demonstrate a strong positive correlation with context retrieval. DeepSeek's Judge Score surged by 17.7% at $k = 3$ (from 4.45 to 5.24). We interpret this as Latent Knowledge Activation: the model already possesses the engineering knowledge to review code, but requires project-specific examples to align its output style. For these models, $k = 3$ represents the optimal signal-to-noise ratio.

5.2.2. Context Collapse in SLMs

In contrast, Small Language Models (SLMs) exhibited context collapse. Phi-3-Mini(3.8B) showed a linear degradation (5.52 $\rightarrow$ 4.74) as k increased to 5. We attribute this to the Attention Bottleneck: limited capacity models struggle to filter relevant signals from dense historical data [49]. At $k = 5$, the retrieved snippets overwhelmed the model's attention mechanism, leading to Negative Transfer, where irrelevant context distracted the model from the actual code change.

5.3. RQ3: Architectural Proficiency and Error Severity Overestimation

RQ3: Do specific LLM architectures demonstrate specialized capabilities across different semantic categories?

Based on the findings in RQ2, we selected a retrieval depth of $k = 3$ for this evaluation. This setting offers the best trade-off: it provides sufficient historical context to guide larger models; yet, it avoids the context collapse observed in smaller models when they are

https://doi.org/10.3390/app16041875

exposed to excessive data. The heatmap in Figure 6 captures these results, showing the comparative quality scores for each model across the tested categories.

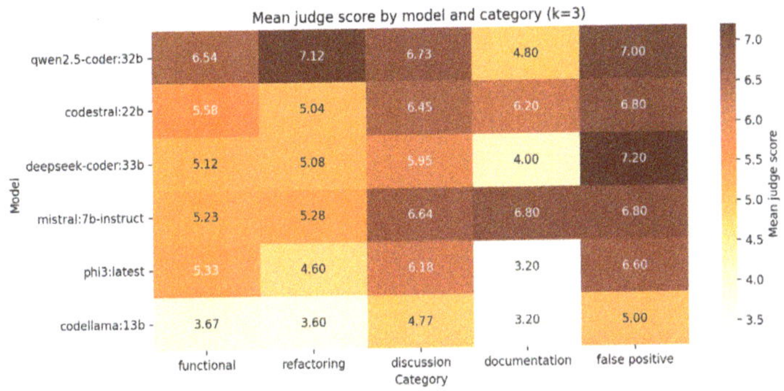

Figure 6. Generation Quality Heatmap (Judge Scores at $k = 3$). Darker cells indicate higher quality. Notice the separation of concerns: "Qwen2.5-Coder-32B" dominates Logic (top-left), while "Mistral-Instruct-7B" dominates Documentation (bottom-right).

Table 7 details the performance breakdown in four semantic categories. The data expose a fundamental trade-off between logical reasoning and language fluency.

Table 7. Model performance (Judge Score 0–10) across semantic categories at $k = 3$. A distinct trade-off is visible: Code-Specialized models (Qwen2.5-Coder-32B) dominate logic tasks, while generic models (Mistral-Instruct-7B) excel in documentation.

Model	Semantic Category ($k = 3$)				Mean
	Functional	Refactoring	Discussion	Docs	
CodeLlama-13B	3.82	3.95	4.10	3.60	3.87
Phi-3-Mini	5.10	5.25	5.40	5.15	5.23
DeepSeek-Coder-33B	5.85	5.90	5.10	4.12	5.24
Mistral-Instruct-7B	5.45	5.50	5.80	**6.80**	5.89
Codestral-22B	5.90	6.10	6.20	6.45	6.16
Qwen2.5-Coder-32B	**6.76**	**7.20**	**7.36**	4.80	**6.53**

Bold indicates the best performance in each category.

5.3.1. The Logic-Fluency Dichotomy

"Qwen2.5-Coder-32B" performs very well in reasoning tasks, scoring 7.20 in Refactoring. This suggests that models trained on code execution traces develop a good understanding of Abstract Syntax Trees (ASTs). However, Qwen scores lower in "Documentation" (5.00), while the generalist "Mistral-Instruct-7B" scores better (6.80). This indicates that documentation is mainly a translation task (Code-to-Natural Language) that relies more on language skills than on strict algorithmic reasoning.

5.3.2. Error Severity Overestimation in Reasoning Models

Despite its precision, "Qwen2.5-Coder-32B" exhibits a behavioral misalignment that we define as Error Severity Overestimation. It systematically misclassified 84.6% of benign stylistic suggestions as serious functional bugs. In practice, models optimized for strict code correctness often treat "invalid code" (technical debt) as "broken code" (system failure), which could lead to too many "False Positive" categories in Continuous Integration and Continuous Delivery (CI/CD) pipelines [50].

https://doi.org/10.3390/app16041875

5.3.3. Quantifying Failure Modes: Hallucination and Severity Overestimation

To further validate our findings, we analyzed the data from our human evaluation ($N = 105$) to quantify two specific failure modes. We defined these metrics using the expert scores and dataset labels as follows:

- **Hallucination Rate:** This assesses the model's reliability regarding factual accuracy. It is defined as the rate at which responses contain verifiable fabrications (such as non-existent APIs, fabricated code elements, or direct contradictions with the code changes), explicitly excluding generic low-quality advice that is technically correct but unhelpful.
- **Severity Overestimation:** This assesses the model's tendency to overstate severity. It is defined as the rate at which innocuous changes (such as Refactoring, Documentation, or Visual Representation) are incorrectly classified as "Functional" defects.

Table 8 presents the "Hallucination Rates" and "Severity Overestimation" across different retrieval depths.

Table 8. Failure rates evaluated by human experts ($N = 105$). Metrics include Hallucination Rate and Severity Overestimation, which measure the error rate specifically on the non-functional subset.

Model	Context (k)	Hallucination Rate (%)	Severity Overestimation (%)
DeepSeek-Coder-33B	0	19.19	20.00
	1	20.61	29.52
	3	**17.69**	**19.05**
	5	21.43	31.43
Phi-3-Mini	0	**10.66**	**20.95**
	1	15.95	20.95
	3	15.00	22.86
	5	20.97	33.33
Codestral-22B	0	16.32	21.90
	1	13.01	20.00
	3	**12.52**	11.43
	5	14.65	**9.52**
Qwen2.5-Coder-32B	0	10.23	20.00
	1	9.69	20.00
	3	**7.86**	**11.43**
	5	11.47	22.86
Mistral-Instruct-7B	0	**9.83**	**36.19**
	1	10.38	37.14
	3	17.30	43.81
	5	15.71	41.90
CodeLlama-13B	0	31.88	36.19
	1	**26.29**	35.24
	3	29.95	**18.10**
	5	37.27	41.90

Bold values indicate the lowest (best) error rate within each model's group.

The results highlight distinct behavioral patterns across the evaluated architectures:

High Precision in Reasoning Models: Qwen2.5-Coder-32B demonstrated the best performance at $k = 3$, with a Hallucination Rate of 7.86% and a Severity Overestimation of 11.43%. This contradicts the assumption that reasoning models are inherently overly strict [50]. It suggests that when provided with sufficient context, these models can accurately distinguish between style suggestions and functional bugs.

Context Collapse in Small Models: Phi-3-Mini showed a clear degradation in performance as we added more context. Its hallucination rate increased from 10.66% at

https://doi.org/10.3390/app16041875

$k = 0$ to 20.97% at $k = 5$. This aligns with the "Lost in the Middle" phenomenon [49], where smaller models struggle to filter relevant information from noisy retrieval contexts.

Bias in Generalist Models: Mistral-Instruct-7B exhibited a consistently high Severity Overestimation rate (>36%) across all settings. Although this model produces fluent text, it lacks the technical nuance to correctly categorize the severity of defects, often marking minor problems as critical failures.

These quantitative findings support the routing logic of our Hybrid Expert Routing (Section 5.4). Although Qwen2.5-Coder-32B exhibits the highest technical stability (lowest error rates), our earlier analysis (Table 7) revealed that it performs poorly in the "Documentation" category (Judge Score: 5.00). In contrast, Mistral-Instruct-7B achieves a significantly higher quality score (6.80) in that domain. Therefore, our routing strategy prioritizes the model with the highest domain-specific utility: we utilize Qwen2.5-Coder-32B for "Functional" tasks to ensure strict correctness, while routing "Documentation" tasks to Mistral-Instruct-7B to maximize the usefulness and relevance of the feedback.

5.4. RQ4: The Efficacy of Hybrid Expert Routing

RQ4: To what extent does a dynamic "Expert Routing" mechanism enhance overall accuracy compared to static and zero-shot baselines?

Our categorical analysis identified a dual limitation in the standard deployment of Large Language Models: generalist models lack depth in logical tasks. In contrast, code-specialized models suffer from severity overestimation and weak documentation skills. To address these deficiencies simultaneously, we evaluated a Hybrid Expert System.

To rigorously isolate the contribution of our routing strategy, we established two distinct benchmarks based on our findings in RQ1 and RQ3:

1. **Composite Zero-Shot Baseline ($k = 0$):** Calculated as the "instance-weighted average" of the constituent models (Qwen2.5 for Logic/Discussion, Mistral for Documentation) at $k = 0$. This yields a baseline score of 6.21, reflecting the system's performance without any retrieval context.
2. **Single Best Model (SBM):** Represents the strongest static configuration available. As shown in Table 7, Qwen2.5-Coder-32B ($k = 3$) achieved the highest standalone score (6.53) among individual models. We use this as the reference point to measure the specific value of dynamic routing.

The Hybrid architecture dynamically routes tasks to the specialist best suited for the semantic category:

- **Logic (Functional/Refactoring):** Routed to Qwen2.5-Coder-32B ($k = 3$) to unlock "Latent Knowledge" and ensure AST level correctness.
- **Documentation:** Routed to Mistral–Instruct-7B ($k = 3$) to take advantage of its superior natural language fluency.

Results and Engineering Implications

As presented in Table 9, the Hybrid Expert System achieves a significant performance gain over both baselines.

Crucially, the Hybrid System ($\mu = 7.03$) significantly outperforms the Single Best Model ($\mu = 6.53$). We validated this 7.7% net gain using a paired samples t-test [51]. To avoid the bias of majority classes present in the full test set ($N = 1625$), we performed this analysis on the human verified balanced dataset ($N = 105$, detailed in Section 4.4.3), ensuring equal representation across all semantic categories. The test confirmed that the difference is statistically significant ($t(104) = 4.48, p < 0.001$) with a Cohen's d of 0.47 [52]. This empirical evidence supports the premise that our hybrid architecture provides superior alignment compared to a monolithic model (SBM).

https://doi.org/10.3390/app16041875

Table 9. The Hybrid System achieves a Mean Score of 7.03, significantly outperforming the Single Best Model (SBM) by 7.7% and the Zero-Shot baseline by 13.2%.

Category	Zero-Shot Baseline ($k = 0$)	Single Best Model (SBM) ($k = 3$)	Hybrid System (Ours)	Routing Strategy
Functional	6.06	6.76	**6.76**	Qwen2.5 ($k = 3$)
Refactoring	6.76	7.20	**7.20**	Qwen2.5 ($k = 3$)
Discussion	7.02	7.36	**7.36**	Qwen2.5 ($k = 3$)
Documentation	5.00	4.80	**6.80**	Mistral ($k = 3$)
Mean Score	6.21	6.53	**7.03** ***	–
Net Gain	*(Reference)*	**+5.2%**	**+13.2%**	–
Gain vs. SBM	–	*(Reference)*	**+7.7%**	–

*** *Statistically significant difference ($p < 0.001$) based on paired t-test.* **Bold** values indicate the highest scores in each category.

To further isolate the effectiveness of the routing logic from chance, we also evaluated the system against a "Random Routing Baseline". This baseline randomly routes tasks between the same constituent experts (Qwen2.5-Coder-32B and Mistral-Instruct-7B) with uniform probability ($p = 0.5$). On the full benchmark, the Hybrid System outperforms this Random Baseline ($\mu = 6.14$) by 14.5%. This advantage was similarly verified on the human verified balanced dataset ($N = 105$, detailed in Section 4.4.3), yielding a statistically significant difference ($t(104) = 4.10, p < 0.001$) with a Cohen's d of 0.40 [52]. This confirms that the routing mechanism provides a robust, systematic advantage over both fixed (SBM) and random policies.

This improvement is driven by two distinct mechanisms:

1. **Contextual Gain (RAG Effect):** In logical tasks (Functional/Refactoring), introducing context ($k = 3$) increased performance compared to the zero-shot baseline (e.g., 6.06 $\rightarrow$ 6.76). This aligns with our findings in RQ1, confirming that retrieval successfully activates the model's latent technical knowledge.
2. **Architectural Gain (Routing Effect):** The Single Best Model (Qwen2.5-Coder-32B) exhibits a critical weakness in the "Documentation" category (Score: 5.00), primarily due to the "Error Severity Overestimation" analyzed in Section 5.3.2. By routing these tasks to Mistral-Instruct, our Hybrid System achieves a 42% surge in this category (4.80 $\rightarrow$ 6.80). This effectively neutralizes the severity overestimation, ensuring that benign documentation updates are not misclassified as functional defects.

Consequently, the total system improvement of 13.2% (vs. Zero-Shot) is not only a result of adding data, but a product of precise architectural alignment. This suggests that for CI/CD integration, a routed ensemble of smaller, specialized models offers a superior trade-off between computational efficiency and defect detection accuracy compared to a single generalist model.

5.5. RQ5: Misalignment Between N-Gram Metrics and Technical Quality

RQ5: How do traditional n-gram metrics (e.g., BLEU, ROUGE) compare with semantic evaluation methods in assessing the quality of automated code reviews?

To identify a reliable evaluation strategy for automated code review, we examined the relationship between traditional reference-based metrics and semantic evaluation methods. As shown in Table 6, the results reveal an apparent mismatch between the lexical overlap scores and the actual technical usefulness.

5.5.1. Limitations of Lexical Metrics

As shown in Table 6, models such as CodeLlama-13B achieved relatively high ROUGE-L scores (0.111 in $k = 0$) while receiving the lowest Judge Scores (3.54). This gap highlights

https://doi.org/10.3390/app16041875

a key weakness of reference-based metrics in open-ended tasks. A technically correct code review can be expressed in many valid ways that do not share surface-level n-grams with a reference answer. As a result, BLEU and ROUGE often penalize meaningful semantic variations, making them poor indicators of technical quality in software engineering settings [53].

5.5.2. Semantic Similarity and Technical Correctness

Embedding-based cosine similarity provides a stronger signal than n-gram metrics, but it remains insensitive to logical correctness. For example, "Mistral-Instruct-7B" maintained a high Semantic Similarity score (0.416) even as its Judge Score dropped (6.01 $\rightarrow$ 5.46) in a noisy context. This suggests that embeddings capture topical relevance, such as identifying that a comment discusses loops, but fail to distinguish correct solutions from incorrect or hallucinated ones.

5.5.3. Effectiveness of Semantic Evaluation

In contrast, LLM-as-a-Judge scores show a strong correlation with human expert ratings ($r = 0.82, p < 0.001$), as discussed in Section 4.4.3. This indicates that semantic evaluation methods are better suited to complex reasoning tasks, as they focus on the usefulness and correctness of feedback rather than surface-level textual similarity.

In conclusion, the proposed hybrid architecture offers a pragmatic solution for CI/CD integration, effectively solving the "logic-frequency Trade-off" without the need for massive, proprietary models.

5.6. Validation with Human Evaluation

To verify the validity of the automated judge, we assessed the alignment between the LLM-generated scores and the human expert ratings (n = 105). While the initial analysis showed a strong linear relationship (Pearson $r = 0.84$, $p < 0.001$), we expanded the evaluation to verify the stability of the model using rank-based and agreement-specific metrics against the human ground truth.

First, we calculated Spearman's rank correlation coefficient to evaluate how well the model preserves the ordering established by human experts. The resulting $\rho = 0.87$ confirms that the judge consistently ranks higher-quality responses above lower-quality ones [54].

Second, to measure inter-annotator agreement while accounting for the ordinal nature of the scoring scale (0–10), we utilized "Cohen's Quadratic Weighted Kappa" [55]. The analysis resulted in $\kappa = 0.78$. Based on the interpretation benchmarks by Landis and Koch [56], this indicates "substantial agreement" between the automated judge and the human evaluators.

These metrics confirm that the performance gains offered by the hybrid system align with the perceptual preferences of the human evaluators (senior software engineers).

5.7. Ablation Study: Standalone Routing Performance

We conducted a standalone ablation study of the categorization module to confirm that the performance gains in comment generation come from our context-aware routing strategy, rather than just the LLM's baseline capabilities. By isolating this component, we verified that the retrieval mechanism accurately identifies the semantic intent of code changes before the prompt is even constructed.

5.7.1. Experimental Setup

We used the manually labeled dataset of 1273 samples, which we originally curated for the offline SVM training phase described in Section 3.4. We created a stratified split from

https://doi.org/10.3390/app16041875

this dataset, keeping approximately 20% ($N = 244$) as a test set dedicated to evaluating performance on previously unseen data.

We focused our quantitative analysis on the four primary semantic categories: "Refactoring", "Functional", "Discussion", and "Documentation". We excluded the "False Positive" category from the aggregate metrics in Table 10 because it represented less than 3% of the test set ($N = 7$). Including such a small sample size would introduce statistical noise; therefore, we discuss these samples qualitatively below instead.

Table 10. Comparison of standalone routing strategies on the test set ($N = 244$). The proposed method demonstrates a 410.2% improvement in Macro-F1 over the baseline.

Strategy	Accuracy	Macro-F1	Weighted-F1	Improvement (Δ)
Fixed Routing (Baseline)	0.344	0.128	0.176	–
Neighbour-Voting (Ours)	**0.664**	**0.653**	**0.657**	**+410.2%**

Bold values indicate the best-performing strategy.

We compared two routing strategies:

1. **Fixed Routing (Baseline):** We assigned all queries to the most frequently observed category in training ("Refactoring"). This serves as the lower bound for performance.
2. **Neighbour-Voting Routing (Proposed):** We aggregated votes from the top-k ($k = 3$) retrieved historical code changes based on cosine similarity.

5.7.2. Results and Analysis

Table 10 presents the comparative results. Our proposed Neighbour-Voting strategy achieved a Macro-F1 score of 0.653, which represents a 410.2% relative improvement (The relative improvement is calculated as $\Delta = \frac{F1_{\text{Proposed}} - F1_{\text{Baseline}}}{F1_{\text{Baseline}}} \times 100$. Given the baseline's low performance (0.128), the proportional gain is substantial) over the Fixed Baseline (Macro-F1: 0.128). The baseline predicted the majority class but yielded zero precision and recall for the remaining three categories, confirming that a dynamic routing mechanism is necessary for this task.

To analyze the stability of our classifier, we present the Confusion Matrix in Table 11 and the detailed per-class metrics in Table 12. We observed high specificity across all categories. Importantly, the system successfully distinguishes between "Refactoring" (Precision: 0.73) and "Functional" (Recall: 0.75) changes. This distinction is challenging because both categories often involve code modifications; however, our retrieval mechanism uses the semantic context from file paths and code diffs to resolve this ambiguity effectively.

Table 11. Confusion Matrix of the Neighbour-Voting Routing module (Primary Categories). Rows represent true labels, columns represent predicted labels.

	Predicted Category			
True Category	**Discussion**	**Documentation**	**Functional**	**Refactoring**
Discussion	**34**	7	11	9
Documentation	6	**31**	2	5
Functional	6	1	**41**	7
Refactoring	8	7	13	**56**

Bold values indicate correct predictions along the diagonal.

Qualitative Analysis of Outliers: Although we excluded the quantitative analysis for the "False Positive" category due to insufficient sample support ($N = 7$), we analyzed these instances manually. We found that the model misclassified most of them as "Refactoring" (4) or "Functional" (2). These errors highlight a challenge inherent to retrieval-based systems: valid code changes often share a high semantic resemblance with actionable ones,

https://doi.org/10.3390/app16041875

making them difficult to distinguish in vector space. We expect that incorporating negative sampling in future work will help reduce this overlap.

Table 12. Detailed Classification Report. The system achieves consistent performance across diverse semantic intents.

Category	Precision	Recall	F1-Score	Support
Discussion	0.63	0.56	0.59	61
Documentation	0.67	0.70	0.69	44
Functional	0.61	0.75	0.67	55
Refactoring	0.73	0.67	0.70	84
Macro Avg	**0.66**	**0.67**	**0.65**	**244**

Italic indicates aggregated metrics; **bold** values highlight overall macro-level performance.

6. Threats to Validity

We identify several potential threats to the validity of our study and discuss the mitigation strategies used to ensure the reliability of our findings.

6.1. Internal Validity

Internal validity concerns factors that might influence the causal relationship between the treatment (RAG/Model Architecture) and the outcome (Review Quality).

- **Data Leakage and Contamination Audit:** A primary concern when evaluating Large Language Models (LLMs) is data contamination—where the test data might have been present in the model's pre-training corpus. To mitigate this, we selected the "Home Assistant Core" repository, specifically focusing on Pull Requests (PRs) created after the knowledge cutoff dates of the evaluated models. To empirically verify the integrity of the split between the retrieval corpus and the evaluation (test) set, we conducted a content-based contamination audit. We generated SHA-256 signatures for the code-comment pairs in both splits and confirmed zero exact overlaps between the retrieval corpus and the test set. Finally, to facilitate external verification and reproducibility, the exact dataset snapshot used in these experiments has been versioned as "experiment_snapshot_v1.0" in the crc-py-dataset repository (https://github.com/busraicoz/crc-py-dataset, accessed on 26 December 2025).
- **Nondeterminism:** LLM generation is inherently stochastic. To reduce run-to-run variance and improve reproducibility, we fixed the decoding configuration in all experiments. This ensures that performance variations are due to architectural differences and retrieval depth (k), rather than random sampling noise.
- **Embedding Limitations:** A potential threat to construct validity is the use of all-MiniLM-L6-v2, which is optimized for natural language. We selected this model because code review comments are primarily natural language explanations. However, we acknowledge that this may miss syntactic nuances in the code diffs. Future iterations of this work could mitigate this by employing code-specific embedding models such as UnixCoder [57] or GraphCodeBERT [58].
- **Retrieval Effectiveness:** Despite the previously mentioned limitation, we validated the practical effectiveness of our retrieval pipeline through the standalone performance of the "Neighbour-Voting Routing" module (Section 5.7). This module achieved a Macro-F1 score of 0.653 using the exact same retrieval inputs, significantly outperforming the zero-shot baseline (+410.2%). This confirms that the retrieved context contains strong semantic signals, supporting our conclusion that the performance degradation at higher depths ($k = 5$) is due to the LLM's attention bottleneck (Context Collapse) rather than retrieval noise.

https://doi.org/10.3390/app16041875

6.2. External Validity

External validity relates to the generalizability of our results to other contexts.

- **Language Bias:** Our dataset consists exclusively of Python code from the Home Assistant Core project. While Python is a dominant language in modern development, our findings regarding "Error Severity Overestimation" or "Context Collapse" may not perfectly transfer to statically typed languages (e.g., Java, C++) or low-resource languages. Future work should validate the proposed Hybrid Expert System in a polyglot dataset.
- **Model Selection:** We limited our evaluation to open-weight models (3B–33B parameters) to ensure accessibility and reproducibility. Consequently, our conclusions may not fully apply to proprietary trillion-parameter models like GPT-5 [59] or Claude 4 [60], which may possess different scaling laws regarding context utilization.

7. Conclusions

In this study, we propose a new automated code review system for Python projects. Unlike standard approaches that treat all code changes equally, our system uses a two-step process. First, we classify the code changes into categories, such as "Functional" or "Refactoring". Then, based on this category, we send the review task to the most suitable language model (expert LLM). We also use Retrieval-Augmented Generation (RAG) to provide relevant historical examples as context.

Our experiments show that adding more context does not constantly improve performance. We found that smaller models often get confused when given too much information, a problem we call "Context Collapse". We also observed a clear trade-off between logic and fluency. Larger models (like Qwen2.5) are good at finding bugs, but can be too strict on minor style issues. Conversely, smaller models (like Mistral) generate fluent feedback, but sometimes lack technical depth.

To address this gap, we evaluated a hybrid expert system. By separating logical verification from document generation and assigning each task to the appropriate specialist ($k = 3$), we achieved a 13.2% improvement in the success rate over the zero-shot baseline ($k = 0$). This suggests that a modular approach is more suitable for CI/CD integration than relying solely on zero-shot models.

In future work, we plan to address the observed error severity overestimation. The next step is to explore Direct Preference Optimization (DPO) [61] as a way to align model output with developer expectations. Additionally, grounded in our qualitative analysis of "False Positive" outliers, we aim to refine the retrieval stage by implementing negative sampling. This will improve the system's ability to distinguish between valid code changes and those that are semantically similar, but do not require actionable feedback. Finally, we plan to extend the hybrid framework to agent-based workflows and multilingual settings, which are critical to scaling automated support in diverse software engineering tasks.

Author Contributions: Conceptualization, B.İ. and G.B.; methodology, B.İ.; software, B.İ.; validation, B.İ. and G.B.; formal analysis, B.İ.; investigation, B.İ.; resources, B.İ.; data curation, B.İ.; writing—original draft preparation, B.İ.; writing—review and editing, B.İ. and G.B.; visualization, B.İ.; supervision, G.B.; project administration, B.İ. All authors have read and agreed to the published version of the manuscript.

Funding: This research received no external funding. The APC was funded by the authors.

Data Availability Statement: The datasets generated and analyzed in this study are publicly available at https://github.com/busraicoz/crc-py-dataset (accessed on 26 December 2025).

Conflicts of Interest: Author Büşra İçöz was employed by the company ING. The remaining authors declare that the research was conducted in the absence of any commercial or financial relationships that could be construed as potential conflicts of interest.

Appendix A. Code Review System Prompt

To ensure reproducibility, we provide the complete prompt and scoring rubric of the system used for the code review LLMs.

System Prompt Configuration:

Role: You are a senior Python developer tasked with reviewing the following pull request code. Your goal is to provide a technical, constructive, and actionable review comment that is clear and helpful to developers.

Code to Review:

```
{code_snippet}
```

Reference Comments (for similar code blocks):

```
{similar code block 1}
{similar review comment 1}
{similar category 1}
{similar subcategory 1}

{similar code block 2}
{similar review comment 2}
{similar category 2}
{similar subcategory 2}

{similar code block 3}
{similar review comment 3}
{similar category 3}
{similar subcategory 3}
```

Instructions:

1. Analyze the code snippet carefully.
2. Assign a subcategory to your review, choosing exactly one from:
```
[
"functional", "logical", "validation", "resource",
"timing", "support issues", "interface",
"solution approach", "alternate output", "code organization",
"variable naming", "visual representation", "documentation",
"design discussion", "question", "praise", "false positive"]
```

Output Format:

- Review Comment: <your detailed feedback here>
- Subcategory: <one of the 17 subcategories>

Appendix B. LLM-as-a-Judge System Prompt

To ensure reproducibility, the system prompt and scoring rubric used for the LLM-as-a-Judge evaluation (Llama-3-70B) are provided below.

LLM-as-a-Judge System Prompt Configuration:

https://doi.org/10.3390/app16041875

Role: You are an expert Senior Software Engineer and Code Reviewer. Your task is to evaluate the quality of a generated code review comment compared to a human-written ground truth based on the rubric defined below.

Input Data:

- `Code Diff:` The code changes introduced in the Pull Request.
- `Ground Truth Comment:` The actual comment written by a human expert.
- `Generated Comment:` The review comment generated by the AI model.

Evaluation Criteria (Scoring Rubric 0–10): Please analyze the generated comment and assign a score based on the following scale:

- 10 (Perfect): Identifies the exact issue, provides a correct fix/suggestion, and matches the technical depth of the ground truth.
- 8–9 (High Quality): Technically correct and helpful, but may have minor differences in tone or phrasing compared to the ground truth.
- 5–7 (Partial): Identifies the general topic or intent correctly, but the solution is incomplete, vague, or lacks specific details.
- 1–4 (Failure): Misses the core issue, provides irrelevant advice, or hallucinates variables/logic not present in the code.
- 0 (Invalid): Factually incorrect, empty response, or nonsensical output.

Output Format: Provide your response in a valid JSON format containing the score and a brief reasoning:

```
{
  "score": <integer>,
  "reasoning": "<short_explanation>"
}
}
```

Appendix C. Reproducibility Protocol

Appendix C.1. Computational Resources

All experiments were conducted on a cloud-based GPU instance provided by RunPod [62]. The environment was configured with the following specifications to ensure consistent inference latency and context handling:

- **GPU:** Single NVIDIA RTX A6000 GP with 48 GB VRAM.
- **Storage:** 100 GB NVMe(Non-Volatile Memory Express) SSD (to accommodate the vector store and model weights).
- **Runtime:** Linux-based container with CUDA drivers pre-installed.

Appendix C.2. Model Artifacts and Runtime Environment

We utilized the `Ollama` runtime (v0.12.7) for serving quantized models.

Appendix C.3. Vector Store Configuration

We utilized `Qdrant` (v1.16.3) as the vector store.

- **Embedding Model:** `sentence-transformers/all-MiniLM-L6-v2`.
- **Retrieval Scope:** Hybrid search (Project History + External Knowledge).

https://doi.org/10.3390/app16041875

Appendix D. Data Selection Protocol

"Daily Trending" Repositories

To ensure reproducibility of the repository selection process, we define the "Daily Trending Heuristic" not by the ephemeral GitHub UI "Trending" tab, but by a deterministic query against the GitHub Search API. A repository was selected for the dataset if it satisfied the **Top-k Star Velocity** criterion during the data collection window.

- **Definition:** A Trending repository is defined as one of the top 10 Python repositories by *total star count* that also exhibited active development.
- **API Endpoint:** `GET https://api.github.com/search/repositories`, accessed on 26 December 2025
- **Exact Query Template:**

```
q = language:python
    +is:public
    +archived:false
    +fork:false
    +stars:>1000
sort = stars
order = desc
per_page = 20
```

- **Filtering Thresholds:**
  1. **Language:** Python.
  2. **Activity:** Must have at least one commit pushed within the query window (e.g., `pushed:>2024-06-01`).
  3. **Popularity Floor:** Minimum 1000 total stars (to filter out low-quality "spam" repositories that often appear in raw trending feeds).
  4. **Exclusions:** Forks and archived repositories were explicitly excluded.

References

1. Bacchelli, A.; Bird, C. Expectations, outcomes, and challenges of modern code review. In *Proceedings of the 2013 International Conference on Software Engineering, San Francisco, CA, USA, 18–26 May 2013*; ICSE '13; IEEE Press: Piscataway, NJ, USA, 2013; pp. 712–721.
2. Sadowski, C.; Söderberg, E.; Church, L.; Sipko, M.; Bacchelli, A. Modern code review: A case study at google. In Proceedings of the 40th International Conference on Software Engineering: Software Engineering in Practice, Gothenburg, Sweden, 27 May–3 June 2018; ICSE-SEIP '18; pp. 181–190. [CrossRef]
3. Bosu, A.; Carver, J.C. Impact of developer reputation on code review outcomes in OSS projects: An empirical investigation. In Proceedings of the 8th ACM/IEEE International Symposium on Empirical Software Engineering and Measurement, Torino, Italy, 18–19 September 2014; ESEM '14. [CrossRef]
4. Rahman, F.; Posnett, D.; Devanbu, P. Recalling the "imprecision" of cross-project defect prediction. In Proceedings of the ACM SIGSOFT 20th International Symposium on the Foundations of Software Engineering, Cary North, CA, USA, 11–16 November 2012; FSE '12. [CrossRef]
5. Johnson, B.; Song, Y.; Murphy-Hill, E.; Bowdidge, R. Why don't software developers use static analysis tools to find bugs? In Proceedings of the 2013 35th International Conference on Software Engineering (ICSE), San Francisco, CA, USA, 18–26 May 2013; pp. 672–681. [CrossRef]
6. Chen, M.; Tworek, J.; Jun, H.; Yuan, Q.; Pondé, H.; Kaplan, J.; Edwards, H.; Burda, Y.; Joseph, N.; Brockman, G.; et al. Evaluating Large Language Models Trained on Code. *arXiv* **2021**, arXiv:2107.03374. [CrossRef]
7. Zhang, Q.; Fang, C.; Xie, Y.; Zhang, Y.; Yang, Y.; Sun, W.; Yu, S.; Chen, Z. A Survey on Large Language Models for Software Engineering. *arXiv* **2024**, arXiv:2312.15223. [CrossRef]
8. Turzo, A.K.; Faysal, F.; Poddar, O.; Sarker, J.; Iqbal, A.; Bosu, A. Towards Automated Classification of Code Review Feedback to Support Analytics. In Proceedings of the 2023 ACM/IEEE International Symposium on Empirical Software Engineering and Measurement (ESEM), New Orleans, LA, USA, 26–27 October 2023; pp. 1–12. [CrossRef]

https://doi.org/10.3390/app16041875

9. Fagan, M.E. Design and code inspections to reduce errors in program development. *IBM Syst. J.* **1976**, *15*, 182–211. [CrossRef]
10. Mateos, P.; Bellogín, A. A systematic literature review of recent advances on context-aware recommender systems. *Artif. Intell. Rev.* **2024**, *58*, 20. [CrossRef]
11. Sadman, N.; Ahsan, M.M.; Mahmud, M.A. ADCR: An Adaptive Tool to select "Appropriate Developer for Code Review" based on Code Context. In Proceedings of the 2020 11th IEEE Annual Ubiquitous Computing, Electronics & Mobile Communication Conference (UEMCON), New York, NY, USA, 28–31 October 2020. [CrossRef]
12. Tufano, M.; Watson, C.; Bavota, G.; Penta, M.D.; White, M.; Poshyvanyk, D. An Empirical Study on Learning Bug-Fixing Patches in the Wild via Neural Machine Translation. *ACM Trans. Softw. Eng. Methodol.* **2019**, *28*, 1–29. [CrossRef]
13. Li, Z.; Lu, S.; Guo, D.; Duan, N.; Jannu, S.; Jenks, G.; Majumder, D.; Green, J.; Svyatkovskiy, A.; Fu, S.; et al. CodeReviewer: Pre-Training for Automating Code Review Activities. *arXiv* **2022**, arXiv:2203.09095. [CrossRef]
14. Lin, H.Y.; Thongtanunam, P.; Treude, C.; Godfrey, M.W.; Liu, C.; Charoenwet, W. Leveraging Reviewer Experience in Code Review Comment Generation. *ACM Trans. Softw. Eng. Methodol.* **2025**, *just accepted*. [CrossRef]
15. Rasheed, Z.; Sami, M.A.; Waseem, M.; Kemell, K.K.; Wang, X.; Nguyen, A.; Systä, K.; Abrahamsson, P. AI-powered Code Review with LLMs: Early Results. *arXiv* **2025**, arXiv:2404.18496. [CrossRef]
16. Rybalchenko, A.; Al-Turany, M. Leveraging Large Language Models for Enhanced Code Review. *EPJ Web Conf.* **2025**, *337*, 01066. [CrossRef]
17. Haroon, S.; Khan, A.F.; Humayun, A.; Gill, W.; Amjad, A.H.; Butt, A.R.; Khan, M.T.; Gulzar, M.A. How Accurately Do Large Language Models Understand Code? *arXiv* **2025**, arXiv:2504.04372. [CrossRef]
18. Lewis, P.; Perez, E.; Piktus, A.; Petroni, F.; Karpukhin, V.; Goyal, N.; Küttler, H.; Lewis, M.; Yih, W.t.; Rocktäschel, T.; et al. Retrieval-augmented generation for knowledge-intensive NLP tasks. In Proceedings of the 34th International Conference on Neural Information Processing Systems, Red Hook, NY, USA, 6–12 December 2020; NIPS '20.
19. Hong, H.; Baik, J. Retrieval-Augmented Code Review Comment Generation. *arXiv* **2025**, arXiv:2506.11591. [CrossRef]
20. Wang, Z.Z.; Asai, A.; Yu, X.V.; Xu, F.F.; Xie, Y.; Neubig, G.; Fried, D. CodeRAG-Bench: Can Retrieval Augment Code Generation? In *Proceedings of the Findings of the Association for Computational Linguistics: NAACL 2025*; Chiruzzo, L., Ritter, A., Wang, L., Eds.; Association for Computational Linguistics: Albuquerque, NM, USA, 2025; pp. 3199–3214. [CrossRef]
21. Qdrant: Vector Database for the Next Generation of AI Applications. Available online: https://qdrant.tech/ (accessed on 23 December 2025).
22. Zhang, Y.; Li, Y.; Cui, L.; Cai, D.; Liu, L.; Fu, T.; Huang, X.; Zhao, E.; Zhang, Y.; Xu, C.; et al. Siren's Song in the AI Ocean: A Survey on Hallucination in Large Language Models. *arXiv* **2025**, arXiv:2309.01219. [CrossRef]
23. Sentence-Transformers/All-MiniLM-L6-v2: Model Card. Available online: https://huggingface.co/sentence-transformers/all-MiniLM-L6-v2 (accessed on 23 December 2025).
24. Manning, C.D.; Raghavan, P.; Schütze, H. *Introduction to Information Retrieval*; Cambridge University Press: Cambridge, UK, 2008.
25. Reimers, N.; Gurevych, I. Sentence-BERT: Sentence Embeddings using Siamese BERT-Networks. In Proceedings of the 2019 Conference on Empirical Methods in Natural Language Processing and the 9th International Joint Conference on Natural Language Processing (EMNLP-IJCNLP), Hong Kong, China, 3–7 November 2019; pp. 3982–3992. [CrossRef]
26. Brown, T.B.; Mann, B.; Ryder, N.; Subbiah, M.; Kaplan, J.; Dhariwal, P.; Neelakantan, A.; Shyam, P.; Sastry, G.; Askell, A.; et al. Language models are few-shot learners. In Proceedings of the 34th International Conference on Neural Information Processing Systems, Red Hook, NY, USA, 6–12 December 2020; NIPS '20.
27. Kalliamvakou, E.; Gousios, G.; Blincoe, K.; Singer, L.; German, D.M.; Damian, D. The promises and perils of mining GitHub. In Proceedings of the 11th Working Conference on Mining Software Repositories, Hyderabad, India, 31 May–1 June 2014; MSR 2014; pp. 92–101. [CrossRef]
28. Salton, G.; Buckley, C. Term-weighting approaches in automatic text retrieval. *Inf. Process. Manage.* **1988**, *24*, 513–523. [CrossRef]
29. Cortes, C.; Vapnik, V. Support-Vector Networks. *Mach. Learn.* **1995**, *20*, 273–297. [CrossRef]
30. Triguero, I.; García, S.; Herrera, F. Self-labeled techniques for semi-supervised learning: Taxonomy, software and empirical study. *Knowl. Inf. Syst.* **2015**, *42*, 245–284. [CrossRef]
31. Home Assistant Community. Home-Assistant/Core: Open Source Home Automation That Puts Local Control and Privacy First. Available online: https://github.com/home-assistant/core (accessed on 23 December 2025).
32. Home Assistant Developer Docs. Integration Architecture. Available online: https://developers.home-assistant.io/docs/architecture_components/ (accessed on 23 December 2025).
33. Home Assistant Developer Docs. Pull Request Review Process. Available online: https://developers.home-assistant.io/docs/review-process/ (accessed on 23 December 2025).
34. Open LLM Leaderboard. Hugging Face. Available online: https://huggingface.co/spaces/open-llm-leaderboard/open_llm_leaderboard (accessed on 22 December 2025).
35. Team, O. Ollama: Large Language Model Runner. 2024. Available online: https://github.com/ollama/ollama (accessed on 23 December 2024).

https://doi.org/10.3390/app16041875

36. Guo, D.; Zhu, Q.; Yang, D.; Xie, Z.; Dong, K.; Zhang, W.; Chen, G.; Bi, X.; Wu, Y.; Li, Y.K.; et al. DeepSeek-Coder: When the Large Language Model Meets Programming—The Rise of Code Intelligence. *arXiv* **2024**, arXiv:2401.14196. [CrossRef]
37. Hui, B.; Yang, J.; Cui, Z.; Yang, J.; Liu, D.; Zhang, L.; Liu, T.; Zhang, J.; Yu, B.; Lu, K.; et al. Qwen2.5-Coder Technical Report. *arXiv* **2024**, arXiv:2409.12186. [CrossRef]
38. Mistral AI Team. Codestral: Hello, World! 2024. Available online: https://mistral.ai/news/codestral/ (accessed on 23 December 2025).
39. Rozière, B.; Gehring, J.; Gloeckle, F.; Sootla, S.; Gat, I.; Tan, X.; Adi, Y.; Liu, J.; Remez, T.; Rapin, J.; et al. Code Llama: Open Foundation Models for Code. *arXiv* **2023**, arXiv:2308.12950.
40. Jiang, A.Q.; Sablayrolles, A.; Mensch, A.; Bamford, C.; Chaplot, D.S.; de las Casas, D.; Bressand, F.; Lengyel, G.; Lample, G.; Saulnier, L.; et al. Mistral 7B. *arXiv* **2023**, arXiv:2310.06825. . [CrossRef]
41. Abdin, M.; Aneja, J.; Awadalla, H.; Awadallah, A.; Awan, A.A.; Bach, N.; Bahree, A.; Bakhtiari, A.; Bao, J.; Behl, H.; et al. Phi-3 Technical Report: A Highly Capable Language Model Locally on Your Phone. *arXiv* **2024**, arXiv:2404.14219. . [CrossRef]
42. Papineni, K.; Roukos, S.; Ward, T.; Zhu, W.J. Bleu: A Method for Automatic Evaluation of Machine Translation. In *Proceedings of the 40th Annual Meeting of the Association for Computational Linguistics*; Isabelle, P., Charniak, E., Lin, D., Eds.; Association for Computational Linguistics: Philadelphia, PA, USA, 2002; pp. 311–318. [CrossRef]
43. Lin, C.Y. ROUGE: A Package for Automatic Evaluation of Summaries. In Proceedings of the Text Summarization Branches Out, Barcelona, Spain, 25–26 July 2004; pp. 74–81.
44. Post, M. A Call for Clarity in Reporting BLEU Scores. In Proceedings of the Conference on Machine Translation, Brussels, Belgium, 31 October–1 November 2018.
45. Zheng, L.; Chiang, W.L.; Sheng, Y.; Zhuang, S.; Wu, Z.; Zhuang, Y.; Lin, Z.; Li, Z.; Li, D.; Xing, E.P.; et al. Judging LLM-as-a-judge with MT-bench and Chatbot Arena. In Proceedings of the 37th International Conference on Neural Information Processing Systems, Red Hook, NY, USA, 10–16 December 2023; NIPS '23.
46. Grattafiori, A.; Dubey, A.; Jauhri, A.; Pandey, A.; Kadian, A.; Al-Dahle, A.; Letman, A.; Mathur, A.; Schelten, A.; Vaughan, A.; et al. The Llama 3 Herd of Models. *arXiv* **2024**, arXiv:2407.21783. [CrossRef]
47. Ouyang, L.; Wu, J.; Jiang, X.; Almeida, D.; Wainwright, C.L.; Mishkin, P.; Zhang, C.; Agarwal, S.; Slama, K.; Ray, A.; et al. Training language models to follow instructions with human feedback. In Proceedings of the 36th International Conference on Neural Information Processing Systems, Red Hook, NY, USA, 6–12 December 2022; NIPS '22.
48. Hu, M.; Wu, H.; Guan, Z.; Zhu, R.; Guo, D.; Qi, D.; Li, S. No Free Lunch: Retrieval-Augmented Generation Undermines Fairness in LLMs, Even for Vigilant Users. *arXiv* **2024**, arXiv:2410.07589. [CrossRef]
49. Liu, N.F.; Lin, K.; Hewitt, J.; Paranjape, A.; Bevilacqua, M.; Petroni, F.; Liang, P. Lost in the Middle: How Language Models Use Long Contexts. *Trans. Assoc. Comput. Linguist.* **2024**, *12*, 157–173. [CrossRef]
50. Askell, A.; Bai, Y.; Chen, A.; Drain, D.; Ganguli, D.; Henighan, T.; Jones, A.; Joseph, N.; Mann, B.; DasSarma, N.; et al. A General Language Assistant as a Laboratory for Alignment. *arXiv* **2021**, arXiv:2112.00861. [CrossRef]
51. Dietterich, T.G. Approximate Statistical Tests for Comparing Supervised Classification Learning Algorithms. *Neural Comput.* **1998**, *10*, 1895–1923. [CrossRef]
52. Cohen, J. *Statistical Power Analysis for the Behavioral Sciences*; Lawrence Erlbaum Associates: Mahwah, NJ, USA, 1988.
53. Ren, S.; Guo, D.; Lu, S.; Zhou, L.; Liu, S.; Tang, D.; Sundaresan, N.; Zhou, M.; Blanco, A.; Ma, S. CodeBLEU: A Method for Automatic Evaluation of Code Synthesis. *arXiv* **2020**, arXiv:2009.10297. [CrossRef]
54. Spearman, C. The proof and measurement of association between two things. *Int. J. Epidemiol.* **2010**, *39*, 1137–1150. [CrossRef]
55. Cohen, J. Weighted kappa: Nominal scale agreement provision for scaled disagreement or partial credit. *Psychol. Bull.* **1968**, *70*, 213–220. [CrossRef]
56. Landis, J.R.; Koch, G.G. The measurement of observer agreement for categorical data. *Biometrics* **1977**, *33*, 159–174. [CrossRef]
57. Guo, D.; Lu, S.; Duan, N.; Wang, Y.; Zhou, M.; Yin, J. UniXcoder: Unified Cross-Modal Pre-training for Code Representation. In *Proceedings of the 60th Annual Meeting of the Association for Computational Linguistics (Volume 1: Long Papers)*; Muresan, S., Nakov, P., Villavicencio, A., Eds.; Association for Computational Linguistics: Dublin, Ireland, 2022; pp. 7212–7225. [CrossRef]
58. Guo, D.; Ren, S.; Lu, S.; Feng, Z.; Tang, D.; Liu, S.; Zhou, L.; Duan, N.; Svyatkovskiy, A.; Fu, S.; et al. GraphCodeBERT: Pre-training Code Representations with Data Flow. *arXiv* **2020**, arXiv:2009.08366. [CrossRef]
59. OpenAI. Introducing GPT-5. OpenAI Blog, 2025. Available online: https://openai.com/index/introducing-gpt-5 (accessed on 26 December 2025).
60. Anthropic. Introducing Claude 4. Anthropic News. 2025. Available online: https://www.anthropic.com/news/claude-4 (accessed on 26 December 2025).

https://doi.org/10.3390/app16041875

61. Rafailov, R.; Sharma, A.; Mitchell, E.; Ermon, S.; Manning, C.D.; Finn, C. Direct Preference Optimization: Your Language Model is Secretly a Reward Model. *arXiv* **2024**, arXiv:2305.18290. [CrossRef]
62. RunPod: GPU Cloud for AI. Available online: https://console.runpod.io (accessed on 15 January 2026).

https://doi.org/10.3390/app16041875

applied sciences

MDPI

Article

A Rule-Based Method for Detecting Discrepancies in Software Project Productivity Analysis

Parag C. Pendharkar [1,*] and James A. Rodger [2]

1 School of Business Administration, Penn State Harrisburg, Middletown, PA 17057, USA
2 Business and Enterprise Division, University of Pittsburgh at Johnstown, Johnstown, PA 15904, USA; jar441@pitt.edu
* Correspondence: pxp19@psu.edu

Abstract

This paper examines traditional data envelopment analysis (DEA), cross efficiency (CE), and game efficiency (GE) models for software productivity analysis and ranking. Additionally, for CE models, secondary objectives of aggressive and benevolent formulations are considered. An entropy criterion is used to identify the best-performing model. Experiments are conducted using the ISBSG dataset. The results show that aggressive CE model formulations have the lowest entropy values and produce unique project rankings. The GE model is computationally intensive and does not provide sufficient benefits to justify the extra effort. A rule-based framework is introduced to identify discrepancies in project rankings across models. This framework helps managers pinpoint truly efficient projects.

Keywords: data envelopment analysis; cross efficiency; game efficiency; rule-based systems; software productivity; project management

1. Introduction

Many studies in the software engineering literature use data envelopment analysis (DEA) to rank software development [1] and maintenance projects [2]. When a software project is evaluated for efficiency under the DEA framework, it can perform a self-assessment by selecting an optimal set of weights to achieve the highest possible efficiency score. Such self-assessments are considered "egoistic" or "narcissistic." The fundamental issue with these self-assessments is that many software projects—also known as decision-making units (DMUs) in DEA terminology—achieve an optimal efficiency score of 1 [3]. The DEA literature refers to this as a problem of total weight flexibility [4]. The problem with weight flexibility is that it prevents further prioritization among the fully efficient subset of projects. This undermines the purpose of efficiency evaluations because, ideally, only a small number of projects should be deemed efficient. Moreover, this small group of efficient projects should also reflect a high level of organizational consensus about their efficiencies.

DEA cross-efficiency (CE) [4] and game-efficiency (GE) [5] models were introduced to address issues with self-evaluations and weight flexibility. CE methods are valued for providing unbiased peer evaluations that lead to a unique ranking of DMUs [4]. However, these techniques have two main limitations. First, CE evaluations can only be obtained under constant-returns-to-scale assumptions, and second, the optimal weights are not unique. While CE models are developed under the variable-returns-to-scale assumption, the resulting models impose additional constraints, and DMU efficiency measured under such constraints has limited interpretation [6]. The non-uniqueness of the optimal CE weights can be further addressed by using secondary objective functions, where the DMU under evaluation uniquely selects its optimal weights using either an aggressive or a benevolent criterion [4]. The GE approach assumes that projects compete for a shared pool of resources and that some direct or indirect competition exists between the projects under evaluation. Under these assumptions, the GE approach estimates DMU efficiencies using traditional CE scores as lower bounds for GE scores. Typical GE score values fall between CE scores and traditional DEA scores. The GE model provides a unique set of DMU rankings and does not require the use of any secondary objective functions. In the context of software engineering projects, the GE model is suitable only when all evaluated software projects come from the same organization and are from the same time frame.

Since software project managers now have several frontier efficiency models to choose from—each offering its own benefits and assumptions—it is crucial to evaluate how these models perform on real-world datasets. After obtaining efficiency scores from each model, they can be averaged into a hybrid ensemble efficiency score, or different performance metrics can be employed to identify DMUs where models diverge in their evaluations [7]. This paper addresses two key issues. First, how to determine the most informative and least biased model when multiple software productivity ranking models are available. Second, since DEA models often identify several projects as fully efficient with the highest average project efficiency scores, while CE models tend to provide the lowest average scores, when both models are used, how can these scores be combined to identify false positives—specifically, high-ranking DEA projects that do not truly merit their rankings? To address the first issue, this paper compares various software productivity ranking models and evaluates them using an entropy-based criterion. The entropy criterion is recognized as maximally informative based on the data. This criterion is frequently employed in the software engineering literature, with recent applications including the development of ensemble classifiers [8] and the measurement of software trustworthiness [9]. To tackle the second issue, this paper uses a rule-based approach to identify discrepancies in project rankings across different models and to detect false positives. Projects that all models agree on can be deemed genuinely efficient. Projects with differing rankings are then scrutinized for false positives.

The rest of the paper is organized as follows. In Section 2, different DEA frontier models and the entropy criterion for model evaluation are presented. Section 3 describes datasets, experiments, and results. Section 4 concludes the paper with a summary and a discussion of limitations.

2. Overview of DEA Efficiency, Cross Efficiency, and Game Efficiency Models

For single-input, single-output measures of software effort in person-months and software size in function points, software productivity is defined as software size divided by software effort (i.e., function points per person-month) [10]. In this research, multiple inputs are used, with software size metric(s) as output(s) and software cost drivers as inputs. Since managers typically attempt to control for cost drivers [11], input-oriented DEA models are more suitable for software project benchmarking. These input-oriented models are described in this section.

The traditional DEA model can be described as n DMUs, each employing m inputs and s outputs. The input vector x and the output vector y take non-negative values. For a DMU $p \in \{1, \ldots, n\}$, its traditional self-evaluation efficiency score, E_{pp}, may be computed by using optimal weights of the following mathematical programming model.

https://doi.org/10.3390/app16031170

$$Max_{u,v}E_{pp} = \frac{\sum_{r=1}^{s} u_{rp}y_{rp}}{\sum_{i=1}^{m} v_{ip}x_{ip}},$$

Subject to the following:

$$\begin{aligned} &\frac{\sum_{r=1}^{s} u_{rp}y_{rj}}{\sum_{i=1}^{m} v_{ip}x_{ij}} \leq 1,\ \forall j = 1,\ldots,n; \\ &u_{rp} \geq 0,\ r = 1,\ldots,s;\ \text{and} \\ &v_{ip} \geq 0,\ i = 1,\ldots,m. \end{aligned} \tag{1}$$

The variables v_{ip} and u_{rp} are input and output vectors for the respective inputs and outputs for DMU_p. Since the model (1) is non-linear and has multiple optimal solutions, it can be linearized as shown below. The linearization guarantees that the optimum solution values are unique.

$$Max_{u,v}E_{pp} = \sum_{r=1}^{s} u_{rp}y_{rp},$$

Subject to the following:

$$\begin{aligned} &\sum_{i=1}^{m} v_{ip}x_{ip} = 1, \\ &\sum_{r=1}^{s} u_{rp}y_{rj} - \sum_{i=1}^{m} v_{ip}x_{ij} \leq 0, \forall\, j = 1,\ldots,n; \\ &u_{rp} \geq 0,\ r = 1,\ldots,s;\ \text{and} \\ &v_{ip} \geq 0,\ i = 1,\ldots,m. \end{aligned} \tag{2}$$

The optimal value obtained by solving model (2), E^*_{pp}, is the traditional DEA efficiency score for DMU_p.

If v^*_{ip} and u^*_{ip} are the optimal solutions chosen by DMUp by using the model (2), then the cross-efficiency scores for all DMUs are computed by evaluating DMU_p's optimal weights as follows:

$$E_{pj} = \frac{\sum_{r=1}^{s} u^*_{rp}y_{rj}}{\sum_{i=1}^{m} v^*_{ip}x_{ij}}, p, j = 1,\ldots,n. \tag{3}$$

Overall cross-efficiency scores are computed by solving problem (2) for each DMU as an evaluator and by computing the corresponding cross-efficiency scores for all DMUs based on the optimal weights of the evaluating DMUs. Once this process is over, the cross-efficiency score for some DMU_j is computed using the following expression:

$$E^c_j = \frac{1}{n}\sum_{p=1}^{n} E_{pj}. \tag{4}$$

A well-known drawback of cross-efficiency scores computed by expression (4) is the presence of alternative optima in the DEA weights [12]. To remove arbitrary optimal weight selections, researchers have suggested secondary objective functions to select a unique set of optimal weights under different secondary criteria. Among these secondary criteria, popular ones are aggressive and benevolent weight selection criteria. Under the aggressive criterion, the rating DMU aims to maximize its simple efficiency score as its primary objective while minimizing the average cross-efficiency score of its peers as its secondary objective. In the benevolent criterion, the primary objective remains the same as before, while the secondary objective is to maximize the average cross-efficiency scores of its peers. Assuming that the simple efficiency of DMU_p is computed using the model (2) and is given as $\theta^* = E^*_{pp}$, the secondary aggressive criterion formulation can be written as follows:

$$Minimize \sum_{j=1, j\neq p}^{n} \left(\sum_{r=1}^{s} u_{rp}y_{rj} - \sum_{i=1}^{m} v_{ip}x_{ij}\right),$$

https://doi.org/10.3390/app16031170

Subject to the following:

$$\begin{gathered}\sum_{i=1}^{m} v_{ip}x_{ip} = 1,\\ \sum_{r=1}^{s} u_{rp}y_{rp} - \theta^{*}\sum_{i=1}^{m} v_{ip}x_{ip} = 0,\\ \sum_{r=1}^{s} u_{rp}y_{rj} - \sum_{i=1}^{m} v_{ip}x_{ij} \leq 0, \forall j = 1,\ldots,n; \& \; j \neq p,\\ u_{rp} \geq 0,\; r = 1,\ldots,s; \text{ and } v_{ip} \geq 0,\; i = 1,\ldots,m.\end{gathered} \tag{5}$$

The corresponding benevolent formulation can be constructed by changing the minimize objective function in the model (5) to the maximize objective function.

Liang et al. [5] defined GE of DMU_j with respect to DMU_p using the following expression:

$$\theta_{pj} = \frac{\sum_{r=1}^{s} u_{rj}^{p*} y_{rj}}{\sum_{i=1}^{m} v_{ij}^{p*} x_{ij}},\; p = 1,\ldots,n, \tag{6}$$

where variables v_{ij}^{p*} and u_{ij}^{p*} are the optimal solutions obtained by solving the following Formulation (7) for an n-dimensional vector α of known values:

$$Max_{u,v}\, \theta_{pj} = \sum_{r=1}^{s} u_{rj}^{p} y_{rj},$$

Subject to the following:

$$\begin{gathered}\sum_{i=1}^{m} v_{ij}^{p}x_{ij} = 1,\\ \sum_{r=1}^{s} u_{rj}^{p}y_{rd} - \sum_{i=1}^{m} v_{ij}^{p}x_{id} \leq 0, \forall\, d = 1,\ldots,n;\\ \alpha_{p}\sum_{i=1}^{m} v_{ij}^{p}x_{ip} - \sum_{r=1}^{s} u_{rj}^{p}y_{rp} \leq 0,\\ u_{rj}^{p} \geq 0,\; r = 1,\ldots,s; \text{ and}\\ v_{ij}^{p} \geq 0,\; i = 1,\ldots,m.\end{gathered} \tag{7}$$

The vector component α_p is a positive number taking values in the interval [0, 1]. The model (7) maximizes the efficiency of DMU_j under the constraint that the cross-efficiency of DMU_p is no less than a value α_p. The model (7) is solved n times each for a different value of $j \in \{1, \ldots, n\}$. The average GE for DMU_j is defined as follows:

$$\alpha_j = \frac{1}{n}\sum_{p=1}^{n} \theta_{pj} = \frac{1}{n}\sum_{p=1}^{n}\sum_{r=1}^{s} u_{rj}^{p*} y_{rj}. \tag{8}$$

Given that the value of θ_{pj} is dependent on α_p, which is a function of $(\alpha_1, \ldots, \alpha_n)$, an iterative algorithm was developed by Liang et al. [5] to obtain the best GE scores at the Nash equilibrium point. This iterative algorithm has the following three steps.

Step 1. Solve (2) and obtain cross-efficiency scores using (3). Set iteration $t = 1$ and $\alpha_p^1 = E_p^c, \forall p = 1, \ldots, n$.

Step 2. Solve model (8) and set

$$\alpha_j^{t+1} = \frac{1}{n}\sum_{p=1}^{n}\sum_{r=1}^{s} u_{rj}^{p*}\left(\alpha_p^t\right) y_{rj}, \tag{9}$$

where $u_{rj}^{p*}\left(\alpha_p^t\right)$ represents an optimal value obtained by solving (7) when $\alpha_p = \alpha_p^t$.

Step 3. If $\left|\alpha_j^{t+1} - \alpha_j^t\right| \geq \varepsilon = 0.001$ for some $j \in \{1, \ldots, n\}$ then $\alpha_j^t = \alpha_j^{t+1}$ and go to Step 2. Otherwise, stop and α_j^{t+1} are the best GE scores of DMU_j for $j = 1, \ldots, n$. Figure 1 illustrates the procedure's flowchart.

https://doi.org/10.3390/app16031170

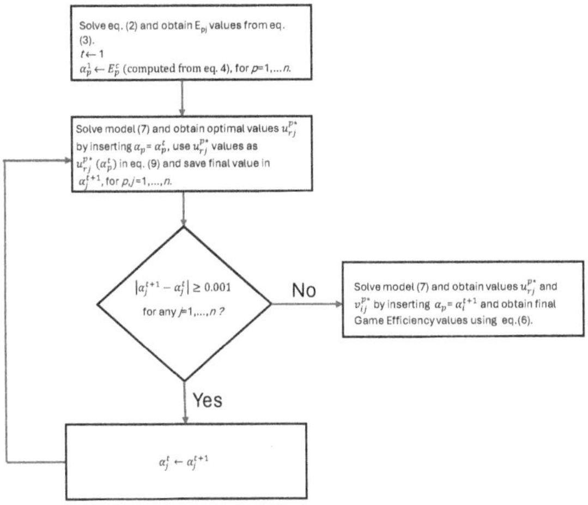

Figure 1. Game efficiency score computation procedure flowchart.

The maximum entropy (ME) principle has been applied to test the DEA DMU ranking distribution bias [13], weight aggregation [14] and comparing different DEA models [15]. Assuming a generic final optimal efficiency score (i.e., any one of traditional, cross efficiency, or game efficiency), notation for DMU_j is denoted as θ_j^*, the entropy score of a given model can be computed by first normalizing the efficiency scores using the following expression:

$$\varphi_j = \frac{\theta_j^*}{\sum_{j=1}^{n} \theta_j^*}, \tag{10}$$

and then computing the entropy score using the following expression:

$$\xi = -\sum_{j=1}^{n} \varphi_j ln(\varphi_j). \tag{11}$$

Higher values of ξ mean lower discrimination power of the model because many DMUs are assigned similar scores. The highest value of ξ is achieved when all DMUs are assigned an efficiency score of 1 and the model has zero discrimination power. Models with lower entropy values are generally desirable because they tend to uniquely rank DMUs and provide for better discrimination among ranked DMUs.

3. Data, Experiments, and Results

Data used for testing the software productivity models were obtained from the International Software Benchmarking Standards Group (ISBSG). The ISBSG dataset is widely used in the software engineering literature and was also employed in the study of production functions [16]. In particular, two software productivity models were tested. The first model was a single-output model in which the software production function produced software size (in function points) as an output, with software effort, project schedule length (in months), and total defects as inputs. The project schedule length was calculated as project elapsed time minus any inactive project time. Total defects were determined as the sum of major and minor defects. Only projects with complete data were included in the analysis; projects with any missing attributes were excluded. As per the ISBSG dataset convention, only projects with data quality ratings A and B were selected for analysis. According to ISBSG, a data quality rating of A indicates all data is seemingly sound, while a rating of B suggests most data attributes are sound except for a few that may not be entirely reliable. A total of 86 projects were used to test the first software productivity model.

https://doi.org/10.3390/app16031170

Figure 2 shows the traditional DEA scores from (2), cross efficiency (CE) scores under an arbitrary criterion using (4), cross efficiency scores with the secondary aggressive (AGG) criterion from (5), and benevolent (Ben) criterion based on the maximum objective function in (5). In the figure, the X-axis lists the DMU numbers, and the Y-axis displays the efficiency scores.

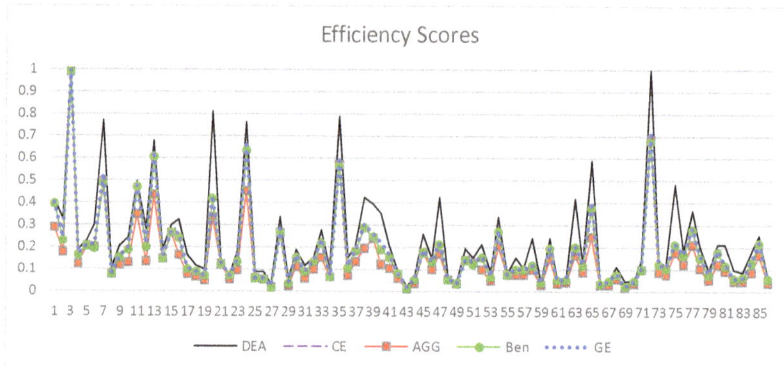

Figure 2. DEA, cross efficiency, and game efficiency scores.

Two expectations exist regarding the results. First, traditional DEA scores will consistently outperform all other scores (i.e., DEA max{CE, GE, AGG, Ben}), and GE scores will always be bounded above by traditional DEA scores and below by CE scores, based on an arbitrary objective function (i.e., DEA GE CE). The results confirmed both expectations. Figure 3 displays the efficiency difference plot comparing DEA and GE scores, as well as GE and CE scores. Similarly to Figure 2, the X-axis shows the DMU numbers, and the Y-axis represents the differences in efficiency scores. The plot indicates that the gap between traditional DEA and GE scores is generally larger than the gap between GE and CE scores. The DEA identified two DMUs as the most efficient, both with an efficiency score of 1. All methods ranked DMU #3 as the highest, with its respective efficiency scores listed in the Max row of Table 1. DMU #3 was a small project with two inputs, taking a low value of the project schedule of one month and zero total defects, against the overall data average project schedule length of approximately 9 months and average total defects of approximately 10 defects. Similarly, all techniques agreed that DMU #43 was the least efficient, with its scores listed in the Min row of Table 1. For this project, the primary reason for the lower efficiency score was a lower value of the output, where its FP value was 16 against a sample average of about 765 function points. The inputs for this DMU had high values of Effort = 465, Schedule = 7, and Defects = 7. Apart from the DEA, all other methods produced unique rankings.

When comparing Ben and AGG secondary objective cross-efficiency models, Ben models mostly had higher scores than the AGG model. Figure 4 illustrates the Ben-AGG efficiency value difference plot. As mentioned earlier, the DEA model efficiency scores were the highest, so no additional comparison between the DEA and secondary objective cross-efficiency models was necessary.

Table 1 summarizes key statistics for all five techniques. The DEA and GE had the highest average efficiency scores, as well as the highest standard deviations. In terms of entropy scores, GE performed the worst with the highest entropy value, while AGG performed the best with the lowest entropy value. Additionally, the mean and standard deviation values for the AGG model were the lowest among all five models.

https://doi.org/10.3390/app16031170

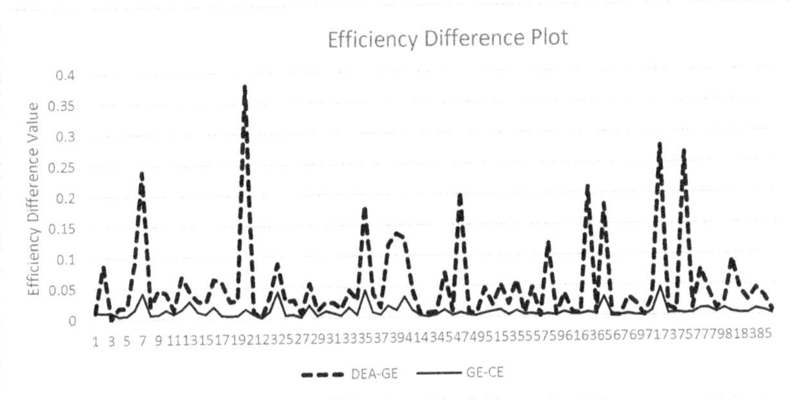

Figure 3. The difference plot of selected efficiency scores.

Table 1. Key summary statistics of model results.

	DEA	CE	AGG	Ben	GE
Max	1	0.9890	0.9890	0.9900	1
Min	0.0228	0.0147	0.0098	0.0146	0.0158
Mean	0.2407	0.1784	0.1473	0.1785	0.1878
St. dev	0.2160	0.1659	0.1538	0.1660	0.1732
Entropy	4.1297	4.1292	4.0812	4.1292	4.1314

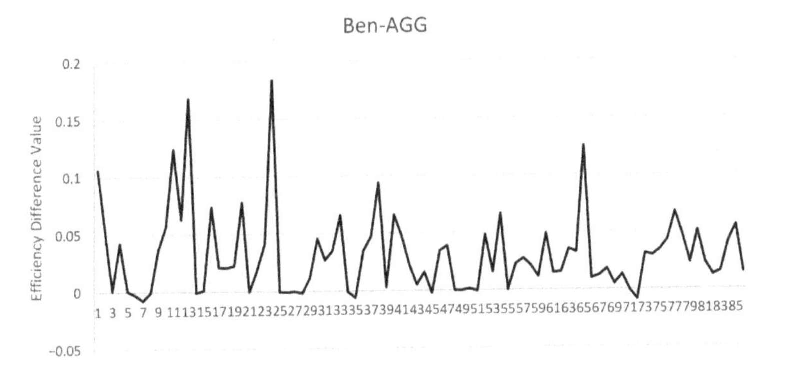

Figure 4. The difference plot of secondary objective cross-efficiency scores.

Table 2 presents the results of a paired-samples t-test comparing efficiency scores across techniques. The table displays |t|-values. All mean differences were significant at the 0.01 level of statistical significance, both for one tail (critical |t|-value = 2.37, df = 85) and two tails (critical |t|-value = 2.63, df = 85). These findings suggest that no two techniques are statistically similar in their rankings.

The second software productivity model examined in the research has two output measures—function points and source lines of code (SLOC). It uses two cost-influencing inputs: software effort and project schedule duration. Due to missing data for SLOC and total defects, including total defects as an input was not feasible, which restricted the dataset to only a few projects. For the model with two inputs and two outputs, 35 projects

https://doi.org/10.3390/app16031170

had complete data for all four variables and were included in the analysis. Figure 5 shows the efficiency scores for these 35 DMUs across all five techniques. The DEA ranked four DMUs as fully efficient with a score of 1. All methods gave the highest score to DMU #10 and the lowest to DMU #31. The highest and lowest scores are listed in Table 3. The high efficiency score for DMU #10 was due to its large size (SLOC = 13,900 and FP = 1106). For DMU #31, its low efficiency score was mainly because of a high effort score (7700) and a lower function points score (182).

Table 2. The t-test for difference in means (|t|-values).

	CE	AGG	Ben	GE
DEA	7.52	9.48	7.51	6.95
CE		7.9	5.11	8.75
AGG			7.92	9.08
Ben				8.66

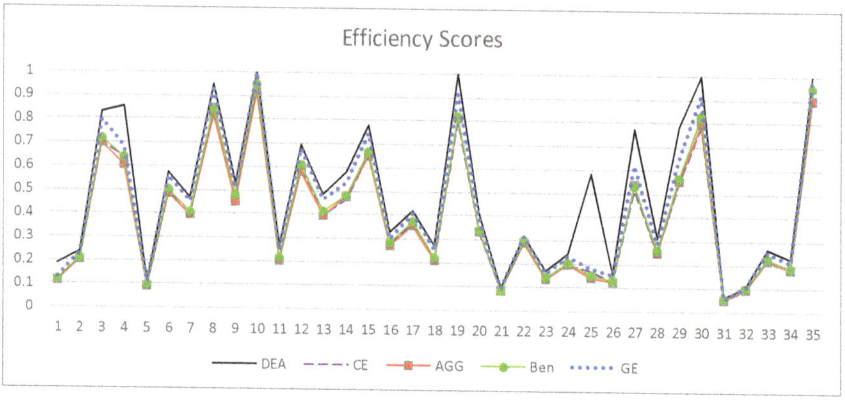

Figure 5. DEA, cross efficiency, and game efficiency scores.

Table 3. Key summary statistics of model results.

	DEA	CE	AGG	Ben	GE
Max	1	0.9415	0.9128	0.9513	1
Min	0.0602	0.0527	0.0516	0.0541	0.0591
Mean	0.4878	0.3927	0.3894	0.4031	0.4439
St. dev	0.3068	0.2619	0.2600	0.2684	0.2909
Entropy	3.3556	3.3394	3.3373	3.3396	3.3439

Figure 6 shows the efficiency difference plot between DEA and GE, and GE and CE. Unlike the single-output software productivity model, in which the difference between DEA and GE mostly overshadowed that between GE and CE, the plot in Figure 5 suggests that GE scores are neither close to DEA nor to CE scores. No clear pattern emerges from the plot.

Figure 7 shows the Ben-AGG efficiency difference plot. Similarly to the results from the previous dataset, the Ben model generally had higher efficiency scores than the AGG model, but the differences were smaller in the second dataset.

https://doi.org/10.3390/app16031170

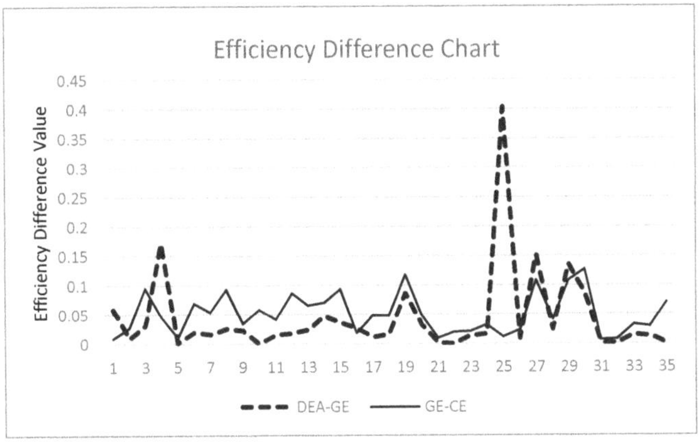

Figure 6. The difference plot of selected efficiency scores.

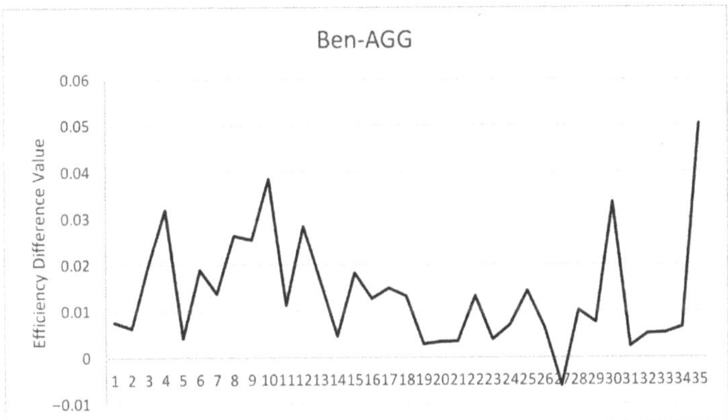

Figure 7. The difference plot of secondary objective cross-efficiency scores.

Table 3 shows key statistics for all five techniques. Similarly to the first experiment, the AGG results had the lowest entropy value and provided the best discrimination between projects and unique DMU rankings. Like the initial experiment, the DEA and GE ranking models showed the highest entropy, mean, and standard deviation values. The Ben ranking model does not seem promising in either single-output or two-output experiments, as its entropy values are not lower than the CE entropy values obtained under the arbitrary criterion. Overall, the AGG results appear consistently the most effective.

Table 4 displays the results of a paired t-test comparing the efficiency scores of different techniques. The table shows $|t|$-values, and most mean differences were statistically significant at the 0.01 level for both one-tail (critical $|t|$-value = 2.44, df = 34) and two-tail tests (critical $|t|$-value = 2.73, df = 34). The difference in means between CE and AGG was only significant at a weaker 0.1 level of significance.

If a manager chooses only one best technique, the experiment results show that AGG is the top choice. It produces a unique set of DMU rankings based on the aggressive secondary criterion, in which a DMU aims not to sacrifice its simple efficiency score so that its peers can improve theirs. Additionally, the AGG efficiency score will be acceptable to all other DMUs and will not be seen as unfair. When managers do not need to explain their results or the assumptions behind them, they can use an ensemble efficiency score by averaging all techniques' scores. However, if a manager prefers to rely only on a traditional

https://doi.org/10.3390/app16031170

DEA method, other techniques can still help identify and highlight projects that deviate significantly from DEA scores. For projects with large score differences between methods, managers may need to reevaluate to prevent unfair ratings. Fortunately, the experiment results show that all methods agree on the highest- and lowest-ranking DMUs, so major disagreements are unlikely. Still, a formal framework is necessary to detect such differences.

Table 4. The t-test for difference in means (| t | -values).

	CE	AGG	Ben	GE
DEA	6.43	6.61	5.80	3.44
CE		1.61 *	6.51	8.68
AGG			6.81	9.91
Ben				8.91

* Significant only at 0.1 level of significance.

The formal evaluation process must distinguish between efficient DMUs and false positives. False positives often occur with ranking methods that assign high-efficiency scores to too many DMUs. The traditional DEA model, with its issue of weight flexibility, frequently overestimates DMU efficiency scores, leading to false positives. While traditional DEA and CE methods are used below to identify false positives, any technique with a high entropy value can be compared to another method with a low entropy value to detect false positives in the high-entropy method. Baker and Talluri [17] proposed the following false-positive index (FPI) metric to measure the false positivity of DMUs. For a DMUj, its FPI can be calculated using the following expression:

$$FPI_j = \frac{E_{jj} - E_j^C}{E_j^C}, \tag{12}$$

where E_{jj} is the traditional DEA efficiency score computed using (2) and E_j^C is the cross-efficiency score calculated using Equation (4). Once FPIs for all DMUs are available, then false positives can be identified by selecting an appropriate threshold value for a parameter η, and running the following rule:

IF $FPI_j > \eta$ THEN DMU_j is False Positive

ELSE DMU_j is Not False Positive.

Figures 8 and 9 illustrate the total false positives for the first and second software productivity models considered in this research. The threshold parameter (η) is varied from 0 in increments of 0.05 until the total false positives drop to zero. Both figures indicate that total false positives fall precipitously until the parameter value of η is about 0.5. After this point, the fall in total false positives is more gradual. Thus, setting the parameter η = 0.5 may be a good idea for identifying false-positive DMUs. When η = 0.5, exactly 18 projects in Model 1 will be identified as false positives, and only three projects from Model 2 will be identified as false positives.

Once the set of false-positive DMUs is identified, managers can review them further, as traditional DEA rankings tend to overestimate the efficiency scores of these DMUs. The lower CE scores for false-positive DMUs suggest that high-efficiency scores from traditional DEA rankings might not be accepted by their peers. The DMUs can also be ranked in descending order based on FPI, and managers may choose to focus only on the top 10% for further examination. In such cases, no threshold is needed to identify false positives.

https://doi.org/10.3390/app16031170

Figure 8. Total false positives for model 1.

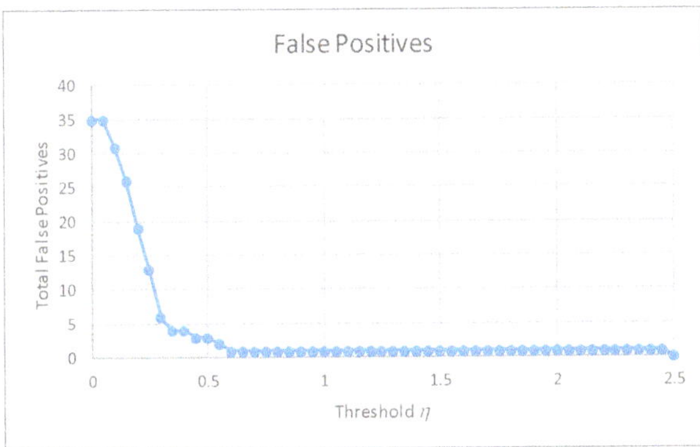

Figure 9. Total false positives for model 2.

4. Summary, Conclusions, and Limitations

This paper compares several non-parametric frontier efficiency models for ranking software project productivity. The models examined include traditional DEA, cross-efficiency DEA models with arbitrary and secondary objectives, and game efficiency models. Experiments used the ISBSG dataset and entropy criteria to select the best model. The study results show that the cross-efficiency model with the aggressive secondary objective is the most effective for software productivity rankings. These CE models provide unique rankings without favoring any particular software project, making their neutral approach potentially more acceptable to organizations. The GE approach appears to be the least effective because it is the most computationally intensive, with CPU runtimes exceeding an hour and resulting in high-entropy efficiency scores. GE models assume competition among projects for shared organizational resources, but this assumption does not seem to hold well in the software industry.

For managers who want to use the traditional DEA model for project ranking, this study offers additional hybrid tools to identify projects that might be unfairly assigned high-efficiency scores. These unjustified high scores occur because of the traditional DEA model's total weight flexibility. By removing these unfair high-ranking DMUs, managers can more confidently identify the best-performing projects.

While nonparametric and free of assumptions about the form of the production function are benefits of the DEA method, the procedure also has some limitations. The principal limitation comes from the assumption of a common production process. An ideal situation for applying the DEA procedure to software engineering datasets would be when

https://doi.org/10.3390/app16031170

all projects come from the same organization and are carried out simultaneously. This way, all projects have access to similar people, tools, procedures, and resources. This will also limit outliers in the analyzed data. Among the different DEA techniques, Game DEA is the most restrictive, as it assumes that software projects compete for common resources in a zero-sum game. The narcissistic nature of the traditional DEA makes it the highest efficiency scoring technique. Peer ranking CE techniques may be suitable when data come from different organizations, as efficiency scores are averaged across peer rankings. In particular, the Benevolent secondary objective CE model, which maximizes the efficiency scores of individual DMUs and the average efficiency of all peer DMUs, is very attractive because it is consistent with the total factor productivity principle. The AGG secondary objective model may be suitable when there is general competition among software projects. Such competition may occur when several companies bid for software projects within a single industry.

The dataset used in this research comes from several companies across different industries. The projects were completed at different times as well. As a result, outliers are expected. Outliers in the dataset will lead to biases in efficiency scores. The entropy- and rule-based procedure proposed in this paper was designed to rank models that are least biased and identify DMUs for which efficiency scores can be considered reliable based on model consensus. The entropy method is just one technique that can be used to deal with outliers. The DEA literature has proposed other bootstrap sampling and robust Bayesian DEA techniques to compute efficiency in the presence of outliers [18]. Future researchers may consider some of these techniques as a possible extension to this research.

Author Contributions: Conceptualization, P.C.P.; methodology, P.C.P.; software, P.C.P.; validation, P.C.P.; formal analysis, P.C.P.; investigation, P.C.P.; data curation/acquisition, J.A.R.; writing—original draft preparation, P.C.P.; writing—review and editing, P.C.P.; visualization, P.C.P.; supervision, P.C.P.; project administration, P.C.P. All authors have read and agreed to the published version of the manuscript.

Funding: This research received no external funding.

Institutional Review Board Statement: Not applicable.

Informed Consent Statement: Not applicable.

Data Availability Statement: The data used in this research are proprietary, but the latest version can be obtained from https://www.isbsg.org/, accessed on 20 January 2026.

Conflicts of Interest: The authors declare no conflicts of interest.

References

1. Banker, R.D.; Kemerer, C.F. Scale Economies in New Software Development. *IEEE Trans. Softw. Eng.* **1989**, *15*, 1199–1205. [CrossRef]
2. Banker, R.D.; Datar, S.M.; Kemerer, C.F. A Model to Evaluate Variables Impacting the Productivity of Software Maintenance Projects. *Manag. Sci.* **1991**, *37*, 1–18. [CrossRef]
3. Pendharkar, P. Scale Economies and Production Function Estimation for Object-Oriented Software Component and Source Code Documentation Size. *Eur. J. Oper. Res.* **2006**, *172*, 1040–1050. [CrossRef]
4. Doyle, J.; Green, R. Efficiency and Cross-Efficiency in DEA: Derivations, Meanings and Uses. *J. Oper. Res. Soc.* **1994**, *45*, 567–578. [CrossRef]
5. Liang, L.; Wu, J.; Cook, W.D.; Zhu, J. The DEA Game Cross-Efficiency Mode and Its Nash Equilibrium. *Oper. Res.* **2008**, *56*, 1278–1288. [CrossRef]
6. Lim, S.; Zhu, J. DEA Cross Efficiency Under Variable Returns to Scale. In *Data Envelopment Analysis A Handbook of Models and Methods*; International Series in Operations Research and Management Science; Springer: Bioston, MA, USA, 2015; Volume 221, pp. 45–66.

https://doi.org/10.3390/app16031170

7. Kalyan, S.; Bansal, P.; Kumar, S. A Novel Hybrid AHP-Entropy Weighted Dynamic Network DEA Framework for Comprehensive Efficiency Assessment. *Expert Syst. Appl.* **2026**, *296*, 129137. [CrossRef]
8. Jiang, F.; Yu, X.; Hu, Q.; Liu, J.; Du, J. An Ensemble Method Using Neighborhood Granular Combination Entropy For Software Defect Prediction. *Inf. Process. Manag.* **2026**, *63*, 104483. [CrossRef]
9. Tao, H.; Liu, H.; Niu, X.; Ding, L.; Chen, Y.; Cao, Q. Software Aging Oriented Trustworthiness Measurement Based on Weighted Boltzmann Entropy. *Inf. Softw. Technol.* **2025**, *178*, 107606. [CrossRef]
10. Subramanian, G.H.; Zarnich, G.E. An Examination of Some Software Development Effort and Productivity Determinants in ICASE Tool Projects. *J. Manag. Inf. Syst.* **1996**, *12*, 143–160. [CrossRef]
11. Menezes, J.; Gusmao, C.; Moura, H. Risk Factors in Software Development Projects: A Systematic Literature Review. *Softw. Qual. J.* **2019**, *27*, 1149–1174. [CrossRef]
12. Ruiz, J.L.; Sirvent, I. Ranking Decision Making Units: The Cross-Efficiency Evaluation. In *Handbook of Operations Analytics Using Data Envelopment Analysis*; Springer: Berlin/Heidelberg, Germany, 2016; pp. 1–29.
13. Soleimani-Damaneh, M.; Zarepisheh, M. Shannon's Entropy for Combining the Efficiency Results of Different DEA Models: Method and Application. *Expert Syst. Appl.* **2009**, *36*, 5146–5150. [CrossRef]
14. Sun, L.; Yu, Y.; He, J.; Li, C.; Yu, X.; Zhang, L.; Lu, Y.; Malik, I.; Wistuba, M. Vulnerability Assessment of Social-Ecological Systems in Arid Regions: A Cross-Efficiency Modified DEA Model with Entropy Weight Aggregation. *Ecol. Indic.* **2025**, *179*, 114149. [CrossRef]
15. Xie, Q.; Dai, Q.; Li, Y.; Jiang, A. Increasing the Discriminatory Power of DEA Using Shannon's Entropy. *Entropy* **2014**, *16*, 1571–1585. [CrossRef]
16. Pendharkar, P.C.; Rodger, J.A.; Subramanian, G.H. An Empirical Study of the Cobb-Douglas Production Properties of Software Development Effort. *Inf. Softw. Technol.* **2008**, *50*, 1181–1188. [CrossRef]
17. Baker, P.C.; Talluri, S. A Closer Look at the Use of Data Envelopment Analysis for Technology Selection. *Comput. Ind. Eng.* **1997**, *32*, 101–108. [CrossRef]
18. Cengiz, M.A.; Senel, T. Bayesian Robust Data Envelopment Analysis With Heavy-Tailed Priors. *J. Math.* **2025**, *2025*, 6484456. [CrossRef]

https://doi.org/10.3390/app16031170

applied sciences

Article

Research on Hybrid Collaborative Development Model Based on Multi-Dimensional Behavioral Information

Shuanliang Gao, Wei Liao, Tao Shu, Zhuoning Zhao and Yaqiang Wang *

College of Software Engineering, Chengdu University of Information Technology, Chengdu 610225, China; 3220704003@stu.cuit.edu.cn (S.G.); liaowei@cuit.edu.cn (W.L.); shutao@cuit.edu.cn (T.S.); zhaozhn@cuit.edu.cn (Z.Z.)

* Correspondence: yaqwang@cuit.edu.cn

Abstract: This paper aims to propose a hybrid collaborative development model based on multi-dimensional behavioral information (HCDMB) to deal with systemic problems in modern software engineering, such as the low efficiency of cross-stage collaboration, the fragmentation of the intelligent tool chain, and the imperfect human–machine collaboration mechanism. This paper focuses on the stages of requirements analysis, software development, software testing and software operation and maintenance in the process of software development. By integrating the multi-dimensional characteristics of the development behavior track, collaboration interaction record and product application data in the process of project promotion, the mixture of experts (MoE) model is introduced to break through the rigid constraints of the traditional tool chain. Reinforcement learning combined with human feedback is used to optimize the MoE dynamic routing mechanism. At the same time, the few-shot context learning method is used to build different expert models, which further improve the reasoning efficiency and knowledge transfer ability of the system in different scenarios. The HCDMB model proposed in this paper can be viewed as an important breakthrough in the software engineering collaboration paradigm, so as to provide innovative solutions to the many problems faced by dynamic requirements and diverse scenarios based on artificial intelligence technology in the field of software engineering involving different project personnel.

Keywords: software engineering; multi-dimensional behavioral information; large language models; mixture of experts

1. Introduction

The revolutionary progress of artificial intelligence technology is driving the paradigm shift of the software engineering discipline from "labor-intensive" to "intelligence-driven". Although the continuous evolution of agile development in the current software development model has broken through the linear constraints of the traditional waterfall model [1], the modern software development process faces systemic challenges such as dynamic evolution of requirements, generalization of application scenarios, and isomerization of project roles, which promote the deep penetration of artificial intelligence technology into the whole process of the software development life cycle. At present, technology integration has gone beyond the tool-assisted stage and entered a new era of process reconstruction and paradigm innovation [2,3].

Traditional methods based on statistical machine learning and deep learning in the field of software engineering often focus on specific problems in a single software development link, resulting in insufficient generalization ability of the model and difficulty in

 https://doi.org/10.3390/app15094907

adapting to the increasing demand for intelligence in the current field of software engineering. Taking the software requirements stage as an example, early studies use deep learning models for requirements classification and feature extraction, which cannot achieve higher-level intelligent processing such as intelligent extraction and summary of requirements elements, modeling of requirements dependencies, and conflict detection. Similarly, in the phase of software operation and maintenance, traditional quality assurance methods rely on manually designed test cases and scripted regression testing, which not only face the challenge of insufficient test coverage, but also suffer from high maintenance costs.

The emergence of large language models (LLM) provides a new technical paradigm for solving the above problems. With its powerful knowledge reasoning ability and context understanding ability, the LLM can be widely used in the whole life cycle of software engineering. Through the training and optimization of the model domain adaptation, the LLM can significantly improve the intelligence level of its domain, and then realize the intelligent analysis of requirements elements, and promote the software quality assurance into a new stage of cognitive intelligence, such as automatically generating test cases, identifying defect patterns of code, etc. This cognitive intelligence method based on LLM not only breaks through the limitations of traditional methods in generalization ability, but also brings a new intelligent solution to software engineering practice. However, there are still several key challenges in the existing technologies. Firstly, it is difficult to dynamically integrate various stages in the software engineering life cycle. Secondly, there is insufficient intelligent support for cross-stage collaborative development. Finally, there is still a cognitive limitation on the value mining of development behavior data, which fails to make full use of behavioral information at each stage of the software life cycle.

In order to solve the above problems, inspired by the MoE model, this paper proposes the HCDMB model. The input data of this model deeply integrates multi-dimensional behavioral information in the whole life cycle of software development. The MoE model is combined to dynamically select the different LLMs of experts, and then a dynamic adaptive intelligent collaboration system is constructed, and the output data are intelligent decision-making suggestions provided according to user behavior, which aims to build a new paradigm for the research of artificial intelligence technology, such as LLM in the field of software engineering.

Specifically, the core innovation of the proposed model is reflected in the following two dimensions:

Firstly, multi-dimensional behavioral information collection and processing: Through the collection of cross-modal software development process behaviors and the modeling of feature extraction, the fragmentation problem of traditional single-dimensional behavior analysis is effectively solved. Secondly, context-aware expert routing mechanism: A gated routing network is constructed based on a large language, and different expert cluster sub-models are selected and activated according to the users' multi-dimensional behavioral information and user intentions. Secondly, reinforcement learning is combined to optimize the routing gate network model, and appropriate expert models are selected based on the users' intentions and related behavioral information to achieve accurate matching between task context and expert capabilities.

The remainder of this paper is organized as follows: Section 2 conducts a literature review on the application of artificial intelligence technology in the field of software engineering and the MoE method. Section 3 presents the proposed HCDMB model, including the architecture design, multi-dimensional behavioral information processing, and the construction of the MoE model with a dynamic routing mechanism based on reinforcement learning from human feedback. Section 4 details the results, covering the experimental configurations, system implementation, and performance evaluations against baseline approaches. Section 5 discusses the limitations of the existing methods and proposes future optimization directions and application scenarios. Finally, Section 6 summarizes this work, discusses the contributions and limitations of the study, and outlines potential future research directions.

2. Literature Review

At present, the research of artificial intelligence technology in the field of software engineering is making significant progress. This section systematically combs the application status of artificial intelligence technology in the field of software engineering, and further analyzes the challenges faced by the existing methods. In view of the above challenges, the advantages of the MoE model and its application in the engineering field are introduced and explored.

2.1. Research on Artificial Intelligence Technology in the Field of Software Engineering

AI-enabled software engineering (AISE) has entered the peak of practical application [4]. The application of AI in software engineering is primarily reflected in three core dimensions: requirements engineering, development paradigms, and quality assurance systems. To be specific, it is manifested as follows:

(1) Semantic deconstruction in requirements engineering. Requirements engineering focuses on constructing functional and non-functional specifications for target systems [5,6]. Early research predominantly centered on model-based classification, for example, Abbas et al. [7] conducted semantic classification of requirement texts based on the Bi-LSTM model, and Marcacini et al. [8] utilized the pre-trained language BERT model [9] to automatically extract requirement features from user comments. With the development of large language models (LLMs), exemplified by GPT [10] and Qwen-VL [11], the demand engineering approach enters a new paradigm: Automated extraction and formalization of requirement elements through semantic correlation analysis, context-aware dynamic generation of requirement documentation, and knowledge graph-enhanced dependency modeling and conflict detection [12–14].

(2) Cognitive reconfiguration and knowledge transfer in development paradigms: The traditional development model uses a linear process to promote the progress of each development stage, which exposes defects such as response delay and experience dependence when facing complex system development [15]. Prior improvements focused narrowly on automating isolated development tasks, Azeem et al. [16] proposed the detection of code anomalies based on machine learning methods, and Sun et al. [17] used Sentent-BERT's recommended code API. The advent of LLMs has fundamentally redefined the technical ecosystem of intelligent development, demonstrating robust capabilities in code generation and autocompletion (e.g., GitHub Copilot [18]), defect pattern recognition (e.g., DeepDebug [19]), and semantic code comprehension [20]. The use of LLMs effectively solves the fragmentation problem of the traditional tool chain, and realizes the systematic precipitation and reuse of development experience.

(3) Intelligent evolution of quality assurance systems. Conventional approaches, constrained by manually designed test cases and scripted regression testing, struggle with inadequate coverage and exponentially rising maintenance costs [21,22]. Current optimizations target isolated techniques, for example, Jones et al. [23] applied a genetic algorithm to automatically generate test datasets, and Zhu et al. [24] generated test cases based on diffusion model. LLMs propel quality assurance into a cognitive intelligence era: Wang et al. [25] use LLMs to implement defect pattern detection and suggestions; reinforcement learning [26] integrated frameworks optimize test data generation through code path coverage reward functions, simultaneously enhancing coverage [27]. This intelli-

gent evolution establishes a novel technical paradigm for quality assurance in continuous delivery scenarios.

The current software development landscape is plagued by fragmented technology integration and isolated toolchains, impeding the transformation of localized task optimization into overall efficiency gains. AI–human interaction remains fragmented both vertically and horizontally, with a lack of dynamic coupling across roles and a deficiency in mutual interpretability and trust between human expertise and AI logic. Additionally, behavioral data from development processes are siloed and underutilized, lacking cross-project knowledge fusion and robust decision support, especially in large-scale distributed systems.

2.2. Application of Mixture of Experts

In response to the above-mentioned systematic contradictions, Jacobs et al. [28] proposed the MoE model, providing an innovative solution for constructing an intelligent software engineering system. Its core mechanism consists of two key components: the expert routing decision layer based on the gating network and the expert sub-model cluster oriented to domain features. The sparsely gated MoE architecture proposed by Google [29], which employs a sparse activation mechanism, lays the foundation for large-scale engineering applications.

The MoE method has high computational efficiency and scalability. MoE enables dynamic resource allocation via conditional computation, achieving exponential parameter scaling (e.g., trillion-parameter models like Switch Transformer [30]). Furthermore, MoE has the capabilities of domain adaptation and task decoupling. It uses multidimensional features to compute expert weights and map tasks to experts. In software engineering, this allows the creation of diverse expert clusters: language-specific compilers, phase-aware controllers for workflows (requirements analysis, code generation, test verification), and cross-role behavior modelers (developer intent recognition, tester pattern mining, requirement tracing). Zhou et al. [31] proposed that the dynamic routing mechanism could solve the capacity bottleneck of the traditional single model architecture in complex task scenarios.

At the level of engineering practice, MoE technology has shown significant application value. For example, Deepseek-v3 [32], GPT-4 [33] and other large models have adopted MoE architecture. This approach can be applied throughout the software development lifecycle: activating requirements experts for specifications in the analysis phase, domain-specific models (e.g., SQL optimization or concurrent programming experts) in the development phase, and quality assurance experts in testing. This dynamic scheduling breaks traditional tool-chain constraints and creates a knowledge enhancement loop through continuous expert experience accumulation.

3. Materials and Methods

This section elaborates the research model of HCDMB. Firstly, the three-level hierarchical architecture design of the system is introduced, including the input layer, the mixed expert (MoE) core layer and the output layer. Secondly, the collection and processing methods of multi-dimensional behavioral information are described in detail, including the development behavior track, collaborative interaction record, feature extraction and semantic embedding of product application data. Then, a dynamic routing mechanism based on the MoE model is proposed to optimize the routing gate network through RLHF, so as to achieve accurate matching between task context and expert capability. In addition, an expert model optimization method based on RAG and few-shot context learning is introduced, which significantly improves the reasoning efficiency and knowledge transfer ability of the system in complex scenarios. Finally, the context-aware reasoning support for the expert model is provided by constructing the project knowledge base and the multi-way recall strategy. As an outcome of the research, we wish to offer a new model and describe that we have developed under the term hybrid collaborative development model based on multi-dimensional behavioral information (HCDMB).

3.1. Design of Research Method's Framework

The HCDMB model adopts a hierarchical and progressive three-level architecture design, which is composed of an input layer, MoE core layer and output layer (as shown in Figure 1).

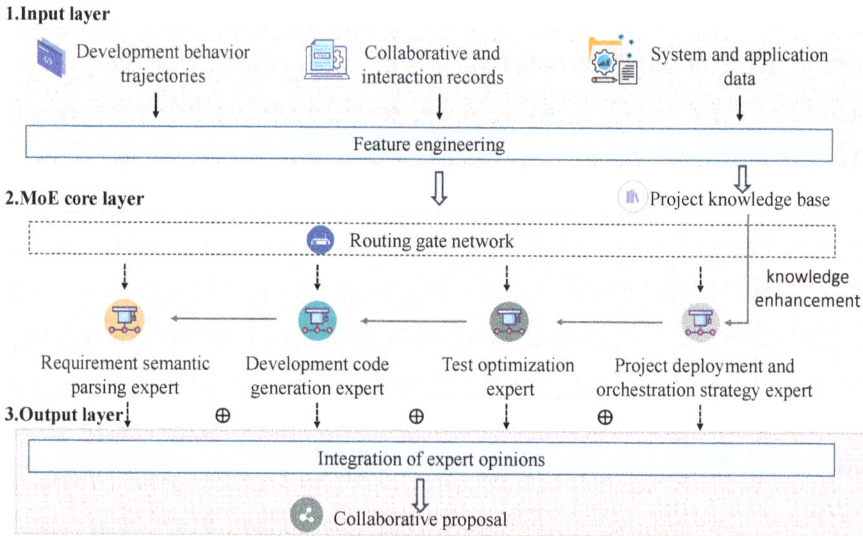

Figure 1. Design of research method's framework.

The input layer mainly realizes the dual functions of multi-dimensional software development behavior data processing and user intention recognition. By integrating multi-source heterogeneous data acquisition pipelines, the behavior data in the whole life cycle of software development are feature extraction and engineering processing. Specifically, the data sources include development behavior trajectories, collaborative and interaction records, system and application data. The feature engineering methods adopted are as follows: for unstructured text data (such as requirements documents, code development, etc.), the embedding models based on BAAI General Embedding (BGE) [34] and CodeBERT [35] are used to encode semantic vectors to build project knowledge bases. For temporal behavior characteristics (such as code submission frequency, test coverage, etc.), key information is extracted and summarized as descriptive text as supplementary knowledge. The input layer is the input data of the model by associating the user's intention with its multi-dimensional behavioral information.

The core layer of the MoE constructs an expert collaborative decision-making system, which includes an expert model group and a routing gate network. The expert model group constructed by this method is configured with four domain specialization modules: requirements semantic parsing expert based on Deepseek v3, development code generation expert based on CodeGeeX4 [36], test optimization expert based on CodeGeeX4, and project deployment and orchestration strategy expert based on Deepseek v3. In the inference stage, each expert model accesses the project knowledge base through the retrieval augmented generation (RAG) method [37], and retrieves the knowledge information related to users' behavior data and intentions in the knowledge base as the context information input to each expert model to enhance and constrain the answers of the model. The routing gate network uses the Deepseek model as the base model, and uses the dynamic routing algorithm to realize the task decomposition and selection of expert models based on user intention and related behavioral information. For example, when high-frequency code commits are identified to be associated with test failures, the gated network will improve the decision weights of the test optimization experts, project deployment and orchestration experts, and trigger the collaborative response of automated test-case generation and team communication suggestions. At the same time, reinforcement learning from human feedback (RLHF) [38] is used to fine-tune the routing gate network and improve its effectiveness.

The output layer fuses the expert opinions of the MoE core layer by constructing an analysis model and generates operational schemes, such as developing process optimization suggestions. The dynamic resource allocation scheme includes the strategic scheduling of computing resources (GPU instance allocation) and human resources (developer task-load balancing), as well as intelligent auxiliary output, covering code autocompletion, fault location and requirements tracking functions.

3.2. Implementation of Key Technologies

This section mainly discusses the key technologies in the model architecture shown in Figure 1, and introduces the data sources of the input layer and the corresponding feature engineering methods. Furthermore, based on the data processed by feature engineering, the project knowledge base and hybrid retrieval method are further constructed to improve the answering ability of the expert model. In addition, for the MoE core layer, this section further introduces the optimization of the routing gate network model by constructing a fine-tuning dataset and the DPO-based method, and the optimization of the expert model by using the few-shot context learning method and the constructed item knowledge base.

3.2.1. Input Layer

The input layer constructs the collection and processing method of multi-dimensional behavioral information data, and realizes the feature extraction and intention association analysis of behavior data in the whole software development life cycle. The data acquisition module covers three types of core data sources: development behavior track, such as Git logs, development process code, etc.; collaborative interaction records, such as requirements documents, interface documentation, etc.; systems and applications data, such as code, system test records, etc. By associating the behavioral development information of different personnel, it provides data support for subsequent personalized services.

In the feature engineering processing part, the feature processing pipeline is constructed according to different types of data. For unstructured text data (submission comments, requirements documents, etc.), after extracting the text content, the key information in the text content is extracted with the help of a large language model through regular expressions; the BGE model is used to obtain the vectorized embedding representation of the text. In addition, the structured coding information, such as development code and test cases, is encoded by vector embedding through CodeBERT. Finally, based on the knowledge base constructed by the above information, the correlation retrieval of multi-dimensional behavioral information is carried out by combining user intention, and the more important input information is selected to participate in the subsequent process, so as to reduce the interference of redundant information in the expert model.

3.2.2. Construction of the Project Knowledge Base

In order to support the context-aware reasoning of the expert model and the hallucination of answer results, we built a knowledge base based on the collected data. The construction process is shown in Figure 2, where the input data of the knowledge base comes from multi-dimensional behavioral information, such as project documents, codes and related description information. After slicing the input data, the segmented data are vectorized through different embedding models, and then the project knowledge base is built by constructing an index mechanism. When the user query is received, the hybrid retrieval method is used to calculate the similarity between the vectors obtained after the user query input into the embedding model and the vectors in the project knowledge base, and the retrieval results based on keyword search are input into the expert model as candidate results as information supplements to support the expert model to generate more accurate responses.

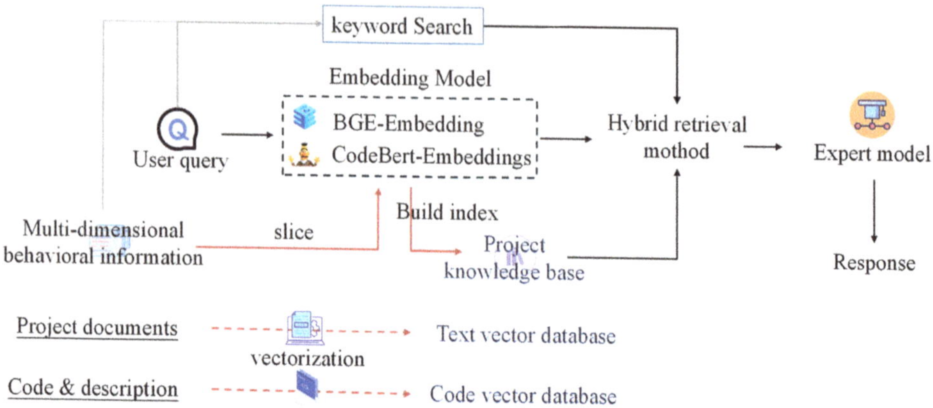

Figure 2. Knowledge base construction process.

Specifically, based on the BGE embedding model, the knowledge document is sliced into blocks and vectorized, and stored in the text vector database. At the same time, the function description of the developed code is extracted and the code's semantic knowledge base is constructed. The embedded representation of the code slice is generated based on CodeBERT and stored in the code vector database. In the retrieval stage, a hybrid retrieval approach is constructed [39]. By designing a multi-way recall strategy, that is, semantic retrieval by calculating the cosine similarity between the user query (user intention) and the text or code vector (Equation (1)). Given the query vector Q, the semantic similarity with the vector S in the knowledge base is calculated to support the demand for deep semantic retrieval. And keyword retrieval is based on the BM25 algorithm [40] to support the retrieval needs of ambiguous query semantics (Equation (2)). These two kinds of methods can complement each other's shortcomings, and then return the retrieved candidate information based on the retrieval fusion module (Equation (4)), where the semantic retrieval threshold is set to 0.75, according to practical application experience and the actual use effect to balance the recall rate and accuracy. Finally, the retrieved information participates in the reasoning of the expert model to obtain together the corresponding model.

$$smi_{cos}(Q,S) = \frac{Q \cdot S}{\|Q\|\|S\|} \tag{1}$$

$$Score(Q,E) = \sum_{i=1}^{n} IDF(q_i) \cdot \frac{f(q_i,E) \cdot (k_1+1)}{f(q_i,E) + k_1 \cdot \left(1 - b + b \cdot \frac{|E|}{lenE_{avg}}\right)} \tag{2}$$

where Q is the query input; $Score(Q,E)$ is the relevance score between the current query Q and the knowledge document E. q_i is the ith word in Q, and $f(q_i,E)$ is the frequency of q_i in

E. $|E|$ is its corresponding length; $lenE_{avg}$ is the average length of different documents. k_1 and b are adjustable parameters and are usually set to 1.2 and 0.75, respectively, referring to the default parameters of related research [41] and ElasticSearch implementation. $IDF(q_i)$ is the inverse document frequency corresponding to q_i (Equation (3)).

$$IDF(q_i) = log\left(\frac{N - n(q_i) + 0.5}{n(q_i) + 0.5} + 1\right) \tag{3}$$

where N is the number of documents; $n(q_i)$ is the number of documents containing q_i.

$$Score = 0.75 * smi_{cos}(Q, S) + 0.25 * Score(Q, E) \tag{4}$$

3.2.3. MoE Routing Gate Networks Optimization

Aiming at the problem of static preference deviation in traditional MoE routing gate networks, this paper proposes a dynamic routing mechanism driven by RLHF. The input datum of this method is Query, and the output data are the expert model of route selection and the description template of Task. According to the above information, the Task information is parsed and passed to the corresponding expert model. In order to construct a route selection model in line with human preferences, this method collects several responses generated by the routing gate network model and constructs $Y = \{Y_w, Y_l\}$, where Y_w is the preferred response output selected by the user, and Y_l is the non-preferred response selected by the user. The MoE routing gate network is optimized by manually constructing training labels to improve the effectiveness of its expert selection.

Specifically, according to the answers generated by different expert models in different scenarios, by sampling multiple model output descriptions, the relevant professionals are coordinated to select the output path of the model. For example, for the requirements analysis expert model, the requirements analysts prefer to select the task description generated by the routing gate network. And the output of other non-preferred models is used as the reject part of the expert model fine-tuning the dataset construction. Finally, a total of 2000 data samples are constructed to fine-tune the model in each scenario.

For the fine-tuning process of the routing gate network model, specifically, considering the computing resources of the system, direct preference optimization (DPO) [42] and QLoRa [43] algorithms are used to realize the pre-training of this model. The dataset is from multiple responses generated by the routing gate network model, and the generated responses are evaluated by manual labeling. Please refer to Appendix A for details of prompt templates and data samples. Its training process is shown in Figure 3, specifically as follows:

(1) Define the policy model and the reference model. The core goal of the policy model is to directly adjust the model parameters by comparing the preference feedback of different policy outputs (such as positive and negative samples selected by users), so that the generated results are more in line with human expectations. The reference model is the given pre-trained model, which is used to provide stability guarantees during the optimization process. The core goal is to constrain the update direction of the policy model to avoid deviating too far from the original distribution and prevent overfitting or performance degradation.

(2) For a given prompt, compute the probabilities of the two routing gate network models for positive and negative samples, where the positive sample is the human-selected response and the negative sample is the rejected response.

(3) Referring to the DPO loss function (Equation (5)) proposed by Rafailov et al. [42], by calculating the difference in the probability of generating content between the policy model and the reference model, the policy model is penalized for the decrease in the probability

of positive samples and the increase in the probability of negative samples, and the model is trained by minimizing the DPO loss.

$$L_{DPO}\left(\pi_\theta;\pi_{ref}\right) = -E_{(x,y_w,y_l,)} \sim D\left[log\sigma\left(\beta log\frac{\pi_\theta(y_w|x)}{\pi_{ref}(y_w|x)} - \beta log\frac{\pi_\theta(y_l|x)}{\pi_{ref}(y_l|x)}\right)\right] \tag{5}$$

where σ is the sigmoid function; x is the *Query*; y_w is user-selected response preference data; y_l is the user's choice of poor response data; π_θ is the policy model; π_{ref} is the reference model; $\pi_\theta(y_w|x)$ represents the cumulative probability of the current policy model generating a good response given the input x; $\pi_{ref}(y_w|x)$ represents the cumulative probability of the current reference model generating a good response given the input x.

$$r_\theta(x,y) = \beta log\frac{\pi_\theta(y|x)}{\pi_{ref}(y|x)} \tag{6}$$

For the update strategy of model parameters, $r_\theta(x,y)$ in Equation (6) is the implicit reward function of the DPO method. Intuitively, the gradient optimization of the loss function increases the possibility of the pre-trained model responding to preference $y_{w,}$, and reduces the possibility of non-preference y_w. Further, by combining QLoRa and DPO, the performance of the routing gate network model is optimized through parametric efficient fine-tuning. QLoRa algorithm is used to compress the structured parameters of the routing gate network model, and the original high-dimensional parameter space is projected to the low-rank subspace through low-rank matrix decomposition. This algorithm converts the full-parameter fine-tuning task into learnable low-rank adapter optimization, significantly reducing the scale of tunable parameters while maintaining the model's representational power.

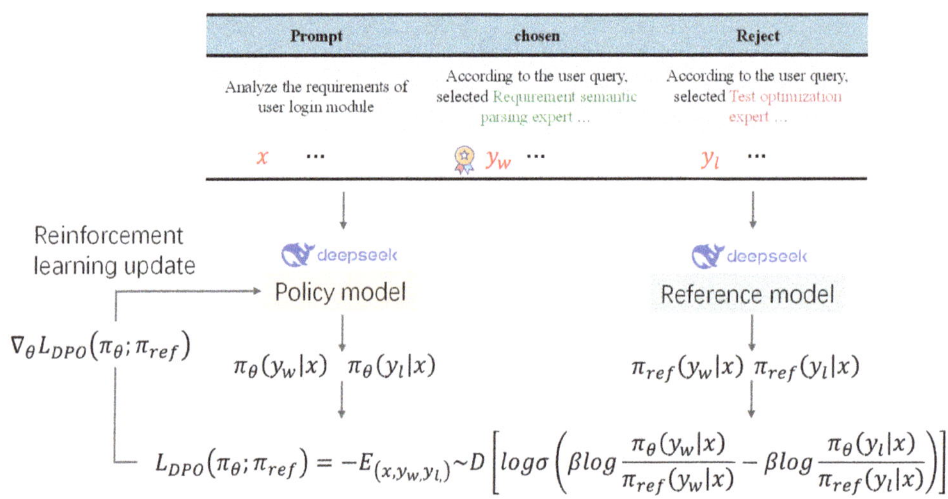

Figure 3. DPO training process.

The directional fine-tuning of routing a gated network is implemented by combining the DPO algorithm. Compared with the traditional RLHF paradigm, DPO restructures the preference learning problem into a classification task and directly optimizes the policy network parameters based on paired preference data, effectively avoiding the computational bottleneck in the training stage of the reward model. This end-to-end optimization approach not only reduces the video memory footprint, but also improves the stability of policy updates through the implicit reward modeling mechanism.

3.2.4. Expert Models with Few-Shot Contextual Learning

In the construction process of the expert model group, considering the limited computing resources on the server side, the background knowledge of the model is enhanced by carrying out upsampling context learning for each expert model. At the same time, the chain of thought (CoT) [44] is used to guide the model to reason, so as to further achieve the balance between computational efficiency and reasoning quality. As shown in Figure 4, in the model inference phase, the problem-solving process is decomposed into an interpretable chain process of knowledge retrieval → logical derivation → decision generation. Specifically, when given a sequence of correlated behaviors $X = \{x_1, x_2, \ldots, x_n\}$, the routing gate network first activates the relevant expert model, and triggers the following process in the expert model by generating the task description and transmitting the corresponding user intention:

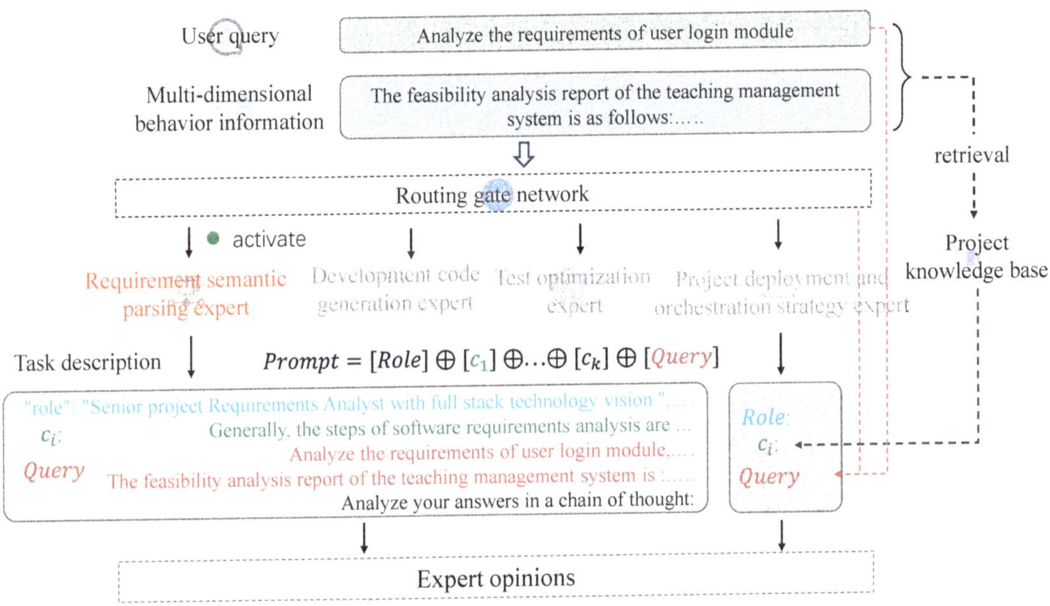

Figure 4. Construction process of expert model based on few-shot context learning.

Firstly, the problem is decomposed, different expert models are triggered according to the input data, and the task description of the response is generated. For example, the requirements analysis task could be described as: original requirements analysis → business rule mapping → architecture impact assessment → use case modeling. Secondly, by retrieving Top-K relevant knowledge $C = \{c_1, c_2, \ldots, c_k\}$ to extract the logical reasoning path in the solution for knowledge injection. After retrieving the relevant outcomes from the knowledge base, it is further injected into the lifting template, and few-shot context learning [45] is used for the LLM to achieve efficient model optimization without parameter training. Specifically, by constructing a structured prompt template (Equation (7)), including task description, retrieved relevant knowledge, user intention, etc., the task instructions are constructed through the above templates, and the displayed requirements of the expert model are divided into logical reasoning and answering. See Appendix A.2 for detailed prompt template settings.

$$Prompt = [Role] \oplus [c_1] \oplus \ldots \oplus [c_k] \oplus [Query] \quad (7)$$

Few-shot context learning is used to guide the optimization of the expert model, which has the following advantages: first, it can optimize the output of the model without parameter update. Compared with the traditional fine-tuning that needs to update millions of parameters, context learning only needs to adjust the example selection strategy in the prompt template, which greatly reduces the consumption of computing resources. Secondly, it can integrate dynamic knowledge, inject domain knowledge through a real-time retrieval mechanism, avoid solidifying vertical domain data to model parameters, and greatly improve the effectiveness of a single expert model. Finally, it has strong interpretability, and the visual reasoning path and retrieval basis of the thinking chain form a double explanation mechanism.

4. Results

The HCDMB model proposed in this study covers a complete, closed-loop system of data acquisition and processing, model construction, model integration and optimization, distributed deployment, system evaluation and optimization, and carries out technical verification in the form of system services. Refer to Appendix B for related model versions and system hardware descriptions. Based on the related methods mentioned above, by encapsulating the methods to provide services for project personnel, this chapter will discuss the implementation details in the actual system construction. As shown in Figure 5, the following will describe the services of each stage of the system.

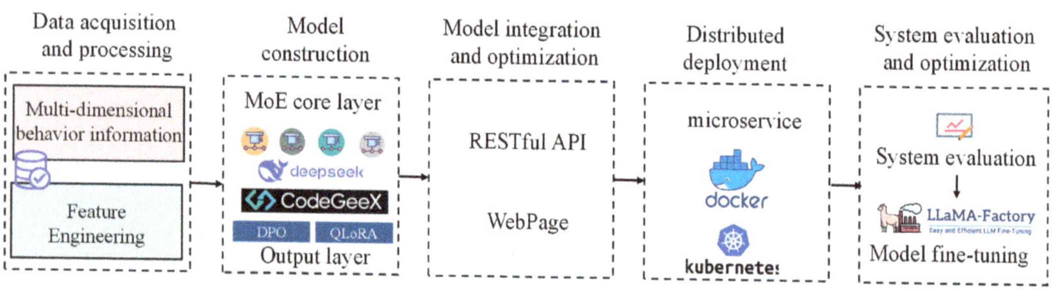

Figure 5. Construction process of system service.

(1) Data acquisition and processing

At the level of data collection and processing, the system realizes the structural integration of behavioral information through the multi-dimensional data processing engine. For the developer behavior data, the semantic correlation mapping between user ID and operation log is established, and the multi-dimensional user portrait supporting personalized service is constructed by establishing the differentiated behavior characteristics of different functional roles. In the aspect of project document processing, the deep learning-based OCR framework (PaddleOCR) [46] was used to realize the semantic parsing of PDF documents, and the standardized document storage format (JSON/Markdown) was formed by combining the layout reconstruction algorithm and the regularization text cleaning mechanism. For unstructured behavioral information, based on the results of feature extraction, the summary generation service of the large model is used to extract and summarize the key information, which effectively reduces the redundancy of knowledge. The construction flow for feature engineering is described in Section 2.

(2) Model construction

In terms of model construction, the system constructed an MoE system based on domain adaptation and on two kinds of large models, CodeGeex and Deepseek, deployed in the cloud. CodeGeex provided code-related services as the base model of code generation and the test-case generation expert model. Due to its excellent reasoning ability, Deepseek can be used as the base model of the expert model for requirements analysis, project scheduling strategy generation, and the opinion summary of each model. In order to support the context-aware reasoning and role differentiation of the expert model, a few-shot context learning paradigm is designed to retrieve and enhance the chain of thinking, and a cross-project knowledge base system is constructed. The knowledge information comes from the relevant milestone document development information and the project development code in the software development process, and guidance services are provided for the model based on this prior knowledge. The above models are deployed in different servers and provide corresponding services for the system through API requests. In addition, for the MoE gating model, a dynamic routing mechanism driven by RLHF was proposed by using the model with the strong reasoning ability of Deepseek. By collecting a number of responses generated by dynamic routes, we will construct the following data: {' prompt ':' ', 'chosen': ' ', 'reject': ' '}, where prompt is the user's intention and related behavioral information, chosen generates a response for the model that the user prefers, and reject is the model response that the user does not prefer. DPO and QLoRa algorithms are used to implement the supervised fine-tuning of the routing gate LLM. To support its selection of expert models that conform to human intuition and provide contextual information, this model is deployed as an independent service.

(3) Model integration and optimization

In the process of model integration and optimization, a two-way interactive interface is designed to meet the needs of human–machine collaboration. A RESTful API interface based on the Flask framework supports the integration of automated workflows. The second is to provide services for users through visual interface, which is developed based on the framework of Open WebUI (Ollama WebUI). Specifically, the process of system integration is as follows: Firstly, the user calls the interactive interface, and the system obtains the relevant behavior trajectory from the database through the user ID, and retrieves the relevant information through the vector representation through the data processing method. Based on the user's intention and its recent behavior trajectory, the decision service of the MoE layer is called, and then a number of appropriate expert models are selected based on the relevant context information and decision suggestions are generated. At the same time, the decision path is visualized to provide users with the interpretability of human–machine collaboration. Users are encouraged to rate the current decision opinions to support the subsequent continuous optimization of the system.

(4) Distributed deployment

In terms of distributed deployment, the system adopts cloud-native architecture to realize elastic resource scheduling, and each expert model is encapsulated as a docker microservice and managed by a Kubernetes container orchestration platform. The dynamic scaling algorithm encapsulates each expert model as an independent microservice according to the real-time load, and its replica number is dynamically adjusted according to the real-time load: when the gating network detects the peak code generation request, the code generation expert instance is automatically expanded. The expert model and the routing gate network model were deployed independently to provide portable services for the optimization and replacement of subsequent models.

(5) System evaluation and optimization

In order to verify the performance of the subsequent system in use, a multi-dimensional evaluation system is established, and the evaluation system of the party is constructed from multiple angles such as data and roles, which will be further incorporated into the evaluation system of the system and optimized for targeted methods. As shown in Table 1, it is evaluated by calculating the selection accuracy of the routing gate network model, the variance analysis of model inference, the user adoption rate and the system response delay, at the same time, the Lamma Factory framework will be used to supervise fine-tuning of each expert model based on the collected data and evaluation indicators in the future.

Table 1. Evaluation index of model effect.

Dimension	Metrics	Measurement Method
Decision quality	expert activation accuracy	F1 value compared with manual annotation
Policy stability	variance of weight assignment	ANOVA for multiple inference of the same scenario
Human collaboration	recommended rate of acceptance	percentage of developers who actually implemented the recommendations
System effectiveness	end-to-end response latency	average elapsed time from input to output

5. Discussion

The HCDMB model proposed in this paper aims to build a dynamic adaptive intelligent cooperative system by deeply integrating multi-dimensional behavioral information in the software development lifecycle. The core innovation of this framework method is embodied in three technical dimensions: multi-dimensional behavioral information fusion, dynamic expert routing mechanism, and continuously evolving learning system. By designing a cross-modal software development behavior feature encoder, modeling and representation of development behavior, management behavior and quality assurance behavior are realized. At the same time, a gated decision network is innovatively constructed, and intelligent model selection is implemented in the expert cluster according to relevant information in the project process, so as to achieve accurate matching between task context and expert ability. In addition, a reinforcement learning method based on human feedback is used to optimize the context-aware routing mechanism.

However, due to the small number of samples of manually annotated datasets in the development process, this study only fine-tuned the gated network model of the core layer of MoE, instead of optimizing each expert model, and only guided the output of the model by means of context learning with a few samples. However, in the face of complex tasks in some specific fields, the generalization ability and adaptability of the model still need to be improved. Therefore, relevant project data will be further collected in the future to further explore more efficient fine-tuning strategies, such as introducing more prior knowledge or adopting more refined parameter adjustment methods, in order to improve the performance of the model in different fields.

Specifically, efficient fine-tuning strategies with partial parameters are used to solve domain adaptability problems. Selecting an expert model that is pre-trained on a general software engineering dataset (such as the GitHub open source project), and then fine-tune the parameters of the vertical domain data efficiently through transfer learning, using LoRA technology to achieve rapid adaptation of private data from different enterprises. This strategy can effectively reduce the computational resources required to fine-tune the new domain while maintaining the generalization ability of the model.

Moreover, the method proposed in this paper only constructs four expert models, which has obvious limitations for the coverage of complex tasks. In order to meet the needs of multi-dimensional collaboration in complex projects, a hierarchical expert cluster architecture is proposed: the existing core expert model is retained in the base layer; adding experts in other vertical fields such as architecture design, performance optimization, and security audit at the extension layer; the expert registration mechanism based on docker container is established in the dynamic extension layer, allowing third-party models to access the system through standardized interfaces.

Finally, the method in this paper has made a certain exploration of human–machine collaboration and interpretability, but in order to better promote the collaboration between human developers and AI systems, further research can be carried out to enhance the interpretability and interactivity of the system in the future. For example, by developing a more intuitive visual interface that allows developers to more clearly understand the decision-making process and basis of the model, or designing a more natural language interaction that allows developers to more easily communicate and collaborate with the system.

Facing the future, the model (HCDMB) proposed, based on this paper, has a wide range of application scenarios. In the application scenario dimension, it could extend to emerging fields such as intelligent operation and maintenance, and build an intelligent ecosystem covering the whole life cycle of software. The direction of model optimization, exploring the dynamic construction mechanism of expert cluster based on neural architecture search, will further improve the adaptive ability of the system. At the same time, the establishment of a multi-dimensional behavioral data federation learning system in the development process will provide new ideas for cross-organization knowledge sharing and privacy protection.

This research is not only a technical breakthrough attempt in the field of software engineering, but also an important exploration of the evolution of human–machine collaborative paradigm. At present, artificial intelligence technology has profoundly changed the form of software development; how to build an intelligent collaborative system with both efficiency and flexibility, and how to realize the complementary advantages of human creativity and machine computing power are still scientific propositions that need to be continuously tackled. The HCDMB model provides a feasible way to solve these problems, and its subsequent development will promote the software engineering discipline to a higher level of intelligence, and lay a solid foundation for building a software ecosystem of independent evolution.

6. Conclusions

The deep integration of artificial intelligence technology and software engineering is reshaping the paradigm system of modern software development. In this paper, a hybrid collaborative development model based on multi-dimensional behavioral information is proposed to solve the problems of the traditional development model, such as the low efficiency of cross-stage collaboration, fragmentation of the intelligent tool chain and imperfect man–machine collaboration mechanisms. This model realizes the organic integration of human intelligence and machine intelligence in the whole life cycle of software development by building a dynamic and adaptive intelligent cooperation system, and provides an innovative solution to the modern software engineering challenges with dynamic demands and diversified scenarios.

The core contribution of this study is to construct an innovative framework of multi-dimensional behavioral feature fusion and dynamic expert collaboration. By integrating multi-dimensional characteristics of development behavior trajectories, collaborative interaction records, and product application data, it breaks through the limitations of traditional single-dimensional analysis. At the level of architecture design, the proposed three-level hierarchical model realizes the closed-loop optimization from data acquisition to decision execution, in which the dynamic routing mechanism, which is based on reinforcement learning and human feedback, effectively balances the domain specialization and task adaptability of the expert model. In addition, retrieval enhances the progressive learning system with the decoupling of thought chain and parameters, which significantly improves the reasoning efficiency and knowledge transfer ability of the system in complex scenarios.

From the perspective of technology evolution, this study provides important methodological enlightenment for the intelligent transformation of software engineering. Firstly, the introduction of the MoE model breaks through the rigid constraints of traditional tool chain, and realizes the flexible reconfiguration of the development process through a dynamic scheduling mechanism. Secondly, the in-depth mining of multi-dimensional behavior characteristics reveals the inherent law of the development process, which lays a theoretical foundation for the construction of a data-driven decision support system. Finally, the bidirectional explanation mechanism of human–machine collaboration effectively bridges the logical gap between domain knowledge and AI decision-making, and provides a technical path for building a trusted intelligent auxiliary system. These innovations mark an important shift in the software engineering collaborative paradigm from experience-driven to data-driven, and from manual coordination to autonomous evolution.

However, due to the realistic conditions, there are still some directions that need to be further explored. At the data level, due to the limitations of sample size and domain coverage, the generalization ability of the current system in specific vertical fields still needs to be improved. In terms of model architecture, the balance between scalability and the task-decoupling efficiency of expert clusters has not been established. In engineering practice, the contradiction between calculation cost and the real-time requirement of dynamic routing mechanisms still needs to be further optimized by hardware acceleration schemes.

In the future, we will further optimize the above directions based on user experience. Specifically, we will carry out targeted optimizations in combination with the evaluation indicators in Table 1 (such as increasing user adoption rate and system response latency, etc.). In addition, a dataset will be further constructed based on the collected user behavioral information to optimize and fine-tune the expert model, enabling it to incorporate more knowledge in the field of software engineering. At the same time, expert models in other stages of the software development process, such as feasibility analysis experts and outline design experts, will also be added, and more intelligent solutions will be designed for the collaborative interaction of each expert model.

Author Contributions: Conceptualization, S.G. and Y.W.; methodology, S.G., Y.W., W.L., T.S. and Z.Z.; software, S.G., Y.W., W.L., T.S. and Z.Z.; data curation, S.G., Y.W., W.L., T.S. and Z.Z.; writing—original draft preparation, S.G.; writing—review and editing, S.G. and Y.W. All authors have read and agreed to the published version of the manuscript.

Funding: This research was funded by the National Key Research and Development Program of China, grant number 2022YFB3305102.

Institutional Review Board Statement: Not applicable.

Informed Consent Statement: Not applicable.

Data Availability Statement: Due to the nature of this research, participants of this study did not agree for their data to beshared publicly, so supporting data is not available.

Conflicts of Interest: The authors declare no conflicts of interest.

Abbreviations

The following abbreviations are used in this manuscript:

HCDMB	Hybrid collaborative development model based on multi-dimensional behavior information
AI	Artificial Intelligence
AISE	AI-enabled software engineering
Bi-LSTM	Bidirectional long- and short-term memory network
LLMs	Large language models

BGE BAAI general embedding
RAG Retrieval augmented generation
RLHF Reinforcement learning from human feedback
BM25 Best matching 25
DPO Direct preference optimization
QLoRa Quantized low-rank adaptation of large language models
CoT Chain of thought

Appendix A

Appendix A.1

In order to improve the selection of MoE expert mixture model, the expert model and the generated task description are more in line with the preferences of relevant practitioners, so the RLHF method is used to optimize the routing gate network model in MoE architecture. The prompt template of this module is shown in the table. Because the fine-tuning data involves the internal information of the project and the information of the developers, it is not disclosed.

Table A1. MoE Architecture routing gate network prompt template.

Prompt Template

"role": "You are an intelligent expert system allocator that automatically matches the most appropriate domain expert model based on user needs and project context",
"available_experts": [
"Requirements semantic parsing expert: Good at parsing natural language requirements and generating structured technical specifications",
"Development code generation expert: automatically generate executable code from technical specifications",
"Test optimization expert: Create test cases and implement performance optimization solutions",
"Project deployment and orchestration strategy expert: Design containerized deployment scenarios and CI/CD pipelines"
],
"input_schema": {
"user_query": "{user_query}",
"project_context": "{ Multi-dimensional behavior infomation}"
},
"output_schema": {
"JSON":
{
"expert": "The name of the selected expert",
"task_describe": " Specific task descriptions for current requirements"
}
},
"processing_logic": [
"1. Semantic parsing: analyze the deep technical appeal of user requirements",
"2. Context matching: Associate technology stack, architecture pattern and other information in project historical behavior data",
"3. Expert selection: routing expert models based on domain matching degree",
"4. Task generation: build atomic tasks that match the ability characteristics of experts"
],
"constraints": [
"The task description fits each expert's ability as much as possible",
"Consider the technical constraints of the project context"
]
}

Table A2. Examples for fine-tuning dataset.

Prompt	Chosen	Rejected
user_query: Please do demand analysis for user login portal project_context: Feasibility analysis of online education system project	{"expert": "Requirements semantic parsing expert", "task_describe": "Combined with the technical constraints of the online education system project, the authentication process, authority management, security audit and other requirements of the user login portal are analyzed, and a structured document containing SSO integration scheme, multi-factor authentication module, and user role authority matrix is generated, which is compatible with the existing OAuth2.0 architecture of the project and meets the GDPR compliance requirements of the education system"}	{"expert": "Requirements semantic parsing expert", "task_describe": "The requirements of users logging in to the portal were semantically parsed to generate structured technical specifications, and the key elements of the login function such as user roles, authentication methods and security requirements were clarified" }
user_query: Generate a test case for this code: xxxxx project_context:	{"expert": "Test optimization expert","task_describe": "Based on the interface definition and business logic of the given code, a complete test suite including boundary value test, abnormal flow test and concurrent stress test is generated. It needs to support the JUnit5/Pytest framework and output code coverage report"}	{ "expert": "Test optimization expert", "task_describe": "Test cases, including unit tests and integration tests, are generated for the provided code to ensure the correctness, stability and performance of the code"}
...	...	...

Appendix A.2

This paper proposes to guide and optimize the expert model by retrieving relevant information and learning from the sample context. The prompt template used is shown in Table A3 below. Specifically, it mainly includes role definition, task analysis process, retrieved relevant knowledge, user intention, task description and analysis constraints. Where task_describe is derived from the output of MoE Architecture routing gate network (Table A1).

Table A3. Prompt templates for different expert models.

Requirements Semantic Parsing Expert Prompt Template

```
{
"role": "Senior requirements semantic parsing expert (full stack technical perspective)",
"analysis_flow": {
  "1. Original requirements deconstruction:": "functional dimension breakdown →
non-functional requirements identification → business value positioning",
  "2. Business rule mapping:": "data verification rule → business process rule → permission
control rule → exception handling rule",
  "3. Architecture impact assessment:": "Technology selection impact assessment, system
boundary redefinition, non-functional support scheme",
  "4. Use case modeling description:": "Participant description, use case analysis"
},
"Reference Information":[c1, c2, ...]
"input_schema": {
  "user_query": "{}",
  "task_describe": "{}"
  },
"constraints": [
  "To reason according to the chain of thought, to analyze logically",
  "Technical constraints of project context to consider"
  "Demand items comply with the INVEST principle",
  "Security Requirements Overlay STRIDE Threat Model",
  "Non-functional requirements satisfy SMART criteria",
  "Use case scenario covers Happy Path/Alternative Path/Exception Path"
  ]
}
```

Table A3. *Cont.*

Requirements Semantic Parsing Expert Prompt Template
Development code generation expert prompt template

```
{
"role": "Senior development code generation expert (full-stack technical perspective)",
"generation_flow": {
  "1. Technical specification analysis:": "Functional requirements analysis → non-functional
requirements adaptation → technical constraints identification",
  "2. Code structure design:": "module division → interface definition → data structure design
→ exception handling mechanism",
  "3. Technology selection adaptation:": "programming language adaptation, framework
selection, library dependency management, code style specification",
  "4. Code implementation and optimization:": "Core function implementation, performance
optimization, security reinforcement, code comments and documentation"
},
"Reference Information": [c1, c2, ...],
"input_schema": {
  "user_query": "{}",
  "task_describe": "{}"
},
"Output_schema": {
  "code":{}
  "code_describe":{}
},
"constraints": [
  "Technical constraints of project context should be considered",
  ">80% code comment coverage",
  "Exception handling covers normal process/exception process/edge case"
  ]
}
```

Test optimization expert prompt template

```
{
"role": "Senior test optimization expert (full stack technical vision)",
"optimization_flow": {
  "1. Test requirement analysis:": "Functional test requirement analysis → non-functional test
requirement identification → test target location",
  "2. Test case design:": "Functional test case → boundary test case → exception test case →
performance test case",
  "3. Test execution and optimization:": "Automated test script generation, performance
bottleneck location, test coverage improvement, exception handling verification"
},
"Reference Information": [c1, c2, c3, c4],
"input_schema": {
  "user_query": "{}",
  "task_describe": "{}"
},
"Output_schema": {
  "test_cases": {},
  "test_results": {},
  "optimization_plan": {}
},
"constraints": [
  "Technical constraints of project context should be considered",
  "The test coverage should reach more than 90%",
  "Exception handling covers normal process/exception process/edge case",
  "Performance testing should meet the SMART criteria",
  "The test report should include defect classification, priority assessment and optimization
recommendations".
  ]
}
```

Table A3. *Cont.*

Requirements Semantic Parsing Expert Prompt Template
Project deployment and orchestration strategy expert prompt template

{
"role": "Senior project deployment and orchestration strategy expert (with full stack technical vision)",
"deployment_flow": {
"1. Deployment requirement analysis:": "Deployment environment analysis → Scalability requirement identification → high availability requirement → technical constraint adaptation",
"2. Technology selection and architecture adaption:": "Selection of containerization technology → adaptation of CI/CD tools → integration of monitoring tools → resource allocation strategy",
"3. Deployment process design and optimization:": "Automatic deployment script generation → rolling update strategy → blue-green deployment scheme → rollback mechanism design",
"4. Deployment execution, performance monitoring, exception handling, feedback optimization closed loop"},
"Reference Information": [],
"input_schema": {
"user_query": "{}",
"task_describe": "{}"
},
"Output_schema": {
"deployment_plan": {},
"execution_results": {},
"optimization_suggestions": {}
},
"constraints": [
"Technical constraints of project context should be considered",
"Deployment needs to support high availability and scalability",
"Deployment flows need to support rolling updates and fast rollbacks",
"Exception handling covers normal deployment/abnormal deployment/edge cases"]
}

Appendix B

The pre-training model adopted by the method proposed in this paper includes: Deepseek v3-32B, CodeGeeX4-all-9B, used for the construction of routing gate network and expert model of MoE framework, BAAI/bge-base-all, microsoft/codebert-base, used for embedded representation of text data and code, To support the construction of knowledge base; ch_PP_OCRv4 is used for extracting knowledge documents.

The hardware devices involved in the implementation process are as follows: The service system is Ubuntu 23.04 (Canonical, London, UK). We have respectively constructed clusters of computing and application services to deploy and fine-tune the model. Among them, the GPU of the computing cluster device is 4 × A100 (80 GB), which is used for model fine-tuning and deployment. Specifically, the GPU device used for the deployment of the fine-tuned routing and gating network model is 2 × A100. In the expert model, the device jointly deployed by DeepSeek v3-32B and CodeGeeX4-all-9B is 2 × A100. The above model adopts FP16 for quantization and multi-card deployment. The GPU device of the application service cluster is 3090 (24 GB), with a memory size of 64 GB, which is used for the deployment of the embedded model in the knowledge base construction and the application deployment of other services.

References

1. Ebert, C.; Gallardo, G.; Hernantes, J.; Serrano, N. DevOps. *IEEE Softw.* **2016**, 33, 94–100. [CrossRef]
2. Xie, T. Intelligent software engineering: Synergy between AI and software engineering. In Proceedings of the 11th Innovations in Software Engineering Conference, Hyderabad, India, 9–11 February 2018; p. 1.

3. Martínez-Fernández, S.; Bogner, J.; Franch, X.; Oriol, M.; Siebert, J.; Trendowicz, A.; Vollmer, A.M.; Wagner, S. Software engineering for AI-based systems: A survey. *ACM Trans. Softw. Eng. Methodol. (TOSEM)* **2022**, *31*, 1–59. [CrossRef]
4. Ozkaya, I. What is really different in engineering AI-enabled systems? *IEEE Softw.* **2020**, *37*, 3–6. [CrossRef]
5. Davis, A.M. *Software Requirements: Analysis and Specification*; Prentice Hall Press: Saddle River, NJ, USA, 1990.
6. Ramesh, B.; Cao, L.; Baskerville, R. Agile requirements engineering practices and challenges: An empirical study. *Inf. Syst. J.* **2010**, *20*, 449–480. [CrossRef]
7. Abbas, J.; Zhang, C.; Luo, B. BET-BiLSTM Model: A Robust Solution for Automated Requirements Classification. *J. Softw. Evol. Process* **2025**, *37*, e70012. [CrossRef]
8. de Araújo, A.F.; Marcacini, R.M. Re-bert: Automatic extraction of software requirements from app reviews using bert language model. In Proceedings of the 36th Annual ACM Symposium on Applied Computing, Virtual, 22–26 March 2021; pp. 1321–1327.
9. Koroteev, M.V. BERT: A review of applications in natural language processing and understanding. *arXiv* **2021**, arXiv:2103.11943.
10. Hurst, A.; Lerer, A.; Goucher, A.P.; Perelman, A.; Ramesh, A.; Clark, A.; Ostrow, A.J.; Welihinda, A.; Hayes, A.; Radford, A.; et al. Gpt-4o system card. *arXiv* **2024**, arXiv:2410.21276.
11. Bai, S.; Chen, K.; Liu, X.; Wang, J.; Ge, W.; Song, S.; Dang, K.; Wang, P.; Wang, S.; Tang, J.; et al. Qwen2. 5-vl technical report. *arXiv* **2025**, arXiv:2502.13923.
12. Son, H.S. Using Large Language Models in Software Requirements Analysis. *Edelweiss Appl. Sci. Technol.* **2025**, *9*, 856–863. [CrossRef]
13. Marques, N.; Silva, R.R.; Bernardino, J. Using chatgpt in software requirements engineering: A comprehensive review. *Future Internet* **2024**, *16*, 180. [CrossRef]
14. Jin, H.; Huang, L.; Cai, H.; Yan, J.; Li, B.; Chen, H. From llms to llm-based agents for software engineering: A survey of current, challenges and future. *arXiv* **2024**, arXiv:2408.02479.
15. Adenowo, A.A.A.; Adenowo, B.A. Software engineering methodologies: A review of the waterfall model and object-oriented approach. *Int. J. Sci. Eng. Res.* **2013**, *4*, 427–434.
16. Azeem, M.I.; Palomba, F.; Shi, L.; Wang, Q. Machine learning techniques for code smell detection: A systematic literature review and meta-analysis. *Inf. Softw. Technol.* **2019**, *108*, 115–138. [CrossRef]
17. Sun, H.; Xu, Z.F.; Li, X. Code Recommendation Based on Deep Learning. In Proceedings of the 2023 12th International Conference of Information and Communication Technology (ICTech), Wuhan, China, 14–16 April 2023; IEEE: Piscataway, NJ, USA; pp. 156–160.
18. Zhang, B.; Liang, P.; Zhou, X.; Ahmad, A.; Waseem, M. Practices and challenges of using github copilot: An empirical study. *arXiv* **2023**, arXiv:2303.08733.
19. Drain, D.; Clement, C.B.; Serrato, G.; Sundaresan, N. Deepdebug: Fixing python bugs using stack traces, backtranslation, and code skeletons. *arXiv* **2021**, arXiv:2105.09352.
20. Nam, D.; Macvean, A.; Hellendoorn, V.; Vasilescu, B.; Myers, B. Using an llm to help with code understanding. In Proceedings of the IEEE/ACM 46th International Conference on Software Engineering, Lisbon, Portugal, 14–20 April 2024; pp. 1–13.
21. Ammann, P.; Offutt, J. *Introduction to Software Testing*; Cambridge University Press: Cambridge, UK, 2016.
22. Orso, A.; Rothermel, G. Software testing: A research travelogue (2000–2014). In *Future of Software Engineering Proceedings*; Association for Computing Machinery: New York, NY, USA, 2014; pp. 117–132.
23. Jones, B.F.; Yang, H.H.S.X.; Eyres, D.E. The automatic generation of software test data sets using adaptive search techniques. *WIT Trans. Inf. Commun. Technol.* **2024**, *14*, 10.
24. Zhu, Y.; Guo, X.; Okamura, H.; Dohi, T. Automated Software Test Input Generation with Diffusion Models. In *International Symposium on Software Fault Prevention, Verification, and Validation*; Springer Nature: Singapore, 2024; pp. 32–48.
25. Wang, J.; Huang, Y.; Chen, C.; Liu, Z.; Wang, S.; Wang, Q. Software testing with large language models: Survey, landscape, and vision. *IEEE Trans. Softw. Eng.* **2024**, *50*, 911–936. [CrossRef]
26. Wiering, M.A.; Van Otterlo, M. Reinforcement learning. *Adapt. Learn. Optim.* **2012**, *12*, 729.
27. Abo-eleneen, A.; Palliyali, A.; Catal, C. The role of Reinforcement Learning in software testing. *Inf. Softw. Technol.* **2023**, *164*, 107325. [CrossRef]
28. Jacobs, R.A.; Jordan, M.I.; Nowlan, S.J.; Hinton, G.E. Adaptive mixtures of local experts. *Neural Comput.* **1991**, *3*, 79–87. [CrossRef]
29. Shazeer, N.; Mirhoseini, A.; Maziarz, K.; Davis, A.; Le, Q.; Hinton, G.; Dean, J. Outrageously large neural networks: The sparsely-gated mixture-of-experts layer. *arXiv* **2017**, arXiv:1701.06538.
30. Fedus, W.; Zoph, B.; Shazeer, N. Switch transformers: Scaling to trillion parameter models with simple and efficient sparsity. *J. Mach. Learn. Res.* **2022**, *23*, 1–39.
31. Zhou, Y.; Lei, T.; Liu, H.; Du, N.; Huang, Y.; Zhao, V.; Dai, A.M.; Le, Q.V.; Laudon, J. Mixture-of-experts with expert choice routing. *Adv. Neural Inf. Process. Syst.* **2022**, *35*, 7103–7114.
32. Liu, A.; Feng, B.; Xue, B.; Wang, B.; Wu, B.; Lu, C.; Zhao, C.; Deng, C.; Zhang, C.; Ruan, C.; et al. Deepseek-v3 technical report. *arXiv* **2024**, arXiv:2412.19437.

33. Achiam, J.; Adler, S.; Agarwal, S.; Ahmad, L.; Akkaya, I.; Aleman, F.L.; Almeida, D.; Altenschmidt, J.; Altman, S.; Anadkat, S.; et al. Gpt-4 technical report. *arXiv* **2023**, arXiv:2303.08774.
34. Chen, J.; Xiao, S.; Zhang, P.; Luo, K.; Lian, D.; Liu, Z. Bge m3-embedding: Multi-lingual, multi-functionality, multi-granularity text embeddings through self-knowledge distillation. *arXiv* **2024**, arXiv:2402.03216.
35. Feng, Z.; Guo, D.; Tang, D.; Duan, N.; Feng, X.; Gong, M.; Shou, L.; Qin, B.; Liu, T.; Jiang, D.; et al. Codebert: A pre-trained model for programming and natural languages. *arXiv* **2020**, arXiv:2002.08155.
36. Zheng, Q.; Xia, X.; Zou, X.; Dong, Y.; Wang, S.; Xue, Y.; Shen, L.; Wang, Z.; Wang, A.; Li, Y.; et al. Codegeex: A pre-trained model for code generation with multilingual benchmarking on humaneval-x. In Proceedings of the 29th ACM SIGKDD Conference on Knowledge Discovery and Data Mining, Long Beach, CA, USA, 6–10 August 2023; pp. 5673–5684.
37. Lewis, P.; Perez, E.; Piktus, A.; Petroni, F.; Karpukhin, V.; Goyal, N.; Küttler, H.; Lewis, M.; Yih, W.T.; Rocktäschel, T.; et al. Retrieval-augmented generation for knowledge-intensive nlp tasks. *Adv. Neural Inf. Process. Syst.* **2020**, *33*, 9459–9474.
38. Kaufmann, T.; Weng, P.; Bengs, V.; Hüllermeier, E. A survey of reinforcement learning from human feedback. *arXiv* **2023**, arXiv:2312.14925.
39. Finardi, P.; Avila, L.; Castaldoni, R.; Gengo, P.; Larcher, C.; Piau, M.; Costa, P.; Caridá, V. The chronicles of rag: The retriever, the chunk and the generator. *arXiv* **2024**, arXiv:2401.07883.
40. Robertson, S.; Zaragoza, H. The probabilistic relevance framework: BM25 and beyond. *Found. Trends Inf. Retr.* **2009**, *3*, 333–389. [CrossRef]
41. Lipani, A.; Lupu, M.; Hanbury, A.; Aizawa, A. Verboseness fission for bm25 document length normalization. In Proceedings of the 2015 International Conference on the Theory of Information Retrieval, Northampton, MA, USA, 27–30 September 2015; pp. 385–388.
42. Rafailov, R.; Sharma, A.; Mitchell, E.; Manning, C.D.; Ermon, S.; Finn, C. Direct preference optimization: Your language model is secretly a reward model. *Adv. Neural Inf. Process. Syst.* **2023**, *36*, 53728–53741.
43. Dettmers, T.; Pagnoni, A.; Holtzman, A.; Zettlemoyer, L. QLoRa: Efficient finetuning of quantized llms. *Adv. Neural Inf. Process. Syst.* **2023**, *36*, 10088–10115.
44. Wei, J.; Wang, X.; Schuurmans, D.; Bosma, M.; Xia, F.; Chi, E.; Le, Q.V.; Zhou, D. Chain-of-thought prompting elicits reasoning in large language models. *Adv. Neural Inf. Process. Syst.* **2022**, *35*, 24824–24837.
45. Geng, M.; Wang, S.; Dong, D.; Wang, H.; Li, G.; Jin, Z.; Mao, X.; Liao, X. Large language models are few-shot summarizers: Multi-intent comment generation via in-context learning. In Proceedings of the 46th IEEE/ACM International Conference on Software Engineering, Lisbon, Portugal, 14–20 April 2024; pp. 1–13.
46. Zhong, X.; Tang, J.; Yepes, A.J. Publaynet: Largest dataset ever for document layout analysis. In Proceedings of the 2019 International Conference on Document Analysis and Recognition (ICDAR), Sydney, Australia, 20–25 September 2019; IEEE: Piscataway, NJ, USA, 2019; pp. 1015–1022.

applied sciences

MDPI

Article

Can Large-Language Models Replace Humans in Agile Effort Estimation? Lessons from a Controlled Experiment

Luka Pavlič *, Vasilka Saklamaeva and Tina Beranič

Faculty of Electrical Engineering and Computer Science, University of Maribor, Koroška Cesta 46, 2000 Maribor, Slovenia; vasilka.saklamaeva@um.si (V.S.); tina.beranic@um.si (T.B.)
* Correspondence: luka.pavlic@um.si

Abstract: Effort estimation is critical in software engineering to assess the resources needed for development tasks and to enable realistic commitments in agile iterations. This study investigates whether generative AI tools, which are transforming various aspects of software development, can improve effort estimation efficiency. A controlled experiment was conducted in which development teams upgraded an existing information system, with the experimental group using the generative-AI-based tool GitLab Duo for estimation and the control group using conventional methods (e.g., planning poker or analogy-based planning). Results show that while generative-AI-based estimation tools achieved only 16% accuracy—currently insufficient for industry standards—they offered valuable support for task breakdown and iteration planning. Participants noted that a combination of conventional methods and AI-based tools could offer enhanced accuracy and efficiency in future planning.

Keywords: software engineering; agile development; iteration planning; effort estimation; generative AI; tool accuracy

1. Introduction

According to the Cambridge Dictionary [1], estimation is an opinion on something, resulting in an estimate (or estimation, noun), which is a guess or calculation about the cost, size, value, etc., of something. Estimates performed in project management and software engineering are far from guesses, since they dictate the project schedules, finances and expected results.

Modern project management sees estimation as a part of the initial project schedule management [2], where estimating the duration of particular project activities leads to assessing the complete project duration, cost and resources that are required to fulfil the project. Project estimation is a well-defined and carefully executed set of activities carried out with a selection of proven tools and techniques that include expert judgement, estimating with analogies, parametric estimation and others [2]. Software engineering is no exception. Estimation is connected to assessing effort, resulting in a finances, schedule and resources plan.

Traditionally, in software engineering, effort is estimated to plan development and maintenance activities. In conventional (i.e., sequential), long-term requirement-driven development projects, effort estimation is usually based on a given set of requirements (or increments). In this setting, effort estimation is targeting longer periods and is, therefore, crucial to the project level and can be a source of many risks connected to misestimation. The issues connected to (mis)estimation have been known for decades and have been exposed and explained in several texts, including Brooks' "The Mythical Man-Month" [3], where he exposed several examples of non-deterministic behaviour in development teams connected to team size, project duration and failed project deliverable acceptance. As he stated, "Estimating the time required for software development tasks accurately is notoriously difficult", which is the result of several interconnected aspects: the high level of complexity and uncertainty in software projects, the overly optimistic nature of software developers and their managers and frequent unexpected technical issues, combined with changing requirements and integration challenges. However, effort estimation in software projects is a well-developed area, full of proven techniques and tools that can be used for accurate estimates [4–10]. The authors include and explain expert judgement, analogy-based methods, use case points, linear regression, robust regression, neural nets, constructive agile estimation algorithms, COSMIC FP, silent grouping, Delphi methods, COCOMO methods, planning poker and others. The mentioned methods [4–10] are either time-consuming or fine-tuned for a particular project and/or development team. A novel approach to effort estimation that is based on generative AI is also emerging. Software development platforms introduced this possibility without fully investigating its potentials and drawbacks (please see Section 3).

As opposed to rigorous effort estimation in conventional development methods, modern methods of agile software development usually take a rather different approach. Some just-in-time-oriented methods (e.g., Kanban) just eliminated the need for a systematic effort estimation during the development of system maintenance. Other iterative and requirement-driven methods do not employ effort estimation to estimate project duration; they rather estimate fine-grained assets frequently (usually user stories). This is the case with the leading methods of agile development [11], e.g., Scrum [12], Scrumban [13], large scale Scrum (LeSS) [14] and development level of scaled agile framework [15]. The approach was also introduced decades ago in agile development methods such as extreme programming (XP) [16] and feature-driven development (FDD) [17]. The aim of such estimation is to give a fair and sincere commitment for an iteration scope, which is usually two weeks long. Decision-making personnel, managers, product owners, etc., in modern projects are usually not interested in assessments on requirements; they are rather interested in the current iteration commitment (i.e., the list of requirements that the team is guaranteeing to be delivered by the end of an iteration). This is why hour-based assessments today are not the only alternative. In addition, development teams use several techniques and tools to carry out the short-term estimations, including story-points, T-shirt size estimation, planning poker and others [11,18]. The usual expert-based methods for effort estimation (including planning poker) are two-fold. Firstly, they include splitting requirements (usually in the form of user stories) into tasks; secondly, requirement estimate is calculated indirectly after estimating and summarising all generated particular tasks [12]. The research presented in this paper employs the same approach.

The changed nature of effort estimation in agile development, having several positive aspects, even resulted from the Brooks advice (e.g., breaking down the task, frequent re-estimation, an iterative approach, systematically added buffers and others), also comes with drawbacks. One of the most obvious is an important slice of the development time devoted for estimations. When teams perform the estimations themselves, planning-Mondays are quite a labour consuming activity, which, in a two-week long iteration, can easily mean 5–10% of the developers' time that could otherwise be used for a development. Several adjustments of by-the-book agile development methods are employed frequently to improve the development team's effectiveness. One of them is also estimation that is not carried out by the development team. Expert judgements, combined with analogies, are a replacement that is employed frequently [8,9]. As we demonstrate in Section 3, several artificial intelligence (AI)-based techniques have already been used for decades for either relieving developers of effort estimation and/or improving estimation accuracy. However, the rapid AI development in recent years, including generative AI and large language models (LLM), resulted in automated tasks that were unimaginable for automation a decade ago. Automated effort estimation in combination with LLM tools is a tempting idea. However, using a novel and nonverified approach in such an important activity with confidence and trust can be risky. On the other hand, even the large group of LLM sceptics [19] have positioned an effort estimation as a task with low risks, when LLM-based chatbot-automated (see Figure 1). Estimates are not hard to verify. However, it is important to have them be accurate, which classifies effort estimation to tasks that can be automated, according to the authors in [19]. At the end of the day, several software development platforms have already included the generative-AI- and LLM-based functionalities that enable task generation and their assessment [20].

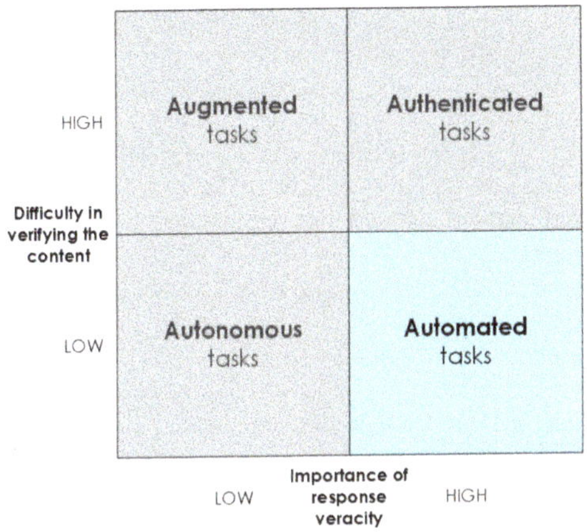

Figure 1. Positioning tasks that can be assisted by the LLM-based chatbots [19].

Based on the presented background, we decided to put a selected generative-AI- and LLM-based (AI-based) effort estimation assistant (see Section 3) on trial by employing a controlled experiment during an iteration-long development. The development teams were asked to split the requirements into tasks and estimate and implement them. We analysed the empirical data that we gathered during the experiment to compare conventional (using years-proven techniques and tools) and generative-AI-based (LLM-based chatbots) effort estimation while answering the following research questions:

- **RQ1**: Is there a difference between tasks created using conventional and generative-AI-supported tools?
  - **RQ1.1**: Is a set of tasks, created by generative-AI-supported tools, comparable to a set of tasks created using conventional methods?
  - **RQ1.2**: Are effort estimations created by generative-AI-supported tools comparable to effort estimations created using conventional methods?
- **RQ2**: How accurate is the effort estimation generated by a generative-AI-supported tool compared to conventional estimation methods?
- **RQ3**: Which aspects of effort estimation can be backed by generative-AI-supported tools?

The rest of the paper is organised as follows. In the next Section, we outline the field of employing AI-related techniques in effort estimation. Next, other authors' research related to ours is highlighted. We are employing generative AI as a tool for creating tasks, their estimation and possible verifications of such an approach. In Section 4, we describe our research method in detail, followed by stating the raw empirical data generated by the controlled experiment. Section 6 challenges the research questions with empirical data, and Section 7 outlines the main threats of validity. We conclude the paper with Section 8.

2. Current AI-Supported Effort Estimation

The history of AI-supported effort estimation is decades old. Since AI was always a field of moving targets, and AI itself is a term that redefines itself every few years, AI-supported tools and methods from the 1990s would not be classified as AI at all today (e.g., decision trees, analogy-recommended systems, case-based reasoning, etc.). There are, however, some exceptions. One such example from 1996 [21] tried to employ artificial neural networks in estimating software development effort and the potential of case-based reasoning for development estimation. Using their simulated dataset, they were rather unsuccessful, with a prediction accuracy of less than 40%.

Later, AI-supported tools and methods employed primarily conventional machine learning models for effort estimation. An example study, reliable machine learning models for estimating effective software development efforts [22], compares the performance of eight different models for effort estimation, which were also not really successful in terms of estimation accuracy, which, in the best cases, reached up to 50% compared to conventional effort assessment methods.

The last five years systematic review [23] presents applications of AI techniques for software effort estimation. The authors compare and evaluate the performance of diverse machine learning models, including artificial neural network, support vector machine, linear regression, random forest, and other techniques. The proposed AI-based framework is claimed to hold the potential to enhance project planning and resource allocation.

In Ref. [24], research was performed, where the authors employed AI to predict an employee's workload from their reported work hours (having a decades long record on their reported working hours). So, the AI-based prediction in this research was on predicting actual effort, not the effort needed to perform a particular task.

Another review [18], which was based on 11 primary studies, was focused on data-driven effort estimation techniques of agile user stories. They identified several possible techniques and algorithms that are employed to enhance effort estimation, among them: Bayesian network, decision trees, support vector machines, long short-term memory and recurrent highway network, stacked autoencoders, variational autoencoders, denoising autoencoders, stacked denoising autoencoders, gradient boosted trees, k-nearest neighbours, artificial neural network, sridge regression, linear regression, naive Bayes, random forest, logistic model tree, and j48 decision tree, fuzzy based model and stepwise regression.

3. Related Work

The last five years systematic review study [23] did not capture any generative-AI-based approaches or tools. The aim of our research is to verify how generative-AI-based methods perform in real-world scenarios. The same applies to another review research [18], where generative-AI-based effort estimation was not identified.

However, we can find research in the field of employing generative AI for effort estimation. In one, the authors [25] describe the conceptual identification of the capabilities of LLM for cost estimation. They used a COSMIC function point estimation model as a prototype. An experiment that they conducted gives a comparison of a manual measurement with trained and untrained models. Their reported findings show that the cost estimation process can be accelerated by using large scale models. They showed how COSMIC function point mapping and measurement can be automated. Another niche study, employing generative AI in effort estimation [26], deals with intelligent interfaces and their user experience. They propose effort estimation based on generative AI in the form of a case study. The limitation of this study is that it is not generic to the field of effort estimation; it is focused towards enhancing the COSMIC function point model.

Arman et al. [27] introduced a conceptual solution designed to improve estimation accuracy and efficiency while minimising manual effort and cost. Their approach involved extracting entities and their relationships from the system, modelling them as semantic triples and developing conceptual micro-services. To enable a more precise functionality breakdown and more accurate effort estimation during microservice development, they incorporated prompt engineering with ChatGPT, enhancing requirements understanding, which, in turn, improved the accuracy of effort estimation. Generative AI in this case was not employed directly to perform the estimations.

A web-based AI chatbot named Alfred is a solution that the authors [28] introduced in their paper. It aids agile software release planning by employing two machine learning models to estimate the duration of tasks and recommend optimal resource assignments for project managers. It is also able to categorise the task estimates based on their confidence level into three groups: low, medium, or high. Chatbot in this case is used as a user-friendly interface for underlying machine learning models. Barcaui and Monat [29] explored the bigger picture of project management in their research paper. They compared GPT-4 and a human project manager in developing project plans, analysing aspects like scope and schedule, as well as cost (effort) and resource estimation, which touched upon our research topic. The study found that AI and human plans have complementary strengths and weaknesses, and it highlighted the importance of human expertise in refining AI outputs. In this sense, the paper outlined similar takeaways as our study. However, our research was focused on task effort estimation carried out by developers using specialised tools.

The potential of generative AI in terms of planning iterations and estimating effort is also articulated clearly in the latest Gartner Research Reports [20]. Among others, they claim that by 2027, the number of platform engineering teams using AI to augment every phase of the SDLC will have increased from 5% to 40%. In addition, they reported in 2024 a list of the state-of-the-art automation tools available in certain points in the DevOps cycle. For planning the iteration based on generative AI, they identified the following tools and providers: Atlassian Intelligence, ClickUp, GitLab Duo and OpenText. Based on their recommendation and our own preliminary tool searching and testing, we decided to use GitLab Duo, which is integrated into GitLab Enterprise. Being listed as one of the leading tools, it gave us the confidence to generalise the findings of our research. Our research is also unique compared to others in terms that we have employed the generative AI tool for splitting user stories into tasks and, in addition, estimate tasks to obtain the complete effort estimation of an user story. This is also the case in several expert-based estimation techniques, e.g., planning poker, which gives our research direct possible validation with the influence on the industry.

4. The Research Method

To challenge the research questions that we defined in the Introduction, we designed a controlled experiment iteratively. We verified the first version using a small-setting pilot and refined the experiment. We followed a proven experiment scoping process, defined and implemented by several empirical research studies in software engineering [30,31]. The controlled experiment design (one factor experiment [30]) followed the objective of evaluating the performance of two competing treatments devoted to the same goal. In our case, it is the planning of an iteration in terms of splitting user stories into tasks and estimating effort. The experiment group was required to use a novel approach—an intelligent agent in a software development platform, while it was challenged by and compared with a control group, which was required to use conventional methods of task splitting and effort estimation of their choice (as they would usually—including planning poker, expert judgement and judgement with analogies). We invited higher-year students, the majority of them already working as developers in companies, to participate in the experiment. For participant profiles, please see Section 5. Figure 2 grabs the essence of our research method, focusing on the controlled experiment, activities, activity flow, independent variables and measured variables.

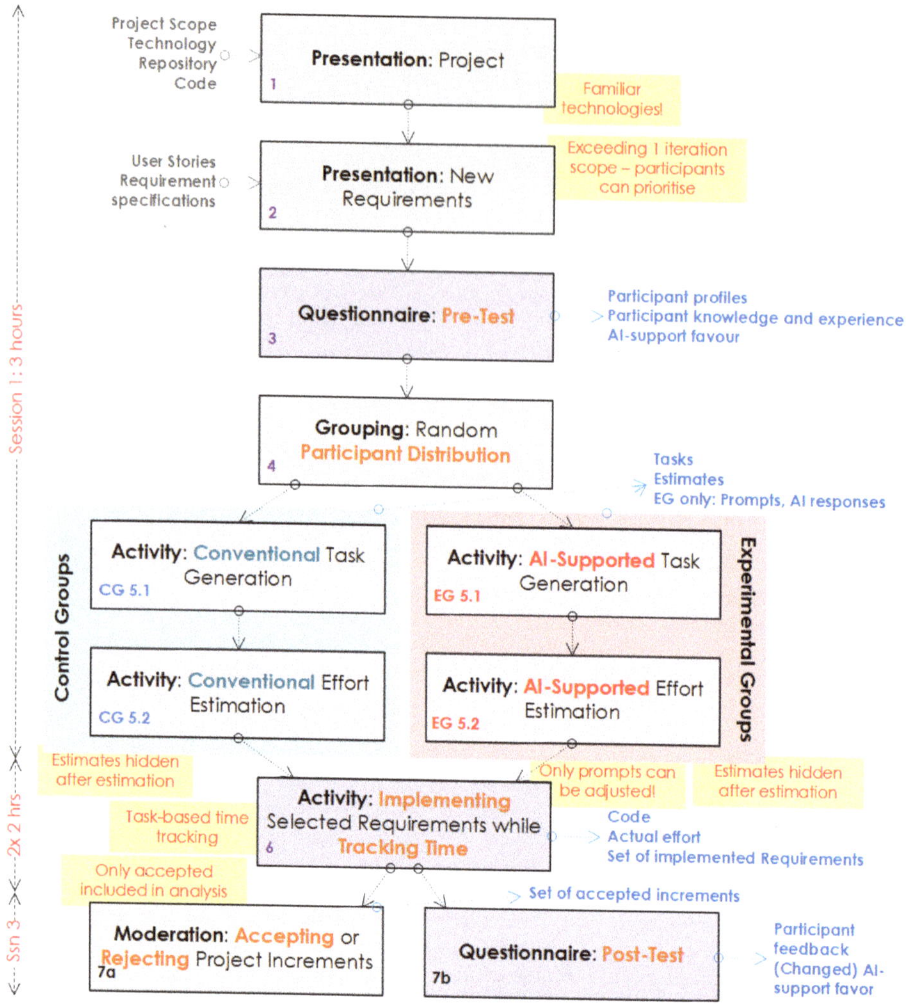

Figure 2. Research method outline with emphasis on controlled experiment.

The controlled experiment consisted, as explained in detail in the next subsection, of three sessions:

- **Session 1**: Requirement presentation, pre-test and participant distribution,
- **Session 2**: Requirement implementation with time tracking and
- **Session 3**: Accepting software increments, post-test.

The research method Figure is colour-coded. The responsibility for activities in the boxes with the gray background (1, 2, 4, 7a) were in the researcher. Purple-coloured boxes (3, 6, 7b) present the activities for participants, where boxes outlined in blue (5.1, 5.2) present activities for participants in the control group and red-outlined boxes (5.1, 5.2) are activities executed by experimental group participants.

The Experiment Setup

During our controlled experiment, the participants were asked to upgrade an existing information system with new functionalities. The system consisted of Jakarta EE (v10) backend, running on a Wildfly/JBoss application server (v.32), storing data in a relational database (configurable H2/MySql/PSql via Java Persistence API) and a simple web-based user interface (Jakarta Server Faces). The architecture and technological stack of the system was standard and familiar to the experiment participants (please see Section 5 for details), which was checked additionally with the pre-test questionnaire (step 3, see Figure 2). Familiar technologies were chosen since we did not want results to be affected by technology-based drawbacks. Functionally, the system was part of a retailer internal application ecosystem with a simple aim: monitoring the temperature at which products are stored and alarming if a particular temperature measurement goes out of the allowed thresholds for the stored product. On the user interface, in this case, the measured temperature is marked as "not OK". Some representative examples of the user interface can be seen in Figure 3.

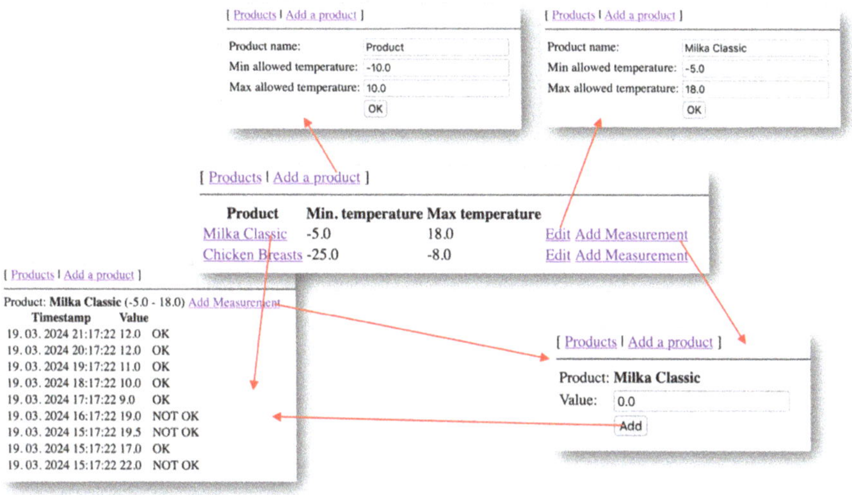

Figure 3. Sample flow of the system that participants were required to upgrade.

As a part of the experiment set-up, we prepared the participants with the initial push to a clean GIT repository (in our case GitLab), where we put all the source code and the documentation related to the system. We also handed them the documentation of the new requirements and the templates (spreadsheets) for the planning phase.

In experimentation session 1 (out of 3), which lasted approximately 3 h, we started with the presentation. During the presentation session (steps 1 and 2, see Figure 2), we presented the system in detail, performed a source code walk-through and demonstrated the development environment setup and initial run. We also presented the new requirements, which consisted of 8 user stories, accompanied by detailed specifications:

- **User Story #1: Email notification** in case of a measurement outside the tolerances. The participants were instructed that the notification should have included the following information: the product, its permitted temperature tolerances, the measurement taken and the exact time of the measurement. Additionally, they had to ensure that the email was sent from a dedicated email address.
- **User Story #2: Monthly reporting** of measurements outside of the allowed tolerances. The monthly report should have included all the measurements, no older than 30 days, that were outside the tolerances. They should have been organised by deviation from the allowed temperature, in descending order, and should have also included the number of improper measurements for each product.
- **User Story #3: Colour coding** of the measurement history. The Table with the measurement history should have highlighted the inappropriate measurements in red and the appropriate measurements in green.

- **User Story #4: Support for the imperial and metric systems.** The participants were instructed to introduce settings in the menu that allowed switching between metric and imperial measurement systems. Depending on the choice, the user interface should also have displayed the label °C or °F throughout.
- **User Story #5: Display products on a graph.** We wanted to have the product graph in the application menu, which showed products based on their allowed temperature tolerances. This graph would later serve as a basis for highlighting products visually (and their temperature tolerances) in terms of their potential for shared storage.
- **User Story #6: Option to import data** from an offline temperature sensor. In case a specific measurement (date, time) has already been imported, the participants were instructed not to import the data again.
- **User Story #7: Temperature trend graph** for each product. Upon selecting a specific product, the participants should have enabled an alternative view of the data (in addition to tabular). They were not limited to a graph type. They were additionally instructed to ensure that the graph presented the tolerances and the actual temperature trends over time clearly.
- **User Story #8: Multilanguage support** (DE/EN/SI). Depending on the selection, the appropriate language of the user interface should have been displayed throughout the application.

The user stories were preliminarily estimated by experts, so we were confident that all user stories will not be implemented by any team. We deliberately proposed more user stories than would fit into a single development iteration so that the participants could make priorities and choose which functionalities to implement.

The next step in the first session was a pre-test questionnaire devoted to capturing the participants' knowledge, experience and possible positive or negative affinity towards generative-AI-based assistants (e.g., if a particular participant would be extremely and subjectively against AI-based assistants), since we wanted to have unencumbered individuals with a sincere intention to verify new methods and tools. The pre-test questionnaire included several questions, among them,

- What is your experience in software development with the Jakarta EE technologies?
- Which technologies do you master?
- How do you think the use of AI tools helps in software development?
- Have you used AI tools in software development before?
- Would you use AI tools to break down user stories into tasks and estimate them?

After the pre-test survey was finished successfully, **we split the participants randomly into two groups** and separated them physically in two different rooms. Both the experimental and control group participants were further combined in teams of three, which is a minimal setting to simulate a team in agile development. The project teams were asked to prepare tasks and estimate them. The same team that was performing the planning was also required to implement the user stories by following the tasks they created. Since the tasks were self-assessed, the team member pre-knowledge and experience were included implicitly in the effort estimation, which is also the case in the majority of the methods of agile development. The estimations were carried out in hours, since our setting was not spanning across many iterations, and, in addition, our research was interested in estimating accuracy, not in sincere iteration promises. The project teams were required to insert generated tasks into a GitLab project as issues and prepare a kanban board for the selected user stories. Although the teams were required to assess all 8 user stories, they were free to pick which and how many user stories they would like to implement in session 2. The estimates that the teams produced were hidden from them since we did not want to have biased time tracking records.

In the case of the experimental group, a short introduction on GitLab Duo was performed before the effort estimation. During the experiment, a limited set of functionalities was used by the tool. The GitLab Duo Chat Boot was employed to provide the user story details and ask for splitting the user story into tasks with task estimates, thus providing a complete effort estimate for the user story. The project teams in that group were obliged to use this intelligent agent to produce both tasks and their estimations. They were not allowed to overrule the suggestions that the tool was giving, the only influence they had were their prompts that they fed to the chatbot. So, their task was also in fine-tuning prompts to obtain a satisfying response. In addition to the tasks and their effort estimates, we also recorded the prompts and responses that were used in the process of effort estimation in the experimental group. For prompts and response examples, please see Section 5.

Activity 6 (see Figure 2)—Implementing selected requirements while tracking time— took place in two separate dedicated timeslots, each approximately 2 h long. During that time, the development teams were asked to implement the tasks of the selected user stories. They were also required to track the time they needed to fulfil a single development task, which was carried out by GitLab—tracking time of moving issues on the kanban board (from "to do" to "in-progress" and from "in-progress" to "done").

After the implementation finished, all the participants were asked to **fill the post-test questionnaire**. At the same time, we reviewed, checked and tested all the delivered user stories from all the development teams to accept the user stories that were claimed to be finished. In the data analysis (regarding the effort estimation accuracy), we only included the tasks and user stories that were accepted as completed correctly and according to requirements. Partially or faultily implemented increments were considered not to be implemented.

This is how our research method and controlled experiment design supported gathering the empirical data that were crucial to answer the research questions. The challenged variable was a method of task generation and their effort estimation, while the dependent variables included estimates (tasks, effort estimates, chatbot prompts, chatbot responses, set of delivered functionalities, actual development efforts) and questionnaire responses.

5. Results

The controlled experiment, in which 42 developers participated, was executed in April 2024. Their background included all the technologies that were used in the information system that they were asked to upgrade (all of them reported to master JSF—Jakarta Server Faces, EJB—Jakarta Enterprise Beans and JPA—Java Persistence API). Their development experience, both in study- or industry-level projects was, majorly, 1–3 years (91%). Three percent of the participants reported up to 5 years of experience, while six percent reported less than 1 year (see Figure 4). The participant involvement in the experiment was voluntary. The entry criterion was successful engagement in previous studying tasks, so only the most proven 42 students (out of 56) participated.

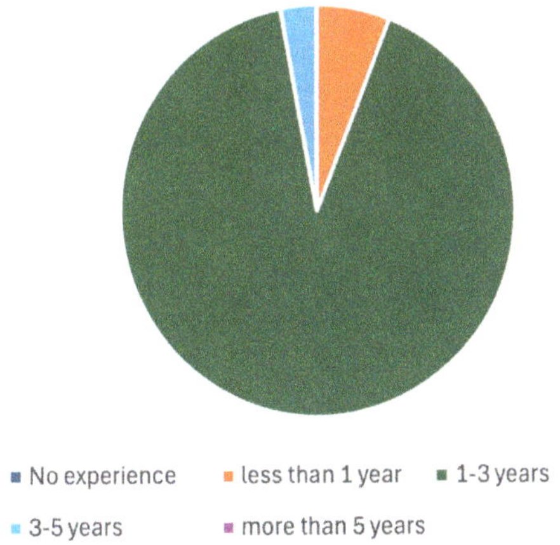

Figure 4. Participant experience.

The participants pre-test question answers are as follows. The majority of the participants had a positive attitude towards AI-based tools in software development, as demonstrated in Figure 5.

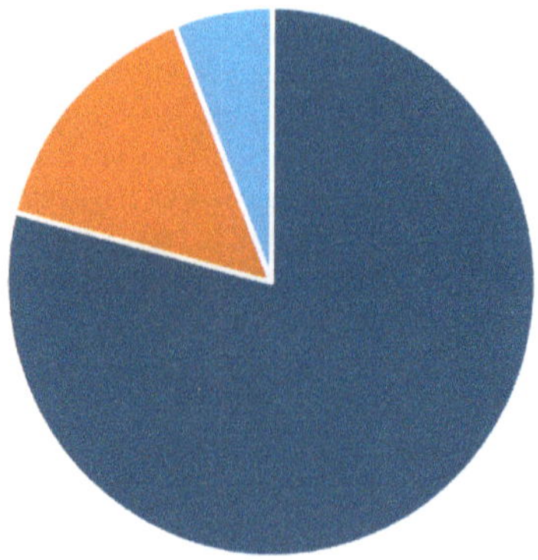

Figure 5. How do you think the use of AI tools helps in software development?

The great majority (82%) also reported that they had already used AI tools in software development. They listed the following tools: ChatGPT, GitHub Copilot, Claude and Superhuman. The participants were eager to use AI tools to break down user stories into tasks and estimate them—85%. Three percent did not like the idea, while twelve percent were undecided.

All 42 participants were divided randomly into the experimental and the control groups; inside the groups, they were also distributed randomly between development teams (7 teams in each group, 3 participants in each team). One team in the experimental group decided not to continue with the experiment, so we included and analysed the empirical data from 39 participants (6 development teams in the experimental group and 7 development teams in the control group).

5.1. Task Generation and Effort Estimation Phase

The participating development teams were given the eight user stories and were asked to prepare a sound set of tasks and their effort estimates. The development teams generated 260 (experimental group) and 184 tasks (control group). As seen in Table 1, the development teams in the experimental group generated 43 tasks on average, while the control group development teams provided 29. An interesting number in Table 1 is also the average task and user story estimate. The user story estimate is calculated as a sum of all task estimates that belong to the user story (see Equation (1)).

$$\text{Estimate}(\text{US}_i) = \sum_{\text{US}_i\text{tasks}} Estimate(task) \tag{1}$$

In the experimental group, the average task effort estimate is 2.5 h, while in the control group, the developers estimated tasks on average at less than half of that: 1 h. This led us to an average user story estimate that was, in the case of the experimental group, 13.5 h and, in the case of the control group, a quarter of that: 3.4 h.

Table 1. The number of generated tasks and estimation summary.

		Experimental Group	Control Group
Development teams		6	7
Estimated user stories per development team		8	8
Estimated user stories		48	56
Generated and estimated development tasks		260	184
Tasks per development team		43.33	26.29
Task estimate	average [h]	2.50	1.03
	st. dev	1.33	0.79
User story estimate	average [h]	13.55	3.37
	st. dev	6.02	1.76

An additional insight into effort estimates is given in Figures 6 and 7. Figure 6 shows the cumulative hours estimated by the experimental group teams (EG1–EG6) and the control group teams (CG1–CG7). We can see that the teams in the experimental group estimated significantly more effort (on average 108 h per team) compared to the control group teams (average 27 h).

Another perspective on cumulative effort estimates is presented in Figure 7. We can see that the user story average effort estimates (all the development teams) are considerably higher in all cases for the experimental group.

Let us demonstrate the difference in task content and individual effort estimates in the case of User Story #2 (Monthly reporting), with representative examples from the development teams in control in the experimental groups. The tasks generated by development team 6 (summarising in 6 h of estimate for User Story #2) in the control group were as follows:

- Monthly report button—0.5 h
- New Table—2 h
- Backend—review of all measurements within 30 days—0.5 h
- Backend—capturing measurements outside the tolerances—0.5 h
- Frontend—arrangement of the covered measurements descending—1 h
- Frontend—show inadequate measurements—1.5 h

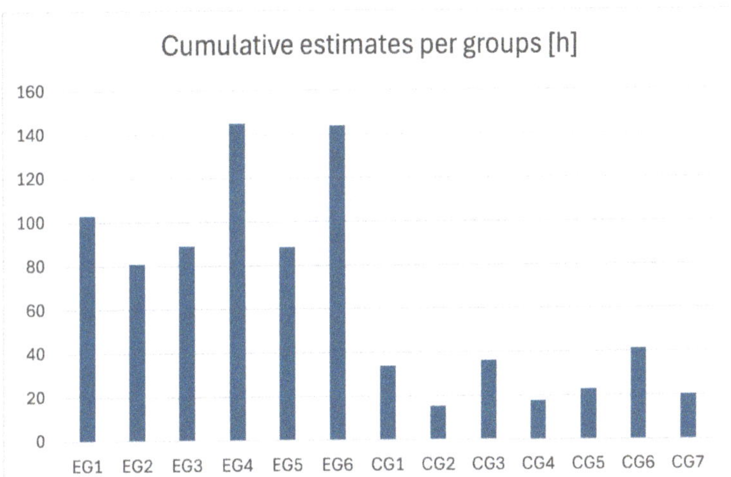

Figure 6. Cumulative effort estimates for all user stories per development teams in hours.

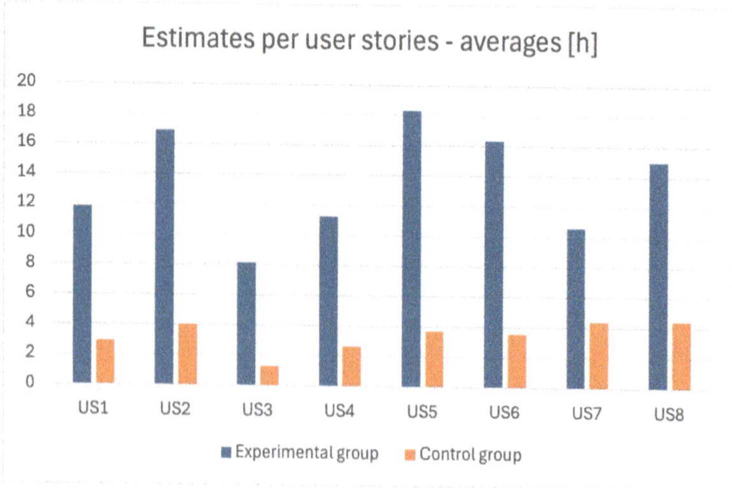

Figure 7. Average user story effort estimates per groups in hours.

While the development teams in the control group were given freedom on creating and estimating tasks (except for AI-tool support), the experimental group development teams had to use Gitlab Duo. They had to report not only the resulting tasks and estimates but also the prompts. Let us see some task sets for the same user story that demonstrate how a prompt plays an important role; we can also see that effort estimates are considerably higher.

Development team 1 used the following prompt to obtain the task set, which summarises a 14 h estimate for User Story #2, more than double compared to the control group development team:

> *Based on the existing code, write me tasks (and their time estimates in hours) to implement the following requirement: I need a new web page that will display a monthly report on how many times a temperature has been out of the tolerance for each product. The data must be displayed in descending order. The report must include several out-of-range measurements for each product. When generating time estimates, be aware that I have some knowledge with the used technologies.*

- Create a new page template and route—2 h
- Create a temperature model—3 h
- Aggregate the data and populate the model—4 h
- Update data aggregation job—2 h
- Display data on a new page—3 h

Another prompt example, used by development team 2, resulted in the tasks that summarise an 11 h estimate for User Story #2.

> *Based on your knowledge of this repository, generate different tasks (and their time estimate in hours) to implement the requirement: Monthly reporting on measurements outside the allowable tolerances. Add the option "monthly report" in the application menu. The monthly report should contain all measurements, up to 30 days old, that were outside the tolerance. They should be sorted by descending deviation from the allowed temperature. The report should also include the number of unacceptable measurements for each product.*

- Add new "Monthly Report" menu option—1 h
- Extend the measurement model with a deviation field—2 h
- Implement monthly report logic—3 h
- Monthly report UI—3 h

- Testing and documentation—2 h

Development team 6 used almost the same prompt, which resulted in a 32h estimate for User Story #2:

- Add an interface for configuring the report parameters—2 h
- Implement a service to query the measurements and generate a report—8 h
- Implement sorting by temperature deviation—4 h
- Group report data by product—3 h
- Identify a location for the new menu option—1 h
- Unit tests for report generation logic—6 h
- Integration tests for end-to-end report generation—4 h
- Call monthly report service on the menu option selection—2 h
- Display the generated report—2 h

We gathered the tasks, effort estimates and prompts (in the case of the experimental group) for all the development teams and user stories. The prompts, cited before, are outlined in order to demonstrate the diversity that was produced not only by human generated tasks but also by the chatbot.

5.2. Implementation and Post-Test Phases

During the implementation, the development teams choose freely which user stories they would implement. After the implementation, we examined their deliverables and accepted or rejected the increments for a particular user story. We analysed only empirical data (the actual time spent on development tasks) generated for user stories that were both reported to be finished and accepted. The summary is shown in Table 2. The data show that despite the different effort estimates, they delivered a comparable number of user stories in the time given to perform the implementation. The actual time that was spent per task and user story was also similar, despite the different estimates.

Table 2. Implemented user stories.

		Experimental Group	Control Group
Developed user stories		17	15
Developed user stories per development team		2.83	2.14
Actual effort per task	average [h]	0.67	0.61
	st. dev	0.91	0.59
Actual effort per user story	average [h]	2	1.92
	st. dev	1.7	1.26

Similarly to user story estimate, the actual effort of the user story is calculated as a sum of all the tasks' actual effort belonging to the user story (see Equation (2)). Please note that all tasks were not necessarily implemented, especially in the case of the experimental group. The unimplemented tasks' actual effort was reported to be 0 h.

$$\text{Actual effort}(US_i) = \sum_{US_i \text{tasks}} \text{Actual effort(task)} \tag{2}$$

Another insight on the average actual effort per user story is shown in Figure 8. In the case of user stories 1 to 5, we can see effort from both the experimental and control groups. User stories 6, 7, and 8 show only the average development time in the control, experimental, or no group. The reason is simple: the actual implementation of User Story #6 was only carried out by development teams in the control group; User Story #8 was implemented only in the experimental group; and no-one decided to implement User Story #7. One can see that five User Stories' implementations, carried out by both groups, were problematic in terms of possible comparison, but, in fact, they were not. The empirical data actually boast of 32 user stories' implementations and 101 implemented tasks to perform the accuracy calculations and comparisons, seen in the next Section 6.

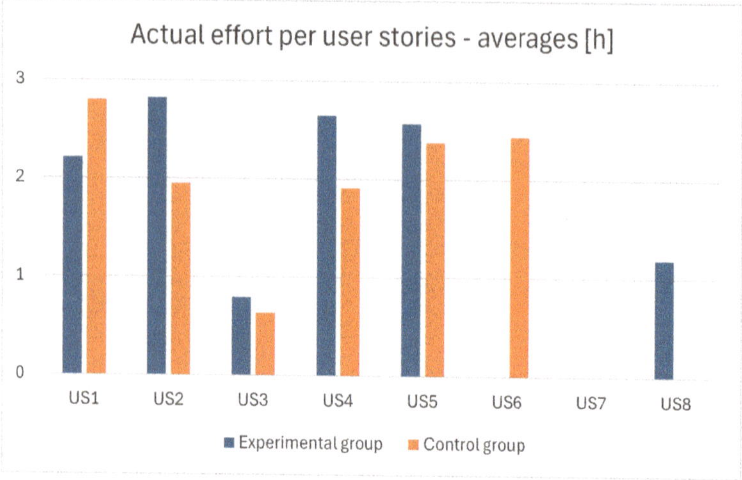

Figure 8. Average user story effort estimates per group in hours.

In parallel with judging the delivered system increments, the developers from the experimental group were asked to participate in a post-test questionnaire (see step 7b in Figure 2). We were interested in two answers:

- Do you think you would prefer to use AI tools, conventional methods or a combination of both in future projects? (Conventional methods—0%; AI tools—0%; A combination of both—100%)
- Do you think AI tools can provide more accurate task estimates compared to conventional methods? (Yes—10%; No—55%; Do not know—35%)

6. Discussion

Based on the research questions and empirical data exposed in the previous Section, we can exercise a grounded discussion. The participating developers demonstrated that they mastered the technologies used in the system, and, therefore, they did not suffer a technology-related handicap. They were also already familiar with AI-enabled tools while developing software—but not for effort estimation. However, they were also keen to try the tools for effort estimation. After the first session, the development teams provided task sets and their effort estimates, which enabled us to answer research question **RQ1: Is there a difference between tasks created using conventional and AI-supported tools?** The answer was positive—both in terms of content and in terms of estimates.

RQ1.1: Is a set of tasks created by generative-AI-supported tools comparable to a set of tasks created using conventional methods?

As demonstrated in Section 5, the most obvious difference between the groups is that the experimental group created 260 tasks (which averaged 5.4 tasks per user story), while the control group created only 184 (3.2 tasks per estimated user story). The task volume implies two conclusions:

- Human-generated tasks are not so fine-grained compared to the AI tool,
- The AI tool can generate more tasks in the same time—which is obviously related to effort estimation, which is time-consuming when carried out manually.

Performing a content-related analysis of tasks, we can see that in our experiment, human-generated tasks, in general, are a subset of AI-generated tasks. In general, the control group teams generated tasks that are required explicitly to fulfil the user story. On the other hand, in the experimental group, the teams reported tasks that were general to the development but were not required explicitly (e.g., unit tests, creating/updating documentation, refactoring existing code). Documentation and testing are tasks that can be found in the majority of experimental group task lists, and they add between 2 to 4 h to the estimate per user story. However, we can also see a lot of general tasks in the task lists that are not really related to user stories (e.g., Create a new page template and routing).

Based on the analysis of the empirical data, we would encourage development teams to start with their own list of tasks, since human-generated tasks would be more related to the context of the user story. Afterwards, an AI-generated task list can be of great help to see if the developers overlooked some tasks that were not so straightforward to spot.

RQ1.2: Are effort estimations, created by generative-AI-supported tools, comparable to effort estimations created using conventional methods?

In addition to the discussion on research question RQ 1.1, the experimental group not only generated considerably more tasks per user story but they were also estimated higher (see Table 1). The conventional effort estimates produced in our experiment were, on average, estimated per user story at 3.37 h, with an average task of 1 h. Contrarily, in the experimental group, we can see the average user story being estimated at 13.5 h, with tasks at an average estimate of 2.5 h. This is why we can see cumulative estimates in the experimental group teams that are considerably higher (108 h on average) compared to the control group (27 h)—see Figure 6.

Speaking strict statistics, when we compared the estimates of the same user stories by the experimental and control groups, the estimates were proven to have significant differences (two-tailed student t-test resulted in a p-value of 3.03×10^{-7}, t-value 6.676—see Table 3).

By analysing the tasks and their estimates closely, we can spot several possible causes for the really high difference between the estimates. Related to the discussion of research question RQ 1.1, an important number of estimates was added by tasks that the teams in the control group did not envision (testing, documentation, refactoring). However, even with those tasks eliminated, we have an average user story estimate over 10 h. Another anomaly that we spotted in the experimental group compared to the control group were tasks that were not really context related, having also quite a high estimate (e.g., user story "Create a new page template and routing" was estimated at 2 h, while this task was not required in the project and was therefore not listed in the control group estimates). A third anomaly when comparing task estimates were the same tasks identified by both group teams but estimated higher by the experimental group teams. The reason for this might have been in (over)confident developers or in the AI-tool, which did not take into account the developers' abilities and/or carried out the estimation in a worst-scenario manner. An example is a task from User Story #1 (Email Notification), which demands the developer prepare a custom, project-dedicated email (creating an email in some free online providers). In the control group teams, this task was estimated between a quarter and a half hour, while the AI-tool estimated this task at over 1 h, in the case of one team also 3 h, which was an obvious overestimate.

Let us discuss the estimate accuracy that we targeted with research question 2 (**RQ2: How accurate is the effort estimation generated by a generative-AI-supported tool compared to conventional estimation methods?**).

In order to address the accuracy, we asked the development teams to perform the actual implementation. The accuracy was then calculated as the ratio between the estimate of task or user story and the actual effort, reported by the developers (see Equation (3)). As stated in Section 5, the developers tracked their development time based on tasks. If a user story was accepted, then the user story's actual effort was calculated as a sum of the fulfilled task efforts (see Equation (2)).

$$\text{Estimation Accuracy}(\text{US}_i) = \frac{\text{Actual effort}(\text{US}_i)}{\text{Estimate}(\text{US}_i)} \times 100\% \tag{3}$$

After the implementation, 32 user stories were accepted, performed by implementing 101 tasks, which were our empirical data body to carry out the accuracy analysis. The accuracy of the experimental group estimates was really low: 16% on average (standard deviation of 9.2%). This is not an acceptable level of accuracy, as expected by the industry [32]. To put this into perspective, the control group's effort accuracy was 60% (standard deviation 24.5%), which correlates to the expected accuracy in the industry [32]. With this, we answered research question 2 partially (RQ 2: How accurate is the effort estimation generated by an AI-supported tool compared to conventional estimation methods?). The accuracy per user stories and groups is shown in Figure 9.

Since the estimation accuracy calculation is carried out with two variables (estimated effort, actual effort), a legitimate debate can also question the correctness of the reported actual effort. To minimise the risk of misreporting, as already explained in Section 4, we hid the estimates from the development teams before the implementation phase. This approach is not uncommon in agile development, where estimates are primarily used during planning meetings to help teams make fair and informed commitments. During the development phase, these estimates are typically "hidden" to ensure developers can focus on delivering high-quality solutions without being influenced by prior estimations, thereby maintaining the integrity of the development process.

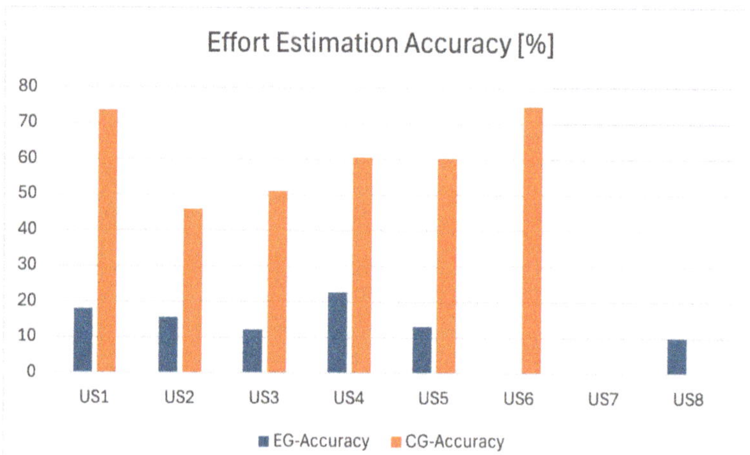

Figure 9. Estimation accuracy in the experimental (EG) and control (CG) groups per user story, in percent.

Another interesting insight, supporting the correctness of reported hours, can be seen in Table 2 of Section 5: regardless of the different task lists and estimates, the development teams of both groups demonstrated similar efforts for implementing user stories to an acceptable level (2 and 1.92 h). All the estimates and actual efforts of both groups per user story are shown in Figure 10, where we can see clearly the similarities between the control group estimates, control group actual effort and experimental group actual effort. The experimental group estimates are obvious outliers.

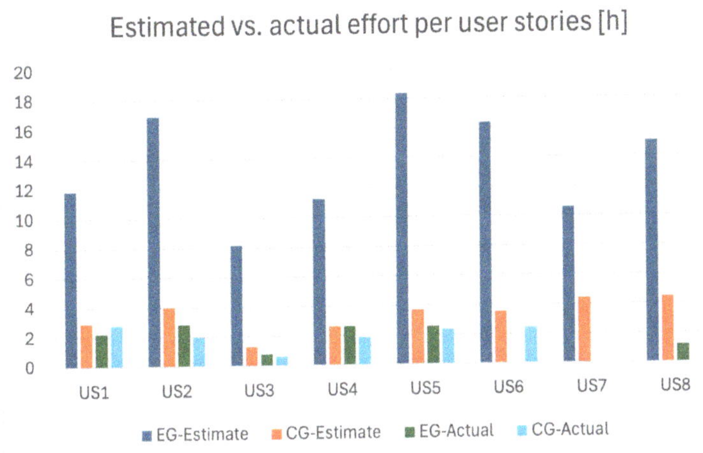

Figure 10. Estimated and actual effort in the experimental (EG) and control (CG) groups per user story in hours.

When exposing development-related empirical data to statistical tests, they showed us interesting insights. As already stated, the estimates from the experimental and control groups demonstrated significant differences. When we compared the estimated and actual effort of the experimental group further, a significant difference was clearly proven: the two-tailed student *t*-test resulted in a *p*-value of 2.2×10^{-9}, *t*-value -7.67. This means that the estimates in the experimental group were all but accurate. When verifying if the development effort was comparable in both groups, the statistical test suggests similarity (a significant difference cannot be proven—$p = 0.675$; $t = 0.424$). The *t*-test also suggested similarity between the estimated and actual effort in the control group: $p = 0.111$; $t = -1.646$.

Table 3. Statistical tests (Student *t*-test) summary.

Data Sets	*p*-Value	*t*-Value	Interpretation
US estimates—CG US estimates—EG	3.03×10^{-7}	6.676	Estimates are proven to have significant differences
US actual effort—EG US estimates—EG	2.2×10^{-9}	7.67	Estimates are significantly different compared to actual effort
US actual effort—CG US estimates—CG	0.111	−1.646	Similarity is suggested between the estimates and actual effort
US actual effort—CG US actual effort—EG	0.675	0.424	Similarity is suggested between the actual efforts in both groups

Let us summarise the discussion by answering research question 3 (**RQ3: Which aspects of effort estimation can be backed by an AI-supported tool?**). Based on RQ1, task generation is a candidate activity that can be improved by generative AI tool support. However, our experiment empirical data did not demonstrate the possibility of carrying it out automatically but, rather, as a helper tool. This outcome is also aligned with the post-test questionnaire results: the participants unanimously saw this activity to be carried out with the combination of conventional methods and AI-supported tools.

When discussing effort estimation, our experimentation shows clearly that the generative AI tools that we used were not mature enough to be used, since the accuracy was not only low but also, importantly, lower than the methods and tools that are used today in the software development industry. This insight has also been reported clearly by the participants in the post-test questionnaire: the majority of the participants were in doubt about the generative-AI-supported estimates or were (more than half) against AI-supported effort estimation (see Section 5 for details).

7. Threats of Validity

7.1. Construct Validity

The research fields of AI, especially generative AI and large language models, are in ascent at the moment. Our experiment, carried out with the tools based on the current state of the art in the field, might not be relevant in years to come or even when improved methods and tools are released. In addition, the tool that we used in the experiment was one of the best on the market. However, the tool was used in the form for a general audience. We believe that if such a tool would be fine-tuned to a particular company and/or domain, it would have performed better. It would also perform better when data feedback in terms of accuracy would be used in future assessments. Unfortunately, the tool does not allow for such adjustments.

In addition, developers' pre-knowledge and experience was implicitly included in the effort estimation due to self-assessment in control group. However, this was not the case in the experimental group, using generative-AI-based estimation, as the prompts do not explicitly contain all the information about the developers' experience. Having generative-AI-based tools aware of pre-knowledge would improve comparability between the groups. When the tools support this functionality, we plan to repeat our research.

7.2. Internal Validity

Although the participants in the research were 4th semester software engineering students who we train from day one in the technologies that were used during the experiment, the fact that they were not full-time developers might affect the results negatively.

Our experimental setup carries some limitations. While the planning meeting closely simulated real industry settings, the development phase was brief, and user stories and tasks were smaller in scale than in typical projects. This was intentional to maintain a controlled environment but may limit generalizability. Not all user stories were implemented, reflecting the agile practice of prioritizing work based on capacity. The teams selected stories in line with iteration commitment, a core agile principle. While this setup may not fully replicate larger projects, it captures key aspects of agile practices, though the limited empirical data might reduce the significance of the results.

7.3. External Validity

We limited ourselves to GitLab Duo for the controlled experiment, which may pose a threat when generalizing our findings. GitLab Duo was identified in 2024, along with Atlassian Intelligence, ClickUp and OpenText, as a leading tool for iteration planning using generative AI. Based on this and our own testing, we chose GitLab Duo, integrated with GitLab Enterprise, which gave us confidence in the tool's relevance. However, using a single tool may limit the broader applicability of our results.

8. Conclusions

An effort estimation, especially in agile software development, is a cornerstone activity. It enables fair judgement of the effort needed to perform a certain development activity and, importantly, to give sincere commitments on the iteration scope. Since proper estimates minimise schedule-, finance-, and resource-related risks, they are carried out carefully, using proven methods and tools. However, effort estimation can not only be time consuming but also occupy the most brilliant minds from the development teams. This is why, for the recent decades, several approaches emerged to introduce help or even automation to the realm of effort estimation. The recent breakthrough in AI, especially in generative AI, that is reshaping a complete software development discipline, implies that novel tools can also be used to estimate effort more efficiently. To put this tempting idea into trial, we designed and executed a controlled experiment.

Considering the key threats that our research is facing (approaching low maturity, estimating with limited pre-knowledge information, student participants, short iteration), we can outline several significant insights. The research takeaways show clearly that the currently leading helper tools, integrated in software development platforms (we used GitLab Duo), are not mature enough to be a replacement for a human estimator. The automated effort estimates, averaged at 16% accuracy, are far from usable in an industry setting. However, our empirical data showed that they can, even in their present form, be used fruitfully as a helper while splitting the requirements of development tasks—let it be task generation or as a help to see if important tasks were left out during the iteration planning.

While analysing the empirical data, we found three clusters of estimates that contributed importantly to the low accuracy. The first tasks were the ones that were not required explicitly and were usually left out by human assessors. Those tasks can be included by conventional task generation activity and re-estimated by human assessors. The second group consisted of tasks that were included in the automatically generated task lists due to ignoring the context of the effort estimation. The last group of tasks that contributed to low accuracy were the ones that were needed explicitly but were overestimated, obviously planned in terms of a worst-case scenario or ignoring the developers' competences.

The research in the field of automating the effort estimation activity is far from finished. Our research into generative AI potential in the field will be extended and possibly repeated after the tools become more mature, to see their impact. The future work we plan to do is to define a sound set of activities built around generative-AI-enabled tools in order to improve effort estimation. The research method to validate them might not only be based on controlled experiments. We plan to test our ideas on industry projects, where development teams exercise effort estimation with discipline and consistency. In this setting, we might experiment with a known codebase at a certain point of time, known requirements that were implemented, and the known effort that was used to implement them. This is how we would have invaluable empirical data used to test competing methods of automated effort estimation. However, we are aware of the threats that this and future research are facing when generalizing the findings.

Currently, we can conclude confidently that generative-AI-based tools are not at the level where they could be used efficiently to estimate effort in software engineering. However, with vigilance, they can be a valuable companion while splitting requirements into development tasks. In conclusion, while our research does not advocate for the use of LLM tools in critical tasks like iteration planning, we recognize their growing presence in the industry. Our evaluation shows that the tools are not yet mature enough to replace human estimators. Although these tools are readily available and often misused for such purposes, our findings emphasize the need for caution and further development before the tools can be relied upon in complex planning tasks.

Author Contributions: Conceptualization, L.P., V.S. and T.B.; methodology, L.P., V.S. and T.B.; software, L.P.; validation, L.P., V.S. and T.B.; formal analysis, L.P. and V.S.; resources, L.P., V.S. and T.B.; data curation, L.P. and V.S.; writing—original draft preparation, L.P., V.S. and T.B.; writing—review and editing, L.P., V.S. and T.B.; visualization, L.P.; supervision, L.P.; project administration, L.P. and T.B.; funding acquisition, L.P. All authors have read and agreed to the published version of the manuscript.

Funding: The authors acknowledge the financial support from the Slovenian Research and Innovation Agency (Research Core Funding No. P2-0057).

Institutional Review Board Statement: Not applicable.

Informed Consent Statement: Informed consent was obtained from all subjects involved in the study.

Data Availability Statement: The raw data supporting the conclusions of this article will be made available by the authors on request.

Conflicts of Interest: The authors declare no conflicts of interest.

References

1. Cambridge University Press. Cambridge Dictionary. Available online: https://dictionary.cambridge.org (accessed on 9 August 2024).
2. PMI. (Ed.) *A Guide to the Project Management Body of Knowledge (PMBOK Guide)*, 5th ed.; Project Management Institute: Newtown Square, PA, USA, 2013.
3. Brooks, F., Jr. *The Mythical Man-Month: Essays on Software Engineering*; Addison-Wesley: Boston, MA, USA, 1995.
4. Fernández-Diego, M.; Méndez, E.R.; González-Ladrón-De-Guevara, F.; Abrahão, S.; Insfran, E. An Update on Effort Estimation in Agile Software Development: A Systematic Literature Review. *IEEE Access* **2020**, *8*, 166768–166800. [CrossRef]
5. Usman, M.; Mendes, E.; Neiva, F.; Britto, R. Effort Estimation in Agile Software Development: A Systematic Literature Review. In Proceedings of the 10th International Conference on Predictive Models in Software Engineering, Turin, Italy, 17 September 2014. [CrossRef]
6. Peluffo-Ordóñez, D.; Sierra Martínez, L.; Timana, J.; Piñeros, C. Effort Estimation in Agile Software Development: A Systematic Map Study. *Inge CUC* **2023**, *14*, 22–36. [CrossRef]
7. Schweighofer, T.; Kline, A.; Pavlič, L.; Heričko, M. How is Effort Estimated in Agile Software Development Projects? In Proceedings of the SQAMIA, 5th Workshop of Software Quality, Analysis, Monitoring, Improvement, and Applications, Budapest, Hungary, 29–31 August 2016.
8. Cohn, M. *Agile Estimating and Planning*; Addison-Wesley Professional: Boston, MA, USA, 2005.
9. Dinwiddie, G. *Software Estimation Without Guessing*; Pragmatic Bookshelf: Raleigh, NC, USA, 2019.
10. Munialo, S.; Muketha, G. A Review of Agile Software Effort Estimation Methods. *Int. J. Comput. Appl. Technol. Res.* **2016**, *5*, 612–618. [CrossRef]
11. Digital.AI. 15th State of Agile Report. Available online: https://digital.ai/resource-center/analyst-reports/state-of-agile-report (accessed on 9 August 2024).
12. Schwaber, K.; Sutherland, J. The Definitive Guide to Scrum: The Rules of the Game. Retrospectiva del Sprint de Nexus. 2017. Available online: https://scrum.org (accessed on 3 November 2024).
13. Agile Alliance. What is Scrumban? Available online: https://www.agilealliance.org/scrumban/ (accessed on 3 November 2024).
14. Large Scale Scrum (LeSS). Available online: https://less.works/ (accessed on 3 November 2024).
15. Scaled Agile Framework. Available online: https://scaledagileframework.com/ (accessed on 3 November 2024).
16. Extreme Programming (XP). Available online: http://www.extremeprogramming.org/ (accessed on 3 November 2024).
17. Feature-Driven Development (FDD). Available online: https://agilemodeling.com/essays/fdd.htm (accessed on 3 November 2024).
18. Alsaadi, B.; Saeedi, K. Data-driven effort estimation techniques of agile user stories: A systematic literature review. *Artif. Intell. Rev.* **2022**, *55*, 5485–5516. [CrossRef]
19. Hannigan, T.R.; McCarthy, I.P.; Spicer, A. Beware of botshit: How to manage the epistemic risks of generative chatbots. *Bus. Horizons* **2024**, *67*, 471–486. [CrossRef]
20. Bhat, M.; Haight, C.; Blosen. B. *How Platform Engineering Teams Can Augment DevOps with AI*; Gartner Reseaerch: Stamford, CT, USA, 2024.
21. Finnie, G.; Wittig, G. AI tools for software development effort estimation. In Proceedings of the 1996 International Conference Software Engineering: Education and Practice, Dunedin, New Zealand, 24–27 January 1996; pp. 346–353. [CrossRef]
22. Jadhav, A.; Shandilya, S.K. Reliable machine learning models for estimating effective software development efforts: A comparative analysis. *J. Eng. Res.* **2023**, *11*, 362–376. [CrossRef]
23. Tran, T.N.; Tran, H.T.; Nguyen, Q.N. Leveraging AI for Enhanced Software Effort Estimation: A Comprehensive Study and Framework Proposal. In Proceedings of the 2023 International Conference on the Cognitive Computing and Complex Data (ICCD), Huaian, China, 21–22 October 2023, pp. 284–289. [CrossRef]
24. Koskinen, K. AI-Assisted Software Development Effort Estimation. Master's Thesis, Department of Computing, University of Turku, Turku, Finland, 2021.
25. Hartenstein, S.; Leroy Johnson, S.; Schmietendorf, A. *Towards a Fast Cost Estimation Supported by Large Language Models*; Technical Report; COSMIC Sizing: Chambly, QC, Canada, 2024.
26. Coelho, C.N., Jr.; Xiong, H.; Karayil, T.; Koratala, S.; Shang, R.; Bollinger, J.; Shabar, M.; Nair, S. Effort and Size Estimation in Software Projects with Large Language Model-based Intelligent Interfaces. *arXiv* **2024**, arXiv:2402.07158. http://arxiv.org/abs/2402.07158.
27. Arman, A.; Di Reto, E.; Mecella, M.; Santucci, G. An Approach for Software Development Effort Estimation Using ChatGPT. In Proceedings of the 2023 IEEE International Conference on Enabling Technologies: Infrastructure for Collaborative Enterprises (WETICE), Paris, France, 14–16 December 2023; pp. 1–7. [CrossRef]
28. Ebrahim, E.; Sayed, M.; Youssef, M.; Essam, H.; El-Fattah, S.A.; Ashraf, D.; Magdy, O.; ElAdawi, R. AI Decision Assistant ChatBot for Software Release Planning and Optimized Resource Allocation. In Proceedings of the 2023 IEEE International Conference on Artificial Intelligence Testing (AITest), Athens, Greece, 17–20 July 2023; pp. 55–60.

29. Barcaui, A.; Monat, A. Who is better in project planning?Generative artificial intelligence or project managers? *Proj. Leadersh. Soc.* **2023**, *4*, 100101. [CrossRef]
30. Wohlin, P. Runeson, M.H.M.C.O.B.R.; Wesslén, A. *Experimentation in Software Engineering*; Springer: Berlin/Heidelberg, Germany, 2012.
31. Ko, A.J.; LaToza, T.D.; Burnett, M.M. A practical guide to controlled experiments of software engineering tools with human participants. *Empir. Softw. Eng.* **2015**, *20*, 110–141. [CrossRef]
32. Jørgensen, M.; Teigen, K.H.; Moløkken, K. Better sure than safe? Over-confidence in judgement based software development effort prediction intervals. *J. Syst. Softw.* **2004**, *70*, 79–93. [CrossRef]

applied sciences

MDPI

Article

AbstractTrace: The Use of Execution Traces to Cluster, Classify, Prioritize, and Optimize a Bloated Test Suite

Ziad A. Al-Sharif [1,*,†,‡] and Clinton L. Jeffery [2,‡]

1 Department of Software Engineering, Faculty of Computer and Information Technology, Jordan University of Science and Technology (JUST), Irbid 22110, Jordan
2 Department of Computer Science and Engineering, New Mexico Institute of Mining and Technology, Socorro, NM 87801, USA; clinton.jeffery@nmt.edu
* Correspondence: zasharif@just.edu.jo or zalsharif@lewisu.edu
† Current address: Department of Engineering, Computing and Mathematical Sciences (*ECaMS*), College of Aviation, Science and Technology (*CoAST*), Lewis University, Romeoville, IL 60446, USA.
‡ These authors contributed equally to this work.

Abstract: Due to the incremental and iterative nature of the software testing process, a test suite may become bloated with redundant, overlapping, and similar test cases. This paper aims to optimize a bloated test suite by employing an execution trace that encodes runtime events into a sequence of characters forming a string. A dataset of strings, each of which represents the code coverage and execution behavior of a test case, is analyzed to identify similarities between test cases. This facilitates the *de-bloating* process by providing a formal mechanism to identify, remove, and reduce *extra* test cases without compromising software quality. This form of analysis allows for the clustering and classification of test cases based on their code coverage and similarity score. This paper explores three levels of execution traces and evaluates different techniques to measure their similarities. Test cases with the same code coverage should generate the exact string representation of runtime events. Various string similarity metrics are assessed to find the similarity score, which is used to classify, detect, and rank test cases accordingly. Additionally, this paper demonstrates the validity of the approach with two case studies. The first shows how to classify the execution behavior of various test cases, which can provide insight into each test case's internal behavior. The second shows how to identify similar test cases based on their code coverage.

Keywords: software engineering; software testing; execution trace; test suite; bloated testing; machine learning; clustering; classification

1. Introduction

Software testing is the process of verifying and validating that a software application or program meets the business and technical requirements that guided its design and development, and works as expected (What is software testing? https://www.ibm.com/topics/software-testing, accessed on 19 November 2024). Software testing also identifies important defects, flaws, or errors in the application code that must be fixed [1]. It is essential to verify functional and non-functional requirements. Functional testing ensures the software performs the actions based on the business or client's requirements. Non-functional testing verifies that the software is performing as expected by the customer, based on the end-user's expectations, including attributes such as performance, reliability, and scalability. Test engineers design and incorporate test cases to reveal as many bugs as possible before the application is deployed and used [2]. The goal of testing is to reduce the risk of software failures and improve the software quality attributes [3]. Inadequate testing negatively affects the quality of the software system. Therefore, testing activities are included in all subsequent phases of the software development life cycle (SDLC). Moreover, software development's iterative and incremental nature requires an iterative and incremental software testing process [4]. Thus, a test suite often includes many test cases, which require effort and time to manage and validate [5].

Test engineers use various testing types such as mutation, regression, stress, security, and load testing to ensure the quality level of various aspects of the software product. Depending on the testing type, engineers create a dedicated test suite, invest in its automation process, and maintain it for a long time. Different test cases can be designed with different goals; each is evaluated, verified, and analyzed during the testing process to ensure the expected output or behavior matches the actual behavior obtained from the application under testing. For instance, when an application is initially developed and tested, a test suite is constructed to ensure its functionality. Test engineers preserve and maintain this test suite for future use. Thus, as changes are made to the application during the development process and maintained afterward, these retained test suites are used to ensure that no new bugs have been introduced into the previously tested features.

On the other hand, over time and due to the nature of the testing process, a test suite can quickly become **bloated** by incorporating redundant and overlapping test cases that could be reduced and eliminated without affecting the overall quality of the software [6–8]. Finding redundant or highly similar test cases may be difficult, considering the number of test cases in a test suite.

However, such a test-suite analysis can be achieved by various means. One method is to employ not the output but instead the execution traces of various test cases. An execution trace is a detailed record of the sequence of *source-code-level* operations executed by a program during its run. This includes function calls, variable uses (read/write), line number changes, dynamic memory allocations, and the flow of control. A sequence of runtime execution events can be used to identify each test case uniquely [9,10]. Then, these unique representations can be analyzed to find the similarities between various test cases incorporated in the test suite. In this paper, we define the similarities between different test cases based on two factors: first, the number of shared statements that different test cases can execute, and second, the order of the executed statements that are shared between different test cases. Therefore, various test cases can be similar or redundant if they execute the same set of statements in the same order, regardless of the differences in the inputs used. It is normal for various test cases to often cover shared parts of the code structure during their execution. For this reason, measuring the similarity or the amount of shared code covered by different test cases can be helpful to the test engineer. Such a measurement can help select and prioritize the test cases based on various criteria. For example, the test engineer may be interested in identifying the root cause of a failure in one of the test cases. Identifying the test cases that may share the most amount of code coverage may help identify and select the set of test cases that are correlated to the failed test case and help in isolating the root cause of the bug. Additionally, in a tight schedule, ranking the test cases based on their similarities in terms of the amount of shared code coverage can help select a subset of test cases that may yield the maximal code coverage with the least amount of test cases. Moreover, it can help focus the testing effort on a specific part of the code where the set of test cases share a high percentage of the code structure.

This paper introduces AbstractTrace, an approach that can assist in software testing to identify test-case similarities and classify its execution behavior. This study confirms the **hypothesis** that utilizing an execution trace facilitates the capture of source-code-level runtime event sequences for each test case. The employed monitoring and tracing framework supports over 120+ types of events. Capturing and recording these events promptly is expected to aid in identifying similarities across different test cases. AbstractTrace encodes each runtime event as one English character; these captured events form strings. In this paper, we use the Greek symbol $\sum$ to denote the set of alphabetic characters used to encode each runtime event. A string can capture and represent the dynamic behavior of executing a test case based on the sequence of the covered source-code statements and structure. Different strings are captured for different test cases. The similarities between these strings reflect similarities in code coverage between various test cases.

Building datasets of these string representations can be started during the validation of the test suite. Then, the dataset analysis should illustrate the similarities between the execution traces and their test cases. For example, one of the uses of this approach is in the context of regression testing, in which selecting an appropriate subset of the test cases to run after implementing new software features can enable test engineers to identify potential faults that may be introduced by these recent changes. However, selecting the subset of test cases to run can be challenging. Classifying and clustering the test cases can assist in the selection and prioritization process [11]. Therefore, this paper introduces an execution trace-based prioritization approach involving code coverage. The similarities between various traces are aligned with the similarities between test cases. This technique can be employed to help understand the execution behavior of a test suite, maximize the code coverage, and minimize the number of test cases. We evaluated various string-similarity algorithms and applied a similarity score-based method to identify similar test cases. Our approach is empirically evaluated using two case studies that use code coverage from runtime events and map the execution traces into the test cases of the investigated code. The results emphasize the value of automatic trace analysis and show the potential for the test-case prioritization and selection process based on execution traces.

Furthermore, this paper investigates three levels of execution traces and evaluates various string-matching algorithms (*techniques*); each level gives different insights about the structure of the executed source code by the test case. The presented approach should facilitate the ability to cluster, classify, and rank test cases based on their code coverage, allowing for the detection of similar and redundant test cases. Labeling each test case in a test suite with a similarity score assists in determining those instances (test cases) to which they have high similarities and those that are less similar.

The remaining parts of the paper are organized as follows. Section 2 sheds some light on the background research and highlights our utilization of the execution trace and source-code-level runtime monitoring. Section 3 presents our research methodology. Section 4 describes the various levels of execution trace, the runtime events and dataset, and the experiments used to validate our methodology. Section 5 describes our experimentation environment and shows how our approach can be applicable in the field for other programming languages and environments. Section 6 presents two case studies, each of which shows the validity of the approach from different angles. Section 7 discusses the implications of the findings. Section 8 highlights the related work. Finally, Section 9 concludes our work, presents its limitations, and highlights the potential for future studies.

2. Background

Assessing the certainty level about the quality of a software product is often needed to build confidence in the quality of the software product. Therefore, testing involves evaluating programs and applications to identify potential software bugs and faults at various levels of the software structure, including units, modules, subsystems, and system levels. Test engineers can use different testing techniques and types at different stages, ranging from white- to black-box testing. Moreover, re-executing and verifying test cases for various modules after a change (*i.e., bug fixing or introducing new features*) requires effort and time. To address this issue, researchers investigated different approaches to handle test-case prioritization and selection [12,13]. Often, their goal is to order test cases based on various factors, optimize the testing process, and ensure its efficiency and effectiveness [14,15].

In this paper, we utilize execution traces produced by a runtime monitoring framework [16] that captures source-code-level events. This monitoring framework can trace more than 120 different kinds of runtime events [17–19]. However, this project only utilizes a set of 70 kinds of events described in Table 1. Some events are triggered from variable references and expression evaluations, and others from various data structures such as lists and associated arrays (dictionaries). In contrast, other events capture syntax and control structures, such as the execution of functions, loops, and source-code line changes. This paper builds on this monitoring framework by introducing two new levels of character encoding. Instead of encoding each event in a structure with a field-encoding event type, as shown in Table 1, each event is further reduced down to one alphabetic character. This allows us to represent the execution of an entire test case as a (possibly long) string that constitutes an abstract view of the source-code coverage and runtime behavior of that test-case execution. Throughout this paper, we utilize the Greek symbol Σ to represent the set of alphabetic characters employed to encode each runtime event. A set of strings is created for each test suite, which is then analyzed to cluster, classify, and rank various related test cases based on their execution behavior. The analysis process yields further insights into the application's internal code structures and runtime behaviors of the software under test, and the relationship between test cases based on their code coverage. It should show how the used test cases cover the application's code and rank these test cases based on their similarities in the code structure covered during its validation process. Similarities between various execution traces will reflect the similarities between the test cases as well as the code that is covered by each of the test cases.

Table 1. The mnemonic codes for the kinds of source-code-level runtime events that are used to capture the code structure and execution behavior of test cases. A total of 70 different kinds of events are used.

Event Type	Source-Code-Level Events (*Event Code*)	#
Variable:	*E_Assign, E_Deref*	2
Expression:	*E_Ecall, E_Eresum, E_Efail, E_Erem, E_Esusp*	5
List/Array:	*E_List, E_Lelem, E_Lsub, E_Lpush, E_Lput, E_Lpop, E_Lpull*	7
Dictionary:	*E_Table, E_Telem, E_Tvsubs, E_Tvtbl,* *E_Tsub, E_Tkey, E_Tinsert, E_Tdelete, E_Tmember*	9
Set:	*E_Set, E_Selem, E_Slots, E_Cset, E_Sinsert, E_Sdelete, E_Smember, E_Sval*	8
Sting:	*E_String, E_Snew, E_Sresum, E_Sfail, E_Ssusp, E_Spos, E_Srem*	7
Reg. Exp.:	*E_PatAttempt, E_PatMatch, E_PatFail, E_PelemAttempt, E_PelemMatch,* *E_PelemFail, E_PatCode, E_PatArg, E_PatVal, E_PatPush, E_PatPop*	11
Struct/Object:	*E_Record, E_Rcreate, E_Rsub, E_Rref*	4
Procedure:	*E_Pcall, E_Presum, E_Pfail, E_Pret, E_Psusp*	5
Function:	*E_Fcall, E_Fresum, E_Ffail, E_Fret, E_Fsusp*	5
Line & Syntax:	*E_Line, E_Syntax*	2
Miscellaneous:	*E_File, E_Lrgint, E_Real, E_Refresh, E_Coexpr*	5

Table 1 shows that variable behavior is captured using two events, one for *read* (*E_Deref*), and the other for *write* (*E_Assign*). Likewise, the behavior of user-defined procedures and built-in functions can be captured by five different events each. Expression evaluation uses five events as well. Additionally, operations on data structures such as lists or arrays, tables or dictionaries, and sets are represented by sets of seven, nine, and eight unique source-code events, respectively. Behavior pertaining to strings and string processing, including pattern matching (e.g., *regular expressions*), can be observed via eighteen events. The behavior of records and objects can be captured using four events. Additionally, line number change and source-code syntactic structures are depicted using two different events. Finally, a set of five events is used for miscellaneous source-code activities such as file handling and co-expression evaluation.

This monitoring framework provides a dynamic filtering mechanism that allows the monitoring program to select a subset of the traced events. Furthermore, each event has a *code* denoting the kind of event and an associated value, and the API enables the tracer program to customize the type and number of traced events based on both the event code and value. There is a direct relationship between the number of traced events and the length of the resulting execution trace. The test engineer can adjust this length by changing the number of monitored events. For example, events such as E_Line can provide insights about the executed line numbers and source-code coverage statements. Such events can be filtered based on a specific source-code file or user-defined procedure. Events reported from user-defined procedures and built-in runtime functions can assist in various control-flow coverage criteria [20]. Whereas, events depicting variable references such as E_Assign and E_Deref can be used to assist in the data-flow coverage criteria, in which the E_Assign can be used to detect variables' ***defs*** and E_Deref can detect variables' ***uses*** or reads [21]. This monitoring framework facilitates the source-code instrumentation with no intrusion of the program under test.

3. Approach and Methodology

This paper employs program execution traces to capture execution behavior and code coverage of test cases. Under the execution trace in the context of this research article, we use source-code-level runtime events, such as function calls, expression evaluations, dynamic memory allocations, etc., to represent the execution behavior of a test case. The set of 70 different runtime events, presented in Table 1, are traced during the execution of the test case. The result of the execution trace of different test cases is used to create a dataset instance that represents the test suite. The execution traces from various test cases are collected and analyzed to detect the similarities between different test cases.

This approach (1) provides a systematic mechanism to study and analyze test suites, (2) simplifies the process of identifying redundant test cases that can be eliminated without impacting the quality of the testing process, and (3) ranks these test cases within a test suite based on their similarity score. The goal is to formalize the process of removing redundant test cases, which should improve the testing process and reduce the overall testing time [22,23]. Therefore, this paper proposes an approach that enables test engineers to score the similarities between various test cases within a test suite.

Experimentation shows that this approach helps identify highly similar test cases and rank these test cases based on their similarity scores [24]. The two case studies provided show that the ranking system allows the engineer to gain insight into the code coverage of the test suite. The approach offers a systematic labeling of test cases in a test suite with a score that indicates the test case and its code coverage score. It also allows the engineer to compare different scores from different test cases in the test suite. This will enable engineers to identify test cases that cover the same set of statements (*share the same code coverage*), which helps to identify the least-impacting test cases in terms of code coverage (*redundant and highly similar test cases*). Therefore, this formal mechanism enables an approach to remove test cases that do not contribute to code coverage within the test suite. This mechanism leads to a reduced number of test cases, reduced effort and time needed to validate these test suites, and an improved overall testing process. Moreover, the approach equips engineers with the ability to prioritize test cases, better select a representative subset of the test cases to run, and eventually estimate the testing time and cost according to the selected quality level.

To achieve these capabilities, the approach uses the execution traces obtained from the test cases; each test case is associated with its string representation of the execution trace: a sequence of letters, each of which represents a unique runtime event. The combined sequence can be unique to represent one of the test cases. A dataset of these *trace strings* is maintained for further analysis using various techniques, including different string-similarity algorithms and modern AI approaches. Trace strings are evaluated to find the similarities between test cases, classify these test cases based on their similarity score, and rank test cases based on their similarity measures. The test engineer can select the subset of test cases to be considered in the next phase of the testing process, which is often included during regression testing.

Figure 1 presents an abstract visual representation of our approach and methodology. During the software development life cycle, the test engineer designs and executes a test suite to verify that the actual outputs and behaviors align with the expected results. Throughout this process, AbstractTrace can be employed. It encapsulates three different phases. First is the **tracing phase**, in which AbstractTrace takes the test suite designed by the test engineer and builds a dataset of execution traces, wherein each trace (string) encapsulates the execution behavior of a passed test case. The second phase is the **analysis phase**, in which the dataset of strings is analyzed using various string-similarity algorithms to identify the similarity score between every pair of test cases. AbstractTrace evaluates this dataset to:

1. Identify redundant test cases;
2. Cluster test cases based on their string similarity scores; and
3. Rank test cases from most to least similar.

Finally, in the **optimization phase**, the test engineer has more insight into the test suite. In this phase, engineers can optimize the test suite by removing similar test cases; those that generate the exact execution trace. Test cases with similar execution behaviors will exhibit comparable string representations. This analysis enables test engineers to eliminate redundant test cases and select a subset that aligns with their testing objectives and goals. Additionally, this execution-trace dataset is updated and maintained during the maintenance of the test suite.

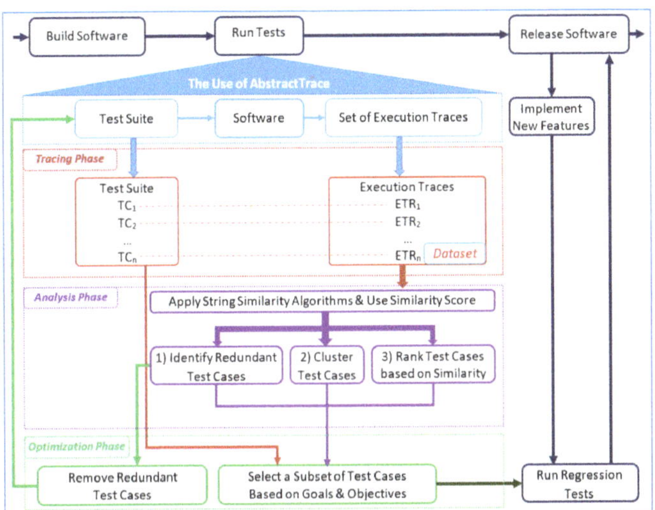

Figure 1. AbstractTrace's approach starts by evaluating a test suite on a program under test, and builds a dataset of execution traces collected for all passed test cases. In the analysis part, all the execution traces are evaluated to find similarities using various algorithms. This similarity score can be used to select and estimate future regression testing whenever it is needed. TC_i stands for test-case number i, and ETR_i stands for the execution-trace number i that is associated with test case i or TC_i.

Figure 2 shows that AbstractTrace employs a hierarchical execution-trace system comprising three levels. The top level utilizes four distinct classes, the mid-level incorporates 16 classes, and the lowest level captures events at the source-code level. Algorithm 1 shows the proposed procedure that can be used to optimize the test suite and improve its code coverage. The approach takes the test suite T_j and the current version of the program under test P_j as inputs. Then, it will run the program with the given test suite, collect execution traces for each of the passed test cases, analyze the traces, and build a similarity matrix SM_{jk} for every dataset of traces. This SM_{jk} will be used to find the redundant test cases. Redundant test cases are those with the similarity $score = 1$. Moreover, a similarity matrix can be built to rank and cluster these test cases. A high similarity score between any two test cases in the matrix indicates a high similarity between the test cases' execution behavior. This similarity score can be based on a clustering mechanism that will help the test engineer select the test cases in future testing rounds, including the regression testing process. It will help better manage the testing process.

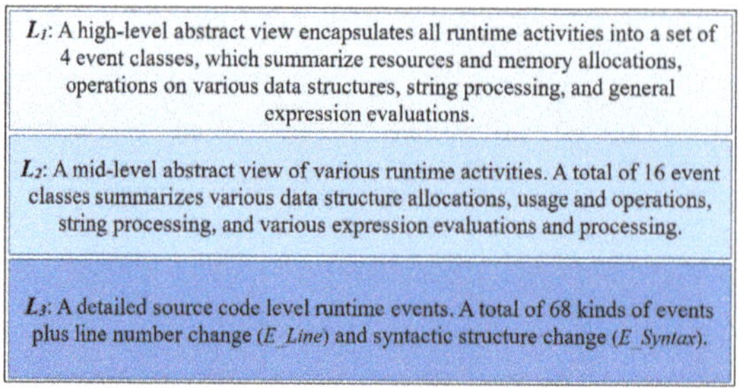

Figure 2. AbstractTrace's hierarchical execution trace: the top level with 4 classes, the mid-level with 16 classes, and the lowest level captures 68 kind of source-code events.

Algorithm 1 AbstractTrace Procedure

Require: $\mathcal{P}_j$: The program under test, *where j is the current version of the program*
Require: $\mathcal{T}_j$: The test suite, *where j is the current version of the test suite $\mathcal{T}$ used to test program $\mathcal{P}_j$*
  Run $\mathcal{P}_j(\mathcal{T}_j)$ and evaluate every $t_i \in \mathcal{T}_j$
  Build and maintain a dataset $\mathcal{D}_j$ from testing program $\mathcal{P}_j$ with test suite $\mathcal{T}_j$

▷ ***Phase#1**: Build datasets by collecting execution traces for each test case in the test suite.*

▷ L_1: *represents the top level; all events are grouped into one of 4 different categories; see Section 4.1.*
▷ L_2: *represents the middle level; all events are grouped into one of 16 different subcategory; see Section 4.2.*
▷ L_2: *represents the lower level; each event is encoded in one of 68 distinct event type; see Section 4.3.*
  for each passed $t_i \in \mathcal{T}_j$ **do**
    Collect execution trace ETR_{i1} of type $\mathcal{L}_1$
    Add ETR_{i1} to $\mathcal{D}_{j1}$

    Collect execution trace ETR_{i2} of type $\mathcal{L}_2$
    Add ETR_{i2} to $\mathcal{D}_{j2}$

    Collect execution trace ETR_{i3} of type $\mathcal{L}_3$
    Add ETR_{i3} to $\mathcal{D}_{j3}$
  end for

▷ ***Phase#2**: Analyze datasets for each of the test suites, and build a similarity matrix SM_{jk}.*
  for each $ETR_i \in \mathcal{D}_{jk}$, *where* $1 \leq i \leq n$ and $k = \{1,2,3\}$ **do**
    for each $ETR_x \in \mathcal{D}_{jk}$, *where* $1 \leq x \leq n$ and $k = \{1,2,3\}$ **do**
      if $i \neq x$ **then**
        Find similarity for ETR_i and ETR_x
        Build similarity vector SV_i for ETR_i and ETR_x
        Add SV_i to SM_{jk}
      end if
    end for
  end for

  for each SM_{jk}, *where* $k = \{\mathcal{L}_1, \mathcal{L}_2, \mathcal{L}_3\}$ **do**
    Analyze and evaluate the SM_{jk}
    Rank/cluster test cases based on their similarity score
▷ ***Phase#3**: Optimize the test suites based on the similarity matrix*
    Remove redundant test case in $\mathcal{T}_j$, ▷ *any two test case with similarity score* $= 1$
    Select a subset of the test cases in future testing.
  end for

---

4. Data Representation: Runtime Events and Dataset

This paper uses execution traces as a representation of test cases. These traces capture aspects of the runtime behavior of test cases. An execution trace provides a comprehensive record of the sequence of source-code-level operations performed by a program during its execution. This trace encompasses function calls, variable accesses (both read and write operations), line number transitions, dynamic memory allocations, and control-flow changes. By analyzing the sequence of runtime execution events, each test case can be uniquely identified. Therefore, the analysis of these traces reveals parts of the test cases' runtime behavior, code structure, and code coverage. The traced execution events are comprehensive enough to represent various code structures, data-structure allocations and operations, source-code evaluations, and built-in operations and functions. This allows a trace to be sensitive to small changes from one test case to another and to depict the similarity in test cases based on their runtime execution behavior and code coverage. Experimentation shows that identical or redundant test cases execute the same code structure in the same order; similar but not identical test cases will share part of the code structure in the same order of execution. Similar runtime characteristics of source-code-level behaviors appear as common substrings in the string representations of the execution traces, which are captured from the sequence of runtime events.

For instance, method calls and returns can become integral parts of a program's execution behavior or test cases. To gain insights into the distribution of these embedded events—specifically, how they are distributed within each test case—we needed to explore whether any execution trace exhibits similar functionalities. Traces with common substrings represent test cases with comparable execution patterns, runtime events, or programs with similar logic or internal design structures. Furthermore, if functions, programs, or test cases significantly deviate from the norm, we can identify this deviation using distinct metrics by utilizing various similarity algorithms and measurement metrics.

Execution traces capture not just the code's similarity but also its order, just like a time series. The captured events in the execution trace can be encoded in three levels of runtime events. These events are triggered by the program under test, obtained, and collected by AbstractTrace based on different aspects of the program under test, such as memory allocations for various resources (*i.e., data-structure allocations such as lists and arrays, tables and dictionaries; sets, etc.*), data-structure utilization, string processing, and the use of various built-in functions and operators, user-defined procedures, and the read and write functions of various program variables. This diversity of runtime events allows for good differentiation between various test cases based on their actual source code and executed statements covered during the test-case validation.

$$\sum_{1} = \{A, D, S, E\} \tag{1}$$

where *A: Resources and Allocations; D: Data-Structure Operations;*
S: String Processing and Operations; E: General Evaluation

The approach introduced in this paper employs program execution traces at three levels; each level captures a defined level of information. For example, level one or L_1 ($\Sigma_{L_1} = \{A, D, S, E\}$) divides the runtime behavior into four classes: (1) 'A': for allocations, (2) 'D': for data-structure usage, (3) 'S': for string-processing activities, and (4) 'E': for general evaluations. See Equation (1), where the Greek symbol $\sum$ is used to represent the set of alphabetic characters. However, if these four major categories are insufficient, the second level, or L_2, can be used. L_2 divides the runtime behavior into sixteen sub-classes, each encoded with a letter in the alphabet ($\Sigma_{L_2} = \{H, U, Z, X, Y, M, L, T, C, O, N, J, G, V, P, F\}$). This allows the analysis process to detect patterns and execution behavior in more detail than the first level; see Table 2. Finally, the third level (or L_3) captures low-level fine-grained execution events; at this level, the tracing language consists of 68 unique execution events that are captured at the virtual machine level or within the runtime system.

Table 2. Major categories of runtime events and their encoding alphabets. Each class and subclass at L_1 and L_2 is encoded with one letter. Events at level L_3 are encoded differently; see Section 4.3.

Class #	Event Type	L_1	L_2	L_3	# of Events
C_1	Resources and Allocations	A		*AllocMask*	
	$C_{1.1}$ Lists Alloc.		H	*ListAlloc*	2
	$C_{1.2}$ Tables Alloc.		U	*TableAlloc*	4
	$C_{1.3}$ Sets Alloc.		Z	*SetAlloc*	4
	$C_{1.4}$ Strings Alloc.		X	*StrAlloc*	1
	$C_{1.5}$ Objects Alloc.		Y	*ObjAlloc*	1
	$C_{1.6}$ Miscellaneous Alloc.		M	*MiscAlloc*	5
C_2	Data-Structure Operations	D		*StructMask*	
	$C_{2.1}$ Lists Oper.		L	*ListMask*	5
	$C_{2.2}$ Tables Oper.		T	*TableMask*	5
	$C_{2.3}$ Sets Oper.		C	*SetMask*	4
	$C_{2.4}$ Objects Oper.		O	*RecordMask*	3
C_3	String Processing and Operations	S		*StrMask*	
	$C_{3.1}$ String Scanning		N	*ScanMask*	6
	$C_{3.2}$ Pattern Matching		J	*PattMask*	11
C_4	General Evaluations and Operations	E		*EvalMask*	
	$C_{4.1}$ Variable Read/Write		V	*VarMask*	2
	$C_{4.2}$ Built-in Operations		G	*OperMask*	5
	$C_{4.3}$ Function Processing		F	*FuncMask*	5
	$C_{4.4}$ Procedure Processing		P	*ProcMask*	5
	No. of Unique Events	4	16		68

These three levels provide test engineers with the flexibility to select the level of detail needed for their test suite. Each of these levels generates a string of execution events with different alphabet sizes and consequently different levels of detail about the actual code executed by the test case or set of test cases. Table 2 presents the three levels of abstract representations used by AbstractTrace. It shows *four* classes of events in L_1, *sixteen* classes of events in L_2, and finally *sixty-eight* types of events in L_3. Additionally, in all three levels, line number and major syntactic structures (two more events: *E_Line* & *E_Syntax*) are used to introduce spaces in between the collected events' codes; *this makes the resulting trace strings consist of tokens based on source-code statements and blocks*—see Figure 3. Moreover, Table 2 shows the unique letters (*event encoding*) used in each level that represent these events in the captured execution trace, in which each level incorporates a specific level of detail. The following three sub-sections give more insights into each of the levels.

```
>computeStats(list=[10])
E  EEE  EE E E EE EEDEEEEE  E EEDEE  EEE E EE EEDEEEEDEEEEEE  EEE
EEEEEE EEEEE EEEEE EEEEE EEEEE EEEEE  E  EE

>computeStats(list=[10 20])
E  EEE  EE E E EE EEDEEEE E EEDEEEEE  E  EEDEEEEAAAEA EEDEEEEAAAE
AE  EEE E EE EEDEEEEDEEEEE E EEDEEEEDEEEEEE  EEE EEEEEE EEEEE
EEEEE EEEEE EEEEE EEEEE  E  EE
```

(**a**) Two samples of *level 1* execution traces for two related unit test cases

```
>computeStats(list=[10])
P  VVP  VV V V VV VVLVVVGG  V VVLVV  VVV V VV VVLVVVVLVVVVGG  VVV
VVGFFV VVGFF VVGFF VVGFF VVGFF VVGFF  P  PG

>computeStats(list=[10 20])
P  VVP  VV V V VV VVLVVVG V VVLVVVGG  V  VVLVVGFXXXFX VVLVVGFXXXF
XV  VVV V VV VVLVVVVLVVVVG V VVLVVVVLVVVVGG  VVV VVGFFV VVGFF
VVGFF VVGFF VVGFF VVGFF  P  PG
```

(**b**) Two samples of *level 2* execution traces for the two related unit cases presented in part (**a**)

Figure 3. Sample execution trace using one character encoding. The two parts represent the same program with two different encoding schemes. Part (**b**) shows more characters than part (**a**).

4.1. Execution Trace (Level 1)

This top level represents all monitored runtime events, which are grouped into one of four different categories. Equation (1) shows the four letters represented in $\sum_1$. An execution trace will be a sequence of these four letters; each letter represents one of the four high-level major classes of runtime execution events. The execution trace can be used to present the runtime execution behavior of the test case. At this level, the details are hidden or encoded in one of four classes: C_1, C_2, C_3, and C_4, with one English letter ($\{A, D, S, E\}$) representing each of these classes. These classes are described as follows:

C_1: **Resources and Allocations.** This major category encompasses most of the allocation activities that may occur during program execution, including the allocations of various data structures, objects, and other miscellaneous resources such as files, large integers, threads, etc. These resources are often needed during the execution of the program under test. Our experimentation shows that different programs and test cases require various execution resources, which may affect the testing time and quality. This category is encoded with one letter A; see Equation (1).

C_2: **Data-Structure Operations.** This major category encompasses most heap activities and operations related to dynamic data structures, excluding the allocation aspects. Some test cases may utilize these data structures in distinct ways. In some instances, these data-structure operations are sub-optimal and require tuning. Different programs and test cases employ different types of data structures and different patterns of access for effective problem-solving. By monitoring, tracing, and evaluating the utilization of these data structures, we can identify algorithm-tuning approaches during software development, potentially impacting software performance optimization, testing time, and quality. This category is encoded with one letter D; see Equation (1).

C_3: **String Processing and Operations.** This major category encompasses most of the specialized operations related to string processing, regular expressions, and pattern matching. Sometimes, these operations play a crucial role in problem-solving techniques, which individuals or groups of test cases can target. Identifying and optimizing these cases can be a challenging task whenever these test cases utilize any of these string-processing techniques as part of their applied solutions. Our experiments reveal that different programs and test cases may require various types of specialized string-related data processing. By identifying and evaluating these specific use cases, we can uncover algorithm-tuning approaches during software development, which may affect the testing time and quality. This category is encoded with the letter S; see Equation (1).

C_4: **General Evaluation and Operations.** This major category encapsulates most of the remaining activities not covered in the previous three categories. Identifying the test cases that are mostly evaluation-focused can be challenging. Various test cases might employ and process the algorithmic solutions differently. Identifying and optimizing these test cases whenever the execution-trace string shows excessive use of these operations can be helpful during testing and development. Identifying and evaluating these test cases can help identify some algorithm-tuning approaches during the solution, which may affect the software quality as well as the testing time and quality. This category is encoded with the letter E; see Equation (1).

4.2. Execution Trace (Level 2)

At this second level (mid-level) of information, the represented execution trace gives more details about the runtime behavior of the test case. For example, considering the *Resources and Allocations* major category represented in one character A in the first level (L_1). At this second level, it is represented or expanded into six subcategories (six different classes) that can specifically depict the allocated resource type. In particular, the data-structure allocations are expressed in their type at this level, such as list allocations, table allocations, and set allocations represented in the letters H, U, and Z, respectively. Moreover, objects' allocations are represented by the letter Y, strings' allocations are represented by the letter X, and every other allocation (Miscellaneous Allocations) is represented in the letter M. In other words, the letter A from the L_1 expands into six letters $\{H, U, Z, Y, X, M\}$ at level L_2, each of which represents one allocation type that the test case can use. The alphabets described in this category are expressed in Equation (2) and Table 2. Other subcategories are expressed in Equations (3)–(5).

In summary, at the top level, we have one letter to depict the complete 17 runtime events in each major category; at this second level, each subcategory has a different number of letters based on its type. In particular, the **first** subcategory $\sum_{2.1}$ that represents the *allocation and resources* has six different letters $\{H, U, Z, Y, X, M\}$, each of which represents one of the six subcategories; see Equation (2). Likewise, the **second** subcategory $\sum_{2.2}$ that represents the *data-structure operations* has four letters $\{L, T, C, O\}$, each of which represents one of the four subcategories; see Equation (3); the **third** subcategory $\sum_{2.3}$ that represents the *string operations* and has two letters $\{N, J\}$, each of which represents one of the two subcategories; see Equation (4); and finally the **fourth** subcategory $\sum_{2.4}$ that represents the *general evaluations and operations* has four letters $\{G, V, P, F\}$, each of which represents one of the four subcategories; see Equation (5).

$$\sum_{2.1} = \{H, U, Z, Y, X, M\} \tag{2}$$

where *H: List Allocations, U: Table Allocations, Z: Set Allocations, Y: Objects/Record Allocations, X: String Allocations, M: Miscellaneous Allocations*

$$\sum_{2.2} = \{L, T, C, O\} \tag{3}$$

where *L: List Operations, T: Table Operations, C: Set Operations, O: Object/Record Operations*

$$\sum_{2.3} = \{N, J\} \tag{4}$$

where *N: String-Scanning Operations, J: Pattern-Matching Operations*

$$\sum_{2.4} = \{G, V, P, F\} \tag{5}$$

where *G: Built-in Operators, V: Variable Read/Write, P: User Procedures, F: Built-in Functions*

4.3. Execution Trace (Level 3)

At this very low level of execution trace, we are using the language-level runtime execution events. This section details each of the four major categories in Section 4.1. A total of 68 different unique runtime events can be captured and represented in the resulting execution trace at this level. Figure 4 shows a sample of execution trace using the low level (L_3) of event monitoring and encoding. It is clear how the one-character encoding mechanism allows the analysis process to be more direct during the string processing and similarity measures, where each character is mapped into one runtime event.

```
>computeStats(list=[10])
E_Pcall  E_DerefE_DerefE_Pcall  E_DerefE_Assign E_Deref E_Assign
E_DerefE_Assign E_DerefE_DerefE_LsubE_DerefE_DerefE_AssignE_EfailE_Efail
E_Deref E_DerefE_DerefE_LsubE_DerefE_Assign  E_DerefE_DerefE_Assign
E_Assign E_DerefE_Assign
E_DerefE_DerefE_LsubE_DerefE_DerefE_DerefE_DerefE_LsubE_DerefE_DerefE_Deref
E_AssignE_EfailE_Efail  E_DerefE_DerefE_Assign
E_DerefE_DerefE_EcallE_FcallE_FretE_Assign
E_DerefE_DerefE_EcallE_FcallE_Fret E_DerefE_DerefE_EcallE_FcallE_Fret
E_DerefE_DerefE_EcallE_FcallE_Fret E_DerefE_DerefE_EcallE_FcallE_Fret
E_DerefE_DerefE_EcallE_FcallE_Fret  E_Pfail  E_PretE_Efail
```

Figure 4. A sample of *level 3* execution traces for a one test case, where the list has only one element.

4.3.1. Allocations and Resources (*AllocMask*)

At this third level, the execution trace includes events that can be represented at the VM (bytecode interpreter) level. For example, a program allocates various resources to facilitate processing and computing; these resources usually include dynamic memory for various data structures, file descriptors, string allocations, thread resources, etc. The execution of different test cases use different resources. Therefore, this level helps identify the similarities and differences between various test cases based on the fine-grain detail of resource allocations for the test cases, which can play a significant role in the testing and profiling process. The following are the major event types that can be traced and monitored; see Table 3 for specific event names and types. The mnemonic *AllocMask* denotes the union of all these various kinds of allocation events.

Table 3. Level 3 runtime events representing Allocations and Resources (*AllocMask*). These 17 kinds of events can be traced to identify the allocation activities of various resources used by a running test case. At *level 3*, each event is uniquely mapped to one type of allocation or resource. *Event codes and descriptions are from* [19].

Category	Event Code	Descriptions
ListAlloc	E_List	List allocation
	E_Lelem	List element allocation
TableAlloc	E_Table	Table allocation
	E_Telem	Table element allocation
	E_Tvsubs	Substring table value allocation
	E_Tvtbl	Table-element value allocation
SetAlloc	E_Set	Set allocation
	E_Selem	Set element allocation
	E_Slots	Hash header allocation
	E_Cset	Cset or character set allocation
StrAlloc	E_String	String allocation
ObjAlloc	E_Record	Record allocation
MiscAlloc	E_File	File allocation
	E_Lrgint	Large integer allocation
	E_Real	Real allocation
	E_Refresh	Refresh allocation
	E_Coexpr	Co-expression allocation

- **Data-Structure Allocations**: this subcategory includes events that represent blocks of memory or resources, such as:
  - *List Allocations*: includes events triggered when a list or a list element is allocated.
  - *Table Allocations (hash tables or dictionaries)*: includes events that can be triggered to indicate that a hash table (*called a dictionary in some languages*) or an element of the table has been allocated.
  - *Set Allocations*: includes events that can be triggered to indicate that a set, set element, or character set has been allocated.
  - *Object Allocations*: includes events that can be triggered to indicate that an instance of a structure, class, or record has been allocated.

- **String Allocations**: includes events that can be triggered to indicate that an Immutable String block has been allocated.
- **Miscellaneous Allocations**: includes all other events that can be triggered to allocate resources such as file handlers, a thread, etc.

4.3.2. Data-Structure Operations (*StructMask*)

This category incorporates all dynamic data structures that are provided as complex data types in the language, including *Lists, Hash Tables, Records, Sets,* and others. Software developers sometimes misuse these dynamic data structures, which may negatively impact the software's performance and other nonfunctional attributes. Some programs are data-structure allocation intensive, whereas this category is focused more on the operations performed on the allocated data structures. Tracing these differences helps the software engineer identify potential bottlenecks while executing various test cases. See Table 4 for specific event names and types.

- **List Operations**: runtime events that can be triggered whenever a dynamic list is used; it captures runtime events defined as a set in *ListMask*.
- **Table Operations**: runtime events that can be triggered whenever a dynamic table, including hash tables or dictionaries. These events are defined as a set in *TableMask*.
- **Set and Character-Set Operations**: runtime events triggered whenever a dynamic set is used; these events are defined as a set in *SetMask*.
- **Object Operations**: runtime events triggered whenever an object is referenced or used; these events are defined as a set in *RecordMask*.

Table 4. Level 3 runtime events representing data-structure operations (*StructMask*). This table shows 17 events that can be traced to identify various data-structure activities of a running test case. At *Level 3*, each event is uniquely mapped to one specific data structure activity. *Event codes and descriptions are from* [19].

Category	Event Code	Descriptions
ListMask	E_Lsub	List subscript
	E_Lpush	List push
	E_Lput	List put
	E_Lpop	List get/pop
	E_Lpull	List pull
TableMask	E_Tsub	Table subscript
	E_Tkey	Table key generation
	E_Tinsert	Table insertion
	E_Tdelete	Table deletion
	E_Tmember	Table membership
SetMask	E_Sinsert	Set insertion
	E_Sdelete	Set deletion
	E_Smembe	Set membership
	E_Sval	Set value
RecordMask	E_Rcreate	Record creation
	E_Rsub	Record subscript
	E_Rref	Record reference

4.3.3. String Operations (*StrMask*)

This major category specializes in string-scanning and pattern-matching operations, which are some of the central features of the Unicon programming language. It might be more appropriate to merge this category with the structure or general operations below in other mainstream languages. See Table 5 for specific event names and types. This category is organized into two subcategories as follows:

- **String-Scanning Operations**: This subcategory covers language-specific operations devoted to string processing and scanning.
- **Pattern-Matching Operations**: This subcategory is dedicated to pattern matching in strings in a way similar to regular expressions.

Table 5. Level 3 runtime events representing string operations (*StrMask*). This table shows 17 events that can be traced to identify the various string-related activities of various resources that the running test case can use. At *Level 3*, each of the runtime events is uniquely mapped to one specific data structure activity. *Event codes and descriptions are from* [19].

Category	Event Code	Descriptions
ScanMask	E_Snew	Scanning environment creation
	E_Sresum	Scanning resumption
	E_Sfail	Scanning failure
	E_Ssusp	Scanning suspension
	E_Spos	Scanning position
	E_Srem	Scanning environment removal
PatternMask	E_PatAttempt	Attempt to Pattern Match
	E_PatMatch	Pattern match success
	E_PatFail	Pattern match failure
	E_PelemAttempt	Pattern element attempt
	E_PelemMatch	Pattern element match succeeded
	E_PelemFail	Pattern element match failed
	E_PatCode	Pattern code
	E_PatArg	Pattern element arguments matched against
	E_PatVal	Result of evaluating uneval expr.
	E_PatPush	Pattern Stack Push indication
	E_PatPop	Pattern Stack Pop indication

4.3.4. General Evaluation and Operations (*EvalMask*)

This category includes various events that can be triggered to indicate the execution of different operations and different types of general and special expression evaluations. See Table 6 for specific event names and types. These events are organized into subcategories as follows:

Table 6. Level 3 runtime events representing General Evaluation and Operations (*EvalMask*). This table shows 17 events that can be traced to identify various runtime events that are uniquely mapped to a specific evaluation-related operation, such as a variable use, function call, etc. *Event codes and descriptions are from* [19].

Category	Event Code	Descriptions
VarMask	E_Assign	Assignment (*Var. Write*)
	E_Deref	De-reference (*Var. Read*)
GenrMask	E_Ecall	Call of operation
	E_Eresum	Resumption of expression
	E_Efail	Failure from expression
	E_Erem	Removal of a suspended generator
	E_Esusp	Suspension from alternation
FuncMask	E_Fcall	Function call
	E_Fresum	Function resumption
	E_Ffail	Function failure
	E_Fret	Function return
	E_Fsusp	Function suspension
ProcMask	E_Pcall	Procedure call
	E_Presum	Procedure resumption
	E_Pfail	Procedure failure
	E_Pret	Procedure return
	E_Psusp	Procedure suspension

- **Procedure Call**: Entry to a user-defined procedure. It is triggered for every procedure call; in this context, a procedure is any function, method or procedure written by the software developer. The event codes are *E_Pcall* and *E_Presum*. Unicon procedures do not always leave via a *return* statement that causes the callee to return to its caller;

a procedure may suspend and save its state, which then can be resumed at a later time.

- **Procedure Return**: Statements representing the return to the caller from the callee of the user-defined procedure. The monitored events are *E_Pfail*, *E_Pret*, and *E_Psusp*.
- **Function Call**: Statements that represent a call for any of the built-in functions in the language runtime system. It is triggered for every function call that the software developer uses. The used events are *E_Fcall* and *E_Fresum*.
- **Function Return**: Statements representing the return to the caller from the called built-in function. The monitored events are *E_Ffail*, *E_Fret*, and *E_Fsusp*.
- **Generator Expression Environment and Operations**: This subcategory covers one of the unique features of the language, which is the support for generator and goal-directed evaluation in expressions. It covers events such as *E_Ecall*, *E_Eresum*, *E_Efail*, *E_Erem*, and *E_Esusp*.
- **Variables**: This major category represents the events of dealing with different variables used in the program source code. It includes subcategories such as:
  - **Variable Write**: This refers to statements that assign values to variables. It is triggered for every variable written or assigned. The used event is *E_Assign*.
  - **Variable Read**: This refers to statements that use (access or read) variables' values. It is triggered for every variable's read. The used event is *E_Deref*.

4.3.5. Code Location Events

Software source code is structured in lines and files. Test engineers can experiment with different runtime events that reflect the structure of the source code. Therefore, information about the source code can help structure the execution trace into tokens (or words) that can reflect the actual structure in the source file. For example, runtime events such as *E_Line* and *E_Loc* can provide insights about the executed line and column numbers within the code coverage of the test case. Other events can be reported from syntactic structures, including loops and conditional statements such as *E_Syntax*. AbstractTrace utilizes the *E_Line* event to break the execution trace into tokens (sub-strings); this event is encoded in white spaces inside the execution trace.

5. Experimentation Environment

Dynamic analysis techniques for software systems can provide valuable information that can help various software engineering activities, including software maintenance, performance analysis, and testing. The runtime information enabling such analysis can be obtained by various means; for example, runtime information can be captured at various levels, such as the business logic, the system level, or the code level. Execution traces can contain different levels of information, depending on the purpose of the trace, the mechanism, and the tool or set of tools involved in obtaining the trace.

This paper argues that execution traces can improve the software testing process. We support our arguments using AbstractTrace, which provides three levels of execution traces. Additionally, we highlight the challenges of software testing and the utilization of execution traces to automate the process of identifying the similarities in code coverage between various test cases within a test suite [25]. This paper experiments with execution traces obtained from monitoring facilities implemented in a research programming language called Unicon [17], which facilitates experimentation and provides a proof of concept for our model of utilizing execution traces to classify, rank, and identify the similarities between various test cases.

5.1. Unicon Language

Unicon [19,26] is an object-oriented dialect of Icon [27], a very high-level programming language with dynamic and polymorphic structure types, generators, and goal-directed evaluation. The main feature of the Unicon language relevant to this paper is an execution monitoring framework called Alamo [18].

The proposed approach is general and applicable during any software testing process. The only requirement is the ability to monitor various execution events in the program under testing. The research in this paper does not require live monitoring at runtime; the availability of postmortem log files is sufficient to complete the tracing and analysis of the test suite after execution.

5.2. Monitoring Framework

In this research, we use the Alamo monitoring framework [28–30] to monitor the execution of the running program. Alamo is a lightweight monitoring architecture originally developed to support program visualization and subsequently shown to be applicable to other dynamic analysis tasks. Alamo provides the Unicon virtual machine with monitoring facilities and the capability for a program to load another program and execute it in a controlled environment. The Alamo architecture is based on a thread model of execution monitoring, where a monitor program and the monitored program are in separate threads in a shared address space. Unicon's threads are called co-expressions. A co-expression is a synchronous thread inside the virtual machine. Evaluating a co-expression requires both an interpreter stack and a C stack separate from the main program's stacks. Alamo extended the Unicon co-expression facility with the ability to load a program and set it up with its code, static data, stack, and heap without linking symbols into the current program. Alamo's execution model minimizes intrusion on the monitored program space, which is ideal for the collection of execution traces of test cases, classical source-level debugging, and program execution visualization tools. Switching between co-expressions is done through a small piece of assembler code that performs a lightweight context switch. The program's state is saved, and the control is transferred to the other program without the operating system's involvement. Because they are synchronous, co-expression switches are much faster than typical thread switches, such as those provided by the *pthreads* library.

5.3. Support for Other Languages

Different monitoring and instrumentation frameworks can support other programming languages. Experimenting with the Unicon programming language does not limit the approach's applicability. Execution traces for other languages can be achieved by different techniques and tools, most of which can be related to the running platform and the used programming language [31]. For example, *DTrace* is a common tracing tool that provides a system-wide tracing capability [32]. Other mainstream programming languages such as *Java*, *Python*, and C provide their tracing tools, frameworks, or packages [33–37]. Additionally, for other researchers to be able to use our approach and utilize our findings and methods, all they need is an instrumentation tool. Other researchers in the field have used these tools. For example, using our approach in Java can be achieved using different tools. In particular, Permata, A. et al. [38] presented an advanced instrumentation technique for Java applications. Mastrangelo, L., and Hauswirth, M. [39] presented JNIF, which is a Java native instrumentation framework. Binder, W. et al. [40] presented Advanced Java bytecode instrumentation.

6. Case Studies

The following two case studies support our methodology and approach. A dataset of execution traces is built for every test suite. Analyzing these datasets helps with understanding their corresponding test cases. For example, the clustering of execution traces can be based on clustering the runtime events gathered from different test cases during the testing process; mapping these clustered events into their test cases can represent the clustering of these traces and the clustering of these test cases based on the similarity with which they execute the same or similar code structures. In other words, the similarities in the sequence of events and event sequence patterns can help cluster execution traces and reflect these cluster traces on the clustered test cases in the test suite.

6.1. Case Study #1: Runtime Behavior and Event Classification

Our methodology employs execution traces to classify programs and their test cases into four categories. This categorization helps test engineers and software developers during various activities of the software development life cycle, including the debugging process. This leads to identifying more of the potential failures by achieving a better testing solution. The approach is divided into four major steps.

First, the sequence of execution traces are assigned into major categories that help the software developer identify various patterns within the source code of the system and its runtime behavior. This leads to identifying, focusing, and prioritizing the testing efforts and resources toward one of these major categories over the others. However, this categorization can be achieved by various means. This paper builds a statistical model that assists with the systematic classification of the test-case strings and, eventually, all programs or software systems into these proposed major classes.

Behavior Classification

Classifying the execution behavior of the running program (during a test case) is achieved using the captured execution trace. A statistical model is used to classify each test case, classify a set of test cases (*test suite*), and eventually classify the complete system or software. The four major classes are:

Class 1: *Resources and Allocations*: In this category, the program is spending a considerable amount of work preparing and allocating resources to the system. These resources are not limited to the dynamic memory allocations frequently needed for processing various requirements. It can be expanded to include all the resources needed to execute the test case or the set of test cases. It may consist of other resources besides the dynamic memory allocations, such as files, network connections, threads, etc. However, the developer can often optimize these resources, which may lead to better software. However, sometimes, most of these resources can be allocated to serve the various dynamic data structures needed to complete the processing of some requirements, leading to the second category.

Class 2: *Data-Structure Operations* is the category where programs spend considerable time processing various dynamic data structures. It differs from the category in *Class 1* above, in that it is not concerned with the allocation itself but with the various data structures used and how frequently they are used. It is more about referencing and managing these data structures that have already been allocated. This major category helps test engineers figure out and focus their testing efforts and resources on the test cases that use more of these data structures. For example, in stress testing, engineers may try to generate test cases that abuse the more expensive structures and measure various nonfunctional requirements in extraordinary situations.

Class 3: *String Processing and Operations* is the text- and string-processing category. It is one of the common techniques used by programmers and software developers to achieve their goals of functional and non-functional requirements. Therefore, this category is designed specifically to address this particular domain. It will help developers and testers identify the test cases and, maybe, eventually, the systems that can be identified as text- and string-processing cases or applications. However, it is very common for various reasons that the developer may need to search for a specific text or sub-string inside another one or, even more so, identify general or specific patterns inside a given text. Therefore, it can be helpful for software testers to identify these cases and evaluate whether their test suite is focused enough on this particular issue needed by the application or system.

Class 4: *General Evaluation* is the category that incorporates all of the program's activities, a specific test case, or a set of test cases. Suppose we exclude the allocation of resources, the processing of various data structures, and the frequently needed test processing and evaluation. In that case, we end up with the remaining operation that can be identified as the general evaluation and processing required to accomplish some task or satisfy functional and non-functional requirements. This category deals with variables, expression evaluations, and calls at the low level and utilizes various user-defined and built-in functions and procedures, libraries, and operators. Identifying the program or the set of test cases in this category would help the test engineer design better test cases and maybe direct resources and efforts into the most-needed places based on time, budgets, and available resources.

This execution trace shows three levels of execution trace to explore. At the top level, there are four major classes with a total of 17 different source-code-level events represented in each sub-class. See Figure 5, in which the distribution of events is somehow uniform between the subclasses. The second (or middle) level of trace provides additional insights into the subcategories or types of events included in each of the four major categories described in the top level; see Figure 6. However, regardless of the tracing level (or the level of detail), the low runtime events divide the test case's runtime behavior into four major classes, each with 17 different runtime events, combined for a total of 68 different kinds of source-code-level events. These runtime events are shown in Tables 3–6.

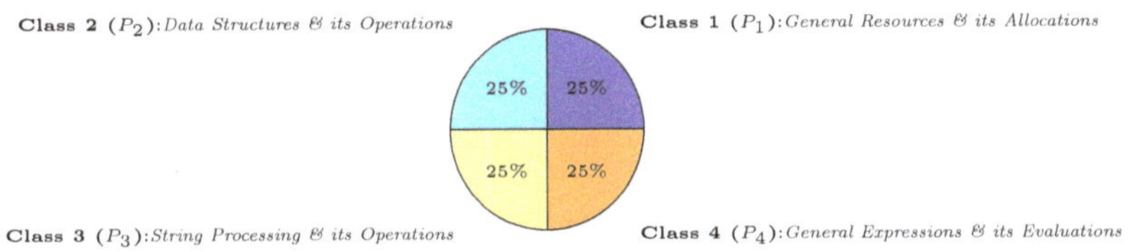

Figure 5. Runtime event classifications. Each category includes 25% of the total number of events that can be captured.

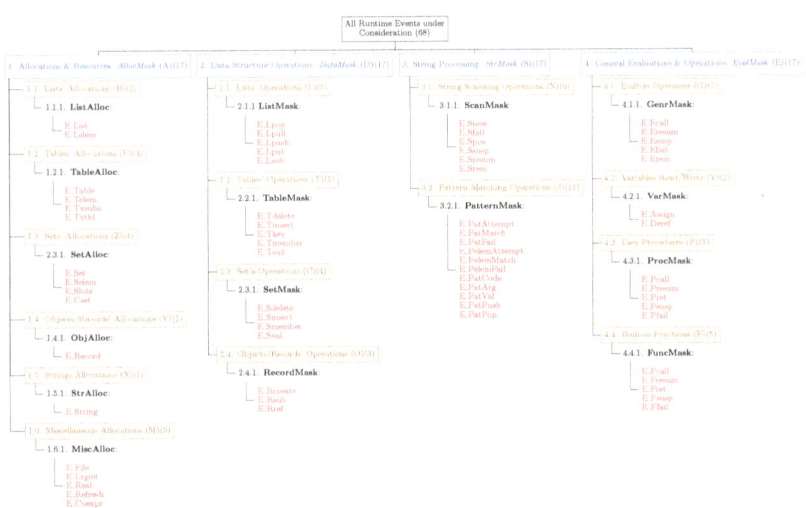

Figure 6. The multilevel runtime events' tree of execution behavior classes. At the top, the blue rectangles present the four top levels ($Level_1$). The second level in the tree, presented in brown rectangles, shows the derived sub-classes of event types that can be captured during the second level ($Level_2$) of the execution trace. Finally, the names presented in red show the names of the actual events ($Level_3$) fired by the actual program under test during its execution trace.

6.2. Case Study #2: Code Coverage and Test-Case Similarity

Our base case of experimentation is to consider one program unit and test this unit to establish the base case of the proposed approach. Figure 7a shows the sample program unit used during this base case of the experiment. Figure 7b shows the graph-based representation of the code presented in Figure 7a. Our experimentation starts with the basic case in which one program is tested with a set of four cases—see Equation (6)—each of which is executing a specific test path presented in Equation (7). These test paths are traced based on the three levels of execution traces defined in this paper. The four test cases are T_1, T_2, T_3, and T_4, and the corresponding set of test paths are P_1, P_2, P_3, and P_4, respectively. A program execution trace is used for each test case; see Figure 11.

```
procedure computeStats(List)
  length := *List

  if length > 0 then{
      sum := 0
      every i := 1 to length do
          sum +:= List[i]

      if length%2 ~= 0 then # Odd Length
          med  := List[(length+1)/2]
      else                   # Even Length
          med  := image(List[length/2])||","||
                  image(List[length/2+1])

      mean := sum/length

      varsum := 0
      every i := 1 to length do
          varsum +:= ((List[i]-mean)*(List[i]-mean))

      var := varsum / length
      sd  := sqrt(var)

      write("length:              ", length)
      write("mean:                ", mean)
      write("median:              ", med)
      write("variance:            ", var)
      write("standard deviation:  ", sd)
  }
  else
      write("Nothing to compute")
end
```

(**a**) Code of the computeStats function

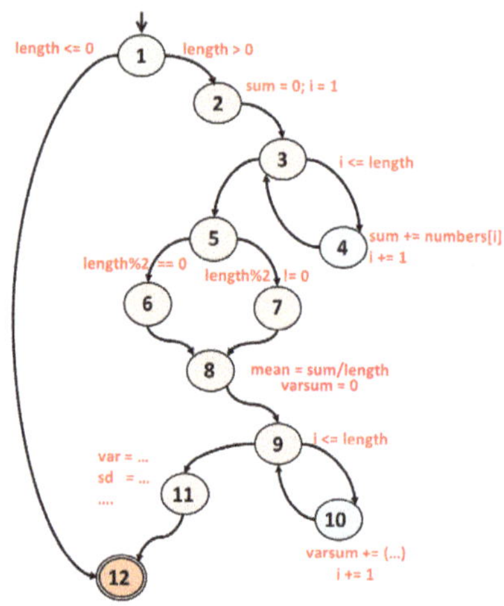

(**b**) CFG of the computeStats function

Figure 7. An example of the *computeStats*() method that takes a list and calculates a set of statistical variables. The Sample function is used to generate a Control-Flow Graph (CFG) representation to demonstrate the use of execution traces for software testing based on graph coverage. Nodes are numbered to indicate different code blocks, while the edges are annotated with their respective conditions.

$$
\begin{aligned}
&T_0 : List = [\ ] \\
&T_1 : List = [10] \\
&T_2 : List = [10, 20] \\
&T_3 : List = [10, 20, 30] \\
&T_4 : List = [10, 20, 30, 40]
\end{aligned}
\tag{6}
$$

$$
\begin{aligned}
&P_0 = [1, 12] \\
&P_1 : [1,2,\ \ 3,4,3,\ \ 5,7,8,\ \ 9,10,9,\ \ 11,12] \\
&P_2 : [1,2,\ \ 3,4,3,4,3,\ \ 5,6,8,\ \ 9,10,9,10,9,\ \ 11,12] \\
&P_3 : [1,2,\ \ 3,4,3,4,3,4,3,\ \ 5,7,8,\ \ 9,10,9,10,9,10,9,\ \ 11,12] \\
&P_4 : [1,2,\ \ 3,4,3,4,3,4,3,4,3,\ \ 5,6,8,\ \ 9,10,9,10,9,10,9,10,9,\ \ 11,12]
\end{aligned}
\tag{7}
$$

- T_1 executes the path P_1 in which the case of the empty list is used, where no calculations can be applied or found on the elements of the list.
- T_2 executes the case when one element is in the list and navigating the test path P_2, where the body of the two loops in the source code is entered once each. It is also good to evaluate this test case, as it covers a new set of statements.

- T_3 executes the case where the list size is more than one and the body of each loop is entered three times. The executed test path P_3 does not add much to the statement coverage included in T_2 and its test path P_2. Thus, the white-box analysis can show that there is a good percentage of redundancy and test-case similarity in terms of statement coverage between the two test cases T_2 and T_3 and their corresponding test paths P_2 and P_3, respectively. **Our evaluation hypothesis is to evaluate and determine if any of the execution-trace similarity measures undertaken will allow us to highlight this fact automatically**. Therefore, to some extent, there is an element of relief for the quality engineer, providing them with the confidence to remove or ignore the use of one of these two test cases due to the overlap between their set of covered program statements.
- T_4 executes the case where the length of the list is more than one, in a situation very similar to the test case presented in T_3, except that this new test case adds to the set of covered statements the scenario where the length of the list is even rather than odd, which leads to having two medians instead of one median in the case of an even number of items in the list. Therefore, this test case has a good similarity with the previous test cases T_2 and T_3, except for having to enter each of the loops four times and, most importantly, covering **node 6** in the abstract graph representation presented in Figure 7b instead of **node 7**, which is covered in the previous two test cases (T_2 and T_3). Therefore, the similarities between this test case and the last two are very high, and only one statement was added to the set of statements covered previously. However, this test case might need to be ranked second for its importance behind test cases 1 and 2.

In this paper, we have evaluated three types of string similarities: (1) edit-based distance; (2) token-based algorithms; and (3) sequence-based algorithms. Each algorithm provides a different perspective on string similarity. That motivated us to evaluate three different algorithms from each category. In particular, edit-based distance measures how dissimilar two strings are by counting the minimum number of operations required to transform one string into the other. These operations typically include insertions, deletions, and substitutions of characters. Token-based algorithms measure the similarity between sets of tokens (words, phrases, or other meaningful units) rather than individual characters. They are particularly useful in text analysis, information retrieval, and clustering, as they compare the presence and frequency of tokens to determine how similar two sets of data are. Sequence-based algorithms measure the similarity between sequences by identifying common subsequences or substrings [41,42]. The Figures 8–10 each show the results from three different algorithms in that subcategory.

Figure 8 shows the results of three of the edit-based algorithms that are used on the five test cases. The figure shows that across all test cases (T_1, T_2, T_3, T_4), the Levenshtein Algorithm [43] seems to consistently perform well. The heat maps distinguished the different test cases in all three levels. Figure 9 shows the results of three of the token-based algorithms that are used in the five test cases. The figure shows that across all test cases (T_1, T_2, T_3, T_4), the Jaccard Algorithm [44] seems to perform well consistently. The heat maps distinguished the different test cases in all three levels. Figure 10 shows the results of three sequence-based algorithms used on the five test cases. The figure shows that across all test cases (T_1, T_2, T_3, T_4), the Ratcliff–Obershelp Algorithm (*Ratcliff–Obershelp pattern recognition*) [45] seems to perform well consistently. The heat maps distinguished the different test cases in all three levels.

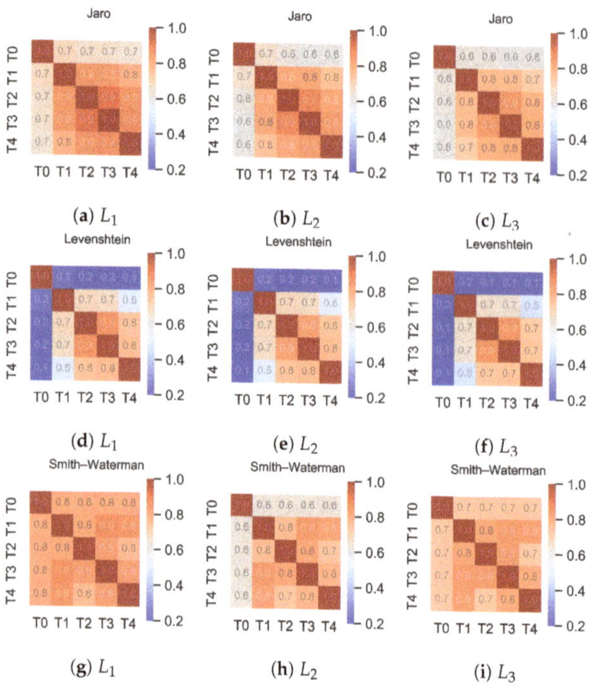

Figure 8. Evaluates three edit-based algorithms: (1) Jaro, (2) Levenshtein, and (3) Smith–Waterman.

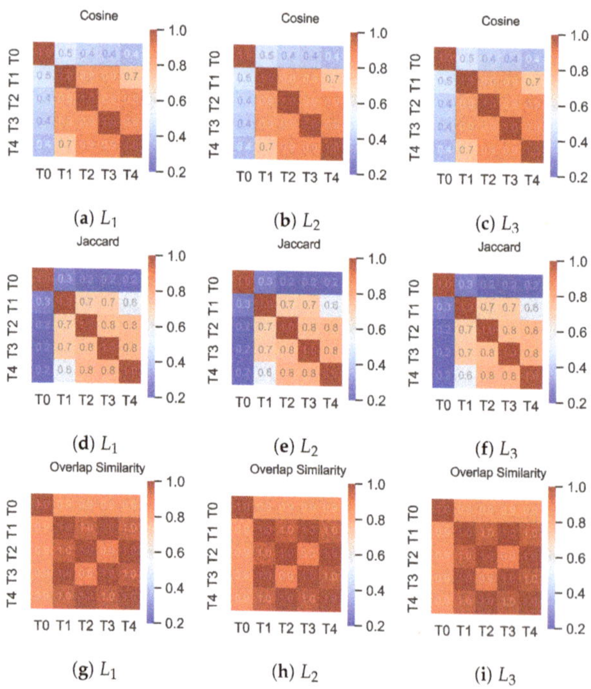

Figure 9. Evaluates three token-based algorithms: (1) Cosine, (2) Jaccard, and (3) Overlap Similarity.

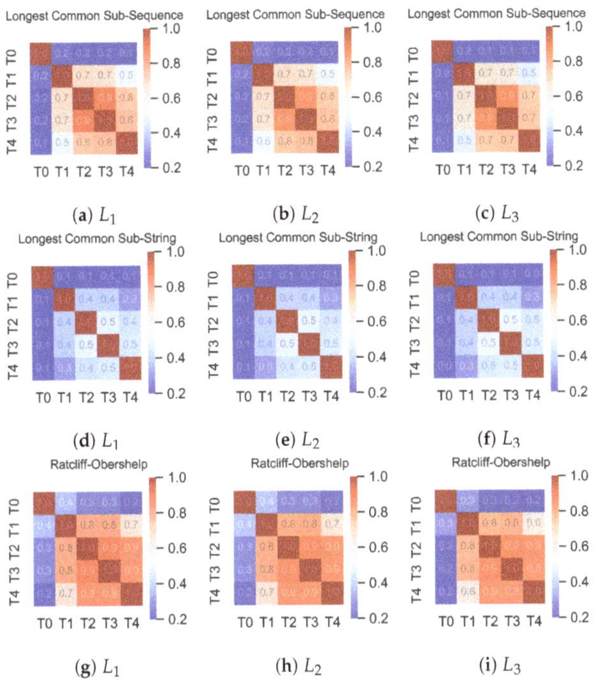

(a) L_1 (b) L_2 (c) L_3 (d) L_1 (e) L_2 (f) L_3 (g) L_1 (h) L_2 (i) L_3

Figure 10. Evaluates three sequence-based algorithms: (1) Longest Common Sub-Sequence, (2) Longest Common Sub-String, and (3) Ratcliff–Obershelp.

7. Discussions

Figure 11 illustrates a sample execution trace, comparing results across three trace levels. The figure's three sections highlight the differences between these levels during a sample run for the same sample function. Similar events are color-coded consistently across all three levels of the trace for the same test case from the same program under test. Figure 11a shows the execution trace from *level 1* for two test cases $computeStats(list = [10])$ and $computeStats(list = [10, 20])$. Figure 11b shows the execution trace from *level 2* for the same two test cases presented in Figure 11a. Figure 11c shows the execution trace from *level 3* for the first test case where $list = [10]$.

In summary, software testing is part of the development activities of every software project [46]. The software testing process aims to evaluate the system to determine whether it meets the specified functional and non-functional requirements. Often, it identifies failures, followed by a debugging process to locate and fix their root causes. The objective is to ensure the system is error-free before it is released and provide users with a high-quality software system [47]. However, to discover as many failures as possible, it is essential to evaluate a set of test cases that can ensure the coverage of all possible usage scenarios. On the other hand, running all potential test cases is infeasible; even running "as many test cases as possible" is time-consuming and imposes a high cost on the development budget and complicates the development process [48].

AbstractTrace presented in this paper utilizes three levels of execution trace; each level utilizes different alphabets for the trace string. Equation 8 shows that the initial alphabet consists of four letters, each encoding one of the major classes of execution events. *Level 2* shows more details about each of the four classes in *level 1*. Finally, *level 3* shows the machine-level events captured from the runtime system, with no classification other than the event type.

$$\sum_{1} = \{A, D, S, E\} \tag{8}$$

$$\sum_{2} = \{H, U, Z, Y, X, M, \quad L, T, C, O, \quad N, J, \quad G, V, P, F\} \tag{9}$$

$$\sum_{3} = AllocMask \cup StructMask \cup StrMask \cup EvalMask \cup \{E\_Line\} \tag{10}$$

```
>computeStats(list=[10])
E  EEE  EE E E EE EEDEEEEE  E EEDEE  EEE E EE EEDEEEEDEEEEEE  EEE
EEEEEE EEEEE EEEEE EEEEE EEEEE EEEEE  E  EE

>computeStats(list=[10 20])
E  EEE  EE E E EE EEDEEEE E EEDEEEEE  E  EEDEEEEAAAEA EEDEEEEAAAE
AE  EEE E EE EEDEEEEDEEEEE E EEDEEEEDEEEEEE  EEE EEEEEE EEEEE
EEEEE EEEEE EEEEE EEEEE  E  EE
```

(**a**)

```
>computeStats(list=[10])
P  VVP  VV V V VV VVLVVVGG  V VVLVV  VVV V VV VVLVVVVLVVVVGG  VVV
VVGFFV VVGFF VVGFF VVGFF VVGFF VVGFF  P  PG

>computeStats(list=[10 20])
P  VVP  VV V V VV VVLVVVG V VVLVVVGG  V  VVLVVGFXXXFX VVLVVGFXXXF
XV  VVV V VV VVLVVVVLVVVVG V VVLVVVVLVVVVGG  VVV VVGFFV VVGFF
VVGFF VVGFF VVGFF VVGFF  P  PG
```

(**b**)

```
>computeStats(list=[10])
E_Pcall  E_DerefE_DerefE_Pcall  E_DerefE_Assign E_Deref E_Assign
E_DerefE_Assign E_DerefE_DerefE_LsubE_DerefE_DerefE_AssignE_EfailE_Efail
E_Deref E_DerefE_DerefE_LsubE_DerefE_Assign  E_DerefE_DerefE_Assign
E_Assign E_DerefE_Assign
E_DerefE_DerefE_LsubE_DerefE_DerefE_DerefE_DerefE_LsubE_DerefE_DerefE_Deref
E_AssignE_EfailE_Efail  E_DerefE_DerefE_Assign
E_DerefE_DerefE_EcallE_FcallE_FretE_Assign
E_DerefE_DerefE_EcallE_FcallE_Fret E_DerefE_DerefE_EcallE_FcallE_Fret
E_DerefE_DerefE_EcallE_FcallE_Fret E_DerefE_DerefE_EcallE_FcallE_Fret
E_DerefE_DerefE_EcallE_FcallE_Fret  E_Pfail  E_PretE_Efail
```

(**c**)

Figure 11. Presents three levels of execution traces. Part (**a**) shows the top-level ($level_1$) execution trace for two sample test cases. Part (**b**) shows two samples of $level_2$ execution traces for the two related unit test cases presented in part (**a**). Part (**c**) shows one sample of $level_3$ execution trace for the first unit test cases presented in parts (**a**,**b**). Samples of similar components across the three levels of traces are highlighted with the same rectangle color to emphasize the differences between these levels.

8. Related Work

Software bugs have a costly impact on the development process [49], requiring time and resources to debug [50]. Thus, software testing is an essential part of the SDLC of any software system. Software testing improves the quality of the software and reduces the risk induced by failures, but does not ensure software correctness [51]. A good testing process should allow engineers to discover errors during an early stage of the development process [52]. Nevertheless, testing can show the presence of errors, not their absence [53]. A good test suite includes a set of test cases executed to verify specific functional and/or non-functional requirements in the software application, and it should be designed based on specific testing criteria [54]. However, any increase in test cases will increase testing time, cost, and needed efforts [55]. A successful run for all test cases in the test suite is required before any new release, whether the changes were fixing an error, modifying functionality, or adding a new feature.

Moreover, regression testing ensures that the modified software is still working. It often employs the entire or part of an existing test suite. Usually, it is re-executed after any code change to confirm that existing functionalities are still working as intended [48,56]. Thus, regression testing can validate and evaluate whether a recent modification has introduced side effects on the existing functionalities. During the regression testing of a system, it is often not feasible, due to time constraints, to evaluate all test cases [57].

New test cases must be added to the existing test suite whenever a modification is conducted in the system's source code. Adding new test cases is needed to check the complete system; it is often proceeded by running regression tests on the modified system. It should be used to ensure that new changes in the code do not affect the functionality nor the quality of the system. The system should work well after new modifications, when existing errors are fixed, or when one or more features are changed. It helps developers ensure that the most recent modifications impose no unexpected side effects. Ngah et al. [58] indicated that regression testing should be considered after a performance optimization is applied, a new system function is added, and even if a system configuration is changed or introduced.

Furthermore, Yoo et al. [59] discussed that regression testing requires an immediate response due to its importance, which lies in detecting errors in an early stage of the system development and modification. It also reduces the cost and effort involved in maintaining the system. Onoma et al. [60] mentioned that regression testing requires a long examination time to discover new features, ensure improvement, and increase quality. Alian et al. [61] pointed out that the testing process helps examine the appropriate software, but it is difficult to test all cases of the system due to the large size of a test suite. They have shown that testing impacts the cost and time of development, and they have emphasized how it is essential to reduce the test cases to minimize the risk of failures and defects in the released system. Additionally, Alian et al. discussed that many regression test-case reduction techniques are classified based on coverage, requirement, genetic algorithms, slicing, hybrid algorithms, fuzzy logic, greedy algorithms, and clustering techniques [61].

On the other hand, runtime execution traces are used in different software systems for debugging [62–64], visualization, program comprehension, reverse engineering, and understanding the behavior of parallel and distributed applications [65]. Additionally, employing execution traces in software testing shows a promising future [66]. This project is intended to facilitate the execution traces in regression testing and evaluate how this would help the test engineer manage, select, and prioritize the set of test cases.

Many researchers agree that removing the redundant and similar test cases is critical in reducing the time needed for executing and validating the test suite [67–70]; it can dramatically reduce the cost of testing [71]. Different techniques have been used to reduce the number of test cases needed. For example, some researchers have employed data-mining techniques such as K-Nearest Neighbors (KNN) [72], Naïve-based [73], K-mean [74], Dynamic Domain Reduction (DDR) [75], and more. Furthermore, recently, researchers have been employing machine learning and deep learning techniques as an approach to tackling complex problems faced by software developers, including software testing. For example, Yuan et al. [76] emphasized that in deep learning, the computer learns to do business and solve problems, learn from experience, and extract the features for large and complex problems. Zhou et al. [77] showed that using deep learning algorithms in many applications could positively impact the testing process and select a subset of test cases to represent the all-test cases for a software system. This study proved that deep learning algorithms have efficiently reduced test cases to 4.6%. Durelli et al. [78] reviewed the use of machine learning (ML) applications in automating and streamlining software testing. The authors analyzed 48 primary studies and categorized them based on study type, testing activity, and ML algorithms. The findings reveal that ML is predominantly applied in test case generation, refinement, and evaluation, as well as in test oracle construction and cost prediction for testing activities. The study also identifies several promising avenues for future research.

However, this paper uses execution traces associated with test cases. We applied machine learning techniques to these execution traces obtained from the dynamic analysis and the execution of different test cases during previous stages. In particular, we used the execution trace (sequence of execution events) to determine the similarity measures and help identify the similarities between different test cases, including identifying redundant and highly similar test cases. AbstractTrace facilitates the execution traces obtained from the test cases; each test case should be associated with its string representation of the execution trace. A dataset of these traces is maintained for further analysis using various techniques, including string-similarity algorithms. AbstractTrace promises to be a valuable addition to the software testing toolkit, enhancing quality and efficiency.

9. Conclusions

Software testing often involves many test cases (*test suites*) that require effort and time to manage and validate. A test suite can easily include redundant and overlapping test cases that can be reduced and eliminated without affecting the overall software quality. Optimizing a *bloated test suite* by identifying, removing, and reducing redundant or non-relevant test cases without compromising the software quality is challenging. Thus, finding these redundant and highly similar test cases is not an easy task considering (1) the number of test cases included in a test site, (2) the dynamic behavior of the execution program, and (3) the high associations between the input value (test case input) and its runtime behaviors concerning code coverage [79,80].

It is clear that analyzing and clustering these traces can result in clustering their test cases. In this study, we introduced the concept of AbstractTrace and its associated execution trace. The presented approach aims at enhancing software testing processes. Our findings reveal several key insights: (1) **Similarity Measures**: AbstractTrace enables test engineers to quantify the similarity between test cases based on code structure and behavior, providing a new view of the test suite. (2) **Ranking and Grouping**: Test engineers can rank test cases based on similarity scores. This ranking informs decisions about test-case execution priority. High-similarity test cases can be grouped, while less similar ones receive individual attention. (3) **Code-Coverage Alignment**: AbstractTrace bridges the gap between similarity and code coverage. It ensures that test cases are executed based on their impact on code structure. No more blind selection; each test case contributes meaningfully to coverage. (4) **Priority-Based Execution**: Our proposed prioritization technique encourages a strategic approach. High-priority test cases take center stage, while common or overlapping cases wait their turn. Finally, (5) **Test-Case Relationships**: AbstractTrace illuminates relationships within the suite beyond individual test cases. It unveils hidden connections, allowing test engineers to identify patterns and dependencies. In summary, AbstractTrace equips test engineers with powerful tools for optimizing testing efforts. By emphasizing differences, aligning with code coverage, and prioritizing strategically, we pave the way for more efficient and effective software validation.

However, this research paper is limited to proving the concept with simple case studies. Future research will be focused on evaluating this approach's practical implementation in software development and testing. Additionally, we plan to evaluate different machine learning models and assess their use during the software testing process.

Author Contributions: Conceptualization, Z.A.A.-S.; Methodology, Z.A.A.-S.; Validation, Z.A.A.-S.; Investigation, Z.A.A.-S.; Resources, C.L.J.; Supervision, C.L.J. All authors have read and agreed to the published version of the manuscript.

Funding: This research was funded by Jordan University of Science and Technology (JUST), Irbid 22110, Jordan, as part of the corresponding author's sabbatical leave.

Institutional Review Board Statement: Not applicable.

Informed Consent Statement: The study did not involve humans.

Data Availability Statement: The original contributions presented in the study are included in the article, further inquiries can be directed to the corresponding author.

Acknowledgments: The authors thank the Department of Software Engineering at Jordan University of Science and Technology for supporting the sabbatical leave. This opportunity allowed the first author, Ziad Al-Sharif, to spend his sabbatical leave as a visiting scholar, collaborating with the second author, Clinton Jeffery, Computer Science and Engineering Department at the New Mexico Institute of Mining and Technology (NMT).

Conflicts of Interest: The authors declare no conflict of interest.

References

1. Spillner, A.; Linz, T. *Software Testing Foundations: A Study Guide for the Certified Tester Exam-Foundation Level-ISTQB® Compliant*; Dpunkt Verlag: Heidelberg, Germany, 2021.
2. Birchler, C.; Khatiri, S.; Derakhshanfar, P.; Panichella, S.; Panichella, A. Single and multi-objective test cases prioritization for self-driving cars in virtual environments. *ACM Trans. Softw. Eng. Methodol.* **2023**, *32*, 1–30. [CrossRef]
3. Kadam, A.K.; Krishna, K.H.; Varshney, N.; Deepak, A.; Pokhariya, H.S.; Hegde, S.K.; Patil, V.H. Design of Software Reliability Growth Model for Improving Accuracy in the Software Development Life Cycle (SDLC). *Int. J. Intell. Syst. Appl. Eng.* **2024**, *12*, 38–50.
4. Tsai, B.Y.; Stobart, S.; Parrington, N.; Thompson, B. Iterative design and testing within the software development life cycle. *Softw. Qual. J.* **1997**, *6*, 295–310. [CrossRef]
5. Cabral, G.G.; Minku, L.L. Towards reliable online just-in-time software defect prediction. *IEEE Trans. Softw. Eng.* **2022**, *49*, 1342–1358. [CrossRef]
6. Buckley, I.A.; Fernandez, E.B. Dependability Patterns: A Survey. *Computers* **2023**, *12*, 214. [CrossRef]
7. Mukherjee, R.; Patnaik, K.S. A survey on different approaches for software test case prioritization. *J. King Saud-Univ.-Comput. Inf. Sci.* **2021**, *33*, 1041–1054. [CrossRef]
8. Chi, J.; Qu, Y.; Zheng, Q.; Yang, Z.; Jin, W.; Cui, D.; Liu, T. Relation-based test case prioritization for regression testing. *J. Syst. Softw.* **2020**, *163*, 110539. [CrossRef]
9. Kong, S.; Lu, M.; Li, L.; Gao, L. Runtime Monitoring of Software Execution Trace: Method and Tools. *IEEE Access* **2020**, *8*, 114020–114036. [CrossRef]
10. Al-Sharif, Z.A.; Abdalrahman, W.F.; Jeffery, C.L. Encoding Test Cases using Execution Traces. In Proceedings of the 2021 12th International Conference on Information and Communication Systems (ICICS), Valencia, Spain, 24–26 May 2021; pp. 239–244.
11. Pan, R.; Bagherzadeh, M.; Ghaleb, T.A.; Briand, L. Test case selection and prioritization using machine learning: A systematic literature review. *Empir. Softw. Eng.* **2022**, *27*, 29. [CrossRef]
12. Almufareh, M.F.; Humayun, M. Improving the Safety and Security of Software Systems by Mediating SAP Verification. *Appl. Sci.* **2023**, *13*, 647. [CrossRef]
13. Krichen, M. A survey on formal verification and validation techniques for internet of things. *Appl. Sci.* **2023**, *13*, 8122. [CrossRef]
14. Chen, Z.; Chen, J.; Wang, W.; Zhou, J.; Wang, M.; Chen, X.; Zhou, S.; Wang, J. Exploring better black-Box test case prioritization via log analysis. *ACM Trans. Softw. Eng. Methodol.* **2023**, *32*, 1–32. [CrossRef]
15. Altiero, F.; Corazza, A.; Di Martino, S.; Peron, A.; Libero Lucio Starace, L. Regression test prioritization leveraging source code similarity with tree kernels. *J. Softw. Evol. Process* **2024**, *36*, e2653. [CrossRef]
16. Jeffery, C.L. The Alamo execution monitor architecture. *Electron. Notes Theor. Comput. Sci.* **2000**, *30*, 198–214. [CrossRef]
17. Jeffery, C.; Mohamed, S.; Al Gharaibeh, J.; Pereda, R.; Parlett, R. *Programming with Unicon*; GNU Free Documentation License. 2018. Available online: http://unicon.org/book/ub.pdf (accessed on 19 November 2024).
18. Jeffery, C.L. *Program Monitoring and Visualization: An Exploratory Approach*; Springer Science & Business Media: New York, NY, USA, 2012.
19. Jeffery, C.L. Unicon: An Extended Dialect of Icon. 2024. Available online: http://unicon.org/ (accessed on 26 February 2024).
20. Rahmani, A.; Min, J.L.; Maspupah, A. An evaluation of code coverage adequacy in automatic testing using control flow graph visualization. In Proceedings of the 2020 IEEE 10th Symposium on Computer Applications & Industrial Electronics (ISCAIE), Penang, Malaysia, 18–19 April 2020; pp. 239–244.
21. Hemmati, H. How effective are code coverage criteria? In Proceedings of the 2015 IEEE International Conference on Software Quality, Reliability and Security, Vancouver, BC, Canada, 3–5 August 2015; pp. 151–156.
22. Jung, P.; Kang, S.; Lee, J. Reducing redundant test executions in software product line testing—A case study. *Electronics* **2022**, *11*, 1165. [CrossRef]
23. Ibrahim, R.; Ahmed, M.; Nayak, R.; Jamel, S. Reducing redundancy of test cases generation using code smell detection and refactoring. *J. King Saud Univ.-Comput. Inf. Sci.* **2020**, *32*, 367–374. [CrossRef]
24. Wu, A.; Wang, Y.; Shu, X.; Moritz, D.; Cui, W.; Zhang, H.; Zhang, D.; Qu, H. Ai4vis: Survey on artificial intelligence approaches for data visualization. *IEEE Trans. Vis. Comput. Graph.* **2021**, *28*, 9495259. [CrossRef]

25. Alawneh, L.; Hamou-Lhadj, A. Execution traces: A new domain that requires the creation of a standard metamodel. In Proceedings of the Advances in Software Engineering: International Conference on Advanced Software Engineering and Its Applications, ASEA 2009 Held as Part of the Future Generation Information Technology Conference, FGIT 2009, Jeju Island, Republic of Korea, 10–12 December 2009; Proceedings; Springer: Berlin/Heidelberg, Germany, 2009; pp. 253–263.
26. Jeffery, C.L. Goal-directed object-oriented programming in Unicon. In Proceedings of the 2001 ACM Symposium on Applied Computing (SAC '01), Las Vegas, NV, USA, 1 March 2001; pp. 306–308. [CrossRef]
27. Griswold, R.E. The Icon Programming Language. 2024. Available online: https://www2.cs.arizona.edu/icon/ (accessed on 26 February 2024).
28. Jeffery, C.; Auguston, M.; Underwood, S. Towards fully automatic execution monitoring. In Proceedings of the International Workshop on Radical Innovations of Software and Systems Engineering in the Future, Venice, Italy, 7–11 October 2002; Springer: Berlin/Heidelberg, Germany, 2002; pp. 204–218.
29. Auguston, M.; Jeffery, C.; Underwood, S. A framework for automatic debugging. In Proceedings of the Proceedings 17th IEEE International Conference on Automated Software Engineering, Edinburgh, UK, 23–27 September 2002; pp. 217–222.
30. Al-Sharif, Z.; Jeffery, C. An extensible source-level debugger. In Proceedings of the 2009 ACM Symposium on Applied Computing (SAC '09), Honolulu, HI, USA, 8–12 March 2009; pp. 543–544. [CrossRef]
31. Bousse, E.; Mayerhofer, T.; Combemale, B.; Baudry, B. Advanced and efficient execution trace management for executable domain-specific modeling languages. *Softw. Syst. Model.* **2019**, *18*, 385–421. [CrossRef]
32. Chen, C.; Ma, J.; Qi, T.; Cui, B.; Qi, W.; Zhang, Z.; Sun, P. Firmware code instrumentation technology for internet of things-based services. *World Wide Web* **2021**, *24*, 941–954. [CrossRef]
33. Golmohammadi, A.; Zhang, M.; Arcuri, A. NET/C# instrumentation for search-based software testing. *Softw. Qual. J.* **2023**, *31*, 1439–1465.
34. Yue, T.; Zhang, F.; Ning, Z.; Wang, P.; Zhou, X.; Lu, K.; Zhou, L. Armor: Protecting Software Against Hardware Tracing Techniques. *IEEE Trans. Inf. Forensics Secur.* **2024**, *19*, 4247–4262. [CrossRef]
35. Lopes, N.P. Torchy: A Tracing JIT Compiler for Pytorch. In Proceedings of the 32nd ACM SIGPLAN International Conference on Compiler Construction (CC '23), Montréal, QC, Canada, 25–26 February 2023; pp. 98–109. [CrossRef]
36. Pekarek, D.; Mössenböck, H. Trcview: Interactive architecture agnostic execution trace analysis. In Proceedings of the 17th International Conference on Managed Programming Languages and Runtimes (MPLR '20), Virtual, UK, 4–6 November 2020; pp. 89–97. [CrossRef]
37. Shimari, K.; Ishio, T.; Kanda, T.; Ishida, N.; Inoue, K. NOD4J: Near-omniscient debugging tool for Java using size-limited execution trace. *Sci. Comput. Program.* **2021**, *206*, 102630. [CrossRef]
38. Permata, A. Advanced Instrumentation Techniques in Java Applications. *Adv. Intell. Inf. Syst.* **2023**, *8*, 21–48.
39. Mastrangelo, L.; Hauswirth, M. JNIF: Java native instrumentation framework. In Proceedings of the 2014 International Conference on Principles and Practices of Programming on the Java Platform: Virtual Machines, Languages, and Tools (PPPJ '14), Cracow, Poland, 23–26 September 2014; pp. 194–199. [CrossRef]
40. Binder, W.; Hulaas, J.; Moret, P. Advanced Java bytecode instrumentation. In Proceedings of the 5th International Symposium on Principles and Practice of Programming in Java (PPPJ07), Lisboa, Portugal, 5–7 September 2007; pp. 135–144. [CrossRef]
41. Kaminsky, Y.; Pena, E.H.; Naumann, F. Discovering similarity inclusion dependencies. *Proc. ACM Manag. Data* **2023**, *1*, 1–24. [CrossRef]
42. Balani, Z.; Varol, C. Combining Approximate String Matching Algorithms and Term Frequency In The Detection of Plagiarism. *Int. J. Comput. Sci. Secur. (IJCSS)* **2021**, *15*, 97–106.
43. Yujian, L.; Bo, L. A normalized Levenshtein distance metric. *IEEE Trans. Pattern Anal. Mach. Intell.* **2007**, *29*, 1091–1095. [CrossRef]
44. Thada, V.; Jaglan, V. Comparison of jaccard, dice, cosine similarity coefficient to find best fitness value for web retrieved documents using genetic algorithm. *Int. J. Innov. Eng. Technol.* **2013**, *2*, 202–205.
45. Hidayat, W.; Utami, E.; Hartanto, A.D. Effect of Stemming Nazief & Adriani on the Ratcliff/Obershelp algorithm in identifying level of similarity between slang and formal words. In Proceedings of the 2020 3rd International Conference on Information and Communications Technology (ICOIACT), Yogyakarta, Indonesia, 24–25 November 2020; pp. 22–27.
46. Akinsola, J.E.; Ogunbanwo, A.S.; Okesola, O.J.; Odun-Ayo, I.J.; Ayegbusi, F.D.; Adebiyi, A.A. Comparative analysis of Software Development Life Cycle models (SDLC). In *Intelligent Algorithms in Software Engineering. CSOC 2020. Advances in Intelligent Systems and Computing*; Springer: Cham, Switzerland, 2020; Volume 1224, pp. 310–322. [CrossRef]
47. Bierig, R.; Brown, S.; Galván, E.; Timoney, J. *Essentials of Software Testing*; Cambridge University Press: Cambridge, UK, 2021. [CrossRef]
48. Khatibsyarbini, M.; Isa, M.A.; Jawawi, D.N.; Tumeng, R. Test case prioritization approaches in regression testing: A systematic literature review. *Inf. Softw. Technol.* **2018**, *93*, 74–93. [CrossRef]
49. Wong, W.E.; Li, X.; Laplante, P.A. Be more familiar with our enemies and pave the way forward: A review of the roles bugs played in software failures. *J. Syst. Softw.* **2017**, *133*, 68–94. [CrossRef]
50. Lee, J.; Kang, S.; Lee, D. Survey on software testing practices. *IET Softw.* **2012**, *6*, 275–282. [CrossRef]
51. Chen, Y.; Li, P.; Xu, J.; Guo, S.; Zhou, R.; Zhang, Y.; Wei, T.; Lu, L. Savior: Towards bug-driven hybrid testing. In Proceedings of the 2020 IEEE Symposium on Security and Privacy (SP), San Francisco, CA, USA, 18–21 May 2020; pp. 1580–1596.

52. Perera, A.; Turhan, B.; Aleti, A.; Böhme, M. How good does a Defect Predictor need to be to guide Search-Based Software Testing? *arXiv* **2021**, arXiv:2110.02682.
53. Shimari, K.; Ishio, T.; Kanda, T.; Inoue, K. Near-omniscient debugging for java using size-limited execution trace. In Proceedings of the 2019 IEEE International Conference on Software Maintenance and Evolution (ICSME), Cleveland, OH, USA, 29 September–4 October 2019; pp. 398–401.
54. Bertolino, A. Software testing research: Achievements, challenges, dreams. In Proceedings of the Future of Software Engineering (FOSE'07), Minneapolis, MN, USA, 23–25 May 2007; pp. 85–103.
55. Hynninen, T.; Kasurinen, J.; Knutas, A.; Taipale, O. Software testing: Survey of the industry practices. In Proceedings of the 2018 41st International Convention on Information and Communication Technology, Electronics and Microelectronics (MIPRO), Opatija, Croatia, 21–25 May 2018; pp. 1449–1454.
56. Labuschagne, A.; Inozemtseva, L.; Holmes, R. Measuring the cost of regression testing in practice: A study of Java projects using continuous integration. In Proceedings of the Joint Meeting of the European Software Engineering Conference and the ACM SIGSOFT Symposium on the Foundations of Software Engineering (ESEC/FSE'17), Paderborn, Germany, 4–8 September 2017; pp. 821–830. [CrossRef]
57. Ahamed, S. Studying the feasibility and importance of software testing: An Analysis. *arXiv* **2010**, arXiv:1001.4193.
58. Ngah, A.; Munro, M.; Abdallah, M. An overview of regression testing. *J. Telecommun. Electron. Comput. Eng. (JTEC)* **2017**, *9*, 45–49.
59. Yoo, S.; Harman, M. Regression testing minimization, selection and prioritization: A survey. *Softw. Test. Verif. Reliab.* **2012**, *22*, 67–120. [CrossRef]
60. Onoma, A.K.; Tsai, W.T.; Poonawala, M.; Suganuma, H. Regression testing in an industrial environment. *Commun. ACM* **1998**, *41*, 81–86. [CrossRef]
61. Alian, M.; Suleiman, D.; Shaout, A. Test case reduction techniques-survey. *Int. J. Adv. Comput. Sci. Appl.* **2016**, *7*, 264–275. [CrossRef]
62. AL-Sharif, Z.; Jeffery, C. An Agent-Oriented Source-Level Debugger on Top of a Monitoring Framework. In Proceedings of the 2009 Sixth International Conference on Information Technology: New Generations, Las Vegas, NV, USA, 27–29 April 2009; pp. 241–247. [CrossRef]
63. Al-Sharif, Z.A.; Jeffery, C.L.; Said, M.H. Debugging with dynamic temporal assertions. In Proceedings of the 2014 IEEE International Symposium on Software Reliability Engineering Workshops, Naples, Italy, 3–6 November 2014; pp. 257–262.
64. Al-Sharif, Z.; Jeffery, C.L. Language Support for Event-based Debugging. In Proceedings of the 21st International Conference on Software Engineering and Knowledge Engineering (SEKE 2009), Boston, MA, USA, 1–3 July 2009; pp. 392–399.
65. Babaei, M.; Bagherzadeh, M.; Dingel, J. Efficient reordering and replay of execution traces of distributed reactive systems in the context of model-driven development. In Proceedings of the 23rd ACM/IEEE International Conference on Model Driven Engineering Languages and Systems (MODELS '20), Virtual Event, 16–23 October 2020; pp. 285–296. [CrossRef]
66. Utting, M.; Legeard, B.; Dadeau, F.; Tamagnan, F.; Bouquet, F. Identifying and generating missing tests using machine learning on execution traces. In Proceedings of the 2020 IEEE International Conference On Artificial Intelligence Testing (AITest), Oxford, UK, 3–6 August 2020; pp. 83–90.
67. Bajaj, A.; Sangwan, O.P. Test case prioritization using bat algorithm. *Recent Adv. Comput. Sci. Commun. (Former. Recent Patents Comput. Sci.)* **2021**, *14*, 593–598. [CrossRef]
68. Gokilavani, N.; Bharathi, B. Test case prioritization to examine software for fault detection using PCA extraction and K-means clustering with ranking. *Soft Comput.* **2021**, *25*, 5163–5172. [CrossRef]
69. Bajaj, A.; Sangwan, O.P. Discrete and combinatorial gravitational search algorithms for test case prioritization and minimization. *Int. J. Inf. Technol.* **2021**, *13*, 817–823. [CrossRef]
70. Messaoudi, S.; Shin, D.; Panichella, A.; Bianculli, D.; Briand, L.C. Log-based slicing for system-level test cases. In Proceedings of the 30th ACM SIGSOFT International Symposium on Software Testing and Analysis (ISSTA '21), Virtual Event, 11–17 July 2021; pp. 517–528. [CrossRef]
71. Panday, A.; Gupta, M.; Singh, M.K.; Ali, N. Test case redundancy detection and removal using code coverage analysis. *MIT Int. J. Comput. Sci. Inf. Technol.* **2013**, *3*, 6–10.
72. Meçe, E.K.; Paci, H.; Binjaku, K. The application of machine learning in test case prioritization—A review. *Eur. J. Electr. Eng. Comput. Sci.* **2020**, *4*, 1.
73. Saifan, A.A. Test Case Reduction Using Data Mining Classifier Techniques. *J. Softw.* **2016**, *11*, 656–663. [CrossRef]
74. Pandey, A.; Malviya, K. Enhancing test case reduction by k-means algorithm and elbow method. *Int. J. Comput. Sci. Eng.* **2018**, *6*, 299–303. [CrossRef]
75. Chaurasia, V.; Chauhan, Y.; Thirunavukkarasu, K. A survey on test case reduction techniques. *Int. J. Sci. Res. (IJSR)* **2014**, *3*, 020131841.
76. Xiao, L.; Miao, H.; Shi, T.; Hong, Y. LSTM-based deep learning for spatial–temporal software testing. *Distrib. Parallel Databases* **2020**, *38*, 687–712. [CrossRef]
77. Zhou, J.; Li, F.; Dong, J.; Zhang, H.; Hao, D. Cost-effective testing of a deep learning model through input reduction. In Proceedings of the 2020 IEEE 31st International Symposium on Software Reliability Engineering (ISSRE), Coimbra, Portugal, 12–15 October 2020; pp. 289–300.

78. Durelli, V.H.; Durelli, R.S.; Borges, S.S.; Endo, A.T.; Eler, M.M.; Dias, D.R.; Guimarães, M.P. Machine learning applied to software testing: A systematic mapping study. *IEEE Trans. Reliab.* **2019**, *68*, 1189–1212. [CrossRef]
79. Soto-Valero, C.; Durieux, T.; Baudry, B. A longitudinal analysis of bloated java dependencies. In Proceedings of the 29th ACM Joint Meeting on European Software Engineering Conference and Symposium on the Foundations of Software Engineering (ESEC/FSE), Athens, Greece, 23–28 August 2021; pp. 1021–1031. [CrossRef]
80. Nagy, S.; Nguyen-Tuong, A.; Hiser, J.D.; Davidson, J.W.; Hicks, M. Same Coverage, Less Bloat: Accelerating Binary-only Fuzzing with Coverage-preserving Coverage-guided Tracing. In Proceedings of the 2021 ACM SIGSAC Conference on Computer and Communications Security (CCS '21), Virtual Event, 15–19 November 2021; pp. 351–365. [CrossRef]

applied sciences

MDPI

Review

Neural Methods for Programming: A Comprehensive Survey and Future Directions

Gebremedhin Gebreslassie Maru [1], Sanghwa Lee [2], Suhwan Ji [3,*], Sang-Ki Ko [4] and Hyeonseung Im [5,*]

1 Department of Computer Science, Kangwon National University, Chuncheon 24341, Republic of Korea; gerie@kangwon.ac.kr
2 Department of Data Science, Kangwon National University, Chuncheon 24341, Republic of Korea; lion0738@kangwon.ac.kr
3 Theory of Computation Laboratory, Yonsei University, Seoul 03722, Republic of Korea
4 Department of Artificial Intelligence, University of Seoul, Seoul 02504, Republic of Korea; sangkiko@uos.ac.kr
5 Department of Computer Science and Engineering, Kangwon National University, Chuncheon 24341, Republic of Korea
* Correspondence: shji@yonsei.ac.kr (S.J.); hsim@kangwon.ac.kr (H.I.)

Abstract

The advancement of neural-based models has driven significant progress in modern code intelligence, accelerating the development of intelligent programming tools such as code assistants and automated software engineering systems. This study presents a comprehensive and systematic survey of neural methods for programming tasks within the broader context of software development. Guided by six research questions, this study synthesizes insights from more than 250 scientific papers, the majority of which were published between 2015 and 2025, with earlier foundational works (dating back to the late 1990s) included for historical context. The analysis spans 18 major programming tasks, including code generation, code translation, code clone detection, code classification, and vulnerability detection. The survey methodologically examines the development and evolution of neural approaches, the datasets employed, and the performance evaluation metrics adopted in this field. It traces the progress in neural techniques from early code modeling approaches to advanced Code-specific Large Language Models (Code LLMs), emphasizing their advantages over traditional rule-based and statistical methods. A taxonomy of evaluation metrics and a categorized summary of datasets and benchmarks reveal both progress and persistent limitations in data coverage and evaluation practices. The review further distinguishes neural models designed for natural language processing and programming languages, highlighting the structural and functional characteristics that influence model performance. Finally, the study discusses emerging trends, unresolved challenges, and potential research directions, underscoring the transformative role of neural-based architectures, particularly Code LLMs, in enhancing programming and software design activities and shaping the future of AI-driven software development.

Keywords: software engineering; neural networks; code translation; code representation and modeling; code-specific Large Language Models (LLMs); datasets and evaluation metrics

1. Introduction

Artificial intelligence (AI) and its subfields, such as machine learning (ML), deep learning (DL), and generative AI, have become integral to modern activities by improving efficiency and quality in daily tasks. DL-based natural language processing (NLP)

enables automation beyond human capabilities [1], including language-related tasks such as autocompletion, long-form text predictions [2], and multilingual translation. The fundamental building blocks of such advancements in the field are neural networks. Hence, they can be considered key drivers of AI-based automation worldwide, enhancing various aspects of daily life. Applications of neural network-based language models, such as ChatGPT [3], showcase improvements in NLP. However, programming, which involves structured instructions to solve computational problems, remains a challenging domain due to its strict syntax, logical complexity, and complexity of semantic analysis. Tasks like writing new code, translating or refactoring existing code, and debugging have traditionally been performed manually or with rigid tools for decades, often struggling to keep up with dynamic and evolving project requirements. This complexity has driven interest in neural approaches for programming tasks, as data-driven models can learn intricate patterns and generalize more effectively to novel problems. Recently, state-of-the-art (SOTA) NLP models—such as OpenAI's Generative Pre-trained Transformer (GPT) models [3]—have been adapted for programming language (PL) tasks [4], and Code-specific Large Language Models (Code LLMs) have been tailored for code-related tasks [5], thereby reducing traditionally time-consuming manual processes such as code editing, comment writing, summarization, and debugging while enabling automation in a range of programming tasks, including source code translation [6,7], code generation [5], summarization [8], automatic code editing [9], decompilation [10], and code similarity detection [11], among others.

Despite the active utilization of neural-based NLP techniques in code-related tasks, there remains a noticeable gap in comprehensive analyses examining the rapid and evolving integration of neural methods into programming-focused applications. Although previous surveys have examined scientific research on neural methods for programming tasks, they often suffer from a limited scope—either focusing on specific tasks [12,13], covering only a narrow subset of neural network-based techniques used in these tasks [14], emphasizing general AI/ML methods with minimal attention to neural techniques [15], or concentrating on broader software engineering (SE) applications with insufficient focus on the programming-centric tasks. Some reviews [16–18] classify the applications of neural models on code into three categories—code generation models, representational models, and pattern mining (code understanding) models—with comparisons of their usage in NLP and programming tasks, whereas others analyze the role of neural models in code understanding, by distinguishing between sequence-based and graph-based approaches. However, many [19–21] omit discussions on the role of neural methods specifically tailored to programming tasks, overlooking the challenges these methods face in capturing the complex syntactic and semantic structures of code and the logical idiom constraints unique to each programming language.

Given the limitations of previous surveys [22–26]—such as their task-specific focus (e.g., code summarization and program repair) and the omission of critical discussions [27,28]—researchers may struggle to identify gaps for further exploration in research themes targeting neural networks applied to programming tasks. To address this, our survey consolidates previous surveys and provides a comprehensive review of existing studies, bridging research gaps and guiding future investigations. In summary, this survey outlines the following concepts and contributions:

- Review existing survey papers on neural methods for programming tasks.
- Compare neural methods applied to NLs and PLs.
- Compare rule-based, statistical, and neural methods for code-related tasks.
- Review 18 programming tasks and outline future research directions for each.
- Examine datasets and benchmarks used in these tasks.
- Analyze performance evaluation metrics for neural models in the reviewed papers.

- Summarize key findings from the reviewed papers on neural models applied to source code.
- Discuss major challenges in applying neural-based models for programming tasks.
- Explore the role of LLMs in programming.
- Identify research gaps and propose future research directions.

This survey serves as a roadmap for researchers interested in the applications of neural networks to programming languages and programming tasks, highlighting the evolution of neural networks from early single-layer models [29] to modern large-scale architectures [30] as depicted in Figure 1. By providing this historical perspective, we contextualize recent achievements and outline directions for future research. To the best of our knowledge, no existing survey is solely dedicated to neural methods with a comprehensive review tracing their application to programming tasks, from early developments to the latest advancements in Code LLMs trained exclusively on code. To maintain consistency and enhance clarity throughout our analysis, we use the term programming tasks to refer to the various code-related activities discussed in this study. While different literature employs a range of terms, such as SE tasks [14], coding tasks [31], code-related tasks, and programming language tasks [32], to describe similar or overlapping concepts, we adopt a unified terminology to reduce ambiguity for readers. However, given the breadth and interdisciplinary nature of these tasks, often involving source code, bug reports, and natural language artifacts, we occasionally use the term SE tasks when appropriate.

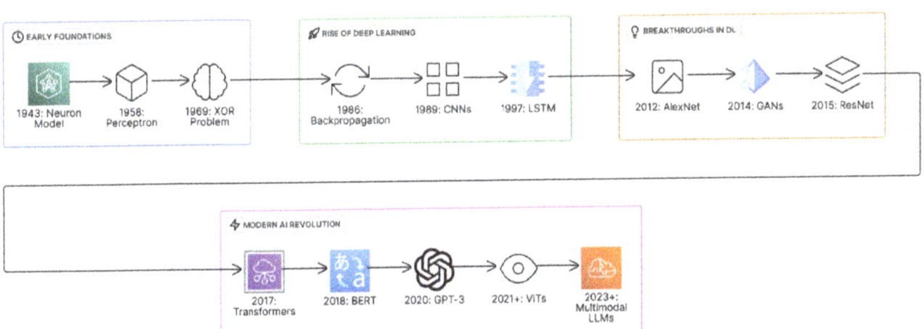

Figure 1. Advancements of neural networks.

Our research scope concentrates on neural methods applied specifically to programming-related SE, as many other SE activities can often be addressed through general-purpose NLP and deep learning surveys. Consequently, this work represents the first comprehensive and systematic review dedicated exclusively to examining how neural approaches have been applied within programming-centric SE domains. To guide this study, we propose the following research questions:

- RQ1: How do neural approaches compare to rule-based and statistical methods in the context of programming tasks?
- RQ2: What is the current landscape of datasets and benchmarks for neural methods in programming tasks, and what are the critical gaps?
- RQ3: Which evaluation metrics best capture model performance on code, both syntactically and functionally, and where do standard NLP metrics fall short?
- RQ4: What roles do LLMs (e.g., GPT-4, LLaMA, Claude) play in programming tasks?
- RQ5: What are the main bottlenecks in scaling and deploying neural-based programming solutions to real-world codebases, and how can they be addressed?
- RQ6: How have neural methods for programming evolved, and which model- and system-level advances have driven this progression?

Finally, we emphasize that our survey follows established systematic review practices—we defined a set of search queries, inclusion/exclusion criteria, and we applied consistent paper collection procedures as noted in Section 3. Our methodology is based on standard guidelines for software engineering systematic literature reviews (e.g., Brereton et al. [33] and Kitchenham and Charters [34]). We extend these practices by including quantitative and qualitative trend analysis to enhance comprehensiveness and rigor, ensuring that our review is reproducible.

To facilitate the discussion, the rest of the paper is structured as follows. Section 2 reviews existing surveys. Section 3 outlines the paper selection process. Section 4 compares the neural models used for NLs and PLs. Section 5 presents neural methods for 18 programming tasks. Section 6 reviews the datasets and evaluation metrics. Section 7 compares neural methods with traditional methods such as rule-based and statistical methods. Section 8 presents answers to the research questions and outlines future research directions, while Section 9 concludes.

2. Related Works

This section reviews prior surveys examining AI approaches in programming and SE, particularly the role of neural methods in programming-related tasks. While some works broadly address AI in SE, they often overlook the huge gains and critical technical challenges specific to neural methods on code-focused applications. Al-Hossami and Shaikh [27] present a taxonomy of AI methods applied to source code and conversational SE systems, spanning traditional neural models such as Multilayer Perceptron, Recurrent Neural Networks (RNNs), and Long Short-Term Memory (LSTM) to Transformers. They categorize tasks into open-domain and task-oriented dialogue systems, referencing datasets like CoNaLa, CodeSearchNet, and other GitHub-derived corpora. Similarly, Watson et al. [35] review DL utilization across SE tasks including defect prediction, program comprehension, and bug fixing. They identify key neural architectures such as autoencoders, Siamese Networks, encoder–decoder models, and CNNs, and common metrics like accuracy, F_1, Mean Reciprocal Rank (MRR), Recall@*k*, and Bilingual Evaluation Understudy (BLEU), while noting limitations include weak reproducibility, preprocessing inconsistencies, and overfitting risks across reviewed works.

Cao et al. [36] survey explainable AI in SE, classifying methods by portability (model-agnostic/specific), timing (ante hoc/post hoc), and scope (local/global). Their dataset coverage includes Devign (Deep Vulnerability Identification via Graph Neural Networks), National Vulnerability Database (NVD), StackOverflow, and CodeSearchNet. They highlight explainable AI's stronger presence in security and defect prediction, its underutilization in early SE phases, and concerns over inconsistent evaluations and lack of standard baselines. The review in [37] emphasizes encoder–decoder architectures in code modeling and generation, exploring a wide array of code representations. Similarly, Samoaa et al. [17] systematically map how DL techniques model code using token, tree, graph, and hybrid formats across classification, clone detection, and summarization tasks. They advocate for standardized benchmarks with industry-level evaluation. Hou et al. [38] discuss the dominance of decoder-only and encoder–decoder architectures (e.g., GPT-3/4, Codex, and CodeT5) with a review on publicly available datasets like HumanEval and Mostly Basic Programming Problems (MBPP). They emphasize the role of prompt engineering and parameter-efficient tuning techniques like Low-Rank Adaptation, prefix-tuning, and adapters, though most models are validated only on academic datasets. Similarly emphasizing LLMs, Fan et al. [39] raise concerns about hallucinations, weak evaluation frameworks, and a lack of rigorous metrics for assessing generated code and other artifacts.

More narrowly scoped reviews target specific programming tasks. Akimova et al. [24] review studies on software defect prediction that utilize RNNs, LSTMs, Tree-LSTMs, GNNs, and Transformer-based models. While neural approaches outperform classical methods, challenges remain in benchmark standardization, class imbalance, and metric selection. Wu et al. [40] analyze vulnerability detection methods, comparing RNN-based and GNN-based models. They stress the need for better code embeddings, representation standards, and interpretability. Xie et al. [25] classify the research works in code search into three taxonomies such as semantic modeling of query, code semantics modeling, and semantic matching phases. Their findings show that pre-trained Transformers like CodeBERT and multi-view inputs significantly improve retrieval, while noting the high training cost and blurred task boundaries with clone detection. Dou et al. [41] empirically review LLMs for code clone detection, comparing open-source (e.g., LLaMA, Vicuna, and Falcon) and proprietary models (e.g., GPT-3.5 and GPT-4) against traditional tools like SourcererCC and NiCad. Using benchmarks such as BigCloneBench and CodeNet (Java, C++, and Python), they examine clone types (1–4) through zero-shot prompts, chain-of-thought prompting, and embedding-based methods (e.g., text-embedding-ada-002 and CodeBERT). LLMs notably outperform classical tools for Type-3/4 clones, especially for Python. GPT-4 demonstrates robustness under multi-step chain-of-thought prompting. Yet, limitations include prompt design constraints, lack of few-shot settings, potential training/evaluation overlap, and computational resource restrictions.

Zhong et al. [42] offer a taxonomy of neural program repair, emphasizing the review of automatic program repair (APR) techniques that leverage various data representation approaches, such as abstract syntax tree (AST) and control flow graph (CFG), to extract context, and employ different neural-based methods, such as encoder–decoder, tree-based, and graph-based architectures, to generate correct or plausible bug-fixing patches. Similarly, Huang et al. [43] trace the APR evolution from search-based to constraint-based, template-based, and learning-based techniques, highlighting models from RNNs and Transformers to static-analysis-integrated encodings, tested on various benchmarks like Defects4J and QuixBugs. Zhang et al. [22] also review learning-based APR tools that frame bug fixing as neural translation, identifying gaps such as limited multi-hunk fix support and inadequate benchmark standardization. Wang et al. [44] provide a broad survey of LLMs in software testing and repair, noting that decoder-only and encoder–decoder models such as GPT-3, Codex, Text-to-Text Transfer Transformer (T5), CodeT5, BART, and LLaMA often outperform traditional techniques. However, they raise caution about benchmark data leakage, privacy risks, and the computational cost of real-world deployment.

Le et al. [28] classify data-driven vulnerability assessment into five themes and subthemes, examining various AI techniques: traditional ML like Support Vector Machine (SVM) and random forest, deep learning like Siamese Neural Networks and GNNs, and knowledge graphs. They also explore datasets like ExploitDB and the Common Vulnerability Scoring Systems, recommending robust validation strategies and evaluation metrics suited for imbalanced data such as Matthews Correlation Coefficient, Mean Absolute Error, and Root Mean Square Error. With a similar research focus, Xiaomeng et al. [23] review ML-based static code analysis for vulnerability detection. Their work spans traditional models like SVMs to deep learning (CNNs, RNNs, and LSTMs), emphasizing reduced manual effort but also highlighting issues like class imbalance and poor generalizability across projects and languages.

Zakeri-Nasrabadi et al. [26] provide a taxonomy of code similarity techniques, covering token-based, tree-based, graph-based, metric-based, and learning-based approaches. They assess benchmarks such as BigCloneBench and metrics like precision, recall, and F1, noting the dominance of languages like Java and C++ and the reproducibility limitations due to some restricted tools for open access. Katsogiannis et al. [45] survey neural approaches for Text-to-SQL translation, reviewing architectures such as seq2seq models, grammar-guided decoders, and GNNs for schema linking. While pre-training-enhanced language models show strong accuracy on benchmarks like WikiSQL and Spider, challenges remain in scalability and generalization to new domains. Grazia and Pradel [46] present a comprehensive review of code search over researches spanned across three decades. They categorize query mechanisms—ranging from NL and code snippets to formal patterns and input/output examples—and discuss indexing strategies, retrieval methods, and ranking techniques. Their survey addresses real-world search behaviors and emphasizes open challenges, such as supporting version history, cross-language search, and more robust evaluation frameworks.

Zheng et al. [47] review 149 studies, comparing those LLMs trained/fine-tuned on code like Codex, CodeLLaMA, and AlphaCode against general LLMs using HumanEval and Automated Programming Progress Standard (APPS) benchmarks. Their findings show that code-specific models typically outperform general models using metrics like Pass@*k* and BLEU. Zan et al. [48] evaluate 27 LLMs for NL-to-code tasks, identifying three key performance drivers: model size, access to premium datasets, and expert fine-tuning. However, they note an overemphasis on short Python snippets, limiting generalization. Wong et al. [49] survey the impact of LLMs trained on "Big Code" in integrated development environment (IDE), examining their ability to support tasks like code autocompletion and semantic comprehension. They also caution about drawbacks such as model bias, security concerns, and latency that may hinder real-time applicability. Similarly, Zheng et al. [50] focus on Transformer-based pre-trained language models and LLMs with parameter size greater than or equal to 0.8B, across seven core tasks such as test generation, defect detection, and code repair. These models perform well in syntax-aware tasks but struggle with semantic understanding. Their review also underscores fragmented benchmarks, limited error analysis, and insufficient attention to ethical and cost-related concerns. Xu and Zhu [51] offer a deep dive into pre-trained langauge models like CodeBERT, GraphCodeBERT, and CodeT5, detailing their distinct learning objectives and use of input structures such as AST and data-flow graph (DFG). However, they note issues including scarce multilingual datasets and underexplored graph-based techniques.

Some surveys have also explored application of AI and its variant for SE life-cycle. Crawford et al. [21] review the integration of AI into software project management, tracing its progression from early expert systems and rule-based planners to contemporary neural network applications. Their findings highlight AI's value in improving estimation accuracy, risk management, and analytics for agile workflow. However, persistent challenges remain, including data privacy concerns and the lack of interpretability in AI models, both of which hinder stakeholder trust and limit industry adoption. Batarseh et al. [52] map AI methods to five SE phases, finding active prototyping in testing and requirements engineering, yet limited industrial validation and evaluation standardization. Durrani et al. [19] take a survey on broad perspective across domains of SE phases. However, their treatment of SE tasks and overreliance on quantitative summaries mined from AI tools (e.g., dimensions.ai) detracts from the unique advances in neural methods specific to programming. Their focus on older models like random forests overlooks the transformative capacity of modern neural models that now even support complex program generation and logical reasoning.

In contrast, our survey concentrates on programming-related SE tasks. While some documentation or design tasks may benefit from lightly fine-tuned general NLP models, we focus on how neural-based architectures are designed to understand, generate, and interact with source code. The limitations of prior surveys—such as narrow benchmarks, limited real-world validation, and fragmented methodologies—underscore the need for a unified, code-centric view of modern neural-based applications in SE. Table 1 compares existing survey and review articles. It outlines each prior work's main focus, key strengths, identified limitations, and basis of validation, allowing readers to quickly compare how existing approaches relate to ours. Based on our review of previous survey studies, we observe that prior works on the application of neural methods and general AI/ML techniques for software engineering and programming tasks can be broadly categorized into four groups as summarized in Table 2.

Our survey distinguishes itself from prior reviews in several key ways. Unlike earlier works that narrowly focus on specific deep learning techniques or isolated SE subdomains, our survey systematically covers almost all types of neural methods across a broad range of programming-centric SE tasks. Additionally, we compare the application of neural methods in both PL and NL, highlighting representative models used in each context. Furthermore, our work stands out by explicitly comparing rule-based, statistical, and neural approaches, offering a holistic understanding of how neural models outperform earlier paradigms as detailed in Section 7. Overall, our survey adopts a broader perspective by integrating both qualitative synthesis and quantitative analysis, examining over 250 papers across 18 distinct programming task domains. We also provide trend-based insights on publication growth, dataset and benchmark usage, and model performance metrics as described in Section 6.

Table 1. Summary of previous survey works' methodologies, strengths, weaknesses, and robustness.

Survey Paper	Methodology	Advantages	Disadvantages	Robustness
Allamanis et al. (2018) [16]	Narrative survey classifying ML models for 'Big Code' and software naturalness using linguistic analogies.	Offers a clear taxonomy of ML models; shows foundational framing about conventional and idiomatic naturalness of code.	Lacks standardized benchmarks; some models (e.g., Transformers) were emerging and not fully covered.	Foundational and widely cited but predates large-scale pre-trained models.
Xiaomeng et al. (2018) [23]	Narrative review on ML in secure code review and vulnerability detection.	Good historical context; contrasts DL with earlier feature-based methods.	Outdated; lacks attention to recent graph neural networks (GNNs)/Transformer models.	Limited coverage and moderately outdated, but contextually informative.
Akimova et al. (2021) [24]	Review on DL-based defect prediction papers, categorized models, datasets, metrics, and investigated trends.	Comprehensive coverage of DL techniques, including data-labeling and generalization issues.	Narrow focus on certain PLs, limited Transformer models coverage.	Moderately useful for defect prediction, limited for closely related SE tasks.
Yang et al. (2022) [14]	Systematic literature review on DL-in-SE papers; organized by DL model architectures, tasks, datasets, and metrics.	Broad task coverage; excellent model categorization; metrics and dataset taxonomy included.	Reproducibility issues; underexplored cross-project transfer learning; lacks deep industrial insights, no coverage of LLMs.	Comprehensive and structured, though no coverage of the emergence of neural-based LLMs.
Zhang et al. (2022) [12]	Structured survey of automatic source code summarization, classifies the task into modeling, generation, and evaluation phases.	Balanced treatment of classic information retrieval and DL methods, covers datasets, metrics, and emerging models.	Limited to code-comment pairs discussion, no critical analysis on the Recall-Oriented Understudy for Gisting Evaluation (ROUGE), Bilingual Evaluation Understudy (BLEU), and other weak metrics issues.	Good for code summarization, well-scoped and methodical, though limited cross-language coverage.
Samoaa et al. (2022) [17]	Systematic mapping study on code representations across SE tasks.	Maps token, tree, graph modalities; clear representation analysis.	Lacks model-specific analysis; omits modern pre-trained models.	Moderately strong on representation types, less on effectiveness.
Xu and Zhu (2022) [51]	Review of pretrained language models in code intelligence.	Covers pre-training and fine-tuning objectives, pre-trained language models' architectures, and preprocessing, and code structure extraction pipelines in pre-trained language models.	Minimal coverage of non-Transformer and structure-based code intelligence models.	Strong overview of pre-trained language models and Transformer-based models, weaker on fine-grained discussion on programming tasks.
Le et al. (2022) [28]	Investigated data-driven vulnerability assessment by examining ML, DL and NLP techniques.	Practical view on the Common Vulnerability Scoring Systems' alignment with reviewed themes and real-world focus.	Lacks depth insight on vulnerability-mitigation related challenges, e.g., patch modeling.	Comprehensive taxonomy of data-driven vulnerability in five themes.
Al-Hossami and Shaikh (2022) [27]	Broad review of AI in source code and conversational systems.	Unique angle on dialogue-based AI; educational application emphasis.	Limited depth on models and benchmarks; no technical coverage related to AI for programming.	Moderately exploratory and broad coverage of AI applications in education, but less technical with respect to PLs.

Table 1. *Cont.*

Survey Paper	Methodology	Advantages	Disadvantages	Robustness
Amalfitano et al. (2023) [18]	Tertiary study synthesizing secondary surveys on AI for software testing.	Provides a holistic, high-level view of AI contributions to software testing; maps AI subdomains to testing tasks.	Lacks depth on datasets, models; omits emerging techniques and several aspects are not yet widely reviewed.	Averagely comprehensive in coverage, but breadth over depth reduces specificity.
Fontes and Gay (2023) [15]	Systematic mapping of studies applying ML to automated test generation; categorized by ML type, task, and metrics.	Captures detailed discussion on test and oracle generation; explores diverse ML methods.	Limited discussion on evaluation quality; limited coverage on neural networks, and no-idea about LLMs; replication gaps.	Strong in breadth but limited by inconsistent evaluation standards.
Xie et al. (2023) [25]	Review of DL-based code search systems with focus on encoding query and source code, and measuring their embedding similarity.	Highlights the concepts of deep code search, benchmarking, model limitations, and practical deployment issues.	Retrieval-centric; lacks broader coverage on SE use cases that align with programmer's workflow focus.	Robust in evaluating code search methods with coverage of popular datasets and benchmarks. But no clue about LLMs.
Zhang et al. (2023) [22]	Review of automatic program repair (APR) structured by pipeline, dataset, and evaluation.	Clear taxonomy of APR approaches, focus on real bug benchmarks.	The review is Java centric, and the evaluation heavily depends on test-suite plausibility.	Highly detailed and accurate for APR pipelines.
Zakeri-Nasrabadi et al. (2023) [26]	Systematic literature review on code clone studies with method and dataset taxonomy.	Broad code similarity and clone detection taxonomy; tools/data gaps clearly identified.	Limited coverage of pre-trained language models and no clue about LLMs.	Excellent for classical clone detection methods.
Uddin et al. (2025) [13]	Analysis of DL for vulnerability detection; introduces a life-cycle from data construction to model deployment.	Life-cycle modeling gives structured perspective; highlights real-world gaps and practical considerations.	Narrower scope, and the analysis is biased toward C/C++ datasets.	Robust within the domain tailored for vulnerability detection, but it is less generalizable.

Table 2. High-level taxonomy of previous survey papers in the field.

Area of Focus	Examples
Task-specific surveys	Code Summarization [12], Comment Generation [53], Code Generation [54], Code Translation [55], Code Clone Detection [56], Code Vulnerability Detection [13], Program Repair [22], etc.
Surveys focused on subsets of neural methods	Review solely on either DL [14,57], LLMs [58], or Code LLMs [47]
Surveys focused on the phases of the Software Development Life Cycle, with limited emphasis on the coding phase.	Software Development Life Cycle phases [19,20] such as Requirement Engineering [52], System Design, and Project Management.
Surveys focused on traditional AI/ML methods with minimal focus on neural methods	Surveys with vast focus on traditional AI/ML methods [18,23] such as Random Forest, Decision Trees, XGBoost, Naive Bayes, Logistic Regression, and SVM.

3. Scientific Paper Selection Process

Our paper selection process is visually summarized in Figure 2. In this study, we have collected and analyzed more than 250 research papers, exploring their primary objectives, contributions, and future research directions. Most of these works were published between 2015 and 2025, covering a decade of intensive research on neural methods for programming tasks. A few earlier foundational studies, dating back to the late 1990s, were also included to provide historical continuity and contextualize recent advances as depicted in Figure 3.

Our investigation delves into various applications of neural methods in programming tasks, including advanced code representation techniques that enhance automation in software development [59]. Table 3 provides an overview of the digital sources in which these papers are published, while Figure 3 highlights that recent years have witnessed a significant increase in publications within this domain.

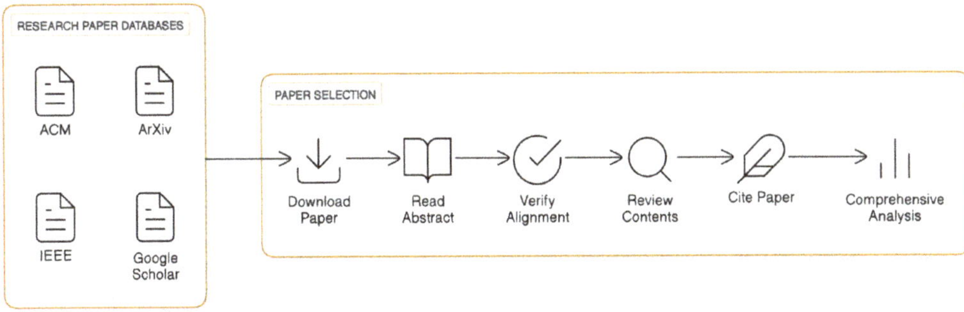

Figure 2. Paper selection process.

The methodology for selecting research papers in this survey aligns with established approaches, such as those employed in [60]. Specifically, we manually defined key phrases and search terms related to various programming tasks to retrieve relevant articles from online digital libraries. Our approach to identifying relevant literature was methodical and targeted. We focused on search phrases involving neural approaches within the context of programming and programming-centric SE. Specifically, we frequently used keyword combinations that included terms like "neural methods", "neural models", and "neural networks", paired with common prepositions followed by the phrases "programming tasks", "programming", and "software engineering", as well as specific code-related task names. The primary search patterns are shown below:

- ("neural methods" | "neural models" | "neural networks") ("in" | "for") ("programming tasks" | "programming" | "software engineering")
- ("neural methods" | "neural models" | "neural networks") ("in" | "for" | "on" | "and") *[specific task]*

where " | " stands for "or", and *[specific task]* is a placeholder for areas such as code translation, code generation, code clone detection, code summarization, program synthesis, and other programming-related tasks.

Table 3. Distribution of collected papers by source.

S.No	Publication Source	Number of Publications
1	ACL, NeurIPS, ICLR	62
2	ACM	53
3	IEEE	49
4	IEEE/ACM (Jointly)	35
5	ArXiV	32
6	Elsevier, MDPI, Springer	29
7	Others	15
	Total	275

Note. IEEE/ACM (Jointly) in the above table indicates those papers published in the conferences or journals that are co-sponsored or jointly organized by both IEEE and ACM.

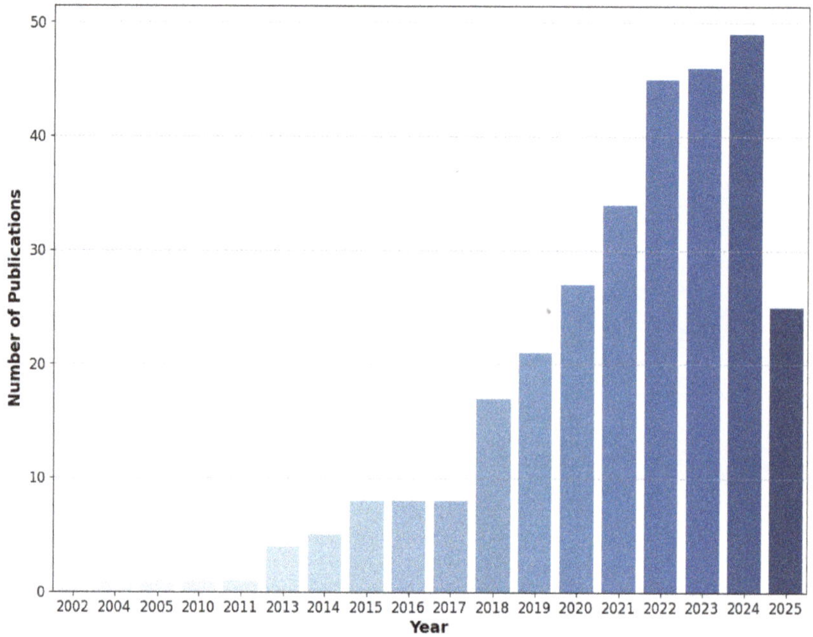

Figure 3. A yearly highlight summary of publications on neural methods for code considered in this survey.

We also applied inclusion and exclusion criteria to refine our selection. Only studies written in English were considered. Furthermore, we specifically included studies that explore the application of neural methods within programming-centric software engineering tasks. Conversely, studies focusing on the reverse, such as applying software engineering techniques to improve AI systems or those discussing neural methods without a clear application to software or programming tasks, were excluded from our review. After the initial collection, we refined the selection by filtering articles based on specific attributes to ensure alignment with our research objectives and focus. The paper selection criteria predominantly include the following aspects:

- Breakthrough research and SOTA approaches: Most selected articles focus on SOTA neural network architectures, including Transformer-based neural networks, encoder–decoder models, and other deep learning frameworks [61]. These studies provide cutting-edge advancements in neural-based code processing.
- Recent publications and citation-based filtering: A significant portion of the papers have been published recently. To ensure that we include impactful research articles, we adopt a citation score-based filtering approach as in [60]. However, for studies published between 2022 and 2025, we prioritize the relevance of the topic without referring to citation counts.

To ensure the inclusion of impactful but recently published studies, we intentionally excluded citation counts as a criterion when selecting papers from 2022 to 2025. Many papers from this period were initially released as preprints on platforms like arXiv and had not accumulated substantial citations, even though they were later accepted by peer-reviewed venues in 2024 and 2025. Relying on citation metrics could have led to the under-representation of valuable studies that were still in the process of gaining visibility. Notably, key contributions—such as OpenAI's GPT-4 and various iterations of Meta's LLaMA models—were disseminated via arXiv rather than formal publication channels [62–64].

This reflects a broader trend toward early sharing in the AI community. To fairly represent the most relevant and innovative research from this evolving landscape, we prioritized the relevance and impact of contributions over citation numbers. During the filtering process, we first reviewed each paper's abstract for relevance. If clarity was insufficient, we further examined the introduction, model architecture and research approach, experimental setup, and discussion sections.

In further illustrating the thematic relationships within the reviewed literature, Figure 4 presents a keyword co-occurrence network generated from the bibliometric analysis of the collected papers. The network highlights how keywords such as code, source code, learning, neural, and language models form the core of the research landscape, demonstrating strong associations with programming tasks including code translation, code generation, code summarization, and other programming tasks. These interlinked clusters reveal the growing convergence between neural methods, neural networks, code understanding and generation, and software engineering automation.

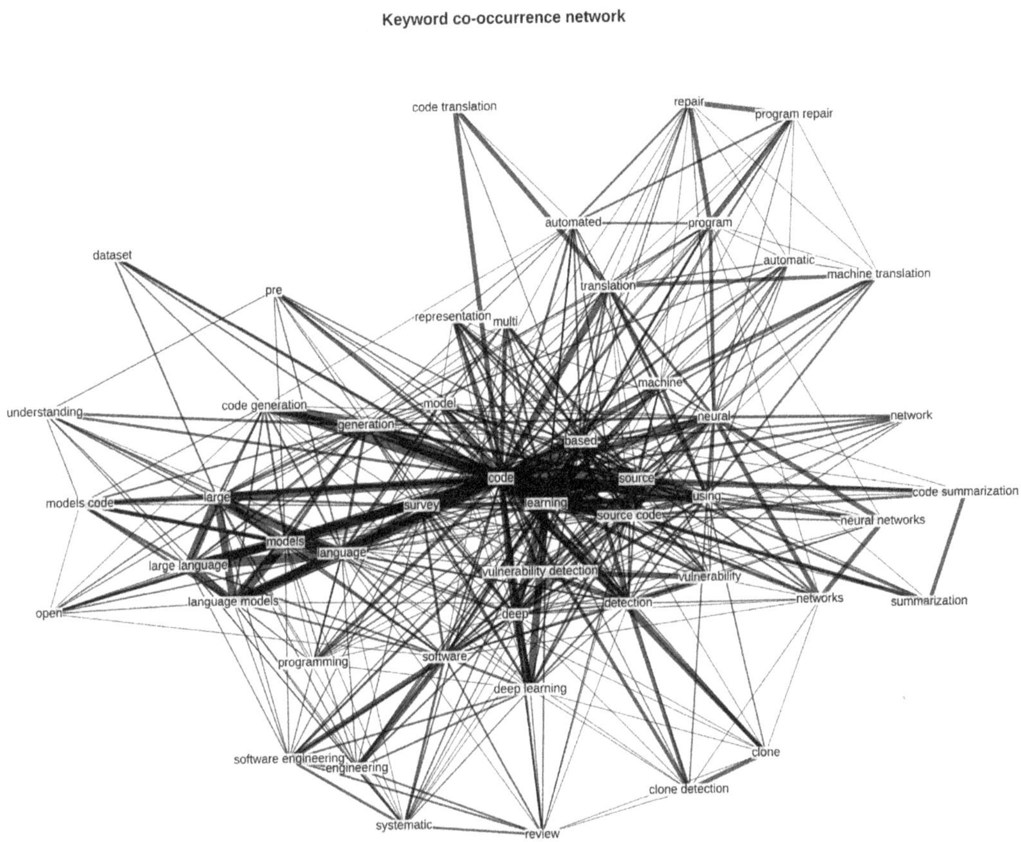

Figure 4. Keyword co-occurrence network of reviewed publications.

4. Neural Methods for Natural Languages vs. Programming Languages

Recent developments in large-scale NLP models have revolutionized human language processing [1,65]. Given the structural and lexical similarities between programming and natural languages, researchers have adapted neural-based NLP techniques to PLs [66].

PLs are essential tools for operating computing devices, enabling application and system development for programmers. Unlike NLs, which evolve through speech and cultural influences, PLs are designed by programmers to serve as a medium of communication between humans and machines. While NLs are analyzed through the norms and grammars of their speakers, PLs are based solely on the syntax, semantics, and grammar rules defined by their designers, making them a specialized subset of NLP. As such, the application of neural-based methods to PLs has benefited from advances in NLP-driven text processing. However, neural approaches tailored to PLs must account for significant differences from those used for NLs.

In terms of using neural methods for PLs, the following are remarkable opportunities we can exploit:

- **Simplified Linguistic Rules:** PLs avoid challenges like pronunciation, accents (e.g., UK vs. US English), writing styles (e.g., formal vs. informal) [67], and text writing direction (e.g., Arabic vs. English), making automation easier than in NLs.
- **Abundant Open-Source Code Corpora:** Repositories like GitHub and coding competitions offer large collections of code written in individual PLs, providing abundant monolingual data that enhance neural model performance on language-specific programming tasks.

On the other hand, there are also some pitfalls in using neural methods for PLs as shown below:

- **Limited Learning Modes:** Unlike NLs, PLs are learned solely through reading and writing, preventing neural-based automation from leveraging voice or speech processing [68].
- **Grammar Sensitivity:** PLs are highly syntax dependent, where minor errors, like missing whitespace in Python or misplaced semicolons in compiled languages, can cause the entire program to fail.

Therefore, the notable distinction between PLs and NLs lies in syntax and ambiguity: PLs are inherently unambiguous and structured to be deterministically parsed, whereas NLs often exhibit ambiguity due to diverse dialects and informal usage. This syntactic rigidity implies that code tokens follow strict formal rules, such as matching braces and consistent indentation that are not typical considerations in NLP tasks. As a result, code tends to be more predictable than human language, given that developers frequently reuse established idioms and avoid non-standard constructs. Consequently, neural models for code often integrate structural representations, such as ASTs or program graphs, rather than processing flat token sequences alone. For instance, GraphCodeBERT [69] enhances a Transformer-based architecture by incorporating DFGs alongside the sequence of tokens to capture variable dependencies and value propagation within the code.

While general-purpose neural language models like BERT [70] have been fine-tuned to apply for both code and NL domains, models trained explicitly for code typically include additional architectural components. These may involve embedding ASTs or data-flow structures using neural network with code-comprehending traits, or using specialized attention masks. Some models also augment input representations with tokens specific to programming constructs, such as language keywords or data types. By contrast, neural models in NLP often emphasize shallow parsing and focus on linguistic challenges such as co-reference resolution and semantic interpretation.

Hence, in this context, we review some prominent NLP models and compare their equivalent models trained for PLs. For example, the Salesforce's CodeT5 model [71] was developed from Google's T5 model. Both employ Byte Pair Encoding tokenization and follow an encoder–decoder architecture. However, while T5 was trained on the C4 corpus, CodeT5 was pre-trained on CodeSearchNet and fine-tuned using CodeXGLUE, enabling it to process both NL and source code. T5 has since evolved into **t5x** and **seqio** models. Similarly, CodeT5 has been extended into CodeT5+, incorporating objectives such as instruction tuning, text-code matching, span denoising, causal language model pre-training, and contrastive learning. Inspired by such development, large multilingual corpora combining natural and programming language tokens are being introduced in the field [72].

Additionally, models derived from BERT have demonstrated strong performance in both NLP and programming tasks. For instance, cuBERT [73] utilizes standard Python tokenization with Word2Vec-based fine-tuning for code classification. CoCLUBERT [74] enhances code clustering through objectives like Deep Robust Clustering, CoCLUBERT-Triplet, and CoCLUBERT-Unsupervised, which outperforms its cuBERT baseline model. Microsoft's CodeBERT [75] employs bimodal Masked Language Modeling with NL and code, along with unimodal (replaced token detection) objectives. Several CodeBERT variant models like GraphCodeBERT [69], UniXcoder [76], LongCoder [77], and others address some programming challenges.

Cross-lingual pre-training and fine-tuning techniques [78] have further enhanced PL models adaptability. A key example is the unsupervised neural machine translation (NMT) approach introduced in [65], which employs Cross-lingual Masked language pre-training, Denoising Autoencoding (DAE), and Back-Translation techniques. This approach forms the backbone for Facebook's (currently known as Meta) TransCoder models, which were designed for code translation [79].

Furthermore, the code summarization research in [8] has introduced mechanisms such as the "copy attention mechanism", improving the quality of code summarization. Unlike its equivalent NLP-based text summarization model presented in [80], which relies on vanilla Transformers and Recall-Oriented Understudy for Gisting Evaluation (ROUGE) scores, the code summarization model integrates multiple performance metrics, including BLEU, Metric for Evaluation of Translation with Explicit ORdering (METEOR), and ROUGE.

A key distinction between neural models for NLs and PLs lies in their training data. Unlike NL corpora, source code cannot be treated as plain text. Therefore, adapting an NLP method for PLs requires specialized preprocessing, tokenization, and model architecture. These differences can help to distinguish why directly transferring NLP models to programming tasks frequently leads to suboptimal results. Neural architectures tailored for programming tasks, through the incorporation of structural features such as ASTs, control and data flow analysis, and type information, tend to outperform their general-purpose counterparts on tasks like code completion, summarization, and bug detection.

To complement the conceptual discussions above, Table 4 provides a comparative summary of neural models designed for natural and programming languages. It distinguishes their representative tasks, data sources, and evaluation metrics. The comparison highlights how PL models (e.g., CodeBERT and CodeT5) extend NL counterparts (e.g., BERT and T5) by incorporating structural information such as ASTs and Data Flow Graphs (DFGs), which enable improved performance in code-related tasks while introducing new challenges in cross-language generalization and semantic correctness.

Table 4. Comparative perspective on neural models for natural and programming languages.

Aspect	NL Models (e.g., BERT, T5)	PL Models (e.g., CodeBERT and CodeT5)
Representative tasks	Question answering, sentiment analysis, abstractive summarization, cross-lingual transfer [65,70,80].	Code search, code summarization, defect prediction, code translation, code completion [8,69,71,75].
Training data and structural bias	Large-scale corpora such as C4 and multilingual web crawls; sequence-focused tokenization with limited structural priors [70,72,80].	Curated repositories (CodeSearchNet, CodeXGLUE) with AST/DFG-aware tokenization and structure-enhanced encoders [69,71,75].
Common metrics	Accuracy, F1, BLEU, ROUGE, cross-lingual transfer scores [65,70,80].	CodeBLEU, BLEU, Mean Reciprocal Rank (MRR), Precision@k, and exact match for code translation [8,71,75].
Empirical comparisons	Fine-tuned BERT variants serve as baselines for syntax-agnostic NLP tasks; performance drops observed on code understanding benchmarks.	CodeBERT improves over BERT on code search; CodeT5 outperforms T5 on summarization and generation tasks tailored to code [71,75].
Observed limitations	Difficulty modeling rigid syntax and long-range dependencies in source code; limited grounding in program semantics.	Sensitive to language-specific idioms and repository noise; struggles with cross-language generalization and semantic correctness without execution feedback [69,78].

5. Neural Methods for Programming and Code-Centric SE Tasks

In this section, we explore neural methods for programming-centric SE tasks in fine-grained detail, covering the research focus, outcomes, and future directions for each task. Table 5 shows an overall summary of the 18 programming tasks, including their main objectives related to utilizing neural methods, along with their open research issues. In selecting these tasks, we prioritized those most frequently addressed in the large volume of literature, capturing widely studied areas with consistent terminology. Tasks mentioned under variant names (e.g., code recommendation vs. code completion; vulnerability prediction vs. vulnerability detection; and static/dynamic analysis vs. code analysis) were mapped to our taxonomy. Unlike some of the prior survey papers, for instance, the review by Durrani et al. [19] where the analysis relies on automated indexing tools such as Dimensions.ai, our review uses a rigorous manual literature collection and researcher-driven analysis. Our approach, which encompasses 18 distinct programming tasks, highlights the multidimensional contributions of neural methods to the field of programming. We emphasize the evolving capabilities of neural models that are the backbone of code assistant tools such as GitHub Copilot, which have not yet been sufficiently acknowledged by recent survey work such as in [19].

5.1. Source Code Translation

Source code translation can be viewed in two ways. First, it refers to the migration of outdated versions of source code to a newer version within the same PL [81]. Second, it involves translating source code from one PL to another [7,79]. In a broader sense, code translation can encompass shifts between different programming paradigms (e.g., declarative to imperative or procedural to object-oriented). It may also involve porting Application Programming Interfaces (APIs) from one language to another [82]. Although early traditional tools for code translation have some limitations, they are cost effective compared to manual translation and provide benefits to businesses across various domains. Source code translation has applications across multiple fields, including high-tech software production, cyber-security, and more. The code translation utilization areas can be seen as follows (but not limited to):

- Platform- or application-specific optimizations for high-performance computing applications [83], especially transitioning software from outdated to modern languages.
- Upgrading software to secure, up-to-date, and well-documented PLs to enhance long-term maintainability and compliance.
- Facilitating the innovation of new PLs by simplifying legacy code migration.
- Advanced program analysis and verification [84].

Existing source code translation methods can be broadly classified into three categories: rule-based, statistical, and neural translation approaches. Additionally, for cases involving a small number of lines of code, manual translation can be a viable option. Similar categorical approaches are also found in other programming tasks, such as code generation, code search, code summarization, etc.

Table 5. An overall summary of programming tasks using neural models, their objectives, and corresponding open research issues.

Task	Objective	Open Research Issues
Automatic Code Edit	Auto-modification of code.	Stable benchmark datasets for evaluation.
Code Analysis	Evaluates structural and runtime behavior of source code.	Need for multiple representations for efficiency.
Code Authorship and Identification	Utilizes neural models to attribute code to developers.	Challenges in coding style variability, multi-language authorship, and AI-generated code identification.
Code Change Detection	Tracks commit updates in large-scale software development.	Potential for IDE integration with push notifications.
Code Classification	Categorizes code based on syntax, semantics, and algorithms.	Demands of expanding classification criteria.
Code Clone Detection	Identifies duplicate or near-duplicate code snippets to maintain software quality.	Demands of distinguishing code clone detection from code similarity detection.
Code Completion	Enhances productivity by auto-completing blocks of codes.	Privacy and security concerns.
Code Generation	Automates code creation using code-assistants.	Ensuring correctness and execution reliability.
Code Modeling and Representation	Uses various representations for better source code understanding.	Designing optimal representation strategies remains an open issue.
Code Search and Retrieval	Enables retrieval of relevant code snippets.	Safety and security of AI-searched code remain a concern.
Code Similarity Detection	Identifies duplicate code using neural networks.	Challenges in dataset reliability.
Code Summarization	Generates human-readable descriptions for code.	Evaluation is highly dependent on NLP metrics.
Code Vulnerability Detection	Uses various neural methods to detect security flaws.	False positives persist and need to integrate neural methods with static/dynamic analysis.
Comment Generation	Generate descriptive comments for code.	Need for multilingual support.

Table 5. *Cont.*

Task	Objective	Open Research Issues
Decompilation	Converts machine-level code into high-level source code.	Need for improving generalization across languages.
Program Repair and Bug Fix	Improve program debugging and efficiency.	Integrating neural methods with program verification systems for runtime bugs.
Program Synthesis	Converts NL instructions into code using neural models.	Evaluation benchmarks remain an issue.
Source Code Translation	Migrates code across different versions of the same language or translates it between different languages [85].	Difficulties in ensuring semantic and functional equivalence between the source and translated programs.

Manual code translation involves an expert translating code between languages, ensuring both source and target languages meet functional requirements. While effective for small functions or short code snippets, this approach is impractical for larger codebases, as it is time-consuming, error-prone, and inefficient.

The rule-based source code translations [86,87], also known as conventional methods, are mainly dependent on the AST of the program's source code [7]. However, there are also variations in the implementation of these code translation approaches.

In [83], the source code's AST is converted to an eXtensible Markup Language (XML), with user-defined rules applied to optimize code translations based on platform-specific features. This research developed the Xevolver tool, built on top of the ROSE compiler infrastructure, which uses XML ASTs to enable code modifications between the source and target languages. Another example is the OP2-Clang tool [88], which utilizes the Clang/LLVM AST matcher to optimize parallel code generation. In [89], a rule-based technique using ASTs is also applied in security and code optimization for Java programs, resulting in an Eclipse plug-in tool.

Statistical methods in source code translation draw from techniques used in statistical machine translation (SMT) for NLP [90]. These approaches comprehend the source code as lexical token sequences, applying statistical language models to map these tokens between source and target languages. For instance, in [90], the source code is modeled using SMT, achieving high BLEU scores when translating Java to C#. Similarly, in [91], a phrase-based language model is applied to translate C# to Java, using a parallel corpus of 20,499 method pairs. In [92], the **S**emantic **LA**nguage **M**odel for Source **C**ode (SLAMC) incorporates semantic information, such as token roles, data types, scopes, and dependencies, to improve SMT-based code translation quality.

Neural networks, particularly neural language models, have greatly advanced source code translation. Numerous neural language models leverage fine-tuning techniques to excel in code-related tasks. Models like CodeBERT and CodeT5 fine-tuned for such tasks, have achieved SOTA performance [71,75].

Facebook's TransCoder [79] employs unsupervised learning to translate between Python, Java, and C++, using monolingual word embeddings, DAE, and BT. Its self-trained extension, TransCoder-ST [93], incorporates automated unit test generation to preserve semantics during code translation. Unit tests play a crucial role not only in code translation but also in a wide range of programming tasks. As such, they are essential for self-supervised neural models to validate the functional correctness of their predictions [94]. PLBART [95] is another versatile model excelling in multiple code-related tasks, including code translation. It outperforms models like RoBERTa and CodeBERT in Java-to-C# translation based on evaluation metrics of BLEU and CodeBLEU [96].

Despite these commendable progress, challenges remain. Traditional NLP metrics like BLEU fail to capture semantic correctness in PL codes, as variations in coding style can yield low scores despite identical functionality. Effective evaluation must consider both syntax and semantics of PL code. Additionally, code translation models are often treated as a supplement to other tasks. A dedicated data pipeline and specialized neural models are needed to refine the defects that arise during code translation and to address the unique complexities of source code translation.

5.2. Code Generation

Automated code generation is crucial for various programming tasks, with diverse demands leveraging generated code's resources [97]. Some methods use code documentation text for code generation, such as doc-strings of Python functions [98], while others integrate back-translation heuristics.

CodeT5 [71], a code model built on top of Google's T5 model [99], incorporates NL and PL tokens, enabling bimodal (NL-PL) and PL-only training for task-specific code generation and understanding.

ASTs play a key role in structured code generation. Abstract Syntax Description Language-based semantic parsing [100], Neural Attribute Machines [101], and other research works have leveraged the AST-based structural representations of a program for code generation. Another approach stated in [102] utilizes an API-driven Java program generation, which leverages combinatorial techniques.

CoDET, short for CODE generation with generated Tests [103], evaluates correctness via test-case based code coverage, although high coverage alone does not guarantee correctness. Execution-based testing such as mutation score evaluation [104] and others offer a more reliable alternative to ensure the correctness of the model-generated codes.

Although improvements have been made over time, generated code often requires manual modifications, and ensuring error-free execution remains an ongoing challenge [105]. Code LLMs enhance efficiently the automation of code generation [106,107]; however, executability issues persist.

5.3. Comment Generation

Code comments in general-purpose programming languages provide a high-level understanding of source code written by developers. Neural models can generate descriptive comment texts for a given program [108].

An empirical study in [109] evaluates T5 and n-gram models in code comment completion tasks. The experimental demonstrations in [110] train a model that learns source code along with its comments written in Japanese NL texts, in which it distinguishes between the code and comments using procedure learning. In this research, LSTM is used for comment generation, leveraging problem statements written in the NL texts to improve program understanding. While the research work in [111] attempts automatic comment generation using NMT models, the performance is suboptimal.

In [108], the Deep Code Comment Understanding and Assessment (DComment) model is proposed to understand and classify generated comments based on their quality. Some studies explore code-to-comment translation [112] as an alternative, while evaluating the generated comments' quality using NLP metrics. However, performance evaluation issues are still concerning as highlighted in Section 6.2.

Most comment generation models produce English-based comments, which can be a barrier for non-English-speaking programmers. Developing models that can generate comments in a multilingual fashion could enhance collaboration in software development.

5.4. Decompilation

Decompilation reverses compilation, converting machine-level code (binary or assembly code) into high-level source code. Traditional rule-based methods are costly with limited performance, prompting exploration of neural methods as alternatives. The research in [10] trains RNNs on machine code compiled from C, which is later extended into a two-phase approach [113]: generating code snippet templates and then populating them with appropriate identifier/variable values.

Neutron [114] applies attention-based NMT techniques for decompilation, while BTC (Beyond the C) [115] offers a platform-independent neural decompiler supporting multiple languages, including Go, Fortran, OCaml, and C. As reported in [116], the researchers have explored the intermediate representations (IR) of program codes with seq2seq Transformers for decompilation.

Most existing tools remain rule-based and limited to specific languages, restricting their effectiveness. While a one-fit-for-all decompiler may be infeasible, future research should focus on leveraging efficient neural models to enhance the generalization of this task across diverse languages.

5.5. Code Search and Retrieval

Developing software from scratch is time-consuming, which requires software engineers to integrate open-source code. However, effective code retrieval requires robust search tools. While traditional search engines excel at NL queries, they struggle with accurate code snippet search. Neural methods offer a promising alternative.

Code-Description Embedding Neural Network (CODEnn) [117] is a deep learning-based code search model that leverages RNN-based sequence embeddings for joint source code and description representations. CARLCS-CNN, short for Co-Attentive Representation Learning Code Search-CNN [118], enhances code search with co-attention mechanism and CNNs to improve search accuracy. The Code-to-Code Search Across Languages (COSAL) model proposed in [119] enables cross-lingual code search using static and dynamic analysis, while Deep Graph Matching and Searching (DGMS) [120] employs Relational Graph Convolutional Networks (RGCNs) and attention mechanisms for unified text-code graph matching.

Traditional information retrieval techniques have also been enhanced with neural approaches. For instance, the study in [121] integrates Word2Vec into retrieval tasks. The Multi-Modal Attention Network (MMAN) in [122] utilizes LSTM, Tree-LSTM, and Gated Graph Neural Networks (GGNNs) to capture syntactic and semantic information. In [123], the authors combine CNNs and joint embeddings for Stack Overflow queries. The Multi-Programming Language Code Search (MPLCS) model proposed in [124] extends retrieval across multiple PLs, benefiting low-resource PLs.

AI-driven tools like Microsoft Copilot and ChatGPT [3] have revolutionized code search, retrieving relevant snippets via NL prompts. Unlike traditional engines, ChatGPT bypasses irrelevant search results but still may return non-executable code. Future improvements could integrate SE tools with neural models to search a code which is ready-made for execution with no errors, enhancing usability and reliability in software development.

5.6. Code Completion

IDEs with auto-completion features significantly enhance software development productivity [125]. Various neural methods have been explored for code completion and related tasks. In [126], LSTMs with attention mechanisms were used for code completion and other group of coding tasks. The study in [66] proposes a pre-trained Transformer-based model with multitask learning to predict code tokens and their types, which is finally fine-tuned for efficient code completion.

Microsoft's IntelliCode Compose [127] is a cloud-based tool that suggests entire lines of code with correct syntax. This model provides monolingual embeddings while leveraging multilingual knowledge, benefiting low-resource programming languages. Additionally, it enhances privacy by preventing exposure of sensitive information, addressing a key limitation in prior auto-completion tools.

Meta's research work in [128] demonstrates the effectiveness of transfer learning for code auto-completion. Their approach is built on top of the GPT-2 and BART Transformer-based models, and applies auto-regressive and DAE objectives to improve predictions.

A critical concern in code completion is privacy and security as noted in [127]. Furthermore, since prompts used for code completion tasks often have similar structures, there is a risk that generated programs will share similar designs, potentially introducing common vulnerabilities. Future research should address these concerns by enhancing model diversity and privacy safeguards in automated code completion. Additionally, most current code auto-completion assistants struggle to retain the long-context of earlier parts of the code written by the programmer. As a result, they often suggest generic and repetitive line completions. To enable more intelligent and context-aware assistance, it is essential to develop code completion systems capable of capturing long-range dependencies, potentially across an entire file or even multiple files within a project. Such capabilities are critical to providing seamless and relevant code suggestions.

5.7. Automatic Code Edit

Editing and fixing awkward parts of code structures are routine yet time-consuming tasks for programmers. These repetitive activities consume significant effort, but recent neural models aim to automate them [129].

CodeEditor [130] is a pre-trained code editing model whose results demonstrate improved performance and generalization capabilities in code-editing tasks. It consists of three stages: collecting code snippets from repositories like GitHub, generating inferior versions (versions somewhat different from the ground truth) of the code for pre-training, and evaluating the pre-trained model under three settings, namely fine-tuning, few-shot, and zero-shot.

The multi-modal NMT-based code editing engine referred as MODIT in [9] processes code in three steps: preprocessing, token representation via an encoder–decoder attention mechanism, and output generation. The preprocessing phase integrates three input modalities: code location, contextual information, and the commit messages, which guide the editing process.

A major challenge in this field is the lack of stable benchmark datasets for source code editing. The exponential growth of demands on software development further compounds this issue, as modern applications span huge numbers of lines of code, making manual code editing tiresome. For automatic code-editing models to be effective and scalable in complex coding environments, they should be trained on diverse and inclusive source code corpora. Addressing this gap is crucial for advancing automated code editing techniques.

5.8. Code Summarization

Programmers frequently read source code written by others, requiring the detailed intuition of a particular program. Automating this process through code summarization, that is, generating human-readable descriptions for code snippets, can significantly enhance efficiency. Neural methods have shown great success in this area.

M2TS, short for Multi-Scale Multi-Modal Approach Based on Transformer for Source Code Summarization [131], utilizes AST structures and token semantics using a cross-modality fusion approach for improved code summarization. Another model in [132] applies reinforcement learning with triplet code representations such as CFG, AST, and plain texts to enhance code summary generations.

In [133], a hybrid model combines token sequences (encoded using c-encoder) with semantic graphs (encoded using g-encoder) for richer context. Structural information from code snippets has inspired research such as AST-Trans [134], which transforms AST graphs into sequences using traversal and linearization techniques, thereby reducing computational costs. In [135], the model predicts action words from code blocks, identifying their intent and job class to enhance summarization.

Although significant improvements have been achieved in the research area of code summarization, evaluating the performance of code summarization models remains challenging. NLP-based metrics fail to capture source code semantics, often leading to misleading results. Research into specialized evaluation metrics tailored for source code is essential to ensure accurate and meaningful assessments of code summarization models.

5.9. Code Change Detection

Tracking updates in large-scale software projects is challenging, especially for a software development distributed across multiple teams, which may require frequent commits and updates from each team. Neural methods have been introduced to assist programmers in efficiently managing code changes.

CORE, short for COde REview engine [136], employs LSTM models with multi-embedding and multi-attention mechanisms to review code changes, effectively capturing semantic modifications. Another model, CC2Vec [137], represents code changes by analyzing modifications across updated source code files. It preprocesses change patches by tokenizing modified code blocks and constructing a code vocabulary. Structural information from added and removed code is then processed via a Hierarchical Attention Network for better representation.

IABLSTM (short for Impact Analysis with Attention Bidirectional Long Short-Term Memory) [138] utilizes a Bidirectional Long Short-Term Memory (Bi-LSTM) with an attention mechanism to detect source code changes. It identifies differences between the original and modified code using cosine similarity, leveraging AST paths and vectorized representations. Another approach in [139] applies NMT techniques to track meaningful code modifications in pull requests, aiding collaborative development.

Along with the previous efforts, code change detection remains an active research area. A promising direction is integrating these models with push notification systems within IDEs, providing real-time alerts about modifications. This would enhance efficiency in team-based software development, ensuring developers stay informed seamlessly.

5.10. Code Similarity Detection

The rising demand for software applications has led to increased source code duplication, where the same code is reused across projects. This issue undermines creativity, infringes upon intellectual property rights, and raises privacy concerns. Neural methods have emerged as promising solutions for detecting code similarity.

The model in [11] applies NLP techniques for code similarity detection. It preprocesses source code through stemming, segmentation, embedding, and feature extraction, generating vectorized representations of code pairs. Cosine distance is then used to compute similarity scores. Another approach in [140] focusing on Scratch, a visual PL, utilizes

Siamese Bi-LSTM model to capture syntactic and semantic code similarities. Manhattan distance metric is utilized to evaluate similarity between the Scratch files.

Cross-language code similarity detection is another active research area. The approach in [141] transforms source code of multiple PLs into control flow charts, applying graph similarity detection techniques to compare them.

A major challenge in code similarity detection research is the reliability of datasets. Open-source repositories may contain default IDE-generated templates, leading to unintentional similarities. Future research should focus on differentiating manually written and machine-generated code to enhance code similarity detection. Addressing these challenges is crucial for maintaining ethical and professional standards in software development.

5.11. Program Synthesis

Ideally, computer-literate end users should be able to interact with machines using clear NL instructions. However, for this to be possible, intelligent systems are needed to convert NL instructions into executable code. Program synthesis [142,143] addresses this challenge by developing models that automatically generate programs based on user-defined instructions.

PATOIS [144] is a program synthesis model which incorporates code idioms via structural components called probabilistic Tree Substitution Grammars (pTSG). Its encoder embeds NL specifications, while its decoder generates token representations of ASTs. LaSynth [145] is an input–output-based program synthesis model, focused on compiled languages like C, by integrating latent execution representations. During training, its loss function combines latent executor loss and token prediction loss. The model also generates input–output pairs to improve supervised program synthesis approaches.

CodeGen [146] is a Salesforce's Code LLM, which employs an auto-regressive method similar to GPT models, predicting code tokens based on prior prompts. Its multi-turn programming benchmark is designed to scale problem sets according to the size of the model and dataset.

However, program synthesis model evaluation benchmarks remain an open challenge. Some studies propose synthetic datasets [147], while others generate domain-specific input–output examples [148]. Further research is needed to establish standardized and versatile evaluation benchmarks, ensure the executability of source code generated by program synthesis, and develop optimal performance evaluation metrics.

5.12. Code Modeling and Representation

This part of our survey presents existing approaches to code representation and modeling in neural-based programming tasks [149]. Effective programming tasks require robust code representation and modeling techniques [150], as these representations directly influence how neural models interpret and process source code.

Several studies have explored different code representation techniques. In [151], source codes are utilized as pair-wise AST node paths, offering a generalizable approach. Another work [152] employs IR and contextual flow graphs (XFG) to enhance semantic code representation. Graph-based methods have also gained attention in the code representation research. Message passing and grammar-based methods in [153] represent the semantics of code structurally. GraphCodeBERT [69] leverages data flow structures to model relationships between variables and computational flow. The Open-vocabulary neural language model (Open Vocab NLM) in [154] integrates Gated Recurrent Units (GRUs) and sub-word tokenization, enabling it to process billions of tokens dynamically. AST-based approaches are evolved in [155], where ST-trees mitigates long-range dependency issues using bidirectional GRUs. Flow2Vec [156] converts code to low-dimensional vector representations using high-order proximity embeddings. CodeDisen [157] leverages a variational autoencoder to disentangle syntax and semantics across PLs. SPT-code [158] incorporates code sequences, ASTs, and NL descriptions for tasks like summarization, completion, bug-fixing, translation, and code search. Another model in [116] aligns embeddings of different PLs augmented along with their IR representations and actual tokens of the source code for the code translation task.

This survey highlights a wide range of representations, from raw source code tokens, ASTs, and CFGs to IR and DFG. While combining various code representations often improves comprehension, systematic research is needed to determine the optimal combination of these possible code representation options. Enhancing the neural-based code-modeling relies on robust, task-specific representation strategies. Hence, exploring the effective augmentation of various code representation alternatives could significantly broaden the research in this field.

5.13. Code Classification

Understanding and identifying source code across multiple PLs requires intuitively grasping the objectives and distinguishing features of programs. Traditional methods, such as manual cross-checking or using predefined rules, are effective but impractical for large-scale projects, especially for developers unfamiliar with multiple PLs. Code classification offers an efficient solution to these challenges by categorizing source code based on syntax, semantics, or other defined characteristics.

In [159], Multinomial Naive Bayes (MNB) is used as the classifier, and the Term Frequency-Inverse Document Frequency (TF-IDF) is employed for feature extraction. This method classifies code snippets from 21 PLs using the Stack Overflow corpus and identifies specific language versions. Deep learning has also further improved classification accuracy. For example, Reyes et al. [160] employs an LSTM with word embeddings and dropout regularization, outperforming traditional classifiers. The research in [161] uses CNNs to classify source code across 60 PLs, achieving high F1 scores. A CNN-based approach in [162] predicts source code categories based on algorithmic structures rather than keywords, using an online judge system as its corpus. In [163], the authors leverage topic modeling and JavaParser preprocessing to identify code block functionalities for Java code classification. Beyond standard code classification tasks, Barr et al. [164] combine deep learning with combinatorial graph analysis to detect and classify code vulnerabilities, using code2vec and LSTM embeddings. The research work in [165] classifies semantic units of machine learning code using LSTM-GRU with attention mechanisms, applying MixUp augmentation to overcome data scarcity.

Code classification methods in the papers reviewed so far can fall into four broad categories such as algorithm or problem domain based, language based, code functionality based, and vulnerability based as shown in Figure 5. However, additional criteria such as coding paradigms (imperative, declarative, functional, and object-oriented) can be a further supplement to code classification models. Future research should focus on expanding classification taxonomies, ensuring a comprehensive categorization basis for an all-inclusive code classification task.

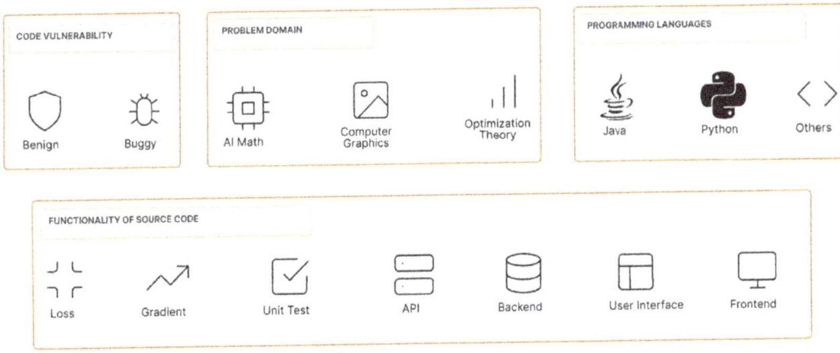

Figure 5. Types of source code classification.

5.14. Code Vulnerability Detection

Source code vulnerabilities arise when errors and security flaws remain unpatched, making automated detection essential for mitigating risks. In [166], CNN and RNN deep learning models are utilized to extract feature representations and detect vulnerabilities in C and C++ code.

The Automated Vulnerability Detection framework based on Hierarchical Representation and Attention Mechanism (AVDHRAM) proposed in [167] improves vulnerability detection by structuring source code into five hierarchical levels: program, function, slice, statement, and token. However, the primary focus of this model is statement-level analysis enhanced by attention mechanisms. Another approach by Mao et al. [168] introduces a Bi-LSTM model that serializes ASTs while incorporating attention mechanisms to improve accuracy in classifying vulnerable functions. Transformer-based vulnerability detection presented in [169] uses fine-grained code slices for analyzing function calls, pointers, and expressions. In [170], three deep learning models combined with multiple code representations improve vulnerability detection.

Graph-based models like the one in [171] employ GGNN and inductive learning, using Common Vulnerability and Exposure (CVE) functions to create code slice graphs. In this work, the attention layer effectively identifies relationships among graph nodes, enhancing vulnerability detection. Wang et al. [172] combine gated graph networks and control flow analysis to distinguish benign from buggy code, addressing data scarcity by leveraging training data from open-source repositories.

Although some remarkable findings are undeniable in this area, vulnerability detection models still face challenges such as false positives and limited generalization to unseen flaws. Identifying vulnerabilities alone is insufficient; thus, classification according to severity, type, and potential impacts is crucial for comprehensive vulnerability management. Integrating neural models with static and dynamic program analysis or formal verification [173] could improve robustness. Future research should explore these integrations experimentally, advancing comprehensive vulnerability detection methodologies.

5.15. Code Analysis

Source code analysis involves multiple stages, serving various purposes and applications [174]. Prior research has explored different attributes for code quality assessment. In [175], static and dynamic properties of CFGs are utilized for code analysis. Ramadan et al. [176] perform code analysis by evaluating the execution speed of a particular program based on AST structures, generating code pairs to identify the snippet with faster execution speed.

A dynamic program analysis algorithm proposed in [177] leverages AST and CFG representations, storing contextual information in Translation Units. In [178], a hybrid analysis tool combines historical and structural schemes, featuring a Java-based parser, a Python-based Code History Miner, and an interactive interface. GENESISP, introduced in [179], integrates source and binary code data for Debian-based environments, employing 13 analysis tools. Though its neural basis is unclear, its user interface facilitates database collection and analysis of open-source software.

Although the current research in source code analysis is commendable, most neural models rely heavily on AST representations. While ASTs capture structural aspects, they fail to convey comprehensive functional and semantic information about the code. Therefore, integrating multiple representations alongside AST information can enhance the robustness of source code analysis.

5.16. Code Authorship Identification

With growing concerns over intellectual property in software development, accurate code authorship identification is essential for innovation and guaranteeing ownership rights [180]. Several studies have explored neural-based approaches to tackle this problem.

Abuhamad et al. [181] introduce a CNN-based method utilizing word embeddings and TF-IDF representations, demonstrating promising authorship attribution results on the Google Code Jam (GCJ) dataset. Kurtukova et al. [182] propose a hybrid neural network combining CNN-Bidirectional GRU (C-BiGRU), LSTM, Bi-LSTM, and other models, training on vectorized datasets before applying them to anonymized source code for authorship identification. Expanding on this, in [180], they tackle more complex real-world scenarios such as multi-language authorship attribution, coding style variations, and AI-generated code identification. Omi et al. [183] introduce a model capable of identifying multiple contributors to a single codebase by converting code snippets into AST paths and using ensemble classifiers. A CNN-based model, along with a KNN classifier, is presented in [184], emphasizing explainability in authorship attribution.

A key challenge in authorship attribution is the variability in coding styles across different PLs. Programmers often write in multiple styles, complicating the identification task. Moreover, IDEs generate code templates, such as ASP.NET MVC scaffolding in Microsoft Visual Studio, and AI-assistants can also produce large amounts of code, making it difficult to distinguish programmer-written and machine-generated code. Although progress has been made, future work should address the evolving programming practices, mixed data sources, and auto-generated code for robust authorship attribution and identification.

5.17. Program Repair and Bug Fix

Troubleshooting errors and fixing bugs in source code are daily challenges for every programmer. Manually handling these tasks for large codebases is cumbersome, necessitating automated tools. Ensemble Learning using Convolution Neural Machine Translation for Automatic Program Repair (ENCORE) is proposed in [185], leveraging a seq2seq encoder–decoder architecture with an attention mechanism and ensemble learning. The model follows three stages: input representation (tokenization), training ensemble models, and validating patches. ENCORE successfully repairs code errors in four PLs and shows potential adaptability for more PLs. Liu et al. [186] address lexical and semantic gaps between bugs and their corresponding fixes by employing lexical and semantic correlation matching, combined with focal loss, to tackle data imbalance in buggy and non-buggy classifications.

While most SOTA approaches fine-tune the pre-trained NLP models for programming tasks, Jiang et al. [187] pre-train a pure PL model on large codebases, then fine-tune it for APR. Their approach introduces a code-aware beam search strategy to manage syntax constraints and sub-word tokenization to mitigate out-of-vocabulary (OOV) issues. CIRCLE

(Continual Repair aCross Programming LanguagEs) [188] is a cross-language APR model, which extends T5-based pre-trained NLP models with continual learning to repair code across multiple PLs. This approach enhances adaptability and generalization.

In real-world software development, bugs are often fixed following the post-failure measures. However, integrating self-healing mechanisms [189] with bug detection and fault localization [190] could revolutionize APR by preventing data loss or system crashes. Despite their promise, LLMs and Code LLMs struggle with runtime bugs unseen during their training stage. Addressing this requires integrating LLMs with external validation systems that provide automatic feedback for invalid patches. Ongoing research explores patch validation and refinement [189], paving the way for end-to-end APR frameworks that enhance the entire software development life cycle.

5.18. Code Clone Detection

Most modern software applications rely heavily on code reuse across their development stage. While this practice accelerates software development and productivity, it can lead to issues such as code bloating and software quality degradation, collectively referred to as code clone problems. Code clone detection models address these challenges. For instance, the research work in [191] proposes a CNN-based model with two convolutional and pooling layers, leveraging the BigCloneBench dataset for evaluation of the model on code clone detection.

Zhang et al. [192] design a clone detection method that aligns similar functionalities between source code snippets, even when their structure is different. This model uses sparse reconstruction and attention-based alignment techniques, relying on similarity scores to detect clones. Meanwhile, Zeng et al. [193] focus on computational efficiency, significantly reducing runtime. They use a weighted Recursive Autoencoder (RAE) and process source code in two phases: feature extraction to generate program vectors and clone detection via Approximate Nearest Neighbor Search (ANNS). They use Euclidean distance as a similarity metric. Functional clone detection, which identifies functionally equivalent but different code implementations, is explored in [194]. This hybrid model combines sequential tokens, syntactical ASTs, and structural CFGs to represent the source code and is evaluated on Java-based clone corpora. Recent research has expanded to cross-language clone detection as demonstrated in [195], which identifies clones across multiple PLs.

While sometimes the term code clone detection overlaps with code similarity detection, they serve distinct purposes. Although code clone detection can be considered a subset of code similarity detection, many studies use these terms interchangeably which may encounter confusion for readers. Future research should clearly distinguish these two tasks while developing an effective clone detection strategy for large-scale projects. Finally, leveraging LLMs or Code LLMs in code clone detection tasks holds promise for enhancing accuracy and scalability. By adopting recently up-to-date methodologies and expanding cross-language code clone detection capabilities, future research can offer robust solutions and clarify the distinction between code clone detection and code similarity detection, thereby improving software quality and maintainability.

To offer a deeper analytical view, we further grouped neural methods across the programming tasks based on their architectural families and learning paradigms. Broadly, these include sequence-based models (e.g., RNNs, LSTMs, and GRUs), Transformer-based large language models (e.g., CodeBERT, CodeT5, and PLBART), and graph-based neural networks (e.g., GGNN and RGCN). Each group exhibits distinct strengths and limitations. Sequence-based models excel at capturing short-range dependencies but struggle with long-contextual understanding; Transformer-based architectures handle long-range dependencies effectively, but they demand extensive computational resources and training data; graph-based approaches model code structure more explicitly but often sacrifice generalization due to task-specific designs. Table 6 summarizes the overall comparison of these neural methods' categories in the context of programming-centric SE tasks.

Table 6. Comparison of major neural method families applied to programming and SE tasks.

Group Name	Advantages	Disadvantages	Common Application Areas
Sequence-based (RNN, LSTM, GRU)	Captures token-level dependencies; effective for small datasets; easy to fine-tune.	Limited context retention; sequential processing slows inference.	Comment generation, code completion, bug-fixing.
Transformer-based (CodeBERT, CodeT5, CodeT5+, PLBART, GPT-family)	Captures long-range context; supports parallel training; high generalization across PLs.	High computational cost; prone to hallucination; sensitive to noisy data.	Code translation, generation, summarization, synthesis.
Graph-based (GGNN, RGCN, AST-GNN)	Encodes structural and semantic information explicitly; interpretable representations.	Task-specific tuning required; limited scalability on large codebases.	Code analysis, clone detection, code search and retrieval.

6. Data, Benchmarks, and Evaluation Metrics

6.1. Datasets and Benchmarks

The scientific literature on the applications of neural networks in programming and SE primarily focuses on model designs and architectural advances. Neural networks form the foundation of deep learning and large parameter size models. The emergence of LLMs and Code LLMs, with a large number of parameters, marks a significant milestone in the field. However, a review of publication trends reveals that datasets and benchmarks often receive less emphasis and are treated as supplementary rather than core components of the research. This neglects the crucial role of data in the advancement of deep learning and AI, particularly in programming tasks, where high-quality training data is essential for model effectiveness.

In this context, we take a chronological deep dive into the major datasets and benchmarks introduced for programming tasks. One such example is the Django dataset introduced in [196], which is a parallel corpus of Python code and corresponding NL text descriptions. Salesforce's encoder–decoder architecture-based CodeT5 model and a retrieval-augmented model kNN-TRANX were among the models evaluated on this dataset [197]. However, this dataset is small in size (18,805 pairs) and is narrowly scoped which ultimately support only the Python-related code generation tasks. Two years later (in 2017), a data corpus consisting of 108,726 Python Code and Doc-string pairs (PCSD) was released, where it incorporates class declarations, class methods, module doc-strings, and commit SHAs in its latest version [98,198]. The M2TS model for code summarization introduced in Section 5.8 is among the models evaluated on this dataset [131]. However, referring to the literature that explores the dataset, we observe that the PCSD data corpus has some noise, and the comments (doc-strings) miss some details.

The CoNaLa dataset is a benchmark comprising approximately 2.4 K curated pairs of English-Python data, extracted from Stack Overflow's programming-related question–answer discussions and documentation [198]. Several neural models were evaluated on this dataset, such as CodeLLaMA, CodeT5+, and CodeGen among others [199].

Another notable dataset is Devign, presented at NeurIPS 2019 and consisting of 27,652 vulnerable and 31,313 non-vulnerable C language functions [200]. As the name suggests, this dataset is dedicated to identifying vulnerability patterns in C programs. It was manually curated from four popular open source C-language projects. The dataset is well-regarded for its quality in vulnerability identification tasks, as data collection and labeling were performed by a team of security experts, requiring approximately 600 man-hours.

Given that neural methods for programming tasks are still evolving, data processing methodologies are largely derived from NLP. Consequently, most of the code corpora utilized in scientific research articles focused on the application of neural methods in SE are mainly dominated by code generation using NL texts [201]. Notable examples include datasets mapping NL to SQL code [202]. In recent related studies, other open-sourced datasets have been designed and released for both NL-to-code and code-to-code generation tasks [203–205]. Semantic parsing is integral to the processing of the code corpus, while static parsing methodologies [206] aid in understanding structural code information.

Recently, numerous large-scale code-specific datasets have been released to boost the neural methods involved in the programming tasks [207,208]. For instance, in [209], a Python class-level code generation dataset containing 842K class skeletons (methods and attributes with doc-strings) has been released. This dataset was extracted from 13,174 real-world GitHub projects.

Online coding competition platforms [210], repositories like GitHub, and technical Q&A forums such as Stack Overflow [198] are key sources of code corpora. However, to date, many of the code corpora released by researchers and practitioners lack standardized dataset pipelines and detailed documentation. In response, commendable efforts have been made to provide well-designed datasets through the HuggingFace Datasets Hub [211].

However, the development of standardized dataset pipelines for programming tasks is still in its early stages. Although many processed code-related datasets are available via the HuggingFace Datasets API, several challenges arise when exploring datasets for the same task. For instance, datasets for tasks like vulnerability detection, code translation, or code generation may come from different contributors. These datasets often suffer from inconsistent data formats, varying feature sets, and undocumented preprocessing steps, making reproducibility difficult for future researchers.

To summarize, Table 7 provides a summary on a significant number of datasets used in programming and SE tasks, arranged in chronological order of their release. It provides a concise summary of each dataset, such as models evaluated on these datasets, targeted tasks, and evaluation metrics used to measure model performance. The critical analyses of various evaluation metrics along with their mathematical formulation are discussed in Section 6.2 below.

Table 7. An overview of datasets curated for programming and software engineering tasks, utilized by neural models in code intelligence research.

Dataset (Year)	Task(s)	Trained/Evaluated Models	Metrics
Defects4J (2014)	Bug detection and repair (Java)	GenProg, Nopol, jKali, ASTOR, RepairAgent [212], ThinkRepair [213]	Repair success rate, Pass@*k*
BigCloneBench (2014)	Code clone detection	GNN, Code2Vec, CodeBERT, GraphCodeBERT	Precision, Recall, F1
Django (2015)	NL-to-code generation, pseudo-code generation	BART, CodeT5, kNN-TRANX	BLEU, CodeBLEU, EM
QuixBugs (2017)	Program repair (buggy algorithms)	GenProg, PolyCoder, Codex	Ranking test-passing patches, BLEU, Pass@*k*
PCSD (2017)	Code summarization, Comment Generation	Seq2Seq, CodeBERT, DECOM	BLEU, ROUGE, METEOR
CoNaLa (2018)	Code generation	CodeLLaMA, CodeGen, CodeGen2, CodeT5	BLEU, CodeBELEU, EM
Concode (2018)	Code generation	Encoder-decoder, Bi-LSTM,	BLEU, EM

Table 7. *Cont.*

Dataset (Year)	Task(s)	Trained/Evaluated Models	Metrics
CodeSearchNet (2019)	Code search and retrieval	Bag-of-words, CNN, RNN, CodeBERT, GraphCodeBERT	MRR, BLEU, ROUGE, Normalized Discounted Cumulative Gain at rank k (NDCG@*k*)
Devign (2019)	Vulnerability detection (C/C++)	GGNN, CNN, LSTM	Accuracy, F1
JuICe (2019)	Contextual code generation, API call	Transformer, LSTM	EM, BLEU, Accuracy, Precision, Recall
Bears (2019)	APR and bug fixing	MUFIN, etc.	Test suite correctness
TransCoder (2020/2022/2023)	Code translation (Java, C++, Python, Go, Rust)	TransCoder, TransCoder-ST, TransCoder-IR, rule-based baselines, GPT-3.5, LLaMA, CodeGen	BLEU, EM, Computational Accuracy (CA), Pass Rate
CodeXGLUE (2021)	Defect detection, code translation, clone detection, and more.	CodeBERT, GraphCodeBERT, CodeGPT, Encoder–Decoder	BLEU, ROUGE, Accuracy, F1, MRR
MBPP (2021)	Python code generation	GPT-3, WizardCoder, etc.	Pass@*k*, BLEU
HumanEval (2021)	Python program synthesis	Codex, GPT-3, GPT-Neo, etc.	Pass@*k*
APPS (2021)	Code generation	GPT-3, GPT-Neo, GPT-J, Codex	Pass@*k*
CodeNet (2021)	Code classification, code similarity, code translation	Multilayer Perceptron, Graph Convolutional Networks (GCNs), GNN, PLBART	Accuracy, BLEU, Runtime metrics
XLCoST (2022)	Code translation, code summarization, code search, and more.	CodeBERT, PLBART, CodeT5, RoBERTa, and more.	BLEU, CodeBLEU, MRR
CodeContests (2022)	Code generation	AlphaCode, GPT-4o mini, Qwen2.5-Coder-7B-Instruct, and more.	Test-case success rate, Pass@*k*
SecurityEval (2022)	Vulnerability detection (Python)	GPT-4o, InCoder, GitHub Copilot, AutoSafeCoder	Vulnerability occurrence rate, Pass@*k*
DiverseVul (2023)	Vulnerability detection (C/C++)	CodeBERT, CodeGPT, PolyCoder, CodeT5, NatGen, and more.	Accuracy, Precision, Recall, F1, False Positive Rate
CodeTransOcean (2023)	Multilingual code translation	GPT-4, CodeT5+, Claude-3.5	EM, BLEU, CodeBLEU, Debugging Success Rate (DSR@*k*), Pass@*k*
DS-1000 (2023)	Data science code generation	CodeGemma, DeepSeek-Coder, CodeLLaMA, Incoder, WizardCoder, and more.	Pass@*k*, Test Cases + Surface-Form Constraints
ClassEval (2023)	Class-level code generation	GPT-4, GPT-3.5, SantaCoder, WizardCoder, Intstruct-CodeGen, CodeGeeX, and more.	Pass@*k*
MCoNaLa (2023)	Multi-NL code generation and summarization on Python	gpt-3.5-turbo, mT5, CodeT5, mBART, PLBART	EM, BLEU, CodeBLEU
PrimeVul (2024)	Vulnerability detection (C/C++)	GPT-3.5, GPT-4, CodeT5, UniXCoder, StarCoder2, and more.	F1, Precision, Recall
EvoCodeBench (2024)	Code generation (Python)	GPT-4, GPT-3.5, StarCoder2, CodeLLaMA-7B, DeepSeekCoder-7B, StarCoder2-7B, and more.	Pass@*k*, Recall@*k*, Debugging Success Improvement (DSI)

Table 7. *Cont.*

Dataset (Year)	Task(s)	Trained/Evaluated Models	Metrics
Statement-level Code Summ. (2024)	Statement-level summarization	GPT-4, GPT-3.5, CodeLLaMA, StarChat	BLEU, SBCS (SentenceBERT + Cosine Similarity), SBED (SentenceBERT + Euclidean Distance), Human Eval
Python ClassGen (2025)	Class-level Python code generation	GPT-4	ROUGE-L, BLEU, Tree Similarity of Edit Distance (TSED)
DEFECTS4J-TRANS [Transformed Defects4J] (2025) [214]	APR	Magicoder-S-DS, WaveCoder-Ultra, CodeQwen1.5, DeepSeek-Coder-Instruct, and more.	plausibility and correctness of patches (plausible patch, correct patch)

6.2. Evaluation Metrics

The progressive development of neural models for programming tasks, particularly those trained on code, is heavily influenced by NLP techniques. Even with the emergence of LLMs and Code LLMs, capable of interpreting code across various PLs, NLP-based evaluation methods remain widely adopted [49]. While not ideally suited for programming tasks, these metrics serve as a foundational baseline in the absence of standardized, code-specific evaluation frameworks. However, recently emerging code-specific evaluation metrics seem to be promising for measuring the rapidly growing range of programming tasks. Based on the evaluation strategies utilized in the major scientific studies reviewed in this survey, the metrics commonly employed to assess model performance in programming tasks can be categorized into five major groups as detailed below.

6.2.1. Text-Match and N-Gram Overlap-Based Metrics

Match-based or n-gram overlapping metrics assess model performance by quantifying the surface-level word matching (n-gram overlap) between model-generated outputs and ground-truth reference outputs. One of these metrics is the **Exact Match (EM)** , which allows no deviation between the generated and reference code. Due to its rigidity, EM is generally not recommended for code generation tasks [215].

A more widely adopted metric is **BLEU** , originally developed for machine translation [216]. BLEU has been applied to programming tasks such as code translation and summarization. However, it overlooks key syntactic and semantic characteristics inherent in PLs.

ROUGE is another metric in this group, primarily used for evaluating code summarization and comment generation. It relies on matching the longest common subsequence between the generated and reference outputs [217]. However, like BLEU, it fails to account for semantically equivalent yet syntactically different code snippets.

To address such limitations, **CodeBLEU** incorporates both syntactic and semantic information through AST matching and data-flow matching [96]. Another alternative evaluation metric is **CrystalBLEU**, which improves upon BLEU and CodeBLEU by ignoring trivial n-gram overlaps that may result in a misleading match between code snippets with different logical purposes. CrystalBLEU has shown efficiency improvements ranging from 1.9 to 4.5 times over BLEU and CodeBLEU and also outperforms other BLEU variants such as Ruby [218,219]. **METEOR**, another widely used metric in this category, incorporates synonymy and stemming and has been adapted to certain code evaluation tasks [220].

Some of the core formulations for these metrics are provided below.

Assume that N denotes the maximum n-gram length (typically 4); w_n, which is commonly computed as $1/N$, represents the weight for each n-gram precision p_n; p_n is the modified n-gram precision; and BP is the brevity penalty. The BLEU score is computed as follows:

$$\text{BLEU} = \text{BP} \cdot \exp\left(\sum_{n=1}^{N} w_n \log p_n\right)$$

$$\text{BP} = \begin{cases} 1 & \text{if } c > r \\ \exp(1 - \frac{r}{c}) & \text{if } c \leq r \end{cases}$$

where c and r denote the lengths of the candidate and reference outputs, respectively.

The CodeBLEU score integrates semantic and structural signals. Assuming $\text{BLEU}_{\text{weight}}$ denotes the token-wise weighted n-gram precision, $\text{Match}_{\text{ast}}$ and Match_{df} compute the syntactic and semantic matches, respectively, and $\alpha, \beta, \gamma, \delta$ are tuning hyperparameters, the CodeBLEU score is computed as follows:

$$\begin{aligned} \text{CodeBLEU} = {} & \alpha \cdot \text{BLEU} + \beta \cdot \text{BLEU}_{\text{weight}} \\ & + \gamma \cdot \text{Match}_{\text{ast}} + \delta \cdot \text{Match}_{\text{df}} \end{aligned}$$

Despite improvements, all these metrics primarily evaluate surface-level match and lack insight into the actual execution or correctness of the model-generated code.

6.2.2. Embedding-Based Similarity and Learned Metrics

Embedding-based and learned metrics aim to capture semantic similarity between generated and reference code by comparing their vector representations or contextual embeddings. These metrics are well-suited for tasks such as code summarization [221], clone detection, code generation, and code search.

A foundational metric in this category is **Cosine Similarity (Embedding CosSim)**, which ranges from -1 to $+1$ and measures the angular similarity between two vectors (e.g., P and Q):

$$\cos(\text{P}, \text{Q}) = \frac{\text{P} \cdot \text{Q}}{\|\text{P}\|\|\text{Q}\|}$$

where $\cdot$ denotes the dot product and $\|\cdot\|$ is the vector norm. Cosine similarity has been widely used in assessing various models like CodeT5+ and GPT-series models. Recent evaluations of these models involve Verilog code generation and comprehension tasks among the notable examples [222].

CodeBERTScore, built upon cosine similarity, utilizes pre-trained CodeBERT embeddings to compare code/comment pairs and has demonstrated high alignment with human judgment [223]. However, its applicability is restricted to a few supported PLs.

Euclidean distance is another metric, defined for two vectors P and Q as shown below:

$$d(\text{P}, \text{Q}) = \sqrt{\sum_i (P_i - Q_i)^2}$$

Manhattan distance, also known as the L1 distance, is defined as

$$d(\mathbf{P}, \mathbf{Q}) = \sum_i |P_i - Q_i|$$

These two distance metrics are often employed in code similarity and clone detection tasks where structural information is less critical.

Another important metric is **MRR** commonly used in code search and retrieval-augmented generation applications. MRR computes the average of the inverse ranks of the first correct result and has been widely adopted in evaluations on CodeSearchNet [224].

BLEURT, a learned regression-based metric initially introduced for NLP evaluation, has recently been adapted for code summarization tasks [225]. Other metrics in this category include **BARTScore**, **GPTScore**, and **NDCG**, each tailored for specific code-related tasks.

Despite their advantages, these metrics face the following limitations:

- They are unsupervised and depend heavily on the quality of the embeddings.
- They often treat code and comments as plain text, disregarding structural and semantic intricacies such as AST nodes and API hierarchies.

Hence, while embedding-based and learned metrics enhance evaluation by moving beyond surface-level token matching, the growing complexity and diversity of programming tasks suggest that structure-aware, execution-based metrics may provide more accurate and holistic assessments.

6.2.3. Classification Metrics

Classification metrics broadly span from binary classification to multi-class and sequence-level accuracy. They are used to evaluate the correctness of classifiers on specific code-related tasks within the context of this survey. The values of classification evaluation metrics typically range from 0 to 1, or 0 to 100%. These evaluation metrics such as **accuracy**, **precision**, **recall**, **F1**, and **AUC (Area Under the ROC Curve)** are widely recognized as standard and reliable classification metrics not only in programming and code-related tasks but also across various other research domains involving classification activities. Several tasks such as code clone detection, code smell detection, source-code classification, and code vulnerability detection depend on such evaluation metrics [166,200,226–230].

Most classification metrics are derived from the following four fundamental attributes of a classification model's inference results:

- **True Positive (TP)**: represents the correct prediction of the positive cases.
- **True Negative (TN)**: represents the correct prediction of the negative cases.
- **False Positive (FP)**: represents the negative cases that are predicted incorrectly as positive ones.
- **False Negative (FN)**: represents the positive cases that are predicted incorrectly as negative ones.

The accuracy, recall, precision and F1 score evaluation metrics are computed as follows:

$$\text{Accuracy} = \frac{TP + TN}{TP + TN + FP + FN}$$

$$\text{Recall} = \frac{TP}{TP + FN}$$

$$\text{Precision} = \frac{TP}{TP + FP}$$

$$\text{F1 score} = 2 \times \frac{Precision \times Recall}{Precision + Recall}$$

Different code-related tasks utilize evaluation metrics based on various scenarios. The accuracy metric is generally recommended when the data classification labels are balanced across classes. The precision metric is best suited for evaluating tasks where minimizing false positives is critical, such as in bug detection since frequently flagging bugs can be costly in such cases. In contrast, the recall metric is essential in tasks where minimizing false negatives is important, such as in assessing overall security coverage, where it is crucial to ensure that all security vulnerabilities are detected. In general, the F1 score and AUC metrics are considered effective in situations where data imbalance is a concern [231].

6.2.4. Security-Specific and Threat-Coverage Metrics

The evaluation metrics in this category are commonly used to assess neural models involved in program security analysis and threat prevention tasks. While a variety of metrics can be applied to such tasks, these particular metrics are distinguished by their specific areas of focus, which are often evident from their name and their computation terminologies. **Threat Coverage** (also known as vulnerability class coverage) serves as a primary example of this group of metrics. It measures the number of known categories of threats or vulnerabilities that a neural model can address or exploit during bug-hunting tasks. The core idea behind this evaluation metric is to quantify the diversity of threats a particular neural model can handle. As recently noted by Google DeepMind, analyzing security threat chains should be a fundamental building block of cyber-security systems, particularly in response to attacks initiated by AI-based incidents [232].

The **Vulnerability Detection Score** is a pairwise evaluation metric in this category [233]. It assesses a model's ability to distinguish between vulnerable and non-vulnerable code, with a focus on minimizing the FN rate while keeping the FP rate below a particular fixed threshold. The **Vulnerability Occurrence Rate** is another example of a security analysis metric. It represents the fraction of code snippet samples in a dataset that contain at least one vulnerability. The study in [234] also explores how other metrics correlate with the vulnerability occurrence rate. Another evaluation metric in this category is the **Attack/Exploit Success Rate**, defined as the number of successful attacks divided by the total number of attack attempts [235]. Additionally, there are other criteria for evaluating the performance of neural models, such as plausibility, fixed bugs count, and correctness of fixed bugs. Most of these require manual intervention to make a final judgment.

6.2.5. Execution-Based and Functional Correctness Metrics

Execution-based evaluation metrics are among the most commendable and ideal metrics for programming-centric tasks involved in the generation of code snippets as model outputs. The top-k metrics, such as **Pass@k**, which are popular program-execution-based evaluation methods, assess a model's performance by determining whether any of the k generated programs pass the given tests. In essence, Pass@k checks whether at least one of the top k model-generated programs passes all test cases, considering the problem to be solved if any of the k model-generated candidate code snippets is correct.

Similarly, the research work in [236] introduces three metrics—Success@k, Build@k, and Average Pass Rate—for evaluating code translation performance across entire repositories. Given M repositories in repository-level code translation benchmarks, we discuss these three metrics below along with their mathematical formulations.

Success@k (Test Pass Rate across Multiple Trials) measures the proportion of repositories that successfully pass all test cases in at least one of the selected k experimental rounds. Given a set T_j of repositories that pass all test cases in the j-th round, the cardinality $|T_j|$ indicates the number of repositories that succeeded in that round. The Success@k metric is computed as shown below, where $\binom{m}{k}$ denotes the binomial coefficient, representing the number of ways to choose k rounds out of m total experimental rounds, and the union captures all repositories that pass in at least one of the selected trials:

$$\text{Success@}k = \frac{1}{\binom{m}{k} \times M} \sum_{1 \leq j_1 < j_2 < \cdots < j_k \leq m} \left| T_{j_1} \cup T_{j_2} \cup \cdots \cup T_{j_k} \right|$$

Build@k (Build Success Rate across Multiple Trials), similar to Success@k, indicates the proportion of repositories that successfully compile in at least one of the k selected rounds. Let B_j denote the set of repositories that were successfully built in the j-th trial, then

$$\text{Build@}k = \frac{1}{\binom{m}{k} \times M} \sum_{1 \le j_1 < j_2 < \cdots < j_k \le m} \left| B_{j_1} \cup B_{j_2} \cup \cdots \cup B_{j_k} \right|$$

Average Pass Rate, also known as the average test case pass rate, measures the mean proportion of test cases passed across all repositories and all experimental rounds. Assuming that $M_{pt}^{(r,s)}$ denotes the number of passed test cases for the r-th repository in the s-th round, and M_{at}^{r} denotes the total number of test cases for the r-th repository, the Average Pass Rate is computed as follows:

$$\text{Average Pass Rate} = \frac{1}{m} \sum_{s=1}^{m} \left(\frac{1}{M} \sum_{r=1}^{M} \frac{M_{pt}^{(r,s)}}{M_{at}^{r}} \right)$$

Another notable example is the **Computational Accuracy (CA)** metric, introduced in 2020 by Meta AI and adapted by other researchers [79,237], which is defined as follows:

$$\text{CA} = \frac{1}{N} \sum_{i=1}^{N} \text{CA}(y_i, \hat{y}_i)$$

$$\text{CA}(y_i, \hat{y}_i) = \begin{cases} 1 & \text{if } \text{Exec}_i(y_i) = \text{Exec}_i(\hat{y}_i) \\ 0 & \text{otherwise} \end{cases}$$

where N denotes the total number of samples, while $\text{Exec}_i(y_i)$ and $\text{Exec}_i(\hat{y}_i)$ represent the execution results of the ground truth sample y_i and the model-predicted sample $\hat{y}_i$, respectively. Given k model-generated candidates, CA@k then evaluates if at least one of them produces the correct output for all test inputs.

In addition, the Test Case Average (TCA@k) [238] quantifies the average number of test cases passed by k generated code fixes per problem. DSR@k proposed in [239] and adapted in [240] defines the proportion of samples whose output is correct within k debugging steps. Repair@k [241] measures the percentage of tasks successfully fixed after k rounds of feedback-driven code repair. Related metrics like DSI and Compilation@k or Repairable Rate (RR) [240] also contribute to the evaluation of a model's iterative fix and recovery abilities. Another related metric, though more common in retrieval-based tasks, is Recall@k [242] which measures the fraction of relevant or ground-truth-equivalent code snippets retrieved within the top-k candidates of the returned results.

The release of HumanEval, a benchmark dataset from the experimental research in [243], marks a shift toward execution-based evaluation. This approach assesses generated code by testing its functionality, addressing the limitations of match based, embedding based, and other metrics that are involved in evaluating model-generated code. Ongoing research continues to refine execution-based metrics, aiming for more reliable evaluation of AI-generated code [238].

While execution-based metrics provide a fine-grained assessment of code correctness, their practical implementation poses significant challenges. These metrics rely heavily on high-quality test cases that are compatible with each generated code sample. For example, the CA metric, originally introduced for evaluating code translation, may encounter limitations in more complex scenarios. In multilingual settings like the research work explored in [239], which involves translation between diverse PLs, applying CA becomes less feasible. The core issue lies in the difficulty of establishing a unified execution framework capable of supporting a broad range of languages and their associated libraries, runtime engines, and dependencies.

Therefore, the adoption and effectiveness of execution-based evaluation could be significantly improved if future research develops standardized and accessible unified frameworks. Such frameworks should provide consistent runtime environments across multiple PLs to facilitate reproducibility and enable more rigorous evaluation in programming tasks.

7. Neural Methods vs. Traditional Approaches in Programming Tasks

This section explores the key advantages of neural networks for programming tasks and examines the challenges of neural-based approaches. It also provides a comparative analysis of the neural methods and other existing methods.

7.1. Rule-Based Approach

In general, rule-based methods rely primarily on predefined "if–then" rules and follow established procedures to guide the knowledge-discovery process to accomplish certain tasks [244–246]. They are powerful for defining structured rules, making them useful as supplementary components in statistical and neural models. However, these approaches suffer from maintainability issues. The programming ecosystem frequently evolves due to business strategy changes and user feedback, requiring continuous updates. Rule-based methods struggle to adapt to these evolving requirements, making them inflexible for long-term scalability.

7.2. Statistical Approach

Several SMT algorithms can serve as benchmarks for adapting NLP-based techniques to programming tasks. SMT approaches basically outperform rule-based methods by incorporating syntactic and semantic representations. For instance, Nguyen et al. [215] utilize phrase-based SMT for program translation in three phases: (1) treating source code as syntactic sequences between source and target languages, (2) integrating semantic information for API migrations, and (3) mapping sememes (semantic units) between PLs. Similarly, other studies have explored the use of SMT methods in generating pseudo-code using the source code of certain languages [53,196]. Such enhancements make SMT approaches superior to rule-based methods, which lack flexibility.

Despite their advantages, statistical models also face challenges. For example, the SLAMC model in [92] does not account for inheritance in object-oriented languages, leading to OOV issues. The mppSMT model in [215], which adopts a divide-and-conquer strategy for code migration, also struggles with dependency learning, API misalignment, and OOV problems. Furthermore, its applicability is primarily limited to Java and C#.

7.3. The Novelty of Neural Methods

Neural networks, inspired by the human brain, offer a novel and promising approach to programming tasks. These models excel in understanding the logic and structure of source code, which itself reflects human cognitive-based solutions. This synergy of analyzing human-created code with human-brain inspired neural net algorithms creates an exciting research intersection [247].

Neural methods leverage vast numbers of neural networks, especially deep neural networks (DNNs) and LLMs, allowing models with billions of parameters to enhance code understanding and generation tasks. While optimal solutions remain an ongoing research challenge, the use of large pre-trained models trained on both NL and PL datasets has significantly improved performance. However, despite their advantages, neural models face several challenges, particularly in the availability of well-structured parallel benchmark datasets.

High-quality training data is essential for the effectiveness of any neural network, but constructing such datasets is resource intensive. Hence, we can say that neural-based approaches provide significant improvements over rule-based and statistical methods, yet overcoming high-quality parallel data limitations and other challenges remains a key area for future research. Table 8 summarizes the pros and cons of these three approaches.

Table 8. Neural methods vs. their counterparts (rule-based and statistical methods).

Method	Strengths	Limitations
Rule-based Methods	Effective for creating precise rules for corpora with complex code patterns.	Hard to maintain and scale. Requires extensive manual effort.
Statistical Methods	Offer more diverse algorithmic implementations than rule-based methods.	Human intervention is needed for better accuracy. SMT methods do not learn from previous experiences.
Neural Methods	Learn patterns from past data, delivering fast and accurate results.	Performance drops with limited training data and requires significant computational resources.

Note: Eighteen studies were examined for this comparison.

8. Discussion and Future Work

In this section, we revisit the research questions that guided our study and highlight potential directions for future work.

8.1. Answers to the Research Questions

8.1.1. RQ1: How Do Neural Approaches Compare to Rule-Based and Statistical Methods in the Context of Programming Tasks?

Neural methods represent the most recent paradigm in applying machine learning to programming tasks, such as source code translation, by leveraging DNNs and large-scale pre-training. In contrast, rule-based approaches rely on manually crafted transformation rules (often operating over ASTs), and statistical methods adapt classical SMT techniques to code (treating programs as literal text sequences).

Neural methods mark a significant leap forward compared to rule-based and statistical approaches for programming tasks, by providing greater adaptability, improved semantic accuracy, and scalable performance on large datasets. However, they demand extensive computational resources, robust parallel or monolingual corpora, and face ongoing challenges in evaluation and interpretability. Rule-based and statistical techniques are still relevant in resource-constrained or safety-critical settings, but for most modern software engineering needs, where languages, libraries, and idiomatic styles rapidly evolve, neural approaches have emerged as the state of the art. As the field progresses, hybrid solutions that integrate symbolic constraints into neural pipelines, alongside richer benchmarks and evaluation frameworks, will likely alleviate the remaining gaps between quality of automated programming tasks and human expert performance.

8.1.2. RQ2: What Is the Current Landscape of Datasets and Benchmarks for Neural Methods in Programming Tasks, and What Are the Critical Gaps?

The landscape of datasets and benchmarks for the application of neural method to programming tasks has expanded dramatically over the past decade, evolving from small, narrowly scoped corpora to large-scale, multi-task corpora. Early efforts (around 2015–2017) focused primarily on mapping NL to code in a single PL, most notably Python, while more recent initiatives (2020–2025) have sought to cover a broader array of tasks (e.g., vulnerability detection, code translation, and code summarization) and multiple PLs (including Java, C/C++, Go, Rust, and other multilingual settings). Despite this progress, several critical gaps remain: most datasets still suffer from limited scope (both in terms of size and language diversity), inconsistent preprocessing and documentation, noisy annotations (particularly in NL annotations or particular task's labels), and a lack of standardized evaluation pipelines.

The field of programming has benefited from a proliferation of datasets and benchmarks spanning several software engineering and programming tasks. Early released code corpora (e.g., Django, PCSD, and CoNaLa) laid the groundwork but often suffered from limited scale and scope. Subsequent benchmarks (e.g., TransCoder, CodeXGLUE, CodeNet, and XLCoST) addressed multi-language and multi-task needs but sometimes at the cost of noisy annotations or inconsistent data format across similar tasks. Most recently, specialized datasets such as [209,242,248,249] have pushed toward class-level generation and real-world repository-level code intelligence tasks along with execution-based evaluation practice. However, critical gaps, such as the lack of standardized preprocessing, detailed documentation, under-representation of many PLs and domains, insufficient benchmarks for multi-file settings, interactivity, and explainability in program repair, as well as real-world performance, still persist. Addressing these gaps will require community-wide efforts to create unified dataset schemas, enrich annotation quality, broaden coverage, and develop richer evaluation methodologies, ultimately enabling more robust, reproducible, and impactful research in the application of neural methods for programming tasks.

8.1.3. RQ3: Which Evaluation Metrics Best Capture Model Performance on Code, Both Syntactically and Functionally, and Where Do Standard NLP Metrics Fall Short?

Evaluating code generation and code understanding models demands metrics that go beyond surface-level text similarity. While traditional NLP metrics (e.g., BLEU, ROUGE, and METEOR) provide a convenient baseline, especially during early stages of model development, their reliance on n-gram overlap prevents them from fully capturing either the syntactic correctness or the functional (execution) behavior of generated code. Even enhanced variants like CodeBLEU and CrystalBLEU, which incorporate AST and data-flow matching, cannot guarantee the generated snippets' compilation or runtime tests. As a result, they serve as convenient proxies during early model inference trials but offer only limited insight into true code correctness.

The most reliable way to assess code model performance combines syntax checks (e.g., Compilation@*k* and Build@*k*) with execution-based metrics such as Pass@*k* and CA. Compilation@*k* ensures that generated programs meet language-grammar requirements, while Pass@*k* and CA verify that at least one of the top-k candidates successfully compiles and produces correct outputs against a comprehensive test suite. Metrics like Success@*k*, Average Pass Rate, and TCA@*k* further enrich this evaluation by measuring test pass rates over multiple trials or averaging partial successes, offering a fine-grained view of both build success and functional correctness of output results.

Standard NLP metrics fall short because they neither enforce compilability nor check whether code handles edge cases or real inputs correctly. In other words, they treat code as "flat text", ignoring compilation requirements and runtime behavior. Embedding-based scores (e.g., CodeBERTScore and Cosine Similarity) improve semantic alignment but still treat code as text and cannot substitute for actual execution checks. Consequently, a robust evaluation framework for code requires prioritizing execution-based measures, backed by reliable test harnesses and multi-language runtime environments, while using text-based and embedding-based metrics only as supplementary signals during early development.

8.1.4. RQ4: What Roles Do LLMs (e.g., GPT-4, LLaMA, and Claude) Play in Programming Tasks?

LLMs originally developed for NLP have been rapidly repurposed to address a wide spectrum of programming tasks, fundamentally altering how code is implemented, reviewed, and maintained. By leveraging the vast corpora of open-source code and documentation, models such as GPT-4, LLaMA, and Claude have demonstrated an ability to generate syntactically correct and often semantically meaningful code snippets from high-level specifications. These models are now routinely employed in interactive, multi-turn dialogues where developers describe functionality or constraints in natural language, and the LLM iteratively refines code to meet functional objective of particular developer defined problem. LLMs generate test cases, and documentations for an entire program. In this capacity, LLMs serve not only as autocompletion engines but also as dynamic programming partners that adapt to evolving requirements and project contexts.

Beyond standalone code generation, LLMs have been integrated into specialized workflows that mirror traditional software-development life-cycle phases [250]. For instance, self-collaborative frameworks distribute subtasks among multiple LLM agents, each responsible for activities such as requirements analysis, architectural design, unit-test creation, and bug-fix proposals; intermediate artifacts generated by one agent become prompts for the next, producing an end-to-end automated pipeline. In parallel, security-oriented studies reveal that LLM outputs can introduce or exacerbate vulnerabilities, prompting the development of hybrid pipelines that combine LLM-driven patch generation with automated test harnesses or static analyzers to validate correctness and security [251]. Furthermore, code-specific LLMs trained and/or fine-tuned on large PL datasets underlie tools such as GitHub Copilot [252] , Cursor, Windsurf, Replit and other programming-specialized AI-chatbots, and utilize LLM-powered AI agents enabling language-agnostic autocompletion, cross-language translation, and even real-time code-review suggestions within integrated development environments.

While LLM-powered development workflows significantly reduce manual implementations, automate boilerplate coding, accelerate test case synthesis, and facilitate rapid prototyping, they also introduce new challenges related to model hallucinations, and hence prompt a need for rigorous validation. Hallucinated library calls, misaligned data-flow assumptions, or omitted edge-case handling can produce code that compiles but behaves incorrectly or insecurely. The computational footprint of large models further constrains on-premises adoption. Despite these limitations, the integration of LLMs into code generation, completion, self-collaborative workflows, and security validation represents a transformative shift in programming, enabling developers to redirect their expertise toward higher-order design and architectural challenges while entrusting routine, syntax-oriented tasks to sophisticated generative models.

8.1.5. RQ5: What Are the Main Bottlenecks in Scaling and Deploying Neural-Based Programming Solutions to Real-World Codebases, and How Can They Be Addressed?

Neural-based programming tasks face several interrelated bottlenecks that hinder their scalability and deployment in real-world codebases. First, the scarcity of high-quality parallel corpora [253] across diverse PLs remains a critical obstacle. The majority of existing datasets are often narrowly focused, covering only a handful of modern PLs along with limited patterns such as NL query and code [254,255], or code–comment pairs, while legacy languages (e.g., COBOL and FORTRAN) and domain-specific languages (e.g., hardware description languages and smart contracts [256]) remain under-represented. Moreover, individual dataset pipelines lack standardization: tokenization strategies, comment handling heuristics, and metadata schemas are often undocumented, hindering reproducibility and fair model comparison. Even when aligned corpora exist (e.g., function-level translations between Java and C#), most corpora are limited to a widely studied couple of language pairs, leaving many language combinations with insufficient supervised data. Additionally, noisy or incomplete annotations, such as shallow doc-strings or heuristically derived vulnerability labels, further degrade model performance, as downstream fine-tuning depends on precise semantic alignments.

Second, the computational and evaluation challenges of neural approaches pose significant barriers to real-world adoption. Transformer-based models trained on massive code corpora require extensive GPU/TPU resources over prolonged periods, imposing both financial and environmental costs that are prohibitive for many academic and industrial settings. Even model inference phase may require optimized set of infrastructure to deliver low-latency, high-throughput code generation, or program understanding services. From an evaluation standpoint, conventional NLP metrics (e.g., BLEU, METEOR, and ROUGE) fail to capture code-specific syntactic and semantic correctness: two semantically equivalent implementations may receive drastically different n-gram scores, while superficially similar, functionally incorrect code can be rewarded [219]. Although specialized metrics such as CodeBLEU [96] have integrated AST-based comparisons, they do not reflect the runtime behaviors of evaluated program. Dynamic evaluation measures such as Pass@*k*, DSK@*k*, and CA incorporate test-based validation [79,257]. However, the availability of comprehensive and end-to-end evaluation pipelines remain scarce—particularly for multi-file projects, which demand integration tests, style readability, and each programming language's coding idiom assessments. Additionally, the black-box nature of neural models presents significant challenges of interpretability and debugging practices. Understanding why a model omits a critical null check or mismatches API calls is far more complex than tracing crashes in traditional programs. Therefore, greater emphasis must be placed on human-in-the-loop evaluation strategies [258,259].

To overcome these bottlenecks, a multifaceted strategy is needed. First, primary efforts should focus on building standardized, end-to-end dataset pipelines that span both modern and legacy PLs, provide rich metadata (e.g., ASTs, DFGs, doc-strings, test cases, and error logs), and automate reproducible preprocessing steps (e.g., tokenization, de-duplication, and splitting). Semi-supervised and synthetic data generation techniques, leveraging unsupervised back-translation, template-based augmentation, and cross-lingual transfer, can help mitigate parallel data scarcity. Second, efficiency-focused model architectures (e.g., distillation, quantization, and efficient-tuning) combined with mixed-precision training can reduce the compute footprint, thereby democratizing access to large-parameter models for resource-constrained researchers. Third, robust evaluation frameworks should integrate both static (e.g., Compilation@*k*) and dynamic (e.g., Pass@*k* and CA) metrics, alongside novel benchmarks for multi-file, long-form code generation, idiomatic constraint, and security vulnerability severity [234]. Finally, enhancing model interpretability through attention visualization, rationale generation, and the integration of symbolically grounded validators or test-based debugging loops will foster greater trust and facilitate the deployment of neural-based solutions in production codebases.

8.1.6. RQ6: How Have Neural Methods for Programming Evolved, and Which Model- and System-Level Advances Have Driven This Progression?

The utilization of neural methods in programming tasks has been progressing rapidly. Examining the trends of utilizing automatic tools in programming and software development methodologies, we observe a transition from rule-based to statistical methods, and ultimately to neural-based approaches. This shift has significantly improved quality, performance, adaptability, and novelty. Neural-based methods, in particular, have experienced rapid growth, with many models achieving SOTA performance. As shown in Figure 6, in the earliest stage (1943–late 1980s), neural methods in programming were largely theoretical: the perceptron, basic neuron models, and backpropagation laid the mathematical foundation. The enhancement of that period was purely conceptual, advancing the understanding of learning algorithms rather than delivering tangible gains in code analysis or generation.

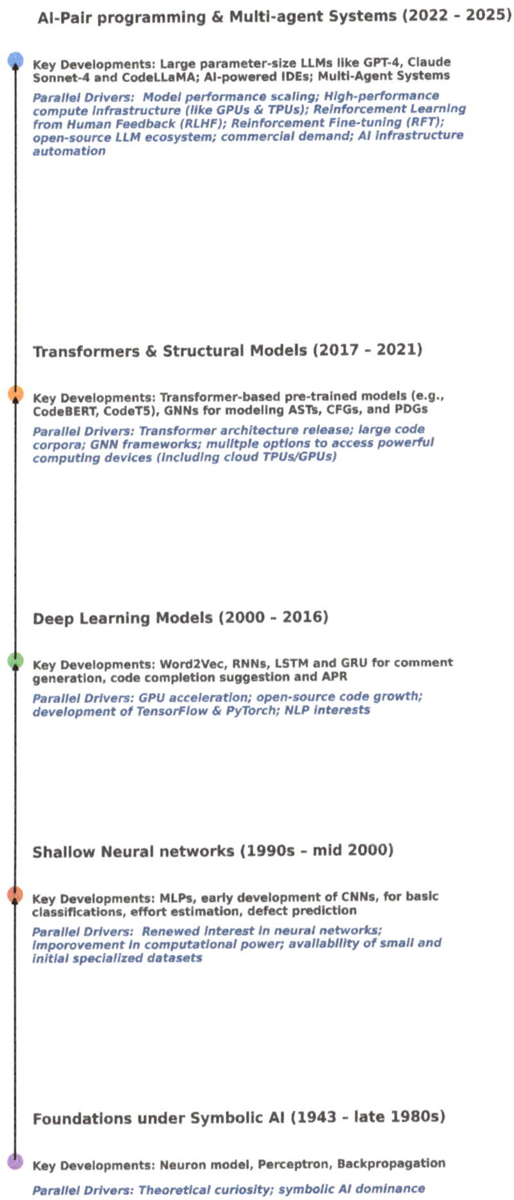

Figure 6. Utilization stages of neural methods in programming and SE tasks.

During the shallow neural network era (1990s–mid 2000), multilayer perceptrons and early convolutional neural networks began to show incremental enhancements over statistical baselines in tasks like code classification, effort estimation, and defect prediction.

From mid 2000 until around 2016, deep learning models, such as Word2Vec, RNNs, LSTM, GRU, and other Seq2Seq models augmented with attention, marked a better improvement for the advancement of neural networks. This gave rise to experimental tools for comment generation, code completion suggestion, code summarization, and automated patch recommendation. Although these systems captured syntactic patterns, they lacked semantic awareness: variable scopes, control flows, and data dependencies across larger contexts remained difficult to represent, limiting their reliability for complex codebases.

Between 2017 and 2021, two parallel streams of innovation converged: graph-based models that embedded ASTs and CFGs into graph neural networks (e.g., GGNN and RGCN), and the Transformer architecture which revolutionized the sequence modeling, enabling parallel processing of long sequences with long-range dependencies, hence marking the significant shift to pre-training various neural models on massive code corpora (e.g., CodeBERT and CodeT5). The former produced richer, semantically grounded embeddings for tasks such as bug localization and code summarization; the latter endowed foundation models with deep contextual understanding and transfer learning capabilities. Systems integrating these models began to automate several tasks such as code search, code translation, and program repair with far greater precision and generality than previous systems.

Since around 2022, large-scale LLMs and Code LLMs (e.g., Codex, CodeGen, CodeLLaMA, and CodeT5+) have advanced the use of neural methods into interactive AI-pair programming and AI-powered software engineering workflows. Embedded in the IDE code-assistants, such as GitHub Copilot, Visual Studio IntelliCode, and CodeWhisperer, these models provide real-time, context-aware code completions, automated reviews, and patch suggestions. Crucially, modern neural-based systems often validate model outputs by running tests or static analyzers before presenting results, ensuring higher correctness. Emerging multi-agent systems further point toward the autonomous orchestration of programming tasks—from requirement parsing to development of functionally correct program codes—transforming neural models from simple code assistants into intelligent co-developers. Hence, the advancement of neural methods in programming and SE represents a rapidly evolving revolution, emerging in recent years and continuing to reshape efficiency and effectiveness across a wide range of tasks, models, and the entire programming ecosystem.

8.2. Future Work and Open Issues

Although neural methods, particularly recent variants such as LLMs, have significantly advanced day-to-day programming tasks, several research challenges remain. We categorize these challenges into five thematic areas, providing concise discussions while preserving the full scope of open research issues investigated during our review.

8.2.1. Evaluation Metric Issues

Code Semantics and Runtime-Behavior-Aware Metrics

Existing NLP metrics (e.g., BLEU and ROUGE) often fail to capture functional equivalence. Syntactic measures such as CodeBLEU, embedding-based metrics, and AST-based distances serve as preliminary filters but require supplementation with dynamic, execution-driven evaluation. Future work should implement end-to-end pipelines that first ensure Compilation@k and then validate runtime behavior via extensive test suites with Pass@k, CA, or DSR@k.

Multi-Objective Scoring

Code quality extends beyond correctness to other factors such as readability, maintainability, robustness, and performance. However, no standard metrics exist for code style, maintainability, or security severity. Benchmarks should integrate the following:

- Readability/Lint Scores: Combine linters (e.g., PEP8 and Checkstyle) and complexity analyzers into aggregate scores.
- Security-severity Evaluations: Quantify vulnerability severity (e.g., exploitability and levels of severity) rather than binary detection.
- Functional Performance Tests: Include runtime and memory benchmarks, especially for large or multi-file projects, to measure efficiency trade-offs.

Interactive and Explainable Evaluation

As interactive code synthesis grows, benchmarks should simulate iterative feedback loops by tracking metrics such as the number of iterations to achieve 100% test pass or the time to convergence. Additionally, when models produce natural-language explanations, new evaluation solutions are required to score logical consistency alongside functional correctness, potentially incorporating human-in-the-loop judgments. Moreover, the rise of LLM-powered AI agents underscores the urgent need for standardized, interactive, real-time evaluation frameworks, an area that remains largely unexplored in the AI research community.

8.2.2. Data Pipelines and Code Representation

Unified Dataset Schema and Code Representation

There is no consensus on a unified representation for code samples (e.g., raw text, raw code, AST, CFG, and IR) and their associated metadata (e.g., NL descriptions, test suites, and error logs). Future datasets should adopt a fine-grained schema for source code, specifying the following:

- Tokenization conventions (e.g., tokenization and comment stripping).
- Possible combinations of code representation formats (e.g., ASTs, CFGs, and DFGs).
- Normalization of NL texts aligned with code (e.g., wording, structure, and phrasing).
- Test-suite inclusion [260], covering unit tests and integration tests.

Reproducible, End-to-End Pipelines

Many published corpora omit detailed preprocessing steps, hindering reproducibility. Future efforts should document all transformations (e.g., code normalization, dataset splits, data-format, filtering and utilized tools) to allow an exact replication of baselines.

Expanding Language and Domain Coverage

Most corpora focus on Python, Java, JavaScript, C/C++, C#, and Go. Under-represented languages (e.g., Rust, Kotlin, Swift, and CUDA) lack large, high-quality parallel datasets. Future research should perform the following:

- Mine and Curate Cross-Lingual/Domain Corpora: Use automatic alignment (e.g., class-level and project-level) to build parallel datasets for less-common pairs (e.g., Solidity—Java).
- Incorporate Non-English NL Data: Collect doc-strings and comments in Arabic, Japanese, Korean, etc., to enable truly multilingual AI-powered programming agents (e.g., Korean—Java).
- Gather Domain-Specific Corpora: Develop benchmarks for Infrastructure-as-Code (e.g., Terraform), hardware design (e.g., Verilog), embedded systems, and financial smart contracts (e.g., Solidity), reflecting their unique syntax and semantics.

8.2.3. Hybrid Neural Methods with Symbolic Architectures

Neuro-symbolic Integration for Semantic Guarantees

Purely neural method generators risk hallucinations, such as improper handling of errors during the reasoning process. Hybrid pipelines can interleave:

- Neuro-symbolic Validators: Post-generation static analysis (e.g., linters, model checkers, formal program verifiers) to flag or correct errors.
- Runtime Test Feedback: Compile and run generated code immediately. On failure, invoke a repair module or re-prompt the model.

Symbolic Augmentation for Certain Tasks

For vulnerability detection, integrating taint analysis, symbolic execution, or fuzzing can lower false positives and improve generalization. Program repair systems benefit from neural-based patch generation combined with symbolic equivalence checking.

8.2.4. Resource Efficiency and Deployment Constraints

Model Compression and Distillation

Larger LLMs achieve state-of-the-art results but are impractical for on-device or resource-constrained settings. Future work should explore the following:

- Knowledge Distillation: Train compact student models to approximate the behavior of larger teacher models.
- Parameter-Efficient Fine-Tuning (PEFT): Apply low-rank updates and quantization to adapt backbone weights, reducing storage and compute overhead [199].
- Edge-Optimized Libraries: Develop inference libraries for mobile or embedded hardware for balancing latency and accuracy when running neural models on edge devices.

8.2.5. Task-Specific Directions

Code Translation and Decompilation

Translation and decompilation should preserve the semantic meaning of code segments in end-to-end migration scenarios across source and target languages. Beyond surface metrics (e.g., BLEU and CodeBLEU), evaluation must incorporate semantic and runtime behavior comparisons, type-checker coverage, and execution outcomes. Architecturally, we have the following:

- Use specialized encoders that align parallel corpora at the function, class, or repository level.
- Employ decoders that enforce the preservation of target-language idioms (e.g., type inference and library-call mapping).
- For neural decompilers, leverage models that can comprehend control-flow and data-flow structures extracted from binaries, supporting multiple architectures (e.g., x86, ARM, and RISC-V) and handling obfuscation (e.g., packing and control-flow flattening).

Large-Scale Generation, Synthesis, and Automated Program Repair

Current benchmarks focus on single functions, but real-world development often spans entire projects. Future datasets should supply the following:

- Complete project skeletons such as minimal web apps with front-end, backend, database scripts, Continuous Integration and Continuous Deployment (CI/CD) configurations, to validate multi-file systems.
- Large, stable program-repair datasets: Curate commit pairs annotated by intent (e.g., bug fix, refactoring, performance optimization, and security patch) and integrate *generate→test→patch* loops where proposed edits are applied and validated against test suites. Coupling LLM outputs with program verification tools and multi-

round repair logic will enable end-to-end automated program repair frameworks that compile and pass correctness checks.

Code Search, Retrieval, and Clone Detection

Future code search systems should ensure that retrieved snippets compile and pass basic program tests by combining static analysis with neural-based techniques, rather than relying on syntax alone. Clone detection should advance beyond the same language heuristics: models should embed joint ASTs, data-flow, and other representations to detect cross-language clones (e.g., C++−Rust). Crucially, systems should differentiate syntactic clones (boilerplate) from intent-based similar programs (semantically equivalent algorithms implemented differently), using semantic-level features (e.g., control-flow and data-flow equivalences) to prioritize intent.

Comment Generation, Code Summarization, and Authorship Attribution

To improve code readability, comment-generation models should support multiple languages: build parallel corpora of code with comments in languages other than English and evaluate multilingual consistency. Code summarization should be semantics-aware, and metrics should verify that generated summaries capture control flow, side effects, and algorithmic complexity by comparing against gold-standard semantic annotations (e.g., CFGs annotated with NL intents). Code authorship and attribution tools should be able to handle code from mixed sources, including human-written code, IDE templates, and AI assistant-generated code. Techniques fusing stylistic features (e.g., code idioms, n-grams, and AST-based style features) with provenance metadata (e.g., commit logs and file metadata) can attribute authorship across PLs.

Code Completion and Privacy

AI-assisted code completion systems should mitigate security and privacy risks. Repeated prompt templates may produce near-identical code segments, propagating flaws. Future systems should introduce controlled stochasticity or template diversification while preserving syntactic and semantic correctness. Training or fine-tuning on proprietary and personal codebases requires confidentiality guarantees; differentially private training algorithms or federated learning frameworks—where model updates are aggregated without exposing raw code elements—are largely unexplored in the programming research domain and should be prioritized to prevent leakage of sensitive source code parts.

By addressing the above-mentioned open issues, such as richer evaluation methods, unified data pipelines, neuro-symbolic integration, high-quality multilingual corpora, and resource-efficient architectures, the research community can advance toward reliable, secure, and accessible AI-driven software development workflows.

8.3. Trends, Risks, and the Road Ahead

While neural-based methods have rapidly advanced the capability of automating various fields across the globe, including programming, the field may encounter subtle risks of trend-driven adoption without rigorous architectural validation and reproducible evaluation. A major challenge lies in the acceleration of model deployment cycles, where experimental prototypes are prematurely promoted to production systems without a robust assessment of long-term reliability, ethical safety, or software quality impacts. This issue is especially critical in programming and software engineering, where neural models directly influence codebases that underpin large-scale industrial and financial infrastructures.

From a statistical perspective, our bibliometric and temporal analyses (Figures 3 and 4) reveal a clear exponential rise in Transformer-based neural models from 2020 onward, with decoder-only architectures (e.g., GPT, LLaMA, and CodeGemma) dominating recent publications. Meanwhile, encoder–decoder and encoder-only designs, which have historically been effective for certain critical tasks, such as semantic and code translation tasks, are showing a relative decline in frequency, signaling a paradigm shift that may inadvertently deprioritize tasks better suited to their structures. The data in our collected publications further indicates that over 62% cited research works published in the year 2024–2025 rely on decoder-only architectures, emphasizing this evolving imbalance.

Emerging research in AI agents and multi-agent systems, integrated with neural code models, illustrates another forward trajectory. However, such agents often lack a defined alignment with the Software Development Life Cycle (SDLC), leading to ad hoc experimentation rather than systematic engineering integration. The next decade is likely to witness "coding agents" capable of generating enterprise-grade applications through high-level natural language instructions. Yet, realizing this vision safely requires verifiable performance measurement frameworks and ethically aware validation procedures that ensure trust, reproducibility, and resilience in code-generation and AI-augmented system-development practices.

In summary, sustainable progress in neural methods for programming depends on bridging three gaps: (1) establishing standard evaluation pipelines; (2) balancing architectural diversity across model families; and (3) embedding AI-agent development within the established SDLC frameworks. Addressing these will transform speculative enthusiasm into scientifically grounded and socially responsible advancement.

9. Conclusions

In synthesizing the reviewed literature, three major conclusions emerge. First, Transformer-based neural architectures, particularly encoder–decoder models such as CodeT5, and decoder-only LLMs such as GPT, Gemini, CodeLLaMA, and CodeGemma represent the most promising and versatile paradigms for programming-related tasks. Their capacity to learn unified representations across natural and programming languages has enabled remarkable progress in code generation, code summarization, code translation, and other SE tasks. Second, despite these advances, several persistent challenges remain unresolved: the absence of semantic and functionality-aware evaluation of generated code, the limited integration of graph-based or structure-aware models with Transformers, and the scarcity of multilingual and multi-paradigm datasets that impede robust cross-language generalization. Third, as outlined in Section 8, future progress will extend on unifying architectural innovation with standard evaluation frameworks and ethically guided deployment. Bridging these dimensions by coupling large-scale models with interpretable and verifiable code representations marks a concrete path toward reliable, safe, and industrially adoptable neural methods for programming tasks.

This survey systematically characterizes the landscape of neural methods in programming and SE, categorizing tasks through an extensive analysis of over 250 scientific papers. It critically examines the objectives, contributions, and limitations of previous surveys while offering a comprehensive comparison of neural methods across natural language and programming language tasks. Furthermore, it contrasts neural approaches with rule-based and statistical paradigms, providing a clear historical and technical evolution of the field. The paper also offers an exhaustive synthetical analysis of datasets and evaluation metrics, which has organized the entire performance evaluation metrics into five taxonomies accompanied by their mathematical formulations and benchmark analyses.

The overall findings indicate that recent advances in LLMs and Code LLMs are fundamentally transforming programming practices. This transformation is amplified by the emergence of multi-agent and context-aware systems that embed LLMs into the broader SE workflow. While the survey encompasses a broad spectrum of representative studies, some recently published breakthroughs are excluded for scope balance, particularly those overlapping with general NLP research. Although no empirical experiments were conducted, the conceptual analyses presented here lay a foundation for evidence-based future studies. Empirical investigations into the limitations of evaluation metrics such as BLEU, CodeBLEU, EM, and ROUGE would further substantiate our claims regarding their insufficiency in capturing semantic correctness.

Persistent challenges remain across most neural methods applied to programming and SE. These include the lack of standard, multi-modal code representations, the limited availability of high-quality parallel datasets, and the non-standardized use of evaluation metrics. Many models continue to rely on surface-level metrics that fail to capture semantic and functional fidelity. Addressing these limitations through improved representation learning, unified evaluation frameworks, and robust multilingual datasets will be pivotal for advancing the reliability, interpretability, and real-world applicability of neural methods for programming.

Author Contributions: Conceptualization, G.G.M. and H.I.; methodology: G.G.M., S.J., and H.I.; investigation: G.G.M.; data curation: G.G.M. and S.L.; writing—original draft preparation: G.G.M. and S.J.; writing—review and editing: G.G.M., S.L., S.J., S.-K.K., and H.I.; visualization: G.G.M. and S.L.; supervision: S.-K.K. and H.I.; project administration: H.I.; funding acquisition: H.I.; All authors have read and agreed to the published version of the manuscript.

Funding: This work was supported by the National Research Foundation of Korea (NRF) grant funded by the Korea government (MSIT) (RS-2023-00208094) and by Basic Science Research Program through the NRF funded by the Ministry of Education (RS-2024-00463967 and No. 25411243). This research was also supported by the Regional Innovation System & Education (RISE) program through the Gangwon RISE Center, funded by the Ministry of Education (MOE) and the Gangwon State (G.S.), Republic of Korea (2025-RISE-10-002).

Conflicts of Interest: The authors declare no conflict of interest.

Abbreviations

The following abbreviations are used throughout this manuscript:

Acronym	Full Form
AI	Artificial Intelligence
ANNS	Approximate Nearest Neighbor Search
API	Application Programming Interface
APR	Automatic Program Repair
APPS	Automated Programming Progress Standard
AST	Abstract Syntax Tree
AUC	Area Under the ROC Curve
AVDHRAM	Automated Vulnerability Detection framework based on Hierarchical Representation and Attention Mechanism
BERT	Bidirectional Encoder Representations from Transformers
Bi-LSTM	Bidirectional Long Short-Term Memory
BLEU	Bilingual Evaluation Understudy
BT	Back-Translation
BTC	Beyond the C
C2RUST	C to Rust Translator
C-BiGRU	Convolutional Neural Network–Bidirectional Gated Recurrent Unit
CA	Computational Accuracy

CARLCS-CNN	Co-Attentive Representation Learning Code Search—Convolutional Neural Network
CFG	Control Flow Graph
CI/CD	Continuous Integration/Continuous Deployment
CIRCLE	Continual Repair aCross Programming LanguagEs
CNN	Convolutional Neural Network
CODEnn	Code-Description Embedding Neural Network
CODIT	Contextualized Code Editing with Neural Machine Translation
CORE	COde REview Engine
COSAL	Code-to-Code Search Across Languages
CVE	Common Vulnerabilities and Exposures
DAE	Denoising Autoencoding
DFG	Data Flow Graph
DGMS	Deep Graph Matching and Searching
DL	Deep Learning
DNN	Deep Neural Network
DSI	Debugging Success Improvement
DSR@*k*	Debugging Success Rate at rank *k*
EM	Exact Match
ENCORE	Ensemble Learning using Convolution Neural Machine Translation for Automatic Program Repair
FP	False Positive
FN	False Negative
GAN	Generative Adversarial Network
GCJ	Google Code Jam
GCN	Graph Convolutional Network
GGNN	Gated Graph Neural Network
GNN	Graph Neural Network
GPT	Generative Pre-trained Transformer
GRU	Gated Recurrent Unit
IABLSTM	Impact Analysis with Attention Bidirectional Long Short-Term Memory
IDE	Integrated Development Environment
IR	Intermediate Representation
LLM	Large Language Model
LSTM	Long Short-Term Memory
MBPP	Mostly Basic Programming Problems
METEOR	Metric for Evaluation of Translation with Explicit ORdering
ML	Machine Learning
MMAN	Multi-Modal Attention Network
MNB	Multinomial Naive Bayes
MPLCS	Multi-Programming Language Code Search
MRR	Mean Reciprocal Rank
NDCG@*k*	Normalized Discounted Cumulative Gain at rank *k*
NLM	Neural Language Model
NLP	Natural Language Processing
NMT	Neural Machine Translation
NVD	National Vulnerability Database
OOV	Out-of-Vocabulary
PATOIS	Probabilistic Tree Grammar–Based Program Synthesizer
PCSD	Python Code and Doc-string pairs
PEFT	Parameter-Efficient Fine-Tuning

PL	Programming Language
pTSG	Probabilistic Tree Substitution Grammar
RAE	Recursive Autoencoder
RGCNs	Relational Graph Convolutional Networks
ResNet	Residual Neural Network (Residual Network)
RNN	Recurrent Neural Network
ROUGE	Recall-Oriented Understudy for Gisting Evaluation
RR	Repairable Rate
SBCS	SentenceBERT + Cosine Similarity
SBED	SentenceBERT + Euclidean Distance
SDLC	Software Development Life Cycle
SE	Software Engineering
SLAMC	Semantic Language Model for Source Code
SMT	Statistical Machine Translation
SOTA	State-of-the-Art
SVM	Support Vector Machine
T5	Text-to-Text Transfer Transformer
TCA@*k*	Test Case Average at rank *k*
TF-IDF	Term Frequency–Inverse Document Frequency
TN	True Negative
TP	True Positive
TSED	Tree Similarity of Edit Distance
ViT	Vision Transformer
XFG	Contextual Flow Graph
XML	eXtensible Markup Language
XOR	Exclusive OR

References

1. Guo, D.; Yang, D.; Zhang, H.; Song, J.; Zhang, R.; Xu, R.; Zhu, Q.; Ma, S.; Wang, P.; Bi, X.; et al. DeepSeek-R1: Incentivizing Reasoning Capability in LLMs via Reinforcement Learning. *arXiv* **2025**, arXiv:2501.12948.
2. Kang, D.; Hovy, E. Plan ahead: Self-Supervised Text Planning for Paragraph Completion Task. In Proceedings of the 2020 Conference on Empirical Methods in Natural Language Processing (EMNLP), Online, 16–20 November 2020; Webber, B., Cohn, T., He, Y., Liu, Y., Eds.; Association for Computational Linguistics: Stroudsburg, PA, USA, 2020; pp. 6533–6543. [CrossRef]
3. OpenAI; Achiam, J.; Adler, S.; Agarwal, S.; Ahmad, L.; Akkaya, I.; Aleman, F.L.; Almeida, D.; Altenschmidt, J.; Altman, S.; et al. GPT-4 Technical Report. *arXiv* **2024**, arXiv:2303.08774.
4. Cao, J.; Li, M.; Wen, M.; Cheung, S. A study on prompt design, advantages and limitations of ChatGPT for deep learning program repair. *Autom. Softw. Eng.* **2025**, *32*, 30. [CrossRef]
5. Zhao, H.; Hui, J.; Howland, J.; Nguyen, N.; Zuo, S.; Hu, A.; Choquette-Choo, C.A.; Shen, J.; Kelley, J.; Bansal, K.; et al. CodeGemma: Open code models based on Gemma. *arXiv* **2024**, arXiv:2406.11409. [CrossRef]
6. Yang, Z.; Liu, F.; Yu, Z.; Keung, J.W.; Li, J.; Liu, S.; Hong, Y.; Ma, X.; Jin, Z.; Li, G. Exploring and Unleashing the Power of Large Language Models in Automated Code Translation. *Proc. ACM Softw. Eng.* **2024**, *1*, 1585–1608. [CrossRef]
7. Ahmad, W.U.; Tushar, M.G.R.; Chakraborty, S.; Chang, K.W. AVATAR: A Parallel Corpus for Java-Python Program Translation. In *Findings of the Association for Computational Linguistics: EACL 2023*; Rogers, A., Boyd-Graber, J., Okazaki, N., Eds.; Association for Computational Linguistics: Stroudsburg, PA, USA, 2023; pp. 2268–2281. [CrossRef]
8. Ahmad, W.; Chakraborty, S.; Ray, B.; Chang, K.W. A Transformer-based Approach for Source Code Summarization. In Proceedings of the 58th Annual Meeting of the Association for Computational Linguistics, Online, 10 July 2020; Jurafsky, D., Chai, J., Schluter, N., Tetreault, J., Eds.; Association for Computational Linguistics: Stroudsburg, PA, USA, 2020; pp. 4998–5007. [CrossRef]
9. Chakraborty, S.; Ray, B. On multi-modal learning of editing source code. In Proceedings of the 36th IEEE/ACM International Conference on Automated Software Engineering, Melbourne, Australia, 15–19 November 2021; IEEE Press: New York, NY, USA, 2021; pp. 443–455. [CrossRef]
10. Katz, D.S.; Ruchti, J.; Schulte, E. Using recurrent neural networks for decompilation. In Proceedings of the 2018 IEEE 25th International Conference on Software Analysis, Evolution and Reengineering (SANER), Campobasso, Italy, 20–23 March 2018; pp. 346–356. [CrossRef]

11. Wu, Y.; Wang, W. Code Similarity Detection Based on Siamese Network. In Proceedings of the 2021 IEEE International Conference on Information Communication and Software Engineering (ICICSE), Chengdu, China, 19–21 March 2021; pp. 47–51. [CrossRef]
12. Zhang, C.; Wang, J.; Zhou, Q.; Xu, T.; Tang, K.; Gui, H.; Liu, F. A Survey of Automatic Source Code Summarization. *Symmetry* **2022**, *14*, 471. [CrossRef]
13. Uddin, M.N.; Zhang, Y.; Hei, X. Deep Learning Aided Software Vulnerability Detection: A Survey. *arXiv* **2025**, arXiv:2503.04002. [CrossRef]
14. Yang, Y.; Xia, X.; Lo, D.; Grundy, J. A Survey on Deep Learning for Software Engineering. *ACM Comput. Surv.* **2022**, *54*, 1–73. [CrossRef]
15. Fontes, A.; Gay, G. The integration of machine learning into automated test generation: A systematic mapping study. *Softw. Test. Verif. Reliab.* **2023**, *33*, e1845. [CrossRef]
16. Allamanis, M.; Barr, E.T.; Devanbu, P.; Sutton, C. A survey of machine learning for big code and naturalness. *ACM Comput. Surv. (CSUR)* **2018**, *51*, 1–37. [CrossRef]
17. Samoaa, H.P.; Bayram, F.; Salza, P.; Leitner, P. A systematic mapping study of source code representation for deep learning in software engineering. *IET Softw.* **2022**, *16*, 351–385. [CrossRef]
18. Amalfitano, D.; Faralli, S.; Hauck, J.C.R.; Matalonga, S.; Distante, D. Artificial Intelligence Applied to Software Testing: A Tertiary Study. *ACM Comput. Surv.* **2023**, *56*, 1–38. [CrossRef]
19. Durrani, U.K.; Akpinar, M.; Adak, M.F.; Kabakus, A.T.; Öztürk, M.M.; Saleh, M. A Decade of Progress: A Systematic Literature Review on the Integration of AI in Software Engineering Phases and Activities (2013–2023). *IEEE Access* **2024**, *12*, 171185–171204. [CrossRef]
20. Sofian, H.; Yunus, N.A.M.; Ahmad, R. Systematic Mapping: Artificial Intelligence Techniques in Software Engineering. *IEEE Access* **2022**, *10*, 51021–51040. [CrossRef]
21. Crawford, T.; Duong, S.; Fueston, R.; Lawani, A.; Owoade, S.; Uzoka, A.; Parizi, R.M.; Yazdinejad, A. AI in Software Engineering: A Survey on Project Management Applications. *arXiv* **2023**, arXiv:2307.15224. [CrossRef]
22. Zhang, Q.; Fang, C.; Ma, Y.; Sun, W.; Chen, Z. A Survey of Learning-based Automated Program Repair. *ACM Trans. Softw. Eng. Methodol.* **2024**, *33*, 1–69. [CrossRef]
23. Xiaomeng, W.; Tao, Z.; Wei, X.; Changyu, H. A survey on source code review using machine learning. In Proceedings of the 2018 3rd International Conference on Information Systems Engineering (ICISE), Shanghai, China, 4–6 May 2018; pp. 56–60.
24. Akimova, E.N.; Bersenev, A.Y.; Deikov, A.A.; Kobylkin, K.S.; Konygin, A.V.; Mezentsev, I.P.; Misilov, V.E. A survey on software defect prediction using deep learning. *Mathematics* **2021**, *9*, 1180. [CrossRef]
25. Xie, Y.; Lin, J.; Dong, H.; Zhang, L.; Wu, Z. Survey of Code Search Based on Deep Learning. *ACM Trans. Softw. Eng. Methodol.* **2023**, *33*, 1–42. [CrossRef]
26. Zakeri-Nasrabadi, M.; Parsa, S.; Ramezani, M.; Roy, C.; Ekhtiarzadeh, M. A systematic literature review on source code similarity measurement and clone detection: Techniques, applications, and challenges. *J. Syst. Softw.* **2023**, *204*, 111796. [CrossRef]
27. Al-Hossami, E.; Shaikh, S. A survey on artificial intelligence for source code: A dialogue systems perspective. *arXiv* **2022**, arXiv:2202.04847. [CrossRef]
28. Le, T.H.; Chen, H.; Babar, M.A. A survey on data-driven software vulnerability assessment and prioritization. *ACM Comput. Surv.* **2022**, *55*, 1–39. [CrossRef]
29. Das, S.; Shah, C. *Contextual Code Completion Using Machine Learning*; Technical Report; Stanford University: Stanford, CA, USA, 2015.
30. Moradi Dakhel, A.; Majdinasab, V.; Nikanjam, A.; Khomh, F.; Desmarais, M.C.; Jiang, Z.M.J. GitHub Copilot AI pair programmer: Asset or Liability? *J. Syst. Softw.* **2023**, *203*, 111734. [CrossRef]
31. Ouyang, S.; Zhang, J.; Sun, Z.; Merono Penuela, A. Knowledge-Enhanced Program Repair for Data Science Code. In Proceedings of the 2025 IEEE/ACM 47th International Conference on Software Engineering (ICSE), Ottawa, ON, Canada, 27 April–3 May 2025; pp. 782–782. [CrossRef]
32. Lu, S.; Guo, D.; Ren, S.; Huang, J.; Svyatkovskiy, A.; Blanco, A.; Clement, C.B.; Drain, D.; Jiang, D.; Tang, D.; et al. CodeXGLUE: A Machine Learning Benchmark Dataset for Code Understanding and Generation. *arXiv* **2021**, arXiv:2102.04664. [CrossRef]
33. Brereton, P.; Kitchenham, B.A.; Budgen, D.; Turner, M.; Khalil, M. Lessons from applying the systematic literature review process within the software engineering domain. *J. Syst. Softw.* **2007**, *80*, 571–583. [CrossRef]
34. Kitchenham, B.; Charters, S. *Guidelines for Performing Systematic Literature Reviews in Software Engineering*; Version 2.3 EBSE Technical Report; EBSE: Rio de Janeiro, Brazil, 2007.
35. Watson, C.; Cooper, N.; Nader-Palacio, D.; Moran, K.; Poshyvanyk, D. A Systematic Literature Review on the Use of Deep Learning in Software Engineering Research. *ACM Trans. Softw. Eng. Methodol.* **2022**, *31*, 1–58. [CrossRef]
36. Cao, S.; Sun, X.; Widyasari, R.; Lo, D.; Wu, X.; Bo, L.; Zhang, J.; Li, B.; Liu, W.; Wu, D.; et al. A Systematic Literature Review on Explainability for Machine/Deep Learning-based Software Engineering Research. *arXiv* **2025**, arXiv:2401.14617.

37. Le, T.H.M.; Chen, H.; Babar, M.A. Deep Learning for Source Code Modeling and Generation: Models, Applications, and Challenges. *ACM Comput. Surv.* **2020**, *53*, 1–38. [CrossRef]
38. Hou, X.; Zhao, Y.; Liu, Y.; Yang, Z.; Wang, K.; Li, L.; Luo, X.; Lo, D.; Grundy, J.; Wang, H. Large language models for software engineering: A systematic literature review. *ACM Trans. Softw. Eng. Methodol.* **2024**, *33*, 1–79. [CrossRef]
39. Fan, A.; Gokkaya, B.; Harman, M.; Lyubarskiy, M.; Sengupta, S.; Yoo, S.; Zhang, J.M. Large language models for software engineering: Survey and open problems. In Proceedings of the 2023 IEEE/ACM International Conference on Software Engineering: Future of Software Engineering (ICSE-FoSE), Melbourne, Australia, 14–20 May 2023; pp. 31–53.
40. Wu, B.; Zou, F. Code vulnerability detection based on deep sequence and graph models: A survey. *Secur. Commun. Netw.*, **2022**, *2022*, 62–73. [CrossRef]
41. Dou, S.; Shan, J.; Jia, H.; Deng, W.; Xi, Z.; He, W.; Wu, Y.; Gui, T.; Liu, Y.; Huang, X. Towards Understanding the Capability of Large Language Models on Code Clone Detection: A Survey. *arXiv* **2023**, arXiv:2308.01191. [CrossRef]
42. Zhong, W.; Li, C.; Ge, J.; Luo, B. Neural program repair: Systems, challenges and solutions. In Proceedings of the 13th Asia-Pacific Symposium on Internetware, Hohhot, China, 11–12 June 2022; pp. 96–106.
43. Huang, K.; Xu, Z.; Yang, S.; Sun, H.; Li, X.; Yan, Z.; Zhang, Y. A Survey on Automated Program Repair Techniques. *arXiv* **2023**, arXiv:2303.18184. [CrossRef]
44. Wang, J.; Huang, Y.; Chen, C.; Liu, Z.; Wang, S.; Wang, Q. Software testing with large language models: Survey, landscape, and vision. *IEEE Trans. Softw. Eng.* **2024**, *50*, 911–936. [CrossRef]
45. Katsogiannis-Meimarakis, G.; Koutrika, G. A survey on deep learning approaches for text-to-SQL. *VLDB J.* **2023**, *32*, 905–936. [CrossRef]
46. Grazia, L.D.; Pradel, M. Code Search: A Survey of Techniques for Finding Code. *ACM Comput. Surv.* **2023**, *55*, 1–31. [CrossRef]
47. Zheng, Z.; Ning, K.; Wang, Y.; Zhang, J.; Zheng, D.; Ye, M.; Chen, J. A Survey of Large Language Models for Code: Evolution, Benchmarking, and Future Trends. *arXiv* **2024**, arXiv:2311.10372. [CrossRef]
48. Zan, D.; Chen, B.; Zhang, F.; Lu, D.; Wu, B.; Guan, B.; Yongji, W.; Lou, J.G. Large language models meet NL2Code: A survey. In Proceedings of the 61st Annual Meeting of the Association for Computational Linguistics (Volume 1: Long Papers), Toronto, ON, Canada, 9–14 July 2023; Association for Computational Linguistics: Stroudsburg, PA, USA, 2023; pp. 7443–7464.
49. Wong, M.F.; Guo, S.; Hang, C.N.; Ho, S.W.; Tan, C.W. Natural Language Generation and Understanding of Big Code for AI-Assisted Programming: A Review. *Entropy* **2023**, *25*, 888. [CrossRef] [PubMed]
50. Zheng, Z.; Ning, K.; Zhong, Q.; Chen, J.; Chen, W.; Guo, L.; Wang, W.; Wang, Y. Towards an understanding of large language models in software engineering tasks. *Empir. Softw. Eng.* **2024**, *30*, 50. [CrossRef]
51. Xu, Y.; Zhu, Y. A Survey on Pretrained Language Models for Neural Code Intelligence. *arXiv* **2022**, arXiv:2212.10079. [CrossRef]
52. Batarseh, F.A.; Mohod, R.; Kumar, A.; Bui, J. The application of artificial intelligence in software engineering: A review challenging conventional wisdom. *Data Democr.* **2020**,179 –232. [CrossRef]
53. Song, X.; Sun, H.; Wang, X.; Yan, J. A Survey of Automatic Generation of Source Code Comments: Algorithms and Techniques. *IEEE Access* **2019**, *7*, 111411–111428. [CrossRef]
54. Ahmed, A.; Azab, S.S.; Abdelhamid, Y. Source-Code Generation Using Deep Learning: A Survey. In *Progress in Artificial Intelligence—22nd EPIA Conference on Artificial Intelligence, EPIA 2023, Faial Island, Azores, September 5–8. 2023, Proceedings, Part II*; Moniz, N., Vale, Z., Cascalho, J., Silva, C., Sebastião, R., Eds.; Lecture Notes in Computer Science; Springer: Berlin/Heidelberg, Germany, 2023; Volume 14116, pp. 467–482. [CrossRef]
55. Chen, X.; Xue, J.; Xie, X.; Liang, C.; Ju, X. A Systematic Literature Review on Neural Code Translation. *arXiv* **2025**, arXiv:2505.07425. [CrossRef]
56. Lei, M.; Li, H.; Li, J.; Aundhkar, N.; Kim, D. Deep learning application on code clone detection: A review of current knowledge. *J. Syst. Softw.* **2022**, *184*, 111141. [CrossRef]
57. Chen, X.; Hu, X.; Huang, Y.; Jiang, H.; Ji, W.; Jiang, Y.; Jiang, Y.; Liu, B.; Liu, H.; Li, X.; et al. Deep learning-based software engineering: Progress, challenges, and opportunities. *Sci. China Inf. Sci.* **2025**, *68*, 111102. [CrossRef]
58. Jiang, J.; Wang, F.; Shen, J.; Kim, S.; Kim, S. A Survey on Large Language Models for Code Generation. *ACM Trans. Softw. Eng. Methodol.* 2025, *accepted*. [CrossRef]
59. Mathai, A.; Sedamaki, K.; Das, D.; Mathews, N.S.; Tamilselvam, S.; Chimalakonda, S.; Kumar, A. CodeSAM: Source Code Representation Learning by Infusing Self-Attention with Multi-Code-View Graphs. *arXiv* **2024**, arXiv:2411.14611.
60. Sharma, T.; Kechagia, M.; Georgiou, S.; Tiwari, R.; Sarro, F. *A Survey on Machine Learning Techniques for Source Code Analysis*; Elsevier Science Inc.: Amsterdam, The Netherlands, 2024.
61. Xiao, Y.; Zuo, X.; Lu, X.; Dong, J.S.; Cao, X.; Beschastnikh, I. Promises and perils of using Transformer-based models for SE research. *Neural Netw.* **2024**, *184*, 107067. [CrossRef]
62. Touvron, H.; Lavril, T.; Izacard, G.; Martinet, X.; Lachaux, M.A.; Lacroix, T.; Rozière, B.; Goyal, N.; Hambro, E.; Azhar, F.; et al. LLaMA: Open and Efficient Foundation Language Models. *arXiv* **2023**, arXiv:2302.13971. [CrossRef]

63. Touvron, H.; Martin, L.; Stone, K.; Albert, P.; Almahairi, A.; Babaei, Y.; Bashlykov, N.; Batra, S.; Bhargava, P.; Bhosale, S.; et al. Llama 2: Open Foundation and Fine-Tuned Chat Models. *arXiv* **2023**, arXiv:2307.09288. [CrossRef]
64. Grattafiori, A.; Dubey, A.; Jauhri, A.; Pandey, A.; Kadian, A.; Al-Dahle, A.; Letman, A.; Mathur, A.; Schelten, A.; Vaughan, A.; et al. The Llama 3 Herd of Models. *arXiv* **2024**, arXiv:2407.21783. [CrossRef]
65. Conneau, A.; Lample, G. Cross-lingual language model pretraining. In Proceedings of the 33rd International Conference on Neural Information Processing Systems, Vancouver, BC, Canada , 8–14 December 2019; pp. 7059–7069.
66. Liu, F.; Li, G.; Zhao, Y.; Jin, Z. Multi-task learning based pre-trained language model for code completion. In *ASE'20: Proceedings of the 35th IEEE/ACM International Conference on Automated Software Engineering*; Association for Computing Machinery: New York, NY, USA, 2020; pp. 473–485. [CrossRef]
67. Jin, D.; Jin, Z.; Hu, Z.; Vechtomova, O.; Mihalcea, R. Deep learning for text style transfer: A survey. *Comput. Linguist.* **2022**, *48*, 155–205. [CrossRef]
68. Pham, Q.N.;Waibel, A.; Niehues, J. Adaptive multilingual speech recognition with pretrained models. In Proceedings of the Conference of the International Speech Communication Association, Incheon, Republic of Korea, 18–22 September 2022.
69. Guo, D.; Ren, S.; Lu, S.; Feng, Z.; Tang, D.; Shujie, L.; Zhou, L.; Duan, N.; Svyatkovskiy, A.; Fu, S.; et al. GraphCodeBERT: Pre-training Code Representations with Data Flow. In Proceedings of the International Conference on Learning Representations, Vienna, Austria, 4 May 2021.
70. Devlin, J.; Chang, M.; Lee, K.; Toutanova, K. BERT: Pre-training of Deep Bidirectional Transformers for Language Understanding. In Proceedings of the 2019 Conference of the North American Chapter of the Association for Computational Linguistics: Human Language Technologies, NAACL-HLT 2019, Minneapolis, MN, USA, 2–7 June 2019; Burstein, J., Doran, C., Solorio, T., Eds.; Association for Computational Linguistics: Stroudsburg, PA, USA, 2019; Volume 1, pp. 4171–4186. [CrossRef]
71. Wang, Y.; Wang, W.; Joty, S.; Hoi, S.C. CodeT5: Identifier-aware Unified Pre-trained Encoder-Decoder Models for Code Understanding and Generation. In Proceedings of the 2021 Conference on Empirical Methods in Natural Language Processing, Virtual, 7–11 November 2021; Moens, M.F., Huang, X., Specia, L., Yih, S.W.t., Eds.; Association for Computational Linguistics: Stroudsburg, PA, USA, 2021; pp. 8696–8708. [CrossRef]
72. Laurençon, H.; Saulnier, L.; Wang, T.; Akiki, C.; del Moral, A.V.; Scao, T.L.; von Werra, L.; Mou, C.; Ponferrada, E.G.; Nguyen, H.; et al. The BigScience ROOTS Corpus: A 1.6TB Composite Multilingual Dataset. *Adv. Neural Inf. Process. Syst.* **2022**, *35*, 31809–31826. [CrossRef]
73. Kanade, A.; Maniatis, P.; Balakrishnan, G.; Shi, K. Learning and evaluating contextual embedding of source code. In Proceedings of the International Conference on Machine Learning, Virtual, 13–18 July 2020; pp. 5110–5121.
74. Hägglund, M.; Pena, F.J.; Pashami, S.; Al-Shishtawy, A.; Payberah, A.H. COCLUBERT: Clustering Machine Learning Source Code. In Proceedings of the 2021 20th IEEE International Conference on Machine Learning and Applications (ICMLA), Pasadena, CA, USA, 13–16 December 2021; pp. 151–158.
75. Feng, Z.; Guo, D.; Tang, D.; Duan, N.; Feng, X.; Gong, M.; Shou, L.; Qin, B.; Liu, T.; Jiang, D.; et al. CodeBERT: A Pre-Trained Model for Programming and Natural Languages. In *Findings of the Association for Computational Linguistics: EMNLP 2020*; Cohn, T., He, Y., Liu, Y., Eds.; Association for Computational Linguistics: Stroudsburg, PA, USA, 2020; pp. 1536–1547. [CrossRef]
76. Guo, D.; Lu, S.; Duan, N.; Wang, Y.; Zhou, M.; Yin, J. UniXcoder: Unified cross-modal pre-training for code representation. In Proceedings of the 60th Annual Meeting of the Association for Computational Linguistics (Volume 1: Long Papers), Dublin, Ireland, 22–27 May 2022; Association for Computational Linguistics: Stroudsburg, PA, USA, 2022.
77. Guo, D.; Xu, C.; Duan, N.; Yin, J.; McAuley, J. LongCoder: A long-range pre-trained language model for code completion. In Proceedings of the International Conference on Machine Learning, Honolulu, HI USA, 23–29 July 2023; pp. 12098–12107.
78. Muennighoff, N.; Wang, T.; Sutawika, L.; Roberts, A.; Biderman, S.; Le Scao, T.; Bari, M.S.; Shen, S.; Yong, Z.X.; Schoelkopf, H.; et al. Crosslingual Generalization through Multitask Finetuning. In Proceedings of the 61st Annual Meeting of the Association for Computational Linguistics (Volume 1: Long Papers), Toronto, ON, Canada, 9–14 July 2023; Association for Computational Linguistics: Stroudsburg, PA, USA, 2023; pp. 15991–16111.
79. Roziere, B.; Lachaux, M.A.; Chanussot, L.; Lample, G. Unsupervised translation of programming languages. In Proceedings of the 34th International Conference on Neural Information Processing Systems, Vancouver, BC, Canada, 6–12 December 2020.
80. Liu, X.; Xv, L. Abstract summarization based on the combination of transformer and LSTM. In Proceedings of the 2019 International Conference on Intelligent Computing, Automation and Systems (ICICAS), Chongqing, China, 6–8 December 2019; pp. 923–927.
81. Aggarwal, K.; Salameh, M.; Hindle, A. Using machine translation for converting Python 2 to Python 3 code. *PeerJ* **2015**, *3*, e1459v1. [CrossRef]
82. Gu, X.; Zhang, H.; Zhang, D.; Kim, S. DeepAM: Migrate APIs with multi-modal sequence to sequence learning. In Proceedings of the 26th International Joint Conference on Artificial Intelligence, Melbourne, Australia, 19–25 August 2017; AAAI Press: Washington, DC, USA, 2017; pp. 3675–3681.

83. Takizawa, H.; Hirasawa, S.; Hayashi, Y.; Egawa, R.; Kobayashi, H. Xevolver: An XML-based code translation framework for supporting HPC application migration. In Proceedings of the 2014 21st International Conference on High Performance Computing (HiPC), Goa, India, 17–20 December 2014; pp. 1–11. [CrossRef]
84. Bhatia, S.; Qiu, J.; Hasabnis, N.; Seshia, S.A.; Cheung, A. Verified Code Transpilation with LLMs. In Proceedings of the 38th Conference on Neural Information Processing Systems (NeurIPS 2024), Vancouver, BC, Canada, 9–15 December 2024.
85. Gebreslassie, M.G.; Ji, S.; Roh, M.; Im, H. Leveraging QLoRA on Code Large Language Models for Multilingual Code Translation. *KIISE Trans. Comput. Pract.* **2025**, *31*, 152–157. [CrossRef]
86. C2Rust—Migrate C code to Rust. GitHub Repository. 2023. Available online: https://github.com/immunant/c2rust.git (accessed on 9 October 2025).
87. J2cstranslator—Java to CSharp Translator. SourceForge Project. 2013. Available online: https://sourceforge.net/projects/j2cstranslator/ (accessed on 9 October 2025).
88. Balogh, G.; Mudalige, G.; Reguly, I.; Antao, S.; Bertolli, C. OP2-Clang: A Source-to-Source Translator Using Clang/LLVM LibTooling. In Proceedings of the 2018 IEEE/ACM 5th Workshop on the LLVM Compiler Infrastructure in HPC (LLVM-HPC), Dallas, TX, USA, 12 November 2018; pp. 59–70. [CrossRef]
89. Hung-Cuong, N.; Quyet-Thang, H.; Ba-Vuong, T. Rule-Based Techniques Using Abstract Syntax Tree for Code Optimization and Secure Programming in Java. In *Context-Aware Systems and Applications*; Vinh, P.C., Alagar, V., Vassev, E., Khare, A., Eds.; Springer: Cham, Switzerland, 2014; pp. 168–177.
90. Nguyen, A.T.; Nguyen, T.T.; Nguyen, T.N. Lexical statistical machine translation for language migration. In *ESEC/FSE 2013: Proceedings of the 2013 9th Joint Meeting on Foundations of Software Engineering*; Association for Computing Machinery: New York, NY, USA, 2013; pp. 651–654. [CrossRef]
91. Karaivanov, S.; Raychev, V.; Vechev, M. Phrase-Based Statistical Translation of Programming Languages. In *Onward! 2014, Proceedings of the 2014 ACM International Symposium on New Ideas, New Paradigms, and Reflections on Programming & Software*; ACM: New York, NY, USA, 2014; pp. 173–184. [CrossRef]
92. Nguyen, T.T.; Nguyen, A.T.; Nguyen, H.A.; Nguyen, T.N. A statistical semantic language model for source code. In *ESEC/FSE 2013: Proceedings of the 2013 9th Joint Meeting on Foundations of Software Engineering*; Association for Computing Machinery: New York, NY, USA, 2013; pp. 532–542. [CrossRef]
93. Roziere, B.; Zhang, J.M.; Charton, F.; Harman, M.; Synnaeve, G.; Lample, G. Leveraging Automated Unit Tests for Unsupervised Code Translation. *arXiv* **2022**, arXiv:2110.06773. [CrossRef]
94. Zhang, Q.; Fang, C.; Zheng, Y.; Zhang, Y.; Zhao, Y.; Huang, R.; Zhou, J.; Yang, Y.; Zheng, T.; Chen, Z. Improving Deep Assertion Generation via Fine-Tuning Retrieval-Augmented Pre-trained Language Models. *ACM Trans. Softw. Eng. Methodol.* 2025, *accepted*. [CrossRef]
95. Ahmad, W.; Chakraborty, S.; Ray, B.; Chang, K.W. Unified Pre-training for Program Understanding and Generation. In Proceedings of the 2021 Conference of the North American Chapter of the Association for Computational Linguistics: Human Language Technologies, online, 6–11 June 2021; Toutanova, K., Rumshisky, A., Zettlemoyer, L., Hakkani-Tur, D., Beltagy, I., Bethard, S., Cotterell, R., Chakraborty, T., Zhou, Y., Eds.; Association for Computational Linguistics: Stroudsburg, PA, USA, 2021; pp. 2655–2668. [CrossRef]
96. Ren, S.; Guo, D.; Lu, S.; Zhou, L.; Liu, S.; Tang, D.; Sundaresan, N.; Zhou, M.; Blanco, A.; Ma, S. CodeBLEU: A Method for Automatic Evaluation of Code Synthesis. *arXiv* **2020**, arXiv:2009.10297. [CrossRef]
97. To, H.; Nguyen, M.; Bui, N. Functional Overlap Reranking for Neural Code Generation. In Proceedings of the Findings of the Association for Computational Linguistics, ACL 2024, Bangkok, Thailand, 11–16 August 2024; Ku, L., Martins, A., Srikumar, V., Eds; Association for Computational Linguistics: Stroudsburg, PA, USA, 2024; pp. 3686–3704. [CrossRef]
98. Miceli-Barone, A.V.; Sennrich, R. A Parallel Corpus of Python Functions and Documentation Strings for Automated Code Documentation and Code Generation. In Proceedings of the Eighth International Joint Conference on Natural Language Processing (Volume 2: Short Papers), Taipei, Taiwan, 27 November 2017; Association for Computational Linguistics: Stroudsburg, PA, USA, 2017; pp. 314–319.
99. Raffel, C.; Shazeer, N.; Roberts, A.; Lee, K.; Narang, S.; Matena, M.; Zhou, Y.; Li, W.; Liu, P.J. Exploring the limits of transfer learning with a unified text-to-text transformer. *J. Mach. Learn. Res.* **2020**, *21*, 1–67.
100. Rabinovich, M.; Stern, M.; Klein, D. Abstract Syntax Networks for Code Generation and Semantic Parsing. In Proceedings of the 55th Annual Meeting of the Association for Computational Linguistics (Volume 1: Long Papers), Vancouver, BC, Canada, 30 July 2017; Association for Computational Linguistics: Stroudsburg, PA, USA, 2017; pp. 1139–1149.
101. Amodio, M.; Chaudhuri, S.; Reps, T.W. Neural Attribute Machines for Program Generation. *arXiv* **2021**, arXiv:1705.09231. [CrossRef]
102. Murali, V.; Qi, L.; Chaudhuri, S.; Jermaine, C. Neural Sketch Learning for Conditional Program Generation. In Proceedings of the 6th International Conference on Learning Representations, ICLR 2018, Vancouver, BC, Canada, 30 April–3 May 2018.

103. Chen, B.; Zhang, F.; Nguyen, A.; Zan, D.; Lin, Z.; Lou, J.G.; Chen, W. CodeT: Code Generation with Generated Tests. In Proceedings of the International Conference on Learning Representations, Kigali, Rwanda, 1–5 May 2023.
104. Liu, J.; Xia, C.S.; Wang, Y.; Zhang, L. Is Your Code Generated by ChatGPT Really Correct? Rigorous Evaluation of Large Language Models for Code Generation. In Proceedings of the Advances in Neural Information Processing Systems 36: Annual Conference on Neural Information Processing Systems 2023, NeurIPS 2023, New Orleans, LA, USA, 10–16 December 2023.
105. Storhaug, A.; Li, J.; Hu, T. Efficient avoidance of vulnerabilities in auto-completed smart contract code using vulnerability-constrained decoding. In Proceedings of the 2023 IEEE 34th International Symposium on Software Reliability Engineering (ISSRE), Florence, Italy, 9–12 October 2023; pp. 683–693.
106. Guo, D.; Zhu, Q.; Yang, D.; Xie, Z.; Dong, K.; Zhang, W.; Chen, G.; Bi, X.; Wu, Y.; Li, Y.K.; et al. DeepSeek-Coder: When the Large Language Model Meets Programming – The Rise of Code Intelligence. *arXiv* **2024**, arXiv:2401.14196.
107. Roziere, B.; Gehring, J.; Gloeckle, F.; Sootla, S.; Gat, I.; Tan, X.E.; Adi, Y.; Liu, J.; Remez, T.; Rapin, J.; et al. Code Llama: Open foundation models for code. *arXiv* **2023**, arXiv:2308.12950.
108. Wang, D.; Guo, Y.; Dong, W.; Wang, Z.; Liu, H.; Li, S. Deep Code-Comment Understanding and Assessment. *IEEE Access* **2019**, *7*, 174200–174209. [CrossRef]
109. Mastropaolo, A.; Aghajani, E.; Pascarella, L.; Bavota, G. An Empirical Study on Code Comment Completion. In Proceedings of the 2021 IEEE International Conference on Software Maintenance and Evolution (ICSME), Bogotá, Colombia, 1–6 October 2021; pp. 159–170.
110. Shiina, H.; Onishi, S.; Takahashi, A.; Kobayashi, N. Automatic Comment Generation for Source Code Using External Information by Neural Networks for Computational Thinking. *Int. J. Smart Comput. Artif. Intell.* **2020**, *4*, 39–61. [CrossRef]
111. Haije, T.; Intelligentie, B.O.K.; Gavves, E.; Heuer, H. Automatic comment generation using a neural translation model. *Inf. Softw. Technol* **2016**, *55*, 258–268.
112. Gros, D.; Sezhiyan, H.; Devanbu, P.; Yu, Z. Code to comment "translation" data, metrics, baselining & evaluation. In Proceedings of the 35th IEEE/ACM International Conference on Automated Software Engineering, Melbourne, Australia, 21–25 September 2020; pp. 746–757.
113. Katz, O.; Olshaker, Y.; Goldberg, Y.; Yahav, E. Towards neural decompilation. *arXiv* **2019**, arXiv:1905.08325. [CrossRef]
114. Liang, R.; Cao, Y.; Hu, P.; Chen, K. Neutron: An attention-based neural decompiler. *Cybersecurity* **2021**, *4*, 5–17. [CrossRef]
115. Hosseini, I.; Dolan-Gavitt, B. Beyond the C: Retargetable Decompilation using Neural Machine Translation. In Proceedings of the Network and Distributed System Security (NDSS) Symposium, San Diego, CA, USA, 24–28 April 2022.
116. Szafraniec, M.; Roziere, B.; Leather, H.J.; Labatut, P.; Charton, F.; Synnaeve, G. Code Translation with Compiler Representations. In Proceedings of the International Conference on Learning Representations (ICLR), Kigali, Rwanda, 1–5 May 2023; pp. 1–20.
117. Gu, X.; Zhang, H.; Kim, S. Deep code search. In Proceedings of the 2018 IEEE/ACM 40th International Conference on Software Engineering (ICSE), Gothenburg, Sweden, 27 May–3 June 2018; pp. 933–944.
118. Shuai, J.; Xu, L.; Liu, C.; Yan, M.; Xia, X.; Lei, Y. Improving code search with co-attentive representation learning. In Proceedings of the 28th International Conference on Program Comprehension, Seoul, Republic of Korea, 13–15 July 2020; pp. 196–207.
119. Mathew, G.; Stolee, K.T. Cross-language code search using static and dynamic analyses. In Proceedings of the 29th ACM Joint Meeting on European Software Engineering Conference and Symposium on the Foundations of Software Engineering, Athens, Greece, 23–28 August 2021; pp. 205–217.
120. Ling, X.; Wu, L.; Wang, S.; Pan, G.; Ma, T.; Xu, F.; Liu, A.X.; Wu, C.; Ji, S. Deep graph matching and searching for semantic code retrieval. *ACM Trans. Knowl. Discov. Data* **2021**, *15*, 1–21. [CrossRef]
121. Van Nguyen, T.; Nguyen, A.T.; Phan, H.D.; Nguyen, T.D.; Nguyen, T.N. Combining Word2Vec with Revised Vector Space Model for Better Code Retrieval. In Proceedings of the 2017 IEEE/ACM 39th International Conference on Software Engineering Companion (ICSE-C), Buenos Aires, Argentina, 20–28 May 2017; pp. 183–185. [CrossRef]
122. Wan, Y.; Shu, J.; Sui, Y.; Xu, G.; Zhao, Z.; Wu, J.; Yu, P. Multi-modal attention network learning for semantic source code retrieval. In Proceedings of the 2019 34th IEEE/ACM International Conference on Automated Software Engineering (ASE), San Diego, CA, USA, 11–15 November 2019; pp. 13–25.
123. de Rezende Martins, M.; Gerosa, M.A. CoNCRA: A Convolutional Neural Networks Code Retrieval Approach. In Proceedings of the 34th Brazilian Symposium on Software Engineering, SBES 2020, Natal, Brazil, 19–23 October 2020; Cavalcante, E., Dantas, F., Batista, T., Eds.; ACM: New York, NY, USA, 2020; pp. 526–531. [CrossRef]
124. Li, W.; Xu, J.; Chen, Q. Knowledge Distillation-Based Multilingual Fusion Code Retrieval. *Algorithms* **2022**, *15*, 25. [CrossRef]
125. Zhang, F.; Chen, B.; Zhang, Y.; Liu, J.; Zan, D.; Mao, Y.; Lou, J.G.; Chen, W. RepoCoder: Repository-level code completion through iterative retrieval and generation. In Proceedings of the 2023 Conference on Empirical Methods in Natural Language Processing, Singapore, 6–10 December 2023.
126. Rahman, M.; Watanobe, Y.; Nakamura, K. A neural network based intelligent support model for program code completion. *Sci. Program.* **2020**, *2020*, 1–8. [CrossRef]

127. Svyatkovskiy, A.; Deng, S.K.; Fu, S.; Sundaresan, N. IntelliCode compose: Code generation using transformer. In Proceedings of the 28th ACM Joint Meeting on European Software Engineering Conference and Symposium on the Foundations of Software Engineering, Virtual, 8–13 November 2020; Association for Computing Machinery, New York, NY, USA, 2020; pp. 1433–1443.
128. Zhou, W.; Kim, S.; Murali, V.; Aye, G.A. Improving code autocompletion with transfer learning. In Proceedings of the 44th International Conference on Software Engineering: Software Engineering in Practice, Pittsburgh, PA, USA, 8–20 May 2022; pp. 161–162.
129. Jimenez, C.E.; Yang, J.; Wettig, A.; Yao, S.; Pei, K.; Press, O.; Narasimhan, K. SWE-bench: Can Language Models Resolve Real-World GitHub Issues? In Proceedings of the Twelfth International Conference on Learning Representations, Vienna, Austria, 7–11 May 2024.
130. Li, J.; Li, G.; Li, Z.; Jin, Z.; Hu, X.; Zhang, K.; Fu, Z. CodeEditor: Learning to edit source code with pre-trained models. *ACM Trans. Softw. Eng. Methodol.* **2023**, *32*, 1–22. [CrossRef]
131. Gao, Y.; Lyu, C. M2TS: Multi-Scale Multi-Modal Approach Based on Transformer for Source Code Summarization. In Proceedings of the 30th International Conference on Program Comprehension, Virtual Event, 16–17 May 2022; Association for Computing Machinery: New York, NY, USA, 2022.
132. Wang, W.; Zhang, Y.; Sui, Y.; Wan, Y.; Zhao, Z.; Wu, J.; Yu, P.S.; Xu, G. Reinforcement-Learning-Guided Source Code Summarization Using Hierarchical Attention. *IEEE Trans. Softw. Eng.* **2022**, *48*, 102–119. [CrossRef]
133. Wang, Y.; Dong, Y.; Lu, X.; Zhou, A. GypSum: Learning Hybrid Representations for Code Summarization. In Proceedings of the 2022 IEEE/ACM 30th International Conference on Program Comprehension (ICPC), Pittsburgh, PA, USA, 16–17 May 2022; pp. 12–23.
134. Tang, Z.; Shen, X.; Li, C.; Ge, J.; Huang, L.; Zhu, Z.; Luo, B. AST-Trans: Code Summarization with Efficient Tree-Structured Attention. In Proceedings of the 44th International Conference on Software Engineering, Pittsburgh, PA, USA, 25–27 May 2022; pp. 150–162.
135. Haque, S.; Bansal, A.; Wu, L.; McMillan, C. Action word prediction for neural source code summarization. In Proceedings of the 2021 IEEE International Conference on Software Analysis, Evolution and Reengineering (SANER), Honolulu, HI, USA, 9–12 March 2021; pp. 330–341.
136. Siow, J.K.; Gao, C.; Fan, L.; Chen, S.; Liu, Y. CORE: Automating review recommendation for code changes. In Proceedings of the 2020 IEEE 27th International Conference on Software Analysis, Evolution and Reengineering (SANER), London, ON, Canada, 18–21 February 2020; pp. 284–295.
137. Hoang, T.; Kang, H.J.; Lo, D.; Lawall, J. CC2Vec: Distributed representations of code changes. In Proceedings of the ACM/IEEE 42nd International Conference on Software Engineering, Seoul, Republic of Korea, 27 June–19 July 2020; pp. 518–529.
138. Pathik, B.; Sharma, M. Source code change analysis with deep learning based programming model. *Autom. Softw. Eng.* **2022**, *29*, 1–25. [CrossRef]
139. Tufano, M.; Pantiuchina, J.; Watson, C.; Bavota, G.; Poshyvanyk, D. On learning meaningful code changes via neural machine translation. In Proceedings of the 41st International Conference on Software Engineering, Montreal, QC, Canada, 25–31 May 2019; pp. 25–36. [CrossRef]
140. Zhang, L.; Feng, Z.; Ren, W.; Luo, H. Siamese-Based BiLSTM Network for Scratch Source Code Similarity Measuring. In Proceedings of the 2020 International Wireless Communications and Mobile Computing (IWCMC), Limassol, Cyprus, 15–19 June 2020; pp. 1800–1805.
141. Zhang, F.; Li, G.; Liu, C.; Song, Q. Flowchart-based cross-language source code similarity detection. *Sci. Program.* **2020**, *2020*; pp. 1–15. [CrossRef]
142. Fried, D.; Aghajanyan, A.; Lin, J.; Wang, S.; Wallace, E.; Shi, F.; Zhong, R.; Yih, S.; Zettlemoyer, L.; Lewis, M. InCoder: A Generative Model for Code Infilling and Synthesis. In Proceedings of the International Conference on Learning Representations, Kigali, Rwanda, 1–5 May 2023.
143. Ji, S.; Choi, S.; Ko, S.; Kim, D.; Im, H. RepCoder: An automated program repair framework for probability-based program synthesis. In Proceedings of the SAC '22: The 37th ACM/SIGAPP Symposium on Applied Computing, Virtual Event, 25–29 April 2022; Hong, J.; Bures, M.; Park, J.W., Cerný, T., Eds.; ACM: New York, NY, USA, 2022; pp. 1554–1561. [CrossRef]
144. Shin, R.; Allamanis, M.; Brockschmidt, M.; Polozov, O. Program synthesis and semantic parsing with learned code idioms. In Proceedings of the 33rd International Conference on Neural Information Processing Systems, Vancouver, BC, Canada, 8–14 December 2019; Curran Associates Inc.: Red Hook, NY, USA, 2019; pp. 10825–10835.
145. Chen, X.; Song, D.; Tian, Y. Latent execution for neural program synthesis. In Proceedings of the 35th International Conference on Neural Information Processing Systems, Online, 6–14 December 2021; Curran Associates Inc.: Red Hook, NY, USA, 2021.
146. Nijkamp, E.; Pang, B.; Hayashi, H.; Tu, L.; Wang, H.; Zhou, Y.; Savarese, S.; Xiong, C. CodeGen: An Open Large Language Model for Code with Multi-Turn Program Synthesis. In Proceedings of the International Conference on Learning Representations, Kigali, Rwanda, 1–5 May 2023.

147. Shin, R.; Kant, N.; Gupta, K.; Bender, C.; Trabucco, B.; Singh, R.; Song, D. Synthetic Datasets for Neural Program Synthesis. In Proceedings of the International Conference on Learning Representations, New Orleans, LA, USA, 6–9 May 2019.
148. Chen, X.; Liu, C.; Song, D. Towards synthesizing complex programs from input-output examples. In Proceedings of the International Conference on Learning Representations, Vancouver, BC, Canada, 30 April–3 May 2018.
149. Wang, X.; Wang, Y.; Wan, Y.; Wang, J.; Zhou, P.; Li, L.; Wu, H.; Liu, J. CODE-MVP: Learning to represent source code from multiple views with contrastive pre-training. In *Findings of the Association for Computational Linguistics: NAACL 2022*; Association for Computational Linguistics: Stroudsburg, PA, USA, 2022.
150. Chakraborty, S.; Ahmed, T.; Ding, Y.; Devanbu, P.T.; Ray, B. NatGen: Generative pre-training by "naturalizing" source code. In Proceedings of the 30th ACM Joint European Software Engineering Conference and Symposium on the Foundations of Software Engineering, Virtual, 14–16 November 2022; Association for Computing Machinery: New York, NY, USA, 2022; pp. 18–30.
151. Alon, U.; Zilberstein, M.; Levy, O.; Yahav, E. A general path-based representation for predicting program properties. In Proceedings of the 39th ACM SIGPLAN Conference on Programming Language Design and Implementation, PLDI 2018, Philadelphia, PA, USA, 18–22 June 2018; Foster, J.S., Grossman, D., Eds.; ACM: New York, NY, USA, 2018; pp. 404–419. [CrossRef]
152. Ben-Nun, T.; Jakobovits, A.S.; Hoefler, T. Neural code comprehension: A learnable representation of code semantics. In *NIPS'18: Proceedings of the 32nd International Conference on Neural Information Processing Systems*; Curran Associates Inc.: Red Hook, NY, USA, 2018; pp. 3589–3601.
153. Brockschmidt, M.; Allamanis, M.; Gaunt, A.L.; Polozov, O. Generative Code Modeling with Graphs. In Proceedings of the International Conference on Learning Representations (ICLR), New Orleans, LA, USA, 6–9 May 2019.
154. Karampatsis, R.M.; Sutton, C. Maybe deep neural networks are the best choice for modeling source code. *arXiv* **2019**, arXiv:1903.05734. [CrossRef]
155. Zhang, J.; Wang, X.; Zhang, H.; Sun, H.; Wang, K.; Liu, X. A novel neural source code representation based on abstract syntax tree. In *ICSE '19: Proceedings of the 41st International Conference on Software Engineering*; IEEE Press: New York, NY, USA, 2019; pp. 783–794. [CrossRef]
156. Sui, Y.; Cheng, X.; Zhang, G.; Wang, H. Flow2Vec: Value-flow-based precise code embedding. *Proc. ACM Program. Lang.* **2020**, *4*, 233. [CrossRef]
157. Zhang, J.; Hong, H.; Zhang, Y.; Wan, Y.; Liu, Y.; Sui, Y. Disentangled Code Representation Learning for Multiple Programming Languages. In *Findings of the Association for Computational Linguistics: ACL-IJCNLP 2021*; Zong, C., Xia, F., Li, W., Navigli, R., Eds.; Association for Computational Linguistics: Stroudsburg, PA, USA, 2021; pp. 4454–4466. [CrossRef]
158. Niu, C.; Li, C.; Ng, V.; Ge, J.; Huang, L.; Luo, B. SPT-code: Sequence-to-sequence pre-training for learning source code representations. In Proceedings of the 44th International Conference on Software Engineering, Pittsburgh, PA, USA, 25–27 May 2022; pp. 2006–2018.
159. Alreshedy, K.; Dharmaretnam, D.; German, D.M.; Srinivasan, V.; Gulliver, T.A. SCC: Automatic classification of code snippets. In Proceedings of the 2018 IEEE 18th International Working Conference on Source Code Analysis and Manipulation (SCAM), Madrid, Spain, 23–24 September 2018.
160. Reyes, J.; Ramírez, D.; Paciello, J. Automatic classification of source code archives by programming language: A deep learning approach. In Proceedings of the 2016 international conference on computational science and computational intelligence (CSCI), Las Vegas, NV, USA, 15–17 December 2016; pp. 514–519.
161. Gilda, S. Source code classification using Neural Networks. In Proceedings of the 2017 14th international joint conference on computer science and software engineering (JCSSE), Nakhon Si Thammarat, Thailand, 12–14 July 2017; pp. 1–6.
162. Ohashi, H.; Watanobe, Y. Convolutional neural network for classification of source codes. In Proceedings of the 2019 IEEE 13th International Symposium on Embedded Multicore/Many-Core Systems-on-Chip (MCSoC), Singapore, 1–4 Octorber 2019; pp. 194–200.
163. Ifham, M.; Kumara, B.S.; Ekanayaka, E.B. Neural Network-based Approach for Source Code Classification to Enhance Software Maintainability and Reusability. In Proceedings of the 2021 From Innovation To Impact (FITI), Colombo, Sri Lanka, 8 December 2021; Volume 1, pp. 1–6.
164. Barr, J.R.; Shaw, P.; Abu-Khzam, F.N.; Yu, S.; Yin, H.; Thatcher, T. Combinatorial code classification & vulnerability rating. In Proceedings of the 2020 Second International Conference on Transdisciplinary AI (TransAI), Irvine, CA, USA, 21–23 September 2020; pp. 80–83.
165. Guseva, P.; Drozdova, A.; Denisenko, N.; Sapozhnikova, D.; Pyaternev, I.; Scherbakova, A.; Ustuzhanin, A. Semantic Code Classification for Automated Machine Learning. *arXiv* **2022**, arXiv:2201.11252. [CrossRef]
166. Russell, R.; Kim, L.; Hamilton, L.; Lazovich, T.; Harer, J.; Ozdemir, O.; Ellingwood, P.; McConley, M. Automated vulnerability detection in source code using deep representation learning. In Proceedings of the 2018 17th IEEE International Conference on Machine Learning and Applications (ICMLA), Orlando, FL, USA, 17–20 December 2018; pp. 757–762.

167. An, W.; Chen, L.; Wang, J.; Du, G.; Shi, G.; Meng, D. AVDHRAM: Automated vulnerability detection based on hierarchical representation and attention mechanism. In Proceedings of the 2020 IEEE Intl Conf on Parallel & Distributed Processing with Applications, Big Data & Cloud Computing, Sustainable Computing & Communications, Social Computing & Networking (ISPA/BDCloud/SocialCom/SustainCom), Exeter, UK, 17–19 December 2020; pp. 337–344.
168. Mao, Y.; Li, Y.; Sun, J.; Chen, Y. Explainable Software vulnerability detection based on Attention-based Bidirectional Recurrent Neural Networks. In Proceedings of the 2020 IEEE International Conference on Big Data (Big Data), Virtual, 10–13 December 2020; pp. 4651–4656.
169. Wu, T.; Chen, L.; Du, G.; Zhu, C.; Shi, G. Self-attention based automated vulnerability detection with effective data representation. In Proceedings of the 2021 IEEE Intl Conf on Parallel & Distributed Processing with Applications, Big Data & Cloud Computing, Sustainable Computing & Communications, Social Computing & Networking (ISPA/BDCloud/SocialCom/SustainCom), New York City, NY, USA, 30 September–3 October 2021; pp. 892–899.
170. Zheng, W.; Semasaba, A.O.A.; Wu, X.; Agyemang, S.A.; Liu, T.; Ge, Y. Representation vs. Model: What Matters Most for Source Code Vulnerability Detection. In Proceedings of the 28th IEEE International Conference on Software Analysis, Evolution and Reengineering, SANER 2021, Honolulu, HI, USA, 9–12 March 2021; IEEE: New York, NY, USA, 2021; pp. 647–653. [CrossRef]
171. Wu, T.; Chen, L.; Du, G.; Zhu, C.; Cui, N.; Shi, G. Inductive Vulnerability Detection via Gated Graph Neural Network. In Proceedings of the 2022 IEEE 25th International Conference on Computer Supported Cooperative Work in Design (CSCWD), Hangzhou, China, 4–6 May 2022; pp. 519–524.
172. Wang, H.; Ye, G.; Tang, Z.; Tan, S.H.; Huang, S.; Fang, D.; Feng, Y.; Bian, L.; Wang, Z. Combining Graph-Based Learning With Automated Data Collection for Code Vulnerability Detection. *IEEE Trans. Inf. Forensics Secur.* **2021**, *16*, 1943–1958. [CrossRef]
173. Du, X.; Wen, M.; Zhu, J.; Xie, Z.; Ji, B.; Liu, H.; Shi, X.; Jin, H. Generalization-Enhanced Code Vulnerability Detection via Multi-Task Instruction Fine-Tuning. In *Findings of the Association for Computational Linguistics: ACL 2024*; Ku, L.W., Martins, A., Srikumar, V., Eds.; Bangkok, Association for Computational Linguistics: Stroudsburg, PA, USA, 2024; pp. 10507–10521. [CrossRef]
174. Wei, J.; Durrett, G.; Dillig, I. TypeT5: Seq2seq Type Inference using Static Analysis. In Proceedings of the The Eleventh International Conference on Learning Representations, Kigali, Rwanda, 1–5 May 2023.
175. Ramu, R.; Upadhyaya, G.; Nguyen, H.A.; Rajan, H. Hybrid traversal: Efficient source code analysis at scale. In Proceedings of the 40th International Conference on Software Engineering: Companion Proceeedings, Gothenburg, Sweden, 27 May–3 June 2018; pp. 412–413.
176. Ramadan, T.; Islam, T.Z.; Phelps, C.; Pinnow, N.; Thiagarajan, J.J. Comparative Code Structure Analysis using Deep Learning for Performance Prediction . In Proceedings of the 2021 IEEE International Symposium on Performance Analysis of Systems and Software (ISPASS), Stony Brook, NY, USA, 28–30 March 2021; pp. 151–161. [CrossRef]
177. Mezhuev, P.; Gerasimov, A.; Privalov, P.; Butkevich, V. A dynamic algorithm for source code static analysis. In Proceedings of the 2021 Ivannikov Memorial Workshop (IVMEM), Nizhny Novgorod, Russian Federation , 24–25 September 2021; pp. 57–60.
178. Qayum, A.; Khan, S.U.R.; Inayat-Ur-Rehman; Akhunzada, A. FineCodeAnalyzer: Multi-Perspective Source Code Analysis Support for Software Developer Through Fine-Granular Level Interactive Code Visualization. *IEEE Access* **2022**, *10*, 20496–20513. [CrossRef]
179. Sargsyan, S.; Vardanyan, V.; Aslanyan, H.; Harutunyan, M.; Mehrabyan, M.; Sargsyan, K.; Hovahannisyan, H.; Movsisyan, H.; Hakobyan, J.; Kurmangaleev, S. GENES ISP: Code analysis platform. In Proceedings of the 2020 Ivannikov Ispras Open Conference (ISPRAS), Moscow, Russia, 10–11 December 2020; pp. 35–39.
180. Kurtukova, A.; Romanov, A.; Shelupanov, A.; Fedotova, A. Complex Cases of Source Code Authorship Identification Using a Hybrid Deep Neural Network. *Future Internet* **2022**, *14*, 287. [CrossRef]
181. Abuhamad, M.; Rhim, J.s.; AbuHmed, T.; Ullah, S.; Kang, S.; Nyang, D. Code authorship identification using convolutional neural networks. *Future Gener. Comput. Syst.* **2019**, *95*, 104–115. [CrossRef]
182. Kurtukova, A.; Romanov, A.; Shelupanov, A. Source Code Authorship Identification Using Deep Neural Networks. *Symmetry* **2020**, *12*, 2044. [CrossRef]
183. Omi, A.M.; Hossain, M.; Islam, M.N.; Mittra, T. Multiple Authors Identification from Source Code Using Deep Learning Model. In Proceedings of the 2021 International Conference on Electronics, Communications and Information Technology (ICECIT), Khulna, Bangladesh, 14–16 September 2021; pp. 1–4.
184. Bogdanova, A.; Romanov, V. Explainable source code authorship attribution algorithm. *J. Phy. Conf. Ser.* **2021**, *2134*, 012011. [CrossRef]
185. Lutellier, T.; Pang, L.; Pham, V.H.; Wei, M.; Tan, L. ENCORE: Ensemble learning using convolution neural machine translation for automatic program repair. *arXiv* **2019**, arXiv:1906.08691.
186. Liu, G.; Lu, Y.; Shi, K.; Chang, J.; Wei, X. Convolutional neural networks-based locating relevant buggy code files for bug reports affected by data imbalance. *IEEE Access* **2019**, *7*, 131304–131316. [CrossRef]

187. Jiang, N.; Lutellier, T.; Tan, L. CURE: Code-Aware Neural Machine Translation for Automatic Program Repair. In *ICSE '21: Proceedings of the 43rd International Conference on Software Engineering*; IEEE Press: New York, NY, USA, 2021; pp. 1161–1173. [CrossRef]
188. Yuan, W.; Zhang, Q.; He, T.; Fang, C.; Hung, N.Q.V.; Hao, X.; Yin, H. CIRCLE: Continual repair across programming languages. In Proceedings of the 31st ACM SIGSOFT International Symposium on Software Testing and Analysis, Daejeon, Republic of Korea, 18–22 July 2022; pp. 678–690. [CrossRef]
189. Charalambous, Y.; Tihanyi, N.; Jain, R.; Sun, Y.; Ferrag, M.A.; Cordeiro, L.C. A new era in software security: Towards self-healing software via large language models and formal verification. *arXiv* **2023**, arXiv:2305.14752. [CrossRef]
190. Ji, S.; Lee, S.; Lee, C.; Han, Y.; Im, H. Impact of Large Language Models of Code on Fault Localization. In Proceedings of the 2025 IEEE Conference on Software Testing, Verification and Validation (ICST), Naples, Italy, 31 March–4 April 2025; pp. 302–313. [CrossRef]
191. Dişli, H.; Tosun, A. Code Clone Detection with Convolutional Neural Networks. *BilişIm Teknol. Derg.* **2020**, *13*, 1–12. [CrossRef]
192. Zhang, A.; Liu, K.; Fang, L.; Liu, Q.; Yun, X.; Ji, S. Learn to align: A code alignment network for code clone detection. In Proceedings of the 2021 28th Asia-Pacific Software Engineering Conference (APSEC), Taipei, Taiwan, 6–9 December 2021; pp. 1–11.
193. Zeng, J.; Ben, K.; Li, X.; Zhang, X. Fast code clone detection based on weighted recursive autoencoders. *IEEE Access* **2019**, *7*, 125062–125078. [CrossRef]
194. Hua, W.; Sui, Y.; Wan, Y.; Liu, G.; Xu, G. FCCA: Hybrid Code Representation for Functional Clone Detection Using Attention Networks. *IEEE Trans. Reliab.* **2021**, *70*, 304–318. [CrossRef]
195. Yahya, M.A.; Kim, D.K. CLCD-I: Cross-Language Clone Detection by Using Deep Learning with InferCode. *Computers* **2023**, *12*, 12. [CrossRef]
196. Oda, Y.; Fudaba, H.; Neubig, G.; Hata, H.; Sakti, S.; Toda, T.; Nakamura, S. Learning to Generate Pseudo-Code from Source Code Using Statistical Machine Translation. In Proceedings of the 30th IEEE/ACM International Conference on Automated Software Engineering, ASE 2015, Lincoln, NE, USA, 9–13 November 2015; Cohen, M.B., Grunske, L., Whalen, M., Eds.; IEEE Computer Society: New York, NY, USA, 2015; pp. 574–584. [CrossRef]
197. Zhang, X.; Zhou, Y.; Yang, G.; Chen, T. Syntax-Aware Retrieval Augmented Code Generation. In Proceedings of the Findings of the Association for Computational Linguistics: EMNLP 2023, Singapore, 6–10 December 2023; Bouamor, H., Pino, J., Bali, K., Eds.; Association for Computational Linguistics: Stroudsburg, PA, USA, 2023; pp. 1291–1302. [CrossRef]
198. Yin, P.; Deng, B.; Chen, E.; Vasilescu, B.; Neubig, G. Learning to mine aligned code and natural language pairs from stack overflow. In Proceedings of the 15thInternational Conference on Mining Software Repositories (MSR), Gothenburg, Sweden, 28–29 May 2018; pp. 476–486.
199. Weyssow, M.; Zhou, X.; Kim, K.; Lo, D.; Sahraoui, H. Exploring parameter-efficient fine-tuning techniques for code generation with large language models. *ACM Trans. Softw. Eng. Methodol.* **2025**, *34*, 1–25. [CrossRef]
200. Zhou, Y.; Liu, S.; Siow, J.K.; Du, X.; Liu, Y. Devign: Effective Vulnerability Identification by Learning Comprehensive Program Semantics via Graph Neural Networks. In *Advances in Neural Information Processing Systems 32: Annual Conference on Neural Information Processing Systems 2019, NeurIPS 2019, December 8–14. 2019, Vancouver, BC, Canada*; Wallach, H.M., Larochelle, H., Beygelzimer, A., d'Alché-Buc, F., Fox, E.B., Garnett, R., Eds.; Curran Associates Inc.: Red Hook, NY, USA, 2019 ; pp. 10197–10207.
201. Wang, Z.; Zhou, S.; Fried, D.; Neubig, G. Execution-Based Evaluation for Open-Domain Code Generation. In *Findings of the Association for Computational Linguistics: EMNLP 2023, Singapore, December 6–10. 2023*; Association for Computational Linguistics: Stroudsburg, PA, USA, 2023; pp. 1271–1290. [CrossRef]
202. Wang, L.; Zhang, A.; Wu, K.; Sun, K.; Li, Z.; Wu, H.; Zhang, M.; Wang, H. DuSQL: A large-scale and pragmatic Chinese text-to-SQL dataset. In Proceedings of the 2020 Conference on Empirical Methods in Natural Language Processing (EMNLP), Online, 16–20 November 2020; pp. 6923–6935.
203. Li, R.; Fu, J.; Zhang, B.W.; Huang, T.; Sun, Z.; Lyu, C.; Liu, G.; Jin, Z.; Li, G. TACO: Topics in algorithmic code generation dataset. *arXiv* **2023**, arXiv:2312.14852. [CrossRef]
204. Jain, N.; Han, K.; Gu, A.; Li, W.D.; Yan, F.; Zhang, T.; Wang, S.; Solar-Lezama, A.; Sen, K.; Stoica, I. LiveCodeBench: Holistic and Contamination Free Evaluation of Large Language Models for Code. In Proceedings of the International Conference on Learning Representations (ICLR), Singapore, 24–28 April 2025.
205. Daghighfarsoodeh, A.; Wang, C.Y.; Taherkhani, H.; Sepidband, M.; Abdollahi, M.; Hemmati, H.; Pham, H.V. Deep-Bench: Deep Learning Benchmark Dataset for Code Generation. *arXiv* **2025**, arXiv:2502.18726. [CrossRef]
206. Oda, Y.; Neubig, G.; Sakti, S.; Toda, T.; Nakamura, S. Syntax-based simultaneous translation through prediction of unseen syntactic constituents. In Proceedings of the 53rd Annual Meeting of the Association for Computational Linguistics and the 7th International Joint Conference on Natural Language Processing (Volume 1: Long Papers), Beijing, China, 26–31 July 2015; Association for Computational Linguistics: Stroudsburg, PA, USA, 2015; pp. 198–207.

207. Kocetkov, D.; Li, R.; Ben Allal, L.; Li, J.; Mou, C.; Muñoz Ferrandis, C.; Jernite, Y.; Mitchell, M.; Hughes, S.; Wolf, T.; et al. The Stack: 3 TB of permissively licensed source code. *Trans. Mach. Learn. Res.* 2023, accepted. Available online: https://arxiv.org/abs/2211.15533 (accessed on 9 October 2025).
208. Lozhkov, A.; Li, R.; Allal, L.B.; Cassano, F.; Lamy-Poirier, J.; Tazi, N.; Tang, A.; Pykhtar, D.; Liu, J.; Wei, Y.; et al. StarCoder 2 and The Stack v2: The Next Generation. *arXiv* **2024**, arXiv:2402.19173. [CrossRef]
209. Rahman, M.; Khatoonabadi, S.; Shihab, E. A Large-scale Class-level Benchmark Dataset for Code Generation with LLMs. *arXiv* **2025**, arXiv:2504.15564.
210. Li, Y.; Choi, D.; Chung, J.; Kushman, N.; Schrittwieser, J.; Leblond, R.; Eccles, T.; Keeling, J.; Gimeno, F.; Lago, A.D.; et al. Competition-level code generation with AlphaCode. *Science* **2022**, *378*, 1092–1097. [CrossRef]
211. Hugging Face. Hugging Face Datasets. 2025. Available online: https://huggingface.co/datasets (accessed on 9 October 2025).
212. Bouzenia, I.; Devanbu, P.; Pradel, M. RepairAgent: An Autonomous, LLM-Based Agent for Program Repair. In Proceedings of the 47th IEEE/ACM International Conference on Software Engineering (ICSE), Ottawa, ON, Canada, 27 April–3 May 2025; pp. 2188–2200. [CrossRef]
213. Yin, X.; Ni, C.; Wang, S.; Li, Z.; Zeng, L.; Yang, X. ThinkRepair: Self-Directed Automated Program Repair. In Proceedings of the 33rd ACM SIGSOFT International Symposium on Software Testing and Analysis, ISSTA 2024, Vienna, Austria, 16–20 September 2024; Christakis, M., Pradel, M., Eds.; ACM: New York, NY, USA, 2024; pp. 1274–1286. [CrossRef]
214. Li, F.; Jiang, J.; Sun, J.; Zhang, H. Evaluating the Generalizability of LLMs in Automated Program Repair. In Proceedings of the 47th IEEE/ACM International Conference on Software Engineering: New Ideas and Emerging Results, ICSE 2025-NIER, Ottawa, ON, Canada, 27 April–3 May 2025; IEEE: New York, NY, USA, 2025; pp. 91–95. [CrossRef]
215. Nguyen, A.T.; Nguyen, T.T.; Nguyen, T.N. Divide-and-conquer approach for multi-phase statistical migration for source code. In *ASE'15: Proceedings of the 30th IEEE/ACM International Conference on Automated Software Engineering*; IEEE Press: New York, NY, USA, 2015; pp. 585–596. [CrossRef]
216. Papineni, K.; Roukos, S.; Ward, T.; Zhu, W. BLEU: A Method for Automatic Evaluation of Machine Translation. In Proceedings of the 40th Annual Meeting of the Association for Computational Linguistics, Philadelphia, PA, USA, 6–12 July 2002; pp. 311–318. [CrossRef]
217. Lin, C.Y. ROUGE: A Package for Automatic Evaluation of Summaries. In *Text Summarization Branches Out*; Association for Computational Linguistics: Stroudsburg, PA, USA, 2004; pp. 74–81.
218. Eghbali, A.; Pradel, M. CrystalBLEU: Precisely and Efficiently Measuring the Similarity of Code. In Proceedings of the 37th IEEE/ACM International Conference on Automated Software Engineering, ASE 2022, Rochester, MI, USA, 10–14 October 2022; ACM: New York, NY, USA, 2022; pp. 1–12. [CrossRef]
219. Tran, N.M.; Tran, H.; Nguyen, S.; Nguyen, H.; Nguyen, T.N. Does BLEU score work for code migration? In Proceedings of the 27th International Conference on Program Comprehension, ICPC 2019, Montreal, QC, Canada, 25–31 May 2019; Guéhéneuc, Y., Khomh, F., Sarro, F., Eds.; IEEE/ACM: New York, NY, USA, 2019; pp. 165–176. [CrossRef]
220. Banerjee, S.; Lavie, A. METEOR: An Automatic Metric for MT Evaluation with Improved Correlation with Human Judgments. In Proceedings of the Workshop on Intrinsic and Extrinsic Evaluation Measures for Machine Translation and/or Summarization@ACL 2005, Ann Arbor, MI, USA, 29 June 2005; Goldstein, J., Lavie, A., Lin, C., Voss, C.R., Eds.; Association for Computational Linguistics: Stroudsburg, PA, USA, 2005; pp. 65–72.
221. Haque, S.; Eberhart, Z.; Bansal, A.; McMillan, C. Semantic similarity metrics for evaluating source code summarization. In Proceedings of the 30th IEEE/ACM International Conference on Program Comprehension, Virtual Event, 16–17 May 2022; pp. 36–47.
222. Liu, Y.; Xu, C.; Zhou, Y.; Li, Z.; Xu, Q. DeepRTL: Bridging Verilog Understanding and Generation with a Unified Representation Model. In Proceedings of the Thirteenth International Conference on Learning Representations, ICLR 2025, Singapore, 24–28 April 2025.
223. Zhou, S.; Alon, U.; Agarwal, S.; Neubig, G. CodeBERTScore: Evaluating Code Generation with Pretrained Models of Code. In Proceedings of the 2023 Conference on Empirical Methods in Natural Language Processing, Singapore, 6–10 December 2023; Bouamor, H., Pino, J., Bali, K., Eds.; Association for Computational Linguistics: Stroudsburg, PA, USA, 2023; pp. 13921–13937. [CrossRef]
224. Husain, H.; Wu, H.H.; Gazit, T.; Allamanis, M.; Brockschmidt, M. CodeSearchNet Challenge: Evaluating the State of Semantic Code Search. *arXiv* **2020**, arXiv:1909.09436.
225. Makharev, V.; Ivanov, V. Code Summarization Beyond Function Level. In Proceedings of the IEEE/ACM International Workshop on Large Language Models for Code (LLM4Code), Ottawa, ON, Canada, 3 May 2025; pp. 153–160. [CrossRef]
226. Agashe, R.; Iyer, S.; Zettlemoyer, L. JuICe: A Large Scale Distantly Supervised Dataset for Open Domain Context-based Code Generation. In Proceedings of the Conference on Empirical Methods in Natural Language Processing and the 9th International Joint Conference on Natural Language Processing (EMNLP-IJCNLP), Hong Kong, China, 3–7 November 2019; Inui, K., Jiang, J., Ng, V., Wan, X., Eds.; Association for Computational Linguistics: Stroudsburg, PA, USA, 2019; pp. 5436–5446. [CrossRef]

227. Abid, S.; Cai, X.; Jiang, L. Measuring model alignment for code clone detection using causal interpretation. *Empir. Softw. Eng.* **2025**, *30*, 46. [CrossRef]
228. Ding, Y.; Fu, Y.; Ibrahim, O.; Sitawarin, C.; Chen, X.; Alomair, B.; Wagner, D.; Ray, B.; Chen, Y. Vulnerability Detection with Code Language Models: How Far are We? In Proceedings of the 47th IEEE/ACM International Conference on Software Engineering (ICSE), Ottawa, ON, Canada, 27 April–3 May 2025; pp. 1729–1741. [CrossRef]
229. Kheria, I.; Gada, D.; Karani, R. A Semisupervised Learning Approach for Code Smell Detection. *SN Comput. Sci.* **2025**, *6*, 143. [CrossRef]
230. He, X.; Asiya; Han, D.; Zhou, S.; Fu, X.; Li, H. An Improved Software Source Code Vulnerability Detection Method: Combination of Multi-Feature Screening and Integrated Sampling Model. *Sensors* **2025**, *25*, 1816. [CrossRef] [PubMed]
231. Kumar, H.; Saxena, V. Software Defect Prediction Using Hybrid Machine Learning Techniques: A Comparative Study. *J. Softw. Eng. Appl.* **2024**, *17*, 155–171. [CrossRef]
232. Rodriguez, M.; Popa, R.A.; Flynn, F.; Liang, L.; Dafoe, A.; Wang, A. A Framework for Evaluating Emerging Cyberattack Capabilities of AI. *arXiv* **2025**, arXiv:2503.11917.
233. Atiiq, S.A.; Gehrmann, C.; Dahlén, K.; Khalil, K. From Generalist to Specialist: Exploring CWE-Specific Vulnerability Detection. *arXiv* **2024**, arXiv:2408.02329. [CrossRef]
234. Wen, J.; Yuan, D.; Ma, L.; Chen, H. Code Ownership in Open-Source AI Software Security. In Proceedings of the 2nd International Workshop on Responsible AI Engineering, Lisbon, Portugal, 16 April 2024; pp. 28–35. [CrossRef]
235. Yang, F.; Wang, Y. Analyzing the Robustness of Complex Networks with Attack Success Rate. *Entropy* **2023**, *25*, 1508. [CrossRef]
236. Wang, Y.; Wang, Y.; Wang, S.; Guo, D.; Chen, J.; Grundy, J.; Liu, X.; Ma, Y.; Mao, M.; Zhang, H.; et al. RepoTransBench: A Real-World Benchmark for Repository-Level Code Translation. *arXiv* **2024**, arXiv:2412.17744.
237. Xie, Y.; Naik, A.; Fried, D.; Rosé, C.P. Data Augmentation for Code Translation with Comparable Corpora and Multiple References. In Proceedings of the Findings of the Association for Computational Linguistics: EMNLP 2023, Singapore, 6–10 December 2023; Bouamor, H., Pino, J., Bali, K., Eds.; Association for Computational Linguistics: Stroudsburg, PA, USA, 2023; pp. 13725–13739. [CrossRef]
238. Anjum Haque, M.M.; Ahmad, W.U.; Lourentzou, I.; Brown, C. FixEval: Execution-based Evaluation of Program Fixes for Programming Problems. In Proceedings of the IEEE/ACM International Workshop on Automated Program Repair (APR), Melbourne, Australia, 16 May 2023; pp. 11–18. [CrossRef]
239. Yan, W.; Tian, Y.; Li, Y.; Chen, Q.; Wang, W. CodeTransOcean: A Comprehensive Multilingual Benchmark for Code Translation. In *Findings of the Association for Computational Linguistics: EMNLP 2023*; Bouamor, H., Pino, J., Bali, K., Eds.; Association for Computational Linguistics: Stroudsburg, PA, USA, 2023; pp. 5067–5089. [CrossRef]
240. Ou, G.; Liu, M.; Chen, Y.; Du, X.; Wang, S.; Zhang, Z.; Peng, X.; Zheng, Z. Enhancing LLM-based Code Translation in Repository Context via Triple Knowledge-Augmented. *arXiv* **2025**, arXiv:2503.18305. [CrossRef]
241. Dai, D.; Liu, M.; Li, A.; Cao, J.; Wang, Y.; Wang, C.; Peng, X.; Zheng, Z. FeedbackEval: A Benchmark for Evaluating Large Language Models in Feedback-Driven Code Repair Tasks. *arXiv* **2025**, arXiv:2504.06939.
242. Li, J.; Li, G.; Zhang, X.; Zhao, Y.; Dong, Y.; Jin, Z.; Li, B.; Huang, F.; Li, Y. EvoCodeBench: An Evolving Code Generation Benchmark with Domain-Specific Evaluations. In Proceedings of the Advances in Neural Information Processing Systems 38: Annual Conference on Neural Information Processing Systems 2024, NeurIPS 2024, Vancouver, BC, Canada, 10–15 December 2024; Globersons, A., Mackey, L., Belgrave, D., Fan, A., Paquet, U., Tomczak, J.M., Zhang, C., Eds.; Association for Computational Linguistics: Stroudsburg, PA, USA, 2024.
243. Chen, M.; Tworek, J.; Jun, H.; Yuan, Q.; Pinto, H.P.d.O.; Kaplan, J.; Edwards, H.; Burda, Y.; Joseph, N.; Brockman, G.; et al. Evaluating large language models trained on code. *arXiv* **2021**, arXiv:2107.03374. [CrossRef]
244. Sridhara, G.; Pollock, L.L.; Vijay-Shanker, K. Automatically detecting and describing high level actions within methods. In Proceedings of the 33rd International Conference on Software Engineering, ICSE 2011, Honolulu , HI, USA, 21–28 May 2011; Taylor, R.N., Gall, H.C., Medvidovic, N., Eds.; ACM: New York, NY, USA, 2011; pp. 101–110. [CrossRef]
245. Liu, H.; Gegov, A.; Cocea, M. Rule-based systems: A granular computing perspective. *Granul. Comput.* **2016**, *1*, 259–274. [CrossRef]
246. Sridhara, G.; Hill, E.; Muppaneni, D.; Pollock, L.L.; Vijay-Shanker, K. Towards automatically generating summary comments for Java methods. In Proceedings of the ASE 2010, 25th IEEE/ACM International Conference on Automated Software Engineering, Antwerp, Belgium, 20–24 September 2010; Pecheur, C., Andrews, J., Nitto, E.D., Eds.; ACM: New York, NY, USA, 2010; pp. 43–52. [CrossRef]
247. Luo, Z.; Xu, C.; Zhao, P.; Sun, Q.; Geng, X.; Hu, W.; Tao, C.; Ma, J.; Lin, Q.; Jiang, D. WizardCoder: Empowering Code Large Language Models with Evol-Instruct. In Proceedings of the International Conference on Learning Representations, Vienna, Austria, 7–11 May 2024.

248. Du, X.; Liu, M.; Wang, K.; Wang, H.; Liu, J.; Chen, Y.; Feng, J.; Sha, C.; Peng, X.; Lou, Y. Evaluating Large Language Models in Class-Level Code Generation. In Proceedings of the 46th IEEE/ACM International Conference on Software Engineering, ICSE 2024, Lisbon, Portugal, 14–20 April 2024; ACM: New York, NY, USA, 2024; pp. 1–13. [CrossRef]
249. Li, J.; Li, G.; Zhao, Y.; Li, Y.; Liu, H.; Zhu, H.; Wang, L.; Liu, K.; Fang, Z.; Wang, L.; et al. DevEval: A Manually-Annotated Code Generation Benchmark Aligned with Real-World Code Repositories. In Proceedings of the Findings of the Association for Computational Linguistics, ACL 2024, Bangkok, Thailand, 11–16 August 2024; Ku, L., Martins, A., Srikumar, V., Eds.; Association for Computational Linguistics: Stroudsburg, PA, USA, 2024; pp. 3603–3614. [CrossRef]
250. Dong, Y.; Jiang, X.; Jin, Z.; Li, G. Self-collaboration Code Generation via ChatGPT. *ACM Trans. Softw. Eng. Methodol.* **2024**, *33*, 1–38. [CrossRef]
251. Khoury, R.; Avila, A.R.; Brunelle, J.; Camara, B.M. How Secure is Code Generated by ChatGPT? In Proceedings of the 2023 IEEE International Conference on Systems, Man, and Cybernetics (SMC), Honolulu, HI, USA, 1–4 October 2023.
252. GitHub. GitHub Copilot is Generally Available to All Developers. 2025. Available online: https://github.blog/news-insights/product-news/github-copilot-is-generally-available-to-all-developers/ (accessed on 9 October 2025).
253. Zhu, M.; Jain, A.; Suresh, K.; Ravindran, R.; Tipirneni, S.; Reddy, C.K. XLCoST: A Benchmark Dataset for Cross-lingual Code Intelligence. *arXiv* **2022**, arXiv:2206.08474.
254. Liu, C.; Wan, X. CodeQA: A question answering dataset for source code comprehension. In *Findings of the Association for Computational Linguistics: EMNLP 2021*; Association for Computational Linguistics: Stroudsburg, PA, USA, 2021.
255. Hasan, M.; Muttaqueen, T.; Ishtiaq, A.A.; Mehrab, K.S.; Haque, M.; Anjum, M.; Hasan, T.; Ahmad, W.U.; Iqbal, A.; Shahriyar, R. CoDesc: A Large Code-Description Parallel Dataset. In *Findings of the Association for Computational Linguistics: ACL-IJCNLP 2021*; Association for Computational Linguistics: Stroudsburg, PA, USA, 2021.
256. Karanjai, R.; Xu, L.; Shi, W. SolMover: Smart Contract Code Translation Based on Concepts. In Proceedings of the 1st ACM International Conference on AI-Powered Software, Galinhas, Brazil, 15–16 July 2024; pp. 112–121. [CrossRef]
257. Dong, Y.; Ding, J.; Jiang, X.; Li, G.; Li, Z.; Jin, Z. CodeScore: Evaluating Code Generation by Learning Code Execution. *ACM Trans. Softw. Eng. Methodol.* **2025**, *34*, 1–22. [CrossRef]
258. Weisz, J.D.; Muller, M.; Houde, S.; Richards, J.; Ross, S.I.; Martinez, F.; Agarwal, M.; Talamadupula, K. Perfection Not Required? Human-AI Partnerships in Code Translation. In Proceedings of the 26th International Conference on Intelligent User Interfaces, College Station, TX, USA, 13–17 April 2021; pp. 402–412. [CrossRef]
259. Justin, D. Weisz and Michael Muller and Steven I. Ross and Fernando Martinez and Stephanie Houde and Mayank Agarwal and Kartik Talamadupula and John T. Richards. Better Together? An Evaluation of AI-Supported Code Translation. In Proceedings of the 27th International Conference on Intelligent User Interfaces, Helsinki, Finland, 22–25 March 2022; pp. 369–391. [CrossRef]
260. Liu, J.; Zhu, Y.; Xiao, K.; FU, Q.; Han, X.; Wei, Y.; Ye, D. RLTF: Reinforcement Learning from Unit Test Feedback. *Trans. Mach. Learn. Res.* 2023, *accepted*. Available online: https://openreview.net/forum?id=hjYmsV6nXZ (accessed on 9 October 2025).

applied sciences

MDPI

Systematic Review

Machine Learning-Based Methods for Code Smell Detection: A Survey

Pravin Singh Yadav [1], Rajwant Singh Rao [1], Alok Mishra [2,3,*] and Manjari Gupta [4]

1 Department of Computer Science and Information Technology, Guru Ghasidas Vishwavidyalaya, Bilaspur 495009, Chhattisgarh, India; pravinsingh1110@gmail.com (P.S.Y.); rajwantrao@gmail.com (R.S.R.)
2 Faculty of Engineering, Norwegian University of Science and Technology (NTNU), 7491 Trondheim, Norway
3 Informatics and Digitalization Group, Molde University College, Specialized University in Logistics, 6402 Molde, Norway
4 Computer Science, DST—Centre for Interdisciplinary Mathematical Sciences, Institute of Science, Banaras Hindu University, Varanasi 221005, Uttar Pradesh, India; manjari@bhu.ac.in
* Correspondence: alok.mishra@ntnu.no

Abstract: Code smells are early warning signs of potential issues in software quality. Various techniques are used in code smell detection, including the Bayesian approach, rule-based automatic antipattern detection, antipattern identification utilizing B-splines, Support Vector Machine direct, SMURF (Support Vector Machines for design smell detection using relevant feedback), and immune-based detection strategy. Machine learning (ML) has taken a great stride in this area. This study includes relevant studies applying ML algorithms from 2005 to 2024 in a comprehensive manner for the survey to provide insight regarding code smell, ML algorithms frequently applied, and software metrics. Forty-two pertinent studies allow us to assess the efficacy of ML algorithms on selected datasets. After evaluating various studies based on open-source and project datasets, this study evaluated additional threats and obstacles to code smell detection, such as the lack of standardized code smell definitions, the difficulty of feature selection, and the challenges of handling large-scale datasets. The current studies only considered a few factors in identifying code smells, while in this study, several potential contributing factors to code smells are included. Several ML algorithms are examined, and various approaches, datasets, dataset languages, and software metrics are presented. This study provides the potential of ML algorithms to produce better results and fills a gap in the body of knowledge by providing class-wise distributions of the ML algorithms. Support Vector Machine, J48, Naive Bayes, and Random Forest models are the most common for detecting code smells. Researchers can find this study helpful in better anticipating and taking care of software development design and implementation issues. The findings from this study, which highlight the practical implications of ML algorithms in software quality improvement, will help software engineers fix problems during software design and development to ensure software quality.

Keywords: antipattern; code smell; code smell detection; identification; machine learning algorithms

1. Introduction

Code smells can indicate deeper problems in the software, adversely affecting the software quality [1–5]. The code smell detection model identifies software issues that may cause severe problems in the future. Identifying code smells is always recommended, which helps to reduce the software maintenance cost and increases the code reusability [3,6]. Software metrics, detection models, pattern-matching approaches, etc., are effective methods for detecting code smells. A variety of software metrics can help to detect code smells. The proper detection of code smells also depends upon how well the model performs and detects various code smells. The domain of code smell detection has witnessed the development of various approaches, from rule-based, metric-based, to machine learning (ML)-based. ML is expanding quickly and finding applications in many different areas.

Solutions based on ML have proven very useful for complicated issues that challenge conventional approaches; because of that, this study is mainly focused on ML-based approaches. In the literature, many ML algorithms are used, such as Decision Tree, Decision Tree (J48), Decision Tree (c4.5), Naive Bayes, Support Vector Machines (SVMs), Random Forest, etc.

Nucci et al. [7] applied thirty-two ML algorithms like AdaBoost, J48, Random Forest, Naive Bayes, JRip, LIBSVM, Sequential Minimal Optimization, etc. They found 96% accuracy and 90% F-measure, the best-known results compared to the other works in this area. Guggulothu et al. [8] applied some ML algorithms with a 10-fold cross-validation method, including the J48 (C4.5) algorithm, Random Forest, JRip, Naive Bayes, Sequential Minimal Optimization, and K-nearest neighbors (where k = 2), and found that tree-based classifiers provide better results among all applied algorithms. Iqbal et al. [9] anticipated two skeletons, one with feature selection and the other without feature selection. They compared their results with techniques such as Multilayer Perceptron, SVM, Rule-Based Learning, Naive Bayes, K-nearest neighbors, Random Forest, etc. They observed that their method performed better than these classification methods. Pecorelli et al. [10] compared ML algorithms with DECOR (DEtection and CORrection), a heuristic-based approach on thirteen open-source software systems, and noticed that DECOR generally provides a better result than ML algorithms.

This study presents a systematic literature review (SLR) to find the applications of ML-based methods in code smell detection. The investigation examined various factors that influence the performance of code smell detection, including the ML algorithm employed, feature selection, evaluation metrics for quality assessment, software metrics, and datasets. This review process involved scrutinizing primary research references from diverse datasets. The code smell detection model is constructed based on an analysis of existing datasets, while the necessary information for the detection model is derived from software metrics. Software practitioners need a quality product that is easily maintainable and error-free. This study will help software professionals to find efficient methods and techniques to eliminate code smells at the early stages of development and ultimately build high-quality products in time. The following are some benefits of code smell detection:

- The better the code smell detection process, the better the software quality.
- Software metrics improve the detection process by focusing on different aspects of the software.
- The possibility of refactoring can be easily identified using this process.

Motivation and Contribution

The existing SLR discussed various ML algorithms, but class-wise categorizations need to be included [11–16]. This SLR illustrates multiple studies of several classes of ML algorithms, the distribution of their subclasses, and the appropriate percentage for each study. This SLR also examined various sources to evaluate the effectiveness of various ML algorithms. Researchers presented and discussed many SLRs, datasets, and performance analysis tools but could not discuss software metrics that are found to be more helpful and the dataset language used in various studies [11,14,16].

The contributions of this SLR are listed below:

i. The survey presents a unique approach to code smell detection, examining the SLR of forty-two papers (ARTN1 to ARTN42) from 2005 to 2024.
ii. This study not only identifies various factors that can impact software quality, such as code smells, software metrics, and datasets, but also provides practical guidelines for addressing these issues. These guidelines include best practices for testing procedures, popular software metrics, and methods for detecting code smells, offering valuable insights for software practitioners. We investigate various factors that may distress any software. The survey also provides some guidelines for handling such problems. These guidelines are theoretical concepts and practical tools that empower professionals to address software quality issues effectively.

iii. We analyzed different issues in the code smell detection space and examined the current solution to those problems. Identifying and analyzing issues involves systematically searching and gathering relevant research articles and popular tools used in code smell detection. Examining the solution involves critically analyzing the methodologies, algorithms, and frameworks developed to address these issues. Based on our rigorous analysis, we identified best practices. This comprehensive approach reassures the audience about the validity and reliability of our findings, instilling confidence in the thoroughness of our research.

iv. Different ML algorithms were analyzed in this field, and it was found that the ML algorithms performed better in most cases. In this SLR, different classes of ML algorithms used for code smell detection (Decision Trees, Ensemble Learners, Bayesian Learners, Rule-Based Learning, Support Vector Machines, neural networks, and miscellaneous) are analyzed with their different algorithms.

The primary goal of conducting this study is to examine, assess, and review the code smell detection methods from the following perspectives:

i. The ML algorithms are used in this field.
ii. Code smells that are being focused on in the literature.
iii. Identification of frequently used metrics.
iv. Identification of the metrics that appeared to be more effective.
v. Identification of various datasets.
vi. Identification of datasets of different languages frequently used in this area.
vii. Outlining the other performance measures used with various ML algorithms.

Figure 1 represents the different SLR states, such as the planning, conducting, and reporting states. The planning stage contains two steps: Step 1: Originate the problem/need to conduct the SLR, define the specific requirement for the survey, and identify the object the SLR seeks to address. Step 2 is to expand the review protocol, which identifies research questions that need to be addressed in the SLR. These research questions are extracted from previously conducted SLRs and motivated by previous studies in this field. The related work is included in Section 2. Section 3 regards conducting the SLR process. In this stage, search questions are framed first (mentioned in Section 3.2); in the next step, these questions are searched in the literature from a list of resources (mentioned in Section 3.2). In the next step, the relevant articles from the previous step are selected. After this step, irrelevant research articles are eliminated by considering a selected research article's abstract, title, and conclusion. The next step is quality evaluations, which check the quality of selected research articles using assessment questions (mentioned in Section 3.3). The evaluation score (mentioned in Table A7) is evaluated, and based on selection criteria (mentioned in Section 4.1.2), the poor-quality papers are eliminated in the next step. After this step, relevant research articles are analyzed, as mentioned in Section 3.4. The primary goal of this analysis is to present facts and figures and answer each research question. Section 4 reports findings and discussions. Section 5 reported possible validity threats. Appendix A illustrates the selected research articles and their scores on different assessment criteria.

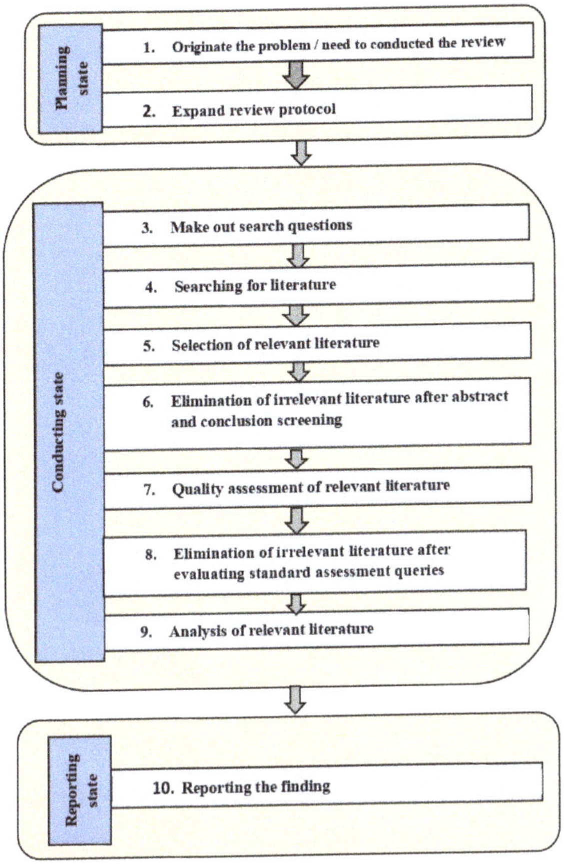

Figure 1. Systematic literature review steps.

2. Related Works

Table 1 shows a comparative analysis of our study with existing literature review studies. Singh et al. [17] analyzed 238 research papers between 1990 and 2015 and discussed the detection of code smells for refactoring. Sobrinho et al. [18] discussed which types of code smells are more extensively researched, reviewed 531 research articles between 1990 and 2017, and connected the researchers studying bad smells other than Duplicate Code using methodological aspects.

Table 1. Comparison with existing studies.

Sr. No.	Author	Year	No. of Research Papers Studied.	Period	Type	Considered Aspects
1	Zhang et al. [19]	2011	39	2000–2009	SLR	Code smell identification, tools, and methods to detect smells. Taxonomy of classifying code smell.
2	Rasool et al. [20]	2015	109	1999–2015	SLR	Code smell detection, classification, comparison, and evaluation detection tools.

Table 1. *Cont.*

Sr. No.	Author	Year	No. of Research Papers Studied.	Period	Type	Considered Aspects
3	Fernandes et al. [21]	2016	107	2005–2014	SLR	Detection tools for code smell, feature evaluation of detection tools, detection techniques, discuss quantitative and qualitative data about the tools.
4	Gupta et al. [22]	2017	60	1996–2016	SLR	The impact of the presence of code smell on the software, as well as the detection method and their correlation.
5	Sharma et al. [23]	2017	445	1999–2016	SLR	Characteristics of code smell, detection methods, tools, the impact of smells on productivity.
6	Sobrinho et al. [18]	2017	351	1990–2017	SLR	Connecting the researchers studying bad smells other than Duplicate Code, methodological aspects, the effect of the combination of bad smells' presence, and improvement in code smell detection.
7	Haque et al. [24]	2018	NA	NA	Survey	Detection approach-based, described its impacts on software, discussed methods to identify the smell.
8	Singh et al. [17]	2018	238	1990–2015	SLR	Detection of code smell for refactoring with different detection approaches.
9	Caram et al. [11]	2019	26	1999–2016	Mapping Study	Used search-based techniques and applied ML algorithms for code smell identification.
10	Kaur et al. [12]	2019	NA	NA	Review	Comparative study on code smell detection, search-based technique.
11	Azeem et al. [13]	2019	15	2000–2017	SLR	ML algorithms are applied for detection and considered independent variables, dependent variables, evaluation metrics, and performance meta-analysis (impact of the independent variable, ML algorithm performance, training strategies).
12	Kaur et al. [12]	2020	20	2005–2020	Review	Frequently used ML algorithms, detected bad smells, and code smell detection using ML and hybrid approaches.
13	Reis et al. [15]	2021	83	2000–2019	SLR	ML algorithms, visualization-based methods, 3D visualization methods, interactive ambient visualization, city metaphors, polymetric views, or graph models.
14	Shaaby et al. [16]	2020	17	2005–2018	SLR	ML algorithm to detect code smells, 27 code smells used for study, 16 ML algorithms, and ensemble techniques.
15	Zhang et al. [25]	2024	86	2010–2023	SLR	Analyzed supervised learning-based code smell detection.
16	Our Work		42	2005–2024	SLR	ML algorithms are used to detect code smells, class-wise categorizations, code smells considered for the study, metrics, datasets, dataset language, and performance measurements of ML algorithms.

Note: NA means 'Not Available'.

Sharma et al. [23] reviewed 445 papers that reported code smell identification tools, techniques, characteristics, and the impact of smells on productivity between 1999 and

2016. Azeem et al. [13] conducted an SLR with the help of ML algorithms and emphasized commonly used methods of independent and dependent variables for code smells. Kaur et al. [14] performed an SLR using ML algorithms and emphasized improvement in software quality. Reis et al. [15] discussed ML algorithms, visualization-based approaches, 3D techniques, and interactive ambient visualization and reviewed 83 relevant papers between 2000 and 2019. Shaaby et al. [16] reviewed 17 articles between 2005 and 2018, studied 27 code smells, and discussed 16 ML and ensemble techniques. The earlier SLRs covered different ML algorithms; however, no class-wise classifications exist. This SLR provides a unique perspective by showing the distribution of subclasses of various ML algorithms, the number of studies in each class, and the correct proportion for each research. The researchers provided and discussed many SLRs, datasets, and performance analysis tools. However, they did not address the language used by the datasets (mentioned in Section 4.2.6).

3. Procedures of Code Smell Detection Approaches

Figure 1 presents a comprehensive methodology for planning, accessing, and analyzing the process. In the planning stage, the problem is organized, and the review protocol, a detailed plan for conducting the literature review, is expanded. This stage involves identifying the problem and steps to find it in the literature, ensuring a thorough understanding of the issue at hand. Furthermore, the conducting stage undertakes the following series of tasks carefully designed to contribute to the overall research process.

Designing search questions, searching for digital libraries, and selecting the relevant literature are based on rigorous and thorough search strategies (discussed below in Section 3.2). The elimination process involves a careful review of the abstract and conclusion of each study. This process ensures that only studies that meet the research objectives and quality standards are included in the review. The process is further refined through the use of assessment queries (discussed below in Section 3.3, Table 2), which are specific questions designed to assess the relevance and quality of each study.

Table 2. Research questions.

RQ-No.	Research Questions	Motivation
RQ-1	Which ML algorithms are used to detect code smell?	Study various sources to evaluate the performance of different ML algorithms [11–16].
RQ-2	Which code smells are measured?	Detection of popular code smells with ML algorithms [11–16].
RQ-3	What software metrics are used for code smell detection?	Identification of metrics frequently used to detect code smells [13,16].
RQ-3.1	Which metrics were found more useful?	Identify the most critical metrics for detecting code smells [13,16].
RQ-4	What are the various datasets used for code smell detection?	Find out which datasets are used to detect code smells [12,14,16].
RQ-4.1	What are the various dataset languages used for code smell detection?	List the different dataset languages that are frequently used [12,14].
RQ-5	What are the performance measurements of the different ML algorithms used?	Find different evaluation techniques to measure the results of various ML algorithms [11,13,14,16].

3.1. Research Questions

After studying many research articles, the questions have been listed in a simplified manner. Table 2 shows the list of research questions (RQ); some questions have sub-questions. RQ-1, RQ-2, and RQ-5 incorporated complete research questions, and RQ-3 and RQ-4 incorporated sub-questions. RQ-1 studies various sources to evaluate the performance of different ML algorithms. This question explores different ML algorithms to detect smells and determine which methods perform better. RQ-2 discovers popular code smells with the ML algorithms. This question aims to collect information about code smells in studies nowadays. RQ-3 identifies critical metrics used for the detection of code smells. RQ-3.1 identifies frequently used software metrics. RQ-4 aims to know the different datasets used for identifying code smells. RQ-4.1 collects information on datasets and the used dataset languages. RQ-5 discusses different evaluation techniques to evaluate the results of various ML algorithms.

In Appendix A, the most relevant 42 research articles are tabulated. These articles are not just a collection of information, but they are the foundation of our study, providing practical insights and guiding our research. Each article has been assigned a unique attribute research article number (ARTN) for this SLR, ensuring their uniqueness, efficiency, and accessibility. Tables A2–A5 include the ARTN, year, tool/technique, smells, algorithms, dataset, performance metrics, and software metrics attributes, all crucial for our research. Tables A2–A5 provide detailed insights into each aspect of the reviewed research articles, facilitating easier navigation and interpretation of the data, thereby enhancing the overall understanding of the research.

3.2. Search Strategy

A robust search strategy is essential for a comprehensive SLR. The search strategy functions as a detailed map, facilitating the identification and selection of relevant study articles. Our search is not only thorough but also comprehensive and accurate, using PICO (Population, Intervention, Comparison, and Outcome). PICO serves as a comprehensive framework for creating research queries. We also employed Boolean expressions 'AND' and 'OR' to expand the scope of our search. These expressions allow for the inclusion of multiple search terms and variations, increasing the likelihood of finding relevant articles. For example, a research query might include questions such as the following:

What are the prevalent code smells [Outcomes/Result] detectable [Population/Space] utilizing ML algorithms? [Intervention]

The alternate string/words of the search question are as follows.

- The following possible words are included in search questions to find articles belonging to 'code smell'.

Code Smells—('code smell' OR 'code smells' OR 'code bad smells' OR 'bad smells' OR 'bad code smells' OR 'anomalies' OR 'antipatterns' OR 'antipattern' OR 'design defect' OR 'design fault' OR 'design-smells' OR 'design flaw').

- The following possible words are included in search questions to find articles belonging to 'machine learning'.

Machine Learning—('machine learning' OR 'supervised learning' OR 'classification' OR 'Machine Learning-based' OR 'regression' OR 'unsupervised learning').

- The following possible words are included in search questions to find articles belonging to 'prediction'.

Prediction—('prediction' OR 'detection' OR 'identification' OR 'prediction model' OR 'detection model' OR 'model').

- All search strings are combined using Boolean operators to make the final search string:

(('code smell' OR 'code smells' OR 'code bad smells' OR 'bad smells' OR 'bad code smells' OR 'anomalies' OR 'antipatterns' OR 'antipattern' OR 'design defect' OR 'design fault' OR 'design-smells' OR 'design flaw') AND/OR ('machine learning' OR 'supervised learning' OR 'classification' OR 'Machine Learning-based' OR 'regression' OR 'unsupervised learning') AND/OR ('prediction' OR 'detection' OR 'identification' OR 'prediction model' OR 'detection model' OR 'model'))

The final search string is searched in the following list of resources to select the research article for the literature review:

i. Springer

ii. ACM Digital Library
iii. IEEE Xplore
iv. Wiley Online Library
v. Google Scholar
vi. Scopus
vii. Science Direct
viii. Web of Science

The inclusion and exclusion of relevant articles are based on several selection and elimination rules. These are the following:

Selection rules:

i. Experimental results are based on ML algorithms.
ii. Results of studies based on non-ML algorithms.
iii. Experimental results are based on comparing statistical techniques and are ML-based.

Elimination rules:

i. Research articles on the ML algorithms without investigational study.
ii. Research articles on ML algorithms other than code smell detection.
iii. The research article results of the same author in a conference or journal are similar.

The research article is placed if any of the conditions in the research article selection rule are met. If any conditions in the research article elimination rule are not met, the research article is not included. The complete selection or elimination rules required are shown in Table 3. This table has three possible values, 'No', 'Partly', and 'Yes', to examine the research papers and assign the score. This is further discussed in Section 3.3.

Table 3. Assessment questions.

Que-No.	Standard Assessment Questions
Que-1	Are the objectives of the research clearly stated?
Que-2	Is the size of the dataset sufficient?
Que-3	Are the results and different evaluation techniques clearly explained?
Que-4	ML algorithms used are sufficiently defined and justified.
Que-5	Different metrics for various code smells are selected.
Que-6	Are there threats to the validity of the research mentioned?
Que-7	Are all independent variables clearly defined?
Que-8	What is the contribution to future research?
Que-9	Is a comparative analysis of different techniques available?

Figure 2 shows the procedure for selecting the research articles from the listed resources. Initially, 311 articles are selected (2005 to 2024) through listed resources with the help of search strategies. In the next step, 265 articles are excluded by considering the articles' titles, abstracts, and conclusions. The remaining 46 articles (2005 to 2022) are focused on for full-text evaluation. A total of 4 articles were eliminated in the quality assessment process because their research score was below 2, and finally, 42 articles were included in the review process. The selection of research articles in this review process depends on the availability of articles in selected databases.

Figure 3 presents the number of research articles reviewed in this SLR and their year of publication. This figure also highlights the impact of the research. In 2019, the graph showed the highest peak, indicating a significant year in which numerous ML algorithms were proposed in research studies. This underscores the importance and relevance of the research findings in the field of machine learning and code smell detection.

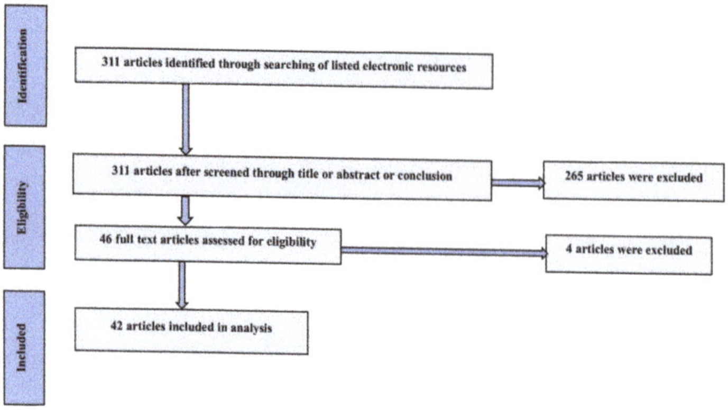

Figure 2. A systematic literature review flow diagram of article inclusion.

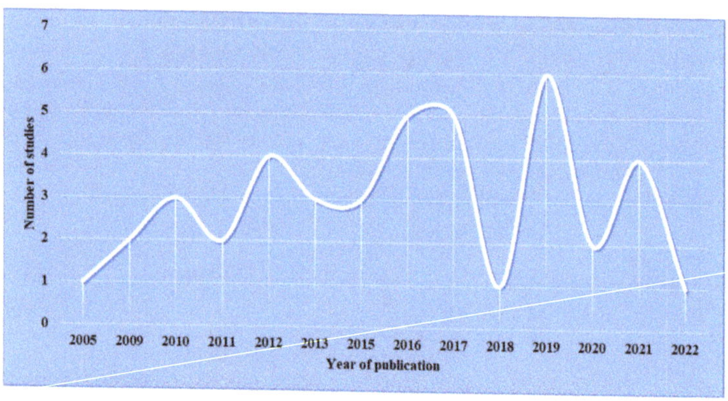

Figure 3. Distribution of studies during different years.

3.3. *Evaluation of Research Article*

Our evaluation process is meticulously designed, with standard assessment questions (Que) formulated (Table 3) to evaluate the correctness and weakness of research articles. This provides a clear and objective basis for assessing the articles' quality. The questions are assigned the research scores 0, 0.5, and 1, where 0, 0.5, and 1 represent the objective of the standard assessment question being not defined, partially defined, and well defined, respectively. The evaluated research score is secured, ranging from 0 to 9. The evaluation for each article is shown in Table A7. After a detailed analysis, selection, and elimination of articles, as shown in Table A1, this study found that 36 belong to above-average and 6 research articles belong to below-average categories.

3.4. *Analysis of the Research Article*

Each research paper undergoes a comprehensive analysis to determine whether the research questions were answered by the initial studies (Table A6 shows the information with assessment query score). The overview of the title, author's name, publication details, dataset information, machine learning algorithm, and metrics utilized are outlined. The details of each research question analysis taken for the SLR have been recorded. The main objective of the analysis is to show facts and figures and address each research question. The performance is evaluated using measures like area under the ROC Curve (AUC ROC), accuracy, etc. This evaluation helps to know the strengths and weaknesses of

ML algorithms, datasets, and feature selection techniques in code smell detection. Column charts and bar charts are used to explain the research.

4. Findings and Discussion

The SLR division conducted a comprehensive discussion of various research articles, recognizing their significant contributions to the field. It provided a summary of the articles, with each section providing a detailed analysis of the research articles. Finally, it concluded with the valuable information and insights gleaned from this study, underscoring the importance of these research articles.

4.1. Description of Articles

This section meticulously explains the most relevant research articles. Forty-two research papers were carefully selected based on their quality. This study exclusively focused on research papers from various journals and conferences where ML algorithms were applied. Each research article was scrutinized to extract critical information and find answers to all research questions.

4.1.1. Publication Sources

The list of publications included in Table 4 is of particular significance from the perspective of code smell detection. The research articles are organized by publication name, type, ISSN number, number of studies, and impact factor. For instance, there are seventeen research articles from IEEE indicating its prominence in this field, and one research paper is from Electronic Notes in Theoretical Computer Science, Software Quality Journal, and Journal of Computer Science and Technology, showcasing their contributions. Four articles from Empirical Software Engineering, etc., further highlight the sources' diversity.

Table 4. Publication summary.

Name of Publication	Type	ISSN Number	Impact Factor	No of Studies
Electronic Notes in Theoretical Computer Science	Journal	15710661	0.357	1
Software Quality Journal	Journal	09639314, 15731367	2.1	1
Journal of Computer Science and Technology	Journal	18604749, 10009000	1.9	1
International Journal of Rough Sets and Data Analysis	Journal	2334-4598	NA	1
International Journal of Electrical and Computer Engineering (IJECE)	Journal	2088-8708	0.376	1
International Journal of Computer Sciences and Engineering	Journal	2347-2693	3.802	1
Elsevier The Journal of Systems and Software	Journal	1641212	2.829	1
IEEE Access	Journal	2169-3536	3.476	2
Empirical Software Engineering	Journal	1382-3256, 1573-7616	3.762	4
Tech Science Press Computers, Materials and Continua Tech Science Press	Conference	NA	NA	1
Scopus, IEEE, and Science Direct	Conference	NA	NA	1
Scopus and IEEE	Conference	NA	NA	2
International Joint Conference on Computer Science and Software Engineering (JCSSE)	Conference	NA	NA	1
International Conference on Quality Software	Conference	NA	NA	1
International Conference on Machine Learning and Data Science	Conference	NA	NA	1
International Conference on Intelligent Computing and Control Systems (ICICCS 2019) IEEE Xplore	Conference	NA	NA	1

Table 4. *Cont.*

Name of Publication	Type	ISSN Number	Impact Factor	No of Studies
International Conference on Enterprise Information Systems (ICEIS 2017)	Conference	NA	NA	1
International Conference on Computer Science and Information Technology (CSIT)	Conference	NA	NA	1
International Conference on Advanced Information Networking and Applications	Conference	NA	NA	1
IEEE Transactions on Software Engineering	Conference	NA	NA	1
IEEE International Conference on Software Maintenance	Conference	NA	NA	1
IEEE	Conference	NA	NA	6
Conference on Software Maintenance and Reengineering	Conference	NA	NA	1
Conference on Reverse Engineering	Conference	NA	NA	1
ASE'16, 3–7 September 2016, Singapore, Singapore	Conference	NA	NA	2
ASE'12, 3–7 September 2012, Essen, Germany	Conference	NA	NA	1
2019 IEEE/ACM 27th International Conference on Program Comprehension (ICPC)	Conference	NA	NA	1
IEEE 24th International Conference on Program Comprehension (ICPC)	Conference	NA	NA	1
International Conference on the Quality of Information and Communications Technology	Conference	NA	NA	1
IEEE ASE 2013, Palo Alto, USA	Conference	NA	NA	1
Conference on Reverse Engineering	Conference	NA	NA	1
Grand Total				42

Note: NA means 'Not Available'.

4.1.2. Quality Evaluation

The assessment queries are used to evaluate the values of the research article. Based on the research score (RS), the article is divided into three categories:

(i) Above average: RS >5;
(ii) Below average: $2 \leq RS \leq 5$;
(iii) Elimination: RS < 2.

4.2. Rationalize the Research Questions

4.2.1. RQ1: Which ML Algorithms Are Used to Detect Code Smells?

The different ML algorithms used are shown below.

i. Decision Trees;
ii. Ensemble Learners;
iii. Bayesian Learners;
iv. Rule-Based Learning;
v. Support Vector Machines;
vi. Neural networks.

Figure 4 illustrates different ML algorithms used to detect code smells. The ML algorithms are divided into subcategories.

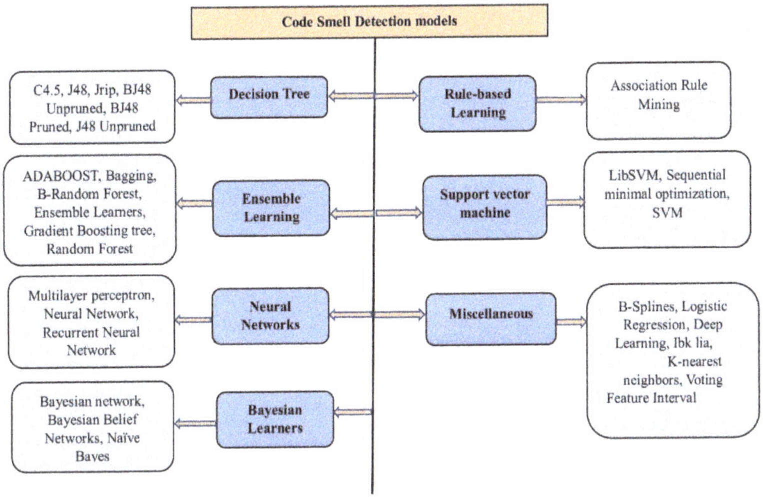

Figure 4. Different ML algorithms used for detecting code smells.

Table 5 shows the different categories of ML algorithms, the number of studies, and their percentage out of 42 (total number of selected articles for this SLR). For example, ensemble learning is used in 21 research articles out of the selected research articles, and their percentage out of 42 is 50%. It also indicates that Decision Tree, SVM, and ensemble learning techniques are often used in code smell detection. Some methods are more often used, so the total percentage is more than 100 in the table, and the number of studies in the table is more than the total number of research articles considered for this study.

Table 5. Machine learning-based code smell detection techniques.

ML Algorithms	Number of Research Studies (Out of 42)	% of Research Studies (Out of 42)
Bayesian learning	18	42.85714286
Decision Tree	27	64.28571429
Ensemble learning	21	50
Miscellaneous	12	28.57142857
Neural network	7	16.66666667
Rule-Based Learning	3	7.142857143
SVM	22	52.38095238

Nucci et al. [7] applied J48, Random Forest, Naive Bayes, LIBSVM, JRip, ADABOOST, and Sequential Minimal Optimization over 74 software systems. Pecorelli et al. [10] used Naive Bayes, J48, Random Forest, JRip, and SVM over JAVA projects and found optimal results. Figures 5 and 6 illustrate the ML algorithms used in code smell detection. Figure 5 indicates the different methods applied in research studies: Decision Tree, Ensemble Learners, Bayesian Learners, Rule-Based Learning, Support Vector Machines, neural networks, and miscellaneous.

The number of studies on Decision Trees, ensemble learning, Bayesian learning, Rule-Based Learning, SVM, neural networks, and miscellaneous based on code smell detection methods are shown in Figure 5a–g.

Figure 6 shows the ML algorithms used in code smell detection. The research studies that make use of subclass techniques of the Decision Tree, ensemble learning, Bayesian learning, SVM, and neural network approaches are J48 (29%), Random Forest (71%), Naive Bayes (72%), SVM (54%), and Multilayer Perceptron (72%). These findings indicate the prevalence of these ML algorithms in code smell detection, providing valuable insights for software engineers and researchers in the field.

The ML algorithms, deep learning, J48, Naive Bayes, SVM, and Random Forest algorithms are employed. The number of research studies performed using these techniques is 15, 13, 12, 2, and 8, respectively.

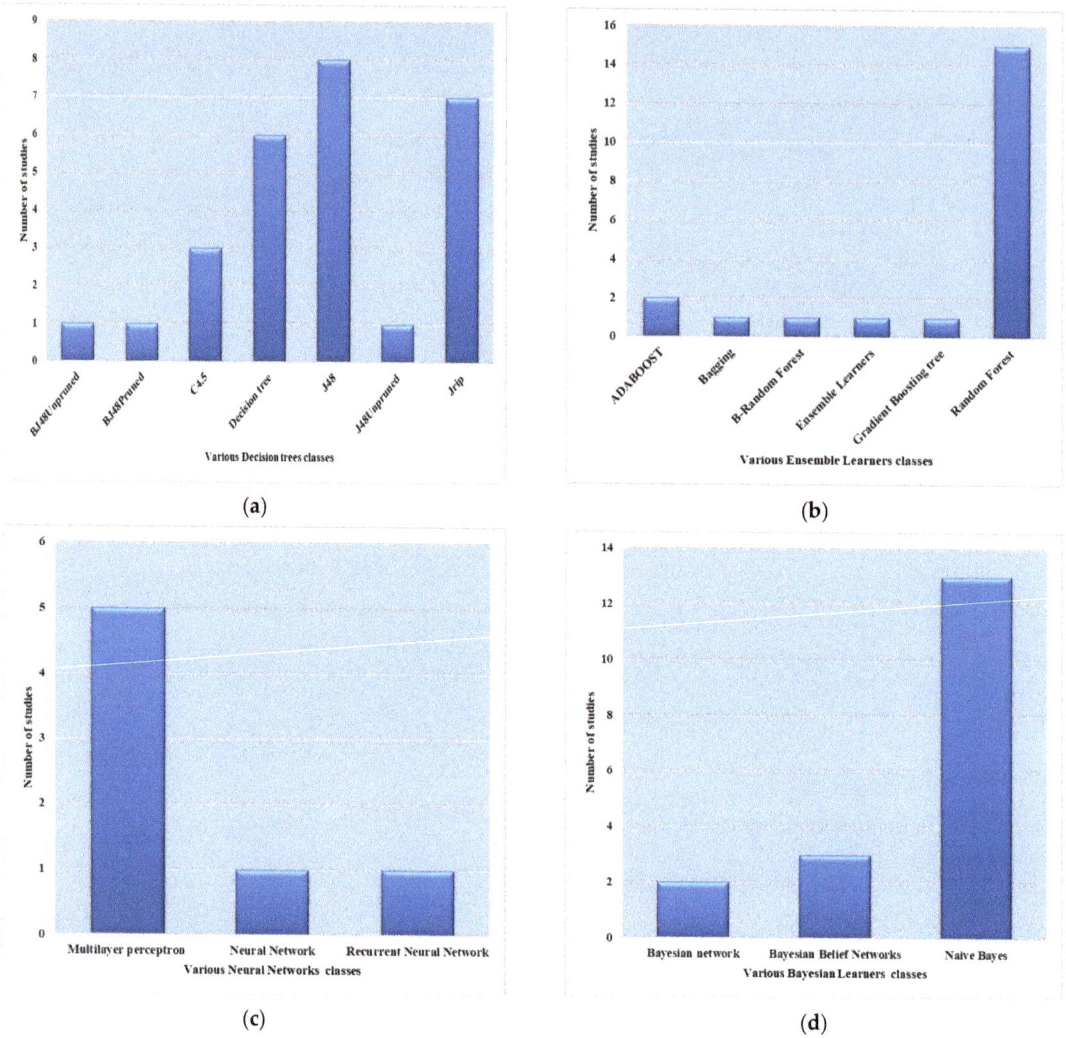

Figure 5. *Cont.*

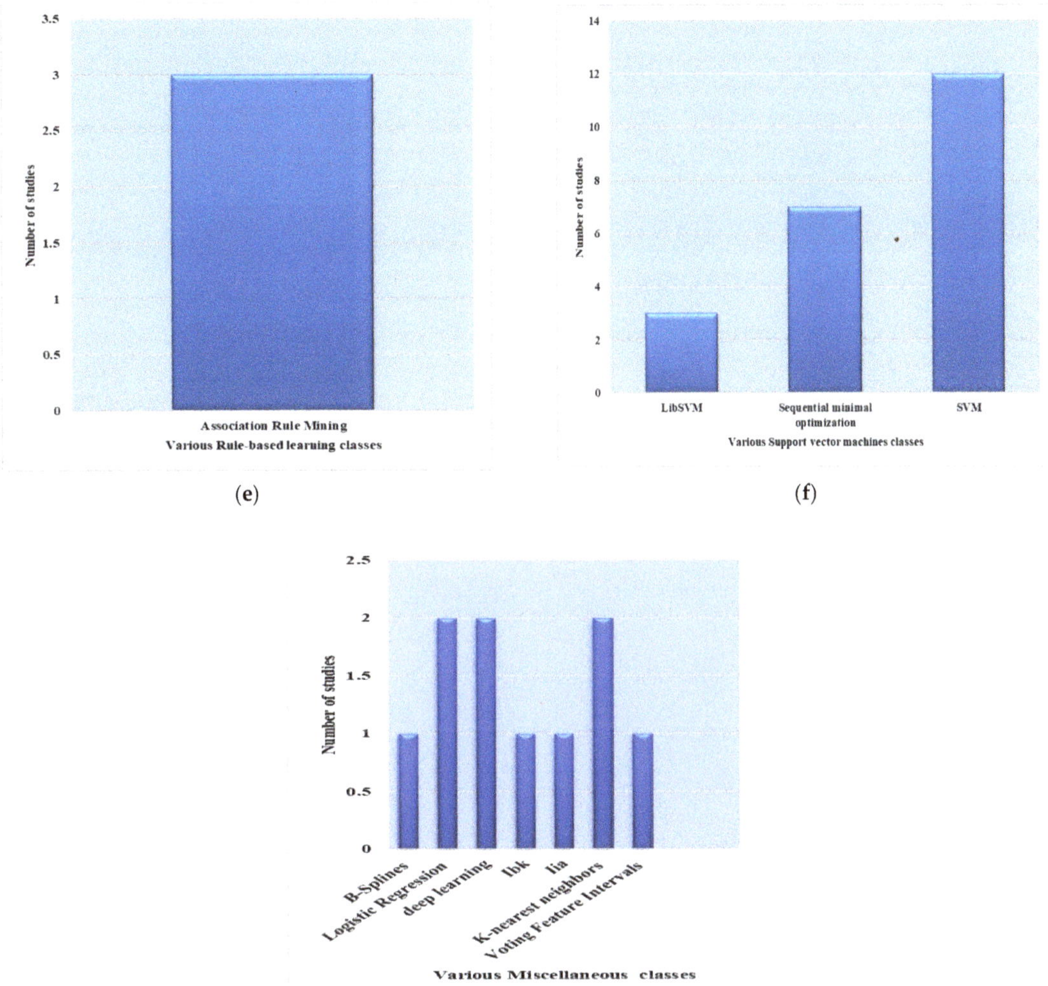

Figure 5. Number of research studies using distinct classes of ML algorithms: (**a**) bar graph of Decision Trees; (**b**) bar graph of Ensemble Learners; (**c**) bar graph of neural networks; (**d**) bar graph of Bayesian Learners; (**e**) bar graph of Rule-Based Learning; (**f**) bar graph of Support Vector Machines; (**g**) bar graph of miscellaneous classes.

Mhawish et al. [3] applied Random Forest, Gradient Boosting Tree, Decision Tree, deep learning, SVM, Multilayer Perceptron, GA (Genetic Algorithm), Naive Bayes, and GA CFS (Correlation-based Feature Selection) over Fontana et al. [26]. Furthermore, 74 open-source systems were used; the highest and precision values are 96.43% and 98.18%, respectively, for the Random Forest algorithm. Guggulothu et al. [8] used the B-Random Forest, Random Forest, B-J48 UnPruned, B-J48 Pruned, and J-48 Unpruned approaches and found 95–98% accuracy. Fontana et al. [26] utilized J48, C4.5 Decision Tree, JRip, Naive Bayes, Random Forest, Sequential Minimal Optimization, LibSVM over Antipattern Scanner, iPlasma, Fluid Tool, Marinescu detection rule, PMD, and the Fluid Tool dataset and found 96–99% accuracy. Kaur et al. [27] proposed an SVM approach over ArgoUML v0.19.8 and Xerces v 2.7.0 datasets and found better results. Nizam et al. [28] developed a deep learning system for code smell detection. They also used K-nearest neighbors and cosine similarity machine learning algorithms for detailed comparison. Shah et al. [29] proposed a CloudScent model, an open-source methodology for detecting code smells. The results demonstrate that the model can accurately detect eight code smells in the cloud.

4.2.2. RQ2: Which Code Smells Are Measured?

This section discusses code smells detected in various research articles. Figure 7 shows a variety of code smells observed in research articles considered in the study. It was found that researchers focused on more than thirty code smells. Data Class, Long Method, Feature Envy, and God Class are the most frequently analyzed code smells. Articles ARTN1, ARTN7, ARTN9, ARTN17, ARTN27, ARTN31, and ARTN39 include a study about the Lazy class. Articles ARTN10, ARTN16, ARTN18, ARTN21, and ARTN31 concentrated on the analysis of Duplicate Code. Spaghetti Code smells are discussed in the research articles ARTN5, ARTN8, ARTN11, ARTN12, ARTN30, and ARTN39. Research article ARTN17 discusses 11 code smells. The code smells are Lazy Class, God Class, Swiss Army Knife, Long Parameter List, etc. In this SLR, God Class code smell detection is found in a maximum number of research articles. Research article ARTN39 discusses nine code smells: Long Method, Spaghetti Code, Feature Envy, Parallel Inheritance, Large Class, Data Class, Lazy Class, Functional Decomposition, and Long Parameter List.

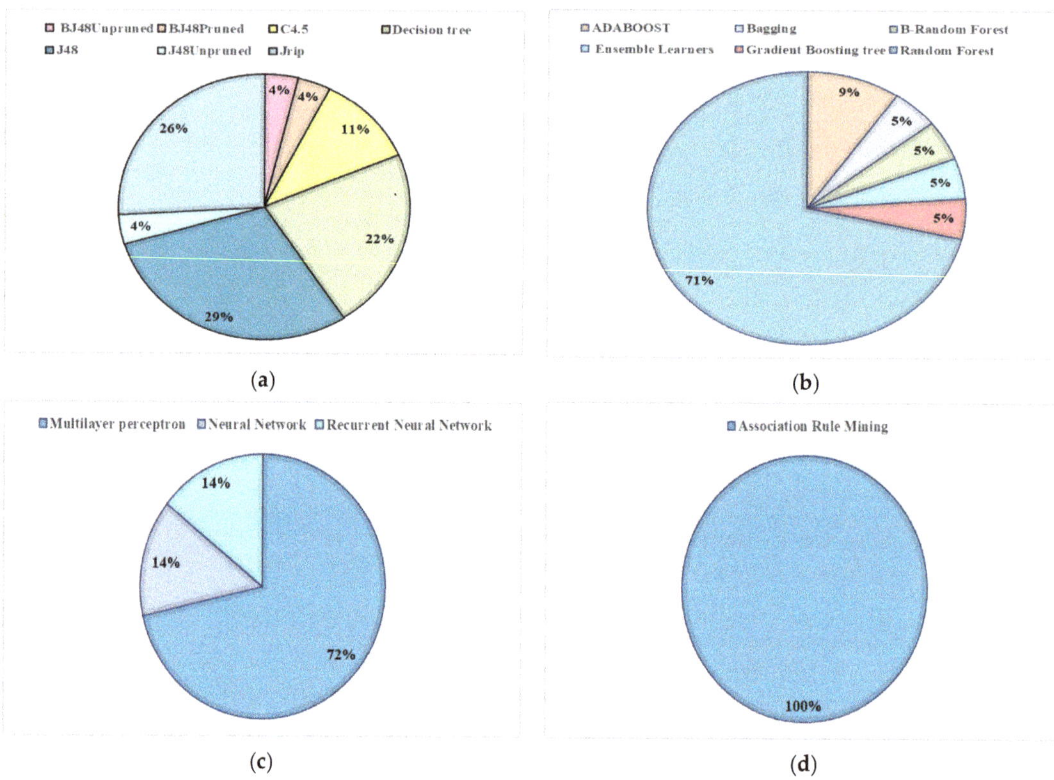

Figure 6. *Cont.*

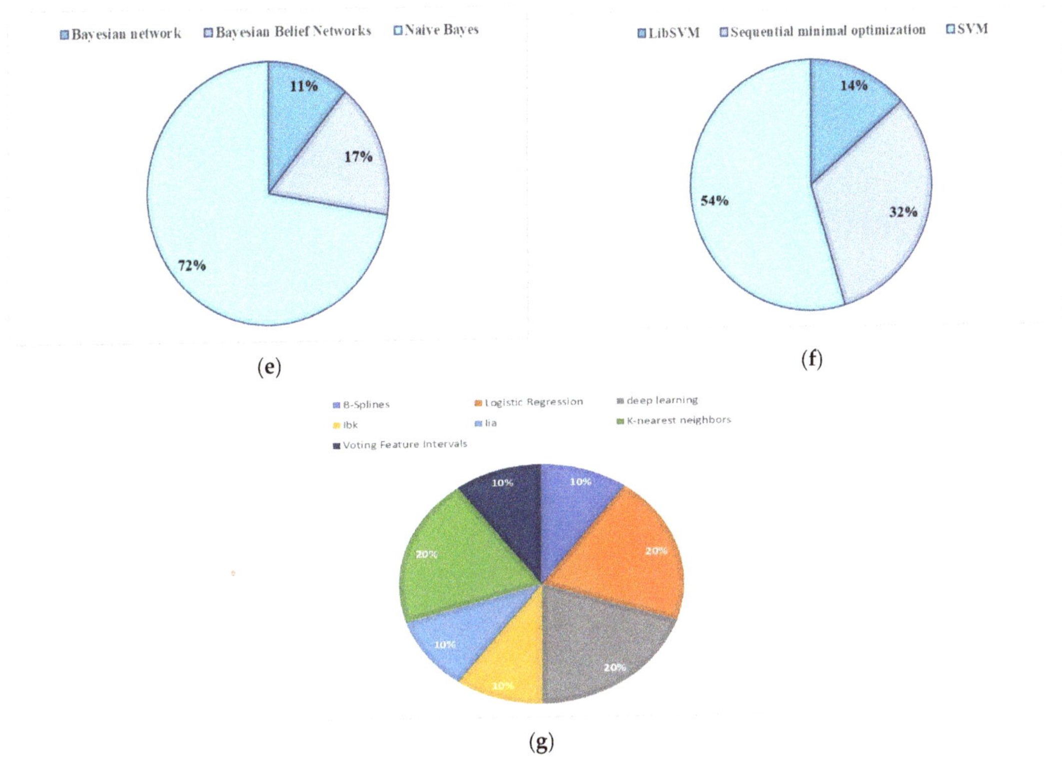

Figure 6. Subclasses' distribution of the Decision Tree, Bayesian learning, ensemble learning, SVM, Rule-Based Learning, neural network, and miscellaneous classification algorithms with appropriate study percentages: (**a**) Decision Tree-based code smell detection techniques; (**b**) Ensemble Learner-based code smell detection; (**c**) neural network-based code smell detection techniques; (**d**) Rule-Based Learning-based code smell detection techniques; (**e**) Bayesian Learner-based code smell detection techniques; (**f**) Support Vector Machine-based code smell detection approaches; (**g**) miscellaneous-based code smell detection techniques.

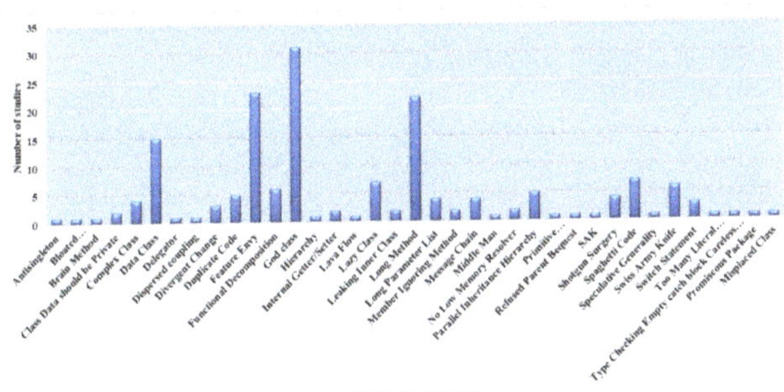

Figure 7. Number of studies of different code smells.

4.2.3. RQ3: What Software Metrics Are Used for Code Smell Detection?

Research articles employ a variety of software metrics, and in this study, more than 290 metrics are used. Figure 8 shows these metrics, arranged from most to least frequently used. This figure includes only the most and least used metrics for clarity. The following section will delve into the significance and application of these software metrics, providing a comprehensive understanding of their use in code smell detection.

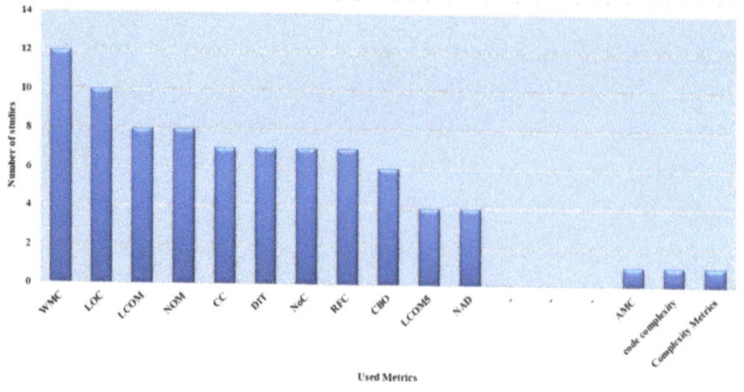

Figure 8. List of frequently used metrics for code smell detection. '-' represents some software metrics between the most and least frequently used metrics for clear visibility.

Object-oriented metrics study various features of object-oriented software like coupling, cohesion, and reusability in articles ARTN1, ARTN4, ARTN6, ARTN7, ARTN9, ARTN11, ARTN12, ARTN13, ARTN15, ARTN16, ARTN23, and ARTN38. The line of code (LOC), a traditional and frequently used software metric, is also considered in this research. Effective line of code (ELOC) is another metric that has been applied in several articles (ARTN13, ARTN17, ARTN21, ARTN27, ARTN30, ARTN31, ARTN32, ARTN34, ARTN38, and ARTN39). LCOM (Lack of COhesion in Methods), a metric that counts the number of method pairs where their class properties are not shared, is used in articles ARTN2, ARTN8, ARTN22, ARTN23, ARTN27, ARTN30, ARTN32, ARTN34, ARTN38, and ARTN39. ARTN34, for instance, considered LOCL with a sampling technique over 629 source project datasets.

Other metrics are applied in article ARTN20, such as the Number of Methods Overridden (NMO), Number Of Public Methods (NOPLM), Number Of Non-Accessor Methods (NONAM), Number Of Protected Attributes (NOPRA), NUMBER OF DEFAULT ATTRIBUTES (NODA), Number Of Static Methods (NOSM), Number Of Static Attributes (NOSA), NUMBER OF NON—CONSTRUCTOR METHODS (NONCM), Number Of Constructor Methods (NOCM), and the NUMBER OF FINAL AND STATIC METHODS (NoFSM). Article ARTN8 proposed the BDTEX (Bayesian Detection EXpert) approach with other metrics such as Coupling Between Objects (CBO), a Goal Question Metric (GQM), and the Number of Attributes Declared (NAD) metrics. Draz et al. [30] proposed a search-based system and employed metrics such as LOC, NAD, McCabe (used for software quality and security such as cyclomatic complexity (CC), actual cyclomatic complexity, etc.), Weighted Methods for Class (WMC), number of children (NOC), CBO, LCOM, CC, Response For A-Class (RFC), Number of Parameters (NOPARAM), and the Depth of Inheritance Tree (DIT). Their method had an average precision and recall of 94.24% and 93.4%, respectively, demonstrating the high effectiveness of these metrics in code smell detection.

The frequently used metrics in articles ARTN3, ARTN8, ARTN13, ARTN16, ARTN17, ARTN20, ARTN21, ARTN22, ARTN23, ARTN27, ARTN30, ARTN31, ARTN32, ARTN34, ARTN36, ARTN38, ARTN39, etc., are LOC, NoC, LCOM, WMC, and DIT. These metrics are widely used because they provide valuable insights into the structure and complexity of the code, which are key factors in code smell detection. The article used coupling and cohesion metrics CBO, SQL software metrics for code smell detection in articles ARTN1, ARTN4, ARTN7, ARTN9, ARTN13, ARTN15, ARTN16, ARTN20, ARTN23, ARTN27, ARTN32, ARTN34, ARTN38, and ARTN39, and also applied data sampling techniques to handle imbalanced data in prediction. LOC, WMC, DIT, LCOM, NoC, CC, NOM (Number of

Methods), etc., are the most commonly employed metrics. So, these metrics belong to the category of thorough utility. It also illustrates that AMC, code complexity, complexity metrics, etc., are rarely applied in identifying code smells and fall under the category of partial utility as a result.

4.2.4. RQ3.1: Which Metrics Are Found More Useful in Code Smell Detection?

Our research delved into the use of various software metrics in code smell detection, a crucial aspect of software quality analysis. These metrics, including object-oriented, coupling, complexity, size, cohesion, quality, GQM, LCOM5, NMD, and NAD metrics, have been extensively used in research articles. Among them, LOC, NOM, LCOM, WMC, CC, DIT, etc., have emerged as the most frequently applied metrics, proving their effectiveness in code smell detection. This comprehensive understanding of software metrics in code smell detection significantly contributes to the field.

4.2.5. RQ4: What Are the Various Datasets Used for Code Smell Detection?

Our study has comprehensively analyzed code smell detection by encompassing many datasets. These datasets, such as Xerces, ArgoUML, Gantt Project, Azureus, Eclipse, and object-oriented metrics datasets, are among the most commonly used ones. These are followed by Apache Ant, Fluid Tool, iPlasma, PMD, etc. This diverse range of datasets, each with unique characteristics and challenges, allowed us to gain a more thorough understanding of code smell detection, making our research findings more robust and insightful. Figure 9 shows a few commonly used datasets.

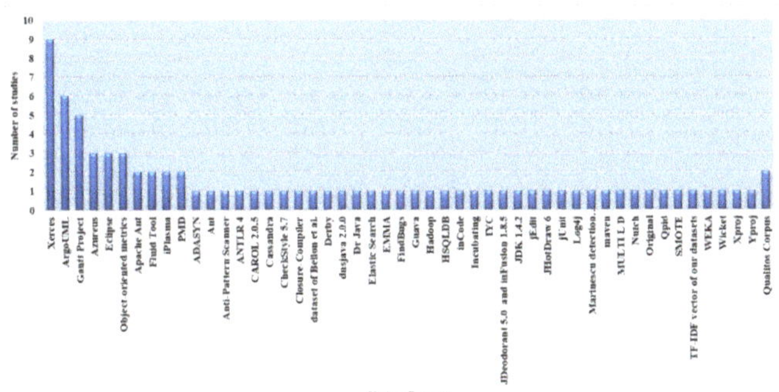

Figure 9. Research conducted on the various datasets used in code smell detection.

4.2.6. RQ4.1: What Are the Various Dataset Languages Used for Code Smell Detection?

A wide variety of dataset languages have been applied in code smell detection. Notably, JAVA emerges as the primary dataset language for code smell detection. The dataset is further categorized into open-source, projects written in JAVA, and any language and varies in size: large, small, and medium. ARTN10 employed C# as the dataset language. ARTN3 used XML with the JAVA dataset language. This diversity in dataset languages underscores the multifaceted nature of code smell detection, as different programming languages may have different code smells and quality issues. Understanding the usage and characteristics of these dataset languages can provide valuable insights for developing language-specific code smell detection techniques. Figure 10 shows the applied dataset languages.

The following are some brief descriptions of a variety of datasets:

- Open-source dataset: It includes freely available software projects such as WEKA, Xerces v2.7.0, IYC, Gantt Project v1.10.2, Eclipse, Guava, Closure Compiler, and jUnit datasets.

- Student dataset: It includes datasets developed by students, such as Fontana et al., who designed datasets using four open-source JAVA projects with the help of three master's degree students [26].
- The language dataset includes a dataset selected from different language projects, such as JAVA, XML, C#, etc. JAVA is the most frequently used language in research articles.
- Others: This study has observed that the main datasets used are open-source datasets belonging to the JAVA language. Researchers in ARTN1, ARTN7, ARTN9, and ARTN10 have also used some private industrial datasets.

This study has observed that the main datasets used are open-source datasets belonging to the JAVA language.

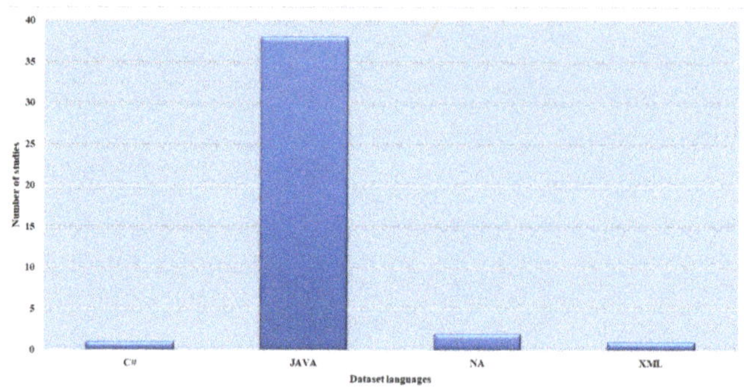

Figure 10. List of dataset languages used for code smell detection.

4.2.7. RQ5: What Are the Performance Measurements of the Different ML Algorithms Used?

Various performance measures are applied in code smell detection, as shown in Figure 11. Some performance measures are effectively used, such as precision (21 times), recall (21 times), accuracy (22 times), and F-measure (18 times). Some rarely used techniques are kept in miscellaneous. Table 6 shows that the performance measures precision, recall, accuracy, F-measure, root mean square error (RMSE), Matthew correlation coefficient (MCC), hamming score, mean absolute error (MAE), etc., are rarely used. ARTN15, ARTN29, ARTN32, ARTN35, ARTN37, and ARTN42 used AUC ROC for performance measurement. ARTN15 and ARTN37 used GMean for performance analysis. These performance measures are crucial in evaluating the effectiveness and efficiency of different ML algorithms in code smell detection.

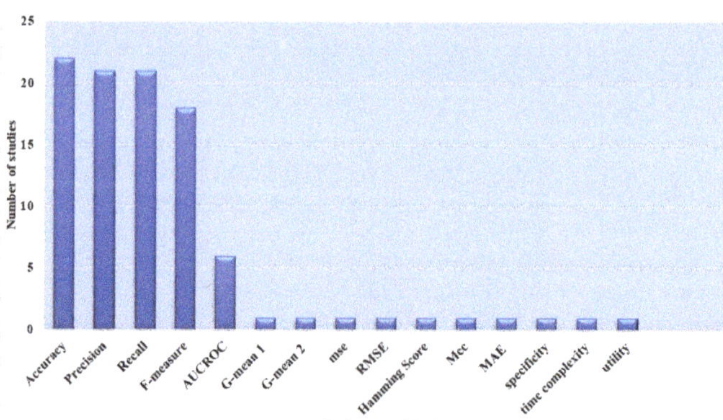

Figure 11. Performance measures used in various types of research.

Table 6. Analyzing performance indicators across studies.

Performance Measures	Description	Research Articles
Accuracy	Out of all projections, how many have been accurate overall?	ARTN1, ARTN2, ARTN6, ARTN7, ARTN9, ARTN15, ARTN18, ARTN20, ARTN22, ARTN24, ARTN27, ARTN29, ARTN32, ARTN33, ARTN34, ARTN35, ARTN36, ARTN37, ARTN38, ARTN40, ARTN41, ARTN42
Precision	It provides data on how well the classifier performs in terms of false positives.	ARTN2, ARTN3, ARTN4, ARTN5, ARTN8, ARTN10, ARTN11, ARTN12, ARTN13, ARTN14, ARTN16, ARTN17, ARTN18, ARTN19, ARTN21, ARTN25, ARTN28, ARTN30, ARTN39, ARTN41, ARTN42
Recall	It provides data on how well the classifier performs in avoiding false negatives.	ARTN2, ARTN3, ARTN4, ARTN5, ARTN8, ARTN10, ARTN11, ARTN12, ARTN13, ARTN14, ARTN16, ARTN17, ARTN18, ARTN19, ARTN21, ARTN25, ARTN28, ARTN30, ARTN39, ARTN41, ARTN42
F-measure	A single score that combines recall and precision.	ARTN13, ARTN14, ARTN15, ARTN16, ARTN17, ARTN19, ARTN29, ARTN30, ARTN32, ARTN33, ARTN34, ARTN35, ARTN36, ARTN37, ARTN38, ARTN40, ARTN41, ARTN42
AUC ROC	The curve between specificity and recall. It calculates the effectiveness.	ARTN15, ARTN29, ARTN32, ARTN35, ARTN37, ARTN42
G-mean (G-mean 1, G-mean 2)	It combines a true positive rate and a true negative rate.	ARTN38
MSE	An average of the square of the differences between the predicted and actual value.	ARTN26
RMSE	It is the MSE value's square root.	ARTN23
Miscellaneous	It includes Hamming Score, Exact Match Ratio, time complexity, standard deviations, effectiveness, and utility.	ARTN7, ARTN8, ARTN10, ARTN23, ARTN24, ARTN26, ARTN30, ARTN31, ARTN35, ARTN37

Our research demonstrated the effectiveness of various ML algorithms in code smell detection. The SVM, Random Forest, J48, and Naive Bayes models have emerged as the most popular and accurate methods, as confirmed by their frequent use in research articles (Table 6). The accuracy, AUC RoC, precision, and recall are manually analyzed from different research articles. The accuracy score, in particular, is often used to measure the model's performance, providing a reliable benchmark for future ML algorithms in code smell detection.

4.3. Opportunities Trends

Software projects are growing more popular due to the digital era's expansion, which has increased the number of modules and the size of these projects. The increased modules can increase the chances of errors in the future and the possibility of severe problems in the software. Code smell detection removes the cause that may create poor performance and future issues in software. It is challenging to find detection rules for code smells; however, some metric-based methods have also been developed. Most of the datasets are from the project/industrial datasets. If various datasets are easily accessible, their detection will be more accurate.

4.4. Insightful Discussion

This section discusses various SLR study findings, which will help software developers to find key points to improve software quality. New researchers can enhance their knowledge for their upcoming research studies. The insights gained from this research include the most effective metrics and dataset languages, the most commonly used datasets, and the performance measurements of different ML algorithms, all of which can guide future research and software development practices.

RQ-1 categorizes ML algorithms into Decision Tree, ensemble learning, Bayesian learning, Rule-Based Learning, SVM, neural network, and miscellaneous. Decision Trees, SVM, ensemble learning, and their subclasses Random Forest, J48, SVM, Naive Bayes, and Multilayer Perceptron are frequently used to identify code smells.

This study found that 27 of 42 research articles used Decision Tree algorithms to identify code smells, as shown in Table 5. Most research studies employ this method because of its excellent performance and widespread availability of relevant software. This study reveals a need for Rule-Based Learning applications to deal with software smells, as only 3 of 42 research articles used this algorithm. More research studies are needed in this area, and future studies may need to use and explore the capability of this algorithm to detect code smells.

RQ-2 discovered that the various researchers employed over 30 code smells more than 140 times in their investigation. Data Class, Feature Envy, God Class, and Long Method are the most frequently used code smells and are given more consideration in recent research, as shown in Figure 7. These code smells may be chosen for the following reasons:

- Many different design concerns are covered.
- They severely compromise the integrity of the program.
- Code smells of these types are the most common type; these code smells are easily recognizable and explained.

Most existing research in ML algorithms has concentrated on a small subset of possible code smells. These studies did not examine all the recommended code smells. Thus, other code smells that significantly impact software quality may need to be noticed. Therefore, there is an opportunity for further research to investigate these unexplored code smells and their effects on software quality [3]. This research gap presents a potential avenue for future improvements in code smell detection and software quality assurance.

RQ-3 discusses various software metrics used in research articles. AMC, code complexity, complexity metrics, etc., are rarely used. In contrast, LOC, WMC, DIT, LCOM, CC, and NoC are frequently used metrics because they provide valuable insights into software code's structural complexity and design issues. These metrics correlate with code smells, which indicate poor code quality and potential maintenance problems.

RQ-4 shows the utilization of datasets in our research. Due to their size and diversity, code smells are often detected using the Xerces, ArgoUML, Gantt Project, Azureus, Eclipse, and object-oriented metrics datasets, which enable the detection of a wide variety of code smells. These datasets are widely used in the software development community and are well documented and simple to utilize.

Based on our findings, earlier studies tended to place more emphasis on the Java language. The majority of these studies used Java-based platforms to test their methodologies. Therefore, further study is required to uncover the efficacy of ML algorithms in detecting code smells in languages other than Java.

RQ-5 discusses the various performance measures. In this study, the most frequently used performance measures are precision (21 times), recall (21 times), accuracy (22 times), and F-measure (18 times).

These performance measures can measure the efficiency of deployed ML algorithms for code smell detection. However, evaluating the model's efficacy by considering recall and precision together is essential.

Furthermore, when dealing with unbalanced datasets in which negative and positive classes are unequal, it is not desirable to rely only on accuracy.

Few research studies have used correlation analysis to calculate the associations between smells. Therefore, more studies are needed to address this issue and create more effective models for detecting code smells.

5. Threats to Validity

This study has not considered all aspects of code smell detection and follows a search strategy to retrieve research articles. The search strategy involved a comprehensive search string encompassing eight digital libraries, including original words, different synonyms, and spellings of the search word. The inclusion/exclusion of relevant articles was carefully considered, depending on their availability and relevance. The selection and elimination rules are discussed in Section 3.2. After analyzing several pertinent articles, it was observed that the recent work is more appropriate. However, it is important to note that the search strategy, while thorough, may have some limitations, such as the potential for missing articles due to inconsistent keywords in different articles or the exclusion of some conference and journal research papers. These limitations should be considered when interpreting this study's results.

This study includes the maximum number of relevant articles on detecting code smell using ML algorithms; so it may be less likely to miss any related articles. This SLR excluded some conference and journal research papers using selection and elimination criteria, as discussed in Section 3.2. The criteria for inclusion were based on the paper's relevance to the research questions and the quality of the research methodology. If a research paper met these criteria, it was included in the study. A few good-quality papers may not meet our selection/inclusion criteria.

In this SLR, during the searching process, it has been observed that various digital libraries are not efficient because of inconsistent keywords in different articles. So, few papers or studies may have been missed. Various researchers followed Kitchenham et al.'s [31] research evaluation and validation method. According to Kitchenham et al., one researcher assesses the quality, and the second performs the validation. In our study, one researcher extracted and evaluated data from randomly chosen articles. The value of research articles is verified from various articles. The parameters set for quality evaluation are not inferior to quality assessment. It may increase the skewness toward quality evaluation because it might require more work to answer the research questions. Despite these challenges, the study's methodology was thorough and rigorous, ensuring the reliability of the results.

6. Conclusions

This study conducted an SLR to analyze and show different aspects of code smell detection with ML algorithms. The SLR covers the class-wise distribution of ML algorithms, a unique aspect not yet present in the literature, providing up-to-date knowledge to researchers for future studies. The class-wise distribution of ML algorithms is significant as it provides insights into the popularity and effectiveness of different ML algorithms in code smell detection. This study offers detailed insights into code smells, primarily focusing on ML algorithms and software metrics applied in studies, which have been found to be beneficial. The review procedure is framed with five research questions. Table A7 shows the evaluation of research articles and their score. Section 3.3 reports various categories of research articles; 36 are above average, and 6 are below average. Tables A2–A5 presents the attributes used to identify the articles. This study aims to facilitate a better understanding of code smell detection with ML algorithms and help researchers identify the popular methods and the methods that perform better.

This SLR summarizes different ML algorithms, performance measures, datasets, and software metrics for detecting code smells. Some main conclusions are as follows:

- Decision Trees, Ensemble Learners, Bayesian Learners, Rule-Based Learning, Support Vector Machines, neural networks, and other miscellaneous ML algorithms are used to detect code smells. The most frequently used ML algorithms from other classes are Naive Bayes, JRip, J48, Random Forest, and SVM.
- This study examined many datasets, some of which are open-source and a few of which are industrial datasets. The datasets are written in different languages, such as C#, JAVA, and XML; of these, JAVA language datasets are more popular.

- A massive range of datasets has been utilized. Xerces, ArgoUML, Gantt Project, Azureus, Eclipse, and object-oriented metrics datasets are frequently used. Apache Ant, Fluid Tool, iPlasma, PMD, etc., are also used in this area.
- Popularly used performance measures are precision, recall, accuracy, and F-measure. MCC, MAE, Hamming score, etc., are also used for performance assessment but are used less frequently than the rest.

This study is a valuable resource for software developers, providing a comprehensive discussion of code smell detection. It enhances developers' understanding of code smells, equipping them with the knowledge to identify and eliminate them. This understanding can be applied to improve software quality and resolve issues. The practical implications of this study's findings are significant, as they can directly impact the quality and maintainability of software, a key concern for developers.

Better code can be written with an understanding of code smells. Over 30 code smells are discussed in this study. The findings of this research study provide insight into how to enhance its quality and maintainability. Software engineers can better apply the most efficient methods of code smell detection by keeping up with the latest developments in this area. This study covers a survey utilizing ML algorithms from 2005 to 2024. Well-known ML algorithms and practical software metrics are included in this research. LOC, WMC, DIT, LCOM, CC, and NoC are the most used metrics for spotting code smells, and 27 articles applied Decision Tree techniques. In this study, the definition, causes, and effects of code smells are provided for the reader. Methods for the detection of code smells are also covered. This knowledge will empower software developers to create more stable and maintainable programs and allow them to identify and fix code smells before releasing them to the public.

The following are future recommendations for software professionals and researchers working in code smell detection. These recommendations are not just suggestions but are crucial for the advancement of code smell detection. These can inspire further research and innovation in this field, providing a roadmap for researchers to contribute to the evolution of code smell detection. By following these recommendations, researchers can feel inspired and motivated to contribute significantly to this field.

(i) Few research studies have investigated how effectively neural networks, Rule-Based Learning, etc., predict outcomes. Some ML algorithms for detecting code smells have never been applied.
(ii) Few datasets are publicly available. Researchers should have unrestricted access to these datasets to conduct more research studies.
(iii) Only a few researchers have conducted generalized analyses; thus, the results of various ML-based algorithms should be more widely applicable. If one adopts this perspective, it will be simple to compare efficiency and performance.
(iv) Overfitting and class imbalance are two major problems in this field. Addressing these is necessary because most of the datasets have a skewed distribution.
(v) The efficacy of ML algorithms should be evaluated with other statistical approaches.

Author Contributions: P.S.Y.: Conceptualization, critical analysis, validation, figure and table preparation, writing review and editing. R.S.R.: Conceptualization, critical analysis, validation, supervision, writing review and editing. A.M.: Supervision, critical analysis, writing review and editing. M.G.: Supervision, writing review and editing. All authors have read and agreed to the published version of the manuscript.

Funding: This research received no external funding.

Data Availability Statement: Not applicable.

Conflicts of Interest: The authors declare no conflicts of interest.

Appendix A

- **Table A1** lists the various types of research articles.
- **Table A2** includes details such as the unique identifier for each article (Article No.), the serial number as listed in the reference section (Ref. no), the year of publication, the name of the journal or conference in which the research article is published (Publication), and whether the research article is a journal or conference paper (Journal/Conference).
- **Table A3** focuses on the dataset used in the reviewed research articles. It contains the unique identifier for each article (Article no.), the name of the dataset (Dataset), the language of the dataset (Dataset Language), and the type of dataset, such as open-source software (OSS) or industrial (Dataset Type).
- **Table A4** addresses the methodologies and tools used in the research articles. It includes the unique identifier for each article (Article no.), the tools or technologies used (Tools/Tech.), the specific code smells covered (Smells), the algorithms used to classify the code smells (Algorithm), and the performance metrics employed to evaluate the methodologies (Performance Metrics).
- **Table A5** details the software metrics utilized in the research articles. It lists the unique identifier for each article (Article no.) and the specific software metrics used in the research (Software Metrics Name).
- **Table A6** checks for the answers to research questions.
- **Table A7**, a comprehensive evaluation, thoroughly examines the research article's performance. This meticulous evaluation instils confidence in the reliability and validity of the research article's findings.

Table A1. Classification and ranking of studies on ML algorithms for code smell detection.

Categories	Research Papers	Score
Above average	ARTN1, ARTN2, ARTN3, ARTN4, ARTN5, ARTN7, ARTN8, ARTN10, ARTN11, ARTN12, ARTN13, ARTN14, ARTN15, ARTN16, ARTN17, ARTN18, ARTN19, ARTN20, ARTN21, ARTN22, ARTN23, ARTN24, ARTN26, ARTN27, ARTN28, ARTN29, ARTN30, ARTN32, ARTN33, ARTN36, ARTN37, ARTN38, ARTN39, ARTN40, ARTN41, ARTN42	>5
Below average	ARTN6, ARTN9, ARTN25, ARTN31, ARTN34, ARTN35	≥2

Table A2. The study's analysis—general information.

Article No.	Ref. no	Year	Publication	Journal/Conference
ARTN1	[32]	2005	Elsevier Electronic notes in Theoretical Computer Science, Science Direct	Journal
ARTN2	[33]	2009	2009 Ninth International Conference on Quality Software	Conference
ARTN3	[34]	2009	2009 16th Working Conference on Reverse Engineering	Conference
ARTN4	[35]	2010	14th European Conference on Software Maintenance and Reengineering	Conference
ARTN5	[36]	2010	2010 Seventh International Conference on the Quality of Information and Communications Technology	Conference
ARTN6	[37]	2010	Scopus and IEEE	Conference

Table A2. *Cont.*

Article No.	Ref. no	Year	Publication	Journal/Conference
ARTN7	[38]	2011	2011 Eighth International Joint Conference on Computer Science and Software Engineering (JCSSE)	Conference
ARTN8	[39]	2011	Elsevier The Journal of Systems and Software	Journal
ARTN9	[40]	2012	IEEE	Conference
ARTN10	[41]	2012	ASE'12, 3–7 September 2012, Essen, Germany	Conference
ARTN11	[42]	2012	ASE'12, 3–7 September 2012, Essen, Germany	Conference
ARTN12	[43]	2012	19th Working Conference on Reverse Engineering	Conference
ARTN13	[44]	2013	IEEE ASE 2013, Palo Alto, USA	Conference
ARTN14	[45]	2013	IEEE Transactions on Software Engineering	Conference
ARTN15	[46]	2013	IEEE International Conference on Software Maintenance	Conference
ARTN16	[47]	2015	IEEE	Conference
ARTN17	[48]	2015	IEEE	Conference
ARTN18	[49]	2015	Empirical Software Eng	Journal
ARTN19	[50]	2016	IEEE 24th International Conference on Program Comprehension (ICPC)	Conference
ARTN20	[26]	2016	Empirical Software Eng, springer	Journal
ARTN21	[51]	2016	ASE'16, 3–7 September 2016, Singapore, Singapore	Conference
ARTN22	[52]	2016	7th International Conference on Computer Science and Information Technology	Conference
ARTN23	[53]	2016	Scopus, IEEE, and Science Direct	Conference
ARTN24	[54]	2017	19th International Conference on Enterprise Information Systems (ICEIS 2017)	Conference
ARTN25	[27]	2017	International Conference on Machine learning and Data Science	Conference
ARTN26	[55]	2017	Knowledge-Based Systems	Journal
ARTN27	[56]	2017	Scopus International Journal of Electrical and Computer Engineering (IJECE)	Journal
ARTN28	[57]	2017	Scopus and IEEE	Conference
ARTN29	[7]	2018	IEEE	Conference
ARTN30	[10]	2019	2019 IEEE/ACM 27th International Conference on Program Comprehension (ICPC)	Conference
ARTN31	[58]	2019	International Conference on Intelligent Computing and Control Systems (ICICCS 2019) IEEE Xplore	Conference
ARTN32	[8]	2019	International Journal of Rough Sets and Data Analysis April–June 2019	Journal
ARTN33	[59]	2019	International Journal of Computer Sciences and Engineering	Journal
ARTN34	[60]	2019	IEEE	Conference
ARTN35	[61]	2019	IEEE	Conference
ARTN36	[3]	2020	Journal of computer science and technology	Journal
ARTN37	[62]	2020	Springer Software Quality Journal	Journal
ARTN38	[63]	2021	IEEE Access	Conference

Table A2. *Cont.*

Article No.	Ref. no	Year	Publication	Journal/Conference
ARTN39	[30]	2021	Tech Science Press Computers, Materials and Continua Tech Science Press	Conference
ARTN40	[64]	2021	International Conference on Advanced Information Networking and Applications, Springer, Cham.	Conference
ARTN41	[65]	2021	IEEE	Journal
ARTN42	[66]	2022	Empirical Software Engineering	Journal

Table A3. The study's analysis—dataset information.

Article No.	Dataset	Dataset Language	Dataset Type
ARTN1	WEKA and IYC	JAVA	OSS, Industrial
ARTN2	Gantt Project v1.10.2 and Xerces v2.7.0	JAVA	OSS
ARTN3	Eclipse JDT and Xerces v2.7.0	XML, JAVA	OSS
ARTN4	NA	JAVA	OSS
ARTN5	Gantt Project v1.10.2 and Xerces v2.7.0	JAVA	OSS
ARTN6	Expert's knowledge and object-oriented metrics	JAVA	OSS
ARTN7	Seven datasets from the previous literature	NA	Industrial
ARTN8	Gantt Project v1.10.2 and Xerces v2.7.0	JAVA	OSS
ARTN9	Electricity calculating program and movie rental program	JAVA	Industrial
ARTN10	Xproj and Yproj	C#	Microsoft Project (Industrial)
ARTN11	Xerces v2.7.1 and Azureus v2.3.0.6, ArgoUML v0.19.8	JAVA	OSS
ARTN12	Xerces v2.7.0 and Azureus v2.3.0.6, ArgoUML v0.19.8	JAVA	OSS
ARTN13	jEdit, Apache Ant, five projects of Android APIs and Apache Tomcat	JAVA	OSS
ARTN14	Twenty open-source software programs	JAVA	OSS
ARTN15	Seventy-six open-source software programs of Qualitas Corpus (two datasets, one for method-level smells, and another one for class-level smells)	JAVA	OSS
ARTN16	Closure Compiler, maven, Guava, Eclipse, and jUnit	JAVA	OSS
ARTN17	CheckStyle 5.7, JDeodorant 5.0, PMD 5.1.1, and inFusion 1.8.5, iPlasma, and inCode	JAVA	OSS
ARTN18	Dataset of Bellon et al., TF-IDF vector of our datasets	JAVA	OSS
ARTN19	Ten open-source projects	JAVA	OSS
ARTN20	Four datasets were acquired (one for each code smell)	JAVA	OSS
ARTN21	ANTLR to tokenize the source code, the RNNLM Toolkit, Apache Ant, Hibernate, JDK, ArgoUML, CAROL, and JHotDraw	JAVA	OSS
ARTN22	BCEL, Maven Core, and Commons 10. Another three projects belong to the biggest airline companies	JAVA	OSS
ARTN23	Object-oriented metrics	JAVA	OSS
ARTN24	Gantt Project	JAVA	OSS

Table A3. *Cont.*

Article No.	Dataset	Dataset Language	Dataset Type
ARTN25	Argo UML v0.19.8 and Xerces v 2.7.0	JAVA	OSS
ARTN26	iPlasma, Antipattern Scanner, Fluid Tool, PMD, and Marinescu detection rule	JAVA	OSS
ARTN27	Object-oriented metrics	JAVA	OSS
ARTN28	Object-oriented metrics	JAVA	OSS
ARTN29	74 software systems	JAVA	OSS
ARTN30	Ant, Cassandra, Derby, ArgoUML, Eclipse, Hadoop, Elastic Search, HSQLDB, Incubating, Qpid, Wicket, Xerces, and Nutch	JAVA	OSS
ARTN31	Implemented in JAVA using Net Beans IDE	JAVA	NA
ARTN32	The dataset objects consist of methods from 74 different JAVA systems	JAVA	NA
ARTN33	Fontana et al. [26]	NA	OSS
ARTN34	Data from 629 open-source projects are accessible on GitHub.	JAVA	OSS
ARTN35	Long Method, Data Class, God Class, and Feature Envy from Fontana et al. [26]	JAVA	OSS
ARTN36	ORI D, REFD D, and MULTI L D	NA	OSS
ARTN37	Four open-source JAVA projects and two method-level datasets from Fontana et al. [26]	JAVA	OSS
ARTN38	Dr JAVA, EMMA, and Find Bugs	JAVA	OSS
ARTN39	Argo UML, Azure, Gantt Project, Log4j, and Xerces-J	JAVA	OSS
ARTN40	Original, SMOTE, and ADASYN datasets	NA	Open-source projects
ARTN41	Qualitas Corpus	JAVA	OSS
ARTN42	18 datasets of different years	JAVA	OSS

Note: NA means 'Not Available'.

Table A4. The study's analysis—smells, tools, algorithm, and evaluation metrics information.

Article No.	Tools/ Tech.	Smells	Algorithm	Performance Metrics
ARTN1	IYC	Delegator, Lazy Class, Long Method, Feature Envy, God Class	C4.5, Decision Tree	Accuracy
ARTN2	Bayesian approach	Blob	Bayesian Belief Networks	Precision, Recall, Accuracy
ARTN3	NA	God Class	Naive Bayes	Precision, Recall
ARTN4	ABS (antipattern identification using B-Splines)	Blob	Bspl	Precision, Recall
ARTN5	IDS (Immune-based Detection Strategy), based on Artificial Immune Systems	Functional Decomposition, Blob, and Spaghetti Code	Immune-inspired Approach	Precision, Recall

Table A4. *Cont.*

Article No.	Tools/ Tech.	Smells	Algorithm	Performance Metrics
ARTN6	Metrics collection tool	Long Method	Eclipse Plugin Binary Logistic Regression (BLR)	Accuracy
ARTN7	A methodology for predicting bad smells from the software design model	Feature Envy, Message Chain, Long Method, Switch Statement, Middle Man, Long Parameter List, and Lazy Class	Random Forest, J48, Naive Bayes, Logistic, IBI, Voting Feature Intervals, and IBk	Hypothesis test, the predictive value of tests, prediction accuracy, and sensitivity and specificity
ARTN8	A GQM-based approach, BDTEX	Blob, Functional Decomposition, and Spaghetti Code	Bayesian Belief Networks	Precision, Recall, and utility
ARTN9	BSDT (BAD SMELL DETECTING TOOL)	Long Method, Switch Statement, Long Parameter List, Parallel Inheritance Hierarchy, Lazy Class, Large Class, and Data Class	A Switch Statement Rules, Naive Bayes	Accuracy
ARTN10	Code clone detection tools	Duplicate Code	Bayesian Network	Precision, Recall, Effectiveness
ARTN11	Support Vector Machine direct	Functional Decomposition, Spaghetti Code, and SAK	SVM	Precision, Recall
ARTN12	SMURF	Blob, Spaghetti Code, Functional Decomposition, and Swiss Army Knife	SVM	Precision, Recall
ARTN13	HIST	Feature Envy, Shotgun Surgery, Blob, Parallel Inheritance Hierarchy, Divergent Change	Association Rule Mining	Precision, Recall, F-measure
ARTN14	HIST	Blob, Divergent Change, Parallel Inheritance Hierarchy, Shotgun Surgery, and Feature Envy	Association Rule Mining	Precision, Recall, F-measure
ARTN15	Code smell detection tool, Weka tool	Data Class, Feature Envy, God Class, and Long Method	LibSVM, J48, Sequential minimal optimization, JRip, Random Forest, Naive Bayes	Accuracy, F-measure, ROC
ARTN16	NA	Duplicate Code, Switch Statement, and Divergent Change	Association Rule Mining	Precision, Recall, and F-measure
ARTN17	Decision Tree (C5.0)	Refused Parent Bequest, Speculative Generality, Complex Class, Antisingleton, Message Chain, Long Parameter List, Class Data should be Private, Lazy Class, Swiss Army Knife, God Class	SVM, Bayesian Belief Networks	Precision, Recall, F-measure
ARTN18	Clone detection tools (CDTs)	Duplicated Code	Bayesian Network	Precision, Recall, Accuracy

Table A4. *Cont.*

Article No.	Tools/ Tech.	Smells	Algorithm	Performance Metrics
ARTN19	TACO (Textual Analysis for Code Smell Detection)	Feature Envy, Blob, Long Method, Misplaced Class, Promiscuous Package	Structural techniques, TACO	Precision, Recall, F-measure
ARTN20	iPlasma, PMD, Fluid Tool, Antipattern Scanner, Marinescu	Long Method, God Class, Data Class, Feature Envy	J48, Naïve Bayes, Sequential minimal optimization, JRip, Random Forest, SVM	The accuracy obtained by the ML-algorithms
ARTN21	RNNLM Toolkit	Duplicated Code	Deep Learning	Precision, Recall
ARTN22	Metric and a rule-based automated antipattern detection	Swiss Army Knife, Blob, and Lava Flow	Three Mechanism Filtering Mechanism, Static Code Analyzer, and Metric Analyzer	Accuracy
ARTN23	DTReg tool	God Class, Feature Envy, Long Method, Empty catch block, Careless cleanup, Type Checking, Nested try statement, Exception thrown in finally block, Unprotected main, Dummy handler, Over logging	SVM, Multilayer Perceptron, Radial Basis Function Neural Networks Linear Regression (LR), Decision Tree Forest (DFT), k-fold cross validation	Root mean square error and mean absolute error
ARTN24	The Weka tool to implement the algorithms analyzed	Data Class, Long Method, Feature Envy, and God Class	J48, JRip, Naive Bayes, Sequential Minimal Optimization, SVM, Random Forest	Accuracy, Efficiency
ARTN25	SVMCSD	Large Class, Feature Envy, Data Class, and Long Method	SVM	Precision, Recall
ARTN26	An approach based on machine learning	Long Method, Data Class, Feature Envy	C4.5, J48, Naive Bayes, JRip, Random Forest, Decision Tree, Sequential Minimal Optimization, LibSVM	Standard deviations, descending values of Spearman's, performance indicators (except Tb), mad, mse, acc
ARTN27	Tensor flow	God Class, Lazy Class, Data Class, Feature Envy, Large Class, Parallel Inheritance Hierarchies	SciTools Understand, JUnit-4.10 Multilayer Perceptron	Accuracy
ARTN28	Weka	God Class, Feature Envy, Long Method, Data Class	Eclipse Plugin, Analyst 4J, Xercesv, ArgoUML SVM, random under sampling	Recall, Precision
ARTN29	NA	God Class, Feature Envy, Data Class, and Long Method	Random Forest, JRip, J48, LIBSVM, ADABOOST, Naive Bayes, Sequential Minimal Optimization	Mean Accuracy, F-Measure, and AUC ROC
ARTN30	ML algorithm with a heuristic	Spaghetti Code, Long Method, Class Data should be private, Complex Class, and God Class	J48, Random Forest, Naive Bayes, SVM, JRip.	Precision, Recall, F-measure, Mcc (Matthews Correlation Coefficient)

Table A4. *Cont.*

Article No.	Tools/ Tech.	Smells	Algorithm	Performance Metrics
ARTN31	Code detection techniques	Lazy Class Detector, Primitive Obsession Detector, Too Many Literal Detectors, Bloated Code Detector, Feature Envy Detector, and Duplicated Code Detector	SVM, Random Forest	Time complexity
ARTN32	Datasets have been prepared based on the tools, manual labeling process.	Shotgun Surgery, Message Chaining	J48, C4.5, Random Forest, JRip, Naive Bayes, Sequential Minimal Optimization, K-nearest neighbors	Area under the ROC, Accuracy, and F-measure
ARTN33	Using a Decision Tree technique and software metrics, detect code smells	Long Method, Data Class, Feature Envy, and God Class	Decision Tree	Accuracy, F-measure
ARTN34	Empirical framework empirically investigates and evaluates different classification techniques, feature selection techniques, and data sampling techniques	Blob Class, Resolver, Member Ignoring Method, Complex Class, Internal Getter/Setter, Long Method, No Low Memory, and Leaking Inner Class	Classification techniques, feature selection techniques, and data sampling techniques to handle imbalanced data in prediction	Accuracy, F-measure, ACC
ARTN35	Especially multi-label classification methods, ML algorithms	Long Method, God Class, Feature Envy, Data Class	Decision Tree, Naive Bayes, Random Forest, Neural Network, SVM	Exact Match Ratio, Hamming Score, AUC ROC, Accuracy, F-measure
ARTN36	A strategy using machine learning and software metrics	Data Class, Feature Envy, Long Method, and God Class	Random Forest, Gradient Boosting Tree, Decision Tree, Deep Learning, SVM, Multilayer Perceptron	Accuracy, F-measure
ARTN37	Design Features and Metrics for JAVA	Long Method, Feature Envy	B-Random Forest, Random Forest, BJ48U, B-J48 Pruned, J48U	Accuracy, F-measure, ROC area
ARTN38	CKJM, JCODODOR, and WEKA	God Class, Brain Method, Shotgun Surgery, Message Chains, Data Class, Dispersed Coupling	Ensemble Learning, Bagging, Random Forest	Accuracy (P1), G-meam2 (P3), G-mean 1(P2), and F-measure (P4)
ARTN39	Search-based approach	Large Class, Long Method, Feature Envy, Spaghetti Code, Data Class, Lazy Class, Functional Decomposition, Parallel Inheritance, and Long Parameter List	Search-based approach	Precision, Recall
ARTN40	Code smell prediction models, feature extraction	Blob Class, Complex Class, Internal Getter/Setter, Leaking Inner Class, Long Method, No Low Memory Resolver, Member Ignoring Method, and Swiss Army Knife	SMOTE, ADASYN sampling methods	Accuracy AUC F-measure

Table A4. *Cont.*

Article No.	Tools/ Tech.	Smells	Algorithm	Performance Metrics
ARTN41	A Novel Approach for the Detection of Code Smells	God Class, Long Method, Data Class, Feature Envy	Naive Bayes, Multilayer Perceptron, KNN, Logistic Regression, Decision Tree, and Random Forest, validation technique: 10-fold cross-validation	Accuracy, Recall, F-measure, and Precision
ARTN42	Crowdsmelling approach	God Class, Feature Envy, Long Method	J48, Random Forest, ADABOOST, Sequential Minimal Optimization, Multilayer Perceptron, Naive Bayes	Accuracy, Precision, Recall, ROC, and F-Measure

Note: NA means 'Not Available'.

Table A5. The study's analysis—S/W metrics.

Article No.	S/W Metrics
ARTN1	Object-oriented metrics IYC, coupling and cohesion, complexity metrics, the size measure, the complexity measure
ARTN2	Goal Question Metric (GQM), LCOM5 metric, and NMD and NAD metrics
ARTN3	NOC, DTT, NMD, and NAD
ARTN4	Quality metrics cohesion, coupling, and complexity
ARTN5	Goal Question Metric (GQM), metric-based heuristics
ARTN6	NBD (Nested Block Depth), VG (cyclomatic complexity), and code complexity metrics- MLOC (Method Lines Of Code) and PAR (Number of Parameters)
ARTN7	Design model metrics: number of members, number of attributes, number of operations, Number of Parameters, response for a class, number of classes, weighted attributes per class, weighted methods per class, appearance in diagrams, Depth of Inheritance Tree, number of children, number of inherited attributes, number of inherited operations, attribute hiding factor, attribute inheritance factor, coupling factor, method hiding factor, method inheritance factor, polymorphism factor, number of actors, number of components, number of name spaces, Coupling Between Objects, number of abstractions, number of times class is used as employment parameter type, and number of dependencies
ARTN8	A Goal Question Metric (GQM) NMD and NAD, LCOM5, and NoDC
ARTN9	Lines of code, Number of Methods, Tree, Depth of Inheritance, Number of Parameters, number of attributes, Method Lines of Code, weighted methods per class, McCabe cyclomatic complexity, Lack of Cohesion of Methods, and number of children
ARTN10	Number of Invocations, Number of Library Invocations, Number of Lines, Number of Local Invocations, Number of Other Invocations, Number of Parameter Accesses, whether it is Test Code4, Number of Field Accesses
ARTN11	Object-oriented metrics, more than 60 metrics
ARTN12	Object-oriented metrics
ARTN13	LOC, weight methods per class (WMC), Coupling Between Objects (CBO), and Number of Methods (NOM)
ARTN14	NA
ARTN15	Complexity, cohesion, size, coupling, and a large set of object-oriented metrics
ARTN16	NOM (Number of Methods), WMC (weight methods per class), and CBO (Coupling Between Objects)

Table A5. *Cont.*

Article No.	S/W Metrics
ARTN17	Number of Parameters (NOParam), the number of lines of code (LOC), Depth of Inheritance Tree (DIT)
ARTN18	Metric-based approach
ARTN19	Structural metrics, like size and complexity metrics.
ARTN20	LOC, NOM, NOPK, LOCNAMM, NOCS, NOA, and WMC, NOMNAMM CYCLO, WMCNAMM, MAXNESTING, AMW, WOC, NOP, NOAV, CLNAMM, ATLD, NOLV, AMWNAMM LCOM5, TCC FANOUT, FDP, RFC, CBO, ATFD, CINT, CDISP, CFNAMM, CC, CM LAA, NOAM, NOPA DIT, NOI, NOC, NMO, NIM, LAA, MaMCL, MeMCL, NODA, NOPVA, NOII, NOPRA, NOFA, NOFSA, NOSA, NONFSA, NOABM, NoNFNSA, NOCM, NOFM, NOFNSM, NoFSM, NONCM, NONFNABM, NONFNSM, NODM, NOPM, NOPRM, NOPLM, NONAM, and NOSM
ARTN21	LOC, AST-based
ARTN22	LCOM RFC NAM NADCs, OPT, and TSCs
ARTN23	LOC, CBO, DIT, RFC, WMC, NOC, LCOM, CC, Dependencies (Dcy and Dcy), Javadoc function (jf), MHF, cyclomatic complexity (Ocavg), Javadoc Javadoc methods (jm), line of code (jLOC), AHF
ARTN24	NA
ARTN25	No. of object-oriented metrics
ARTN26	Measured through Spearman's
ARTN27	LOC, CC, NOC, RFC, DIT, WMC, CBO, and LCOM
ARTN28	Static code metrics-based approach
ARTN29	61 source code metrics were computed at class level and 82—at method level
ARTN30	LCOM, NOPA, NMNOPARAM, ELOC, LOC_METHOD, NOA, NOM, NP, and WMC
ARTN31	NA
ARTN32	LOC, NOM, NOCS, NOPK, LOCNAMM, NOA, NOMNAMM CYCLO, WMCNAMM, WMC, MAXNESTING, WOC, CLNAMM, NOP, NOAV, ATLD, NOLV, AMWNAMM, LCOM5, TCC, FANOUT, AMW, ATFD, RFC, CBO, CFNAMM, FDP, CINT, CDISP, CM, CC, NOAM, NOPA DIT, LAA, NOI, NMO, NIM, NOC, and NOII
ARTN33	82 software metrics and 61 software metrics in the class-level code smells
ARTN34	NOC, NOCH, WMC, IPM, CC, NBI, NOM, NOCH, DIT, LCOM, PPIV, LOCL, APD, XML, BSMC, NTO, WKL, GPS, BMAP, SQL, NET, and I/O
ARTN35	82 features (software metrics), MLC evaluation metrics
ARTN36	In the method-level code smells, 82 software metrics are computed; in the class-level code smells, 61 software metrics are computed
ARTN37	There are 82 measures in the created MLD training dataset, 25 are class metrics, 5 are package metrics, and 6 are project-level metrics
ARTN38	Weighted methods per class, Number of Methods, Depth of the Inheritance Tree, and response for a class. Coupling between object classes, lack of cohesion in methods, the normalized version of LCOM inheritance coupling, coupling between methods, average method complexity, number of public methods for a class, also known as CIS (class interface size), data access metric, measure of aggregation, measure of functional abstraction, cohesion among methods of a class, cyclomatic complexity, lines of code, afferent coupling, efferent coupling, maximum cyclomatic complexity, average cyclomatic complexity
ARTN39	LOC, NAD, McCabe, NOC, CBO, LCOM, CC, LCOM, WMC, NOPARAM, NOM, RFC, DIT, and NMO
ARTN40	Android-oriented metrics, complexity metrics, object-oriented metrics, and dimensional metrics
ARTN41	61 software metrics for the class-level and 82 software metrics for the method-level code smells
ARTN42	For God Class, a set of 61 metrics was used, and for the other two code smells

Note: NA means 'Not Available'.

Table A6. Mapping of research question with the score.

Article No.	RQ1	RQ2	RQ3	RQ4	RQ5	Score
ARTN30	√	√	√	√	√	8
ARTN29	√	√	√	√	√	8
ARTN12	√	√	√	√	√	8
ARTN42	√	√	√	√	√	8
ARTN37	√	√	√	√	√	7.5
ARTN32	√	√	√	√	√	7.5
ARTN10	√	√	√	√	√	7.5
ARTN11	√	√	√	√	√	7.5
ARTN41	√	√	√	√	√	7.5
ARTN38	√	√	√	√	√	7
ARTN39	√	√	√	√	√	7
ARTN36	√	√	√	√	√	7
ARTN26	√	√	√	√	√	7
ARTN23	√	√	√	√	√	7
ARTN16	√	√	√	√	√	7
ARTN14	√	√	×	√	√	7
ARTN8	√	√	√	√	√	7
ARTN3	√	√	√	√	√	7
ARTN28	√	√	√	√	√	6.5
ARTN20	√	√	√	√	×	6.5
ARTN21	√	√	√	√	√	6.5
ARTN17	√	√	√	√	√	6.5
ARTN18	√	√	√	√	√	6.5
ARTN13	√	√	√	√	√	6.5
ARTN15	√	√	√	√	√	6.5
ARTN7	√	√	√	√	√	6.5
ARTN5	√	√	√	√	√	6.5
ARTN33	√	√	√	√	√	6
ARTN19	√	√	√	√	√	6
ARTN22	√	√	√	√	√	6
ARTN2	√	√	√	√	√	6
ARTN1	√	√	√	√	√	6
ARTN40	√	√	√	√	√	5.5
ARTN24	√	√	×	√	√	5.5
ARTN27	√	√	√	√	√	5.5
ARTN4	√	√	√	×	√	5.5
ARTN34	√	√	√	√	√	5
ARTN35	√	√	√	√	√	5
ARTN25	√	√	√	√	√	5
ARTN9	√	√	√	√	√	5
ARTN6	√	√	√	√	√	5
ARTN31	√	√	×	√	√	4

Table A7. Assessment query score and total score.

Article No.	Q1	Q2	Q3	Q4	Q5	Q6	Q7	Q8	Q9	Q1	Total Score
ARTN30	0.5	1	1	1	1	1	1	0.5	1	0.5	8
ARTN29	1	1	1	0.5	0.5	1	1	1	1	1	8
ARTN12	1	1	1	1	0.5	1	1	0.5	1	1	8
ARTN42	1	1	1	1	0	1	1	1	1	1	8
ARTN37	1	0.5	1	1	0.5	1	0.5	1	1	1	7.5
ARTN32	1	0.5	1	1	1	0.5	1	1	0.5	1	7.5
ARTN10	1	0.5	1	1	1	0.5	1	0.5	1	1	7.5
ARTN11	1	1	0.5	1	0.5	1	0.5	1	1	1	7.5

Table A7. *Cont.*

Article No.	Q1	Q2	Q3	Q4	Q5	Q6	Q7	Q8	Q9	Q1	Total Score
ARTN41	1	1	1	1	0	1	0.5	1	1	1	7.5
ARTN38	1	0.5	0.5	1	1	0	1	1	1	1	7
ARTN39	1	0.5	1	1	1	0.5	0	1	1	1	7
ARTN36	1	0.5	1	1	0.5	1	1	0	1	1	7
ARTN26	1	1	1	1	0	1	1	0	1	1	7
ARTN23	1	0.5	1	1	1	0	1	0.5	1	1	7
ARTN16	1	1	0.5	1	1	0	0.5	1	1	1	7
ARTN14	1	1	1	1	0	1	0.5	1	0.5	1	7
ARTN8	1	1	1	1	1	0.5	0.5	0.5	0.5	1	7
ARTN3	1	0.5	1	1	1	0	1	0.5	1	1	7
ARTN28	1	0.5	1	1	0.5	0.5	0.5	0.5	1	1	6.5
ARTN20	1	1	1	0.5	1	0	1	0.5	0.5	1	6.5
ARTN21	1	1	0	1	0.5	1	0.5	1	0.5	1	6.5
ARTN17	1	0.5	1	1	1	0	1	0.5	0.5	1	6.5
ARTN18	1	0.5	1	1	0.5	0.5	0.5	0.5	1	1	6.5
ARTN13	1	0	1	0.5	1	1	0.5	1	0.5	1	6.5
ARTN15	1	0.5	1	1	0.5	0	1	0.5	1	1	6.5
ARTN7	1	1	1	1	1	0	0.5	0	1	1	6.5
ARTN5	1	0.5	0.5	1	1	0.5	0.5	0.5	1	1	6.5
ARTN33	1	0	1	1	0.5	0.5	1	0	1	1	6
ARTN19	1	0.5	0.5	1	0	0.5	0.5	1	1	1	6
ARTN22	1	0.5	1	0.5	1	0	0	1	1	1	6
ARTN2	1	0.5	1	0.5	1	0	0.5	0.5	1	1	6
ARTN1	1	0.5	1	0.5	1	0	0.5	0.5	1	1	6
ARTN40	1	0.5	1	1	0.5	0.5	0	0	1	1	5.5
ARTN24	1	0.5	1	1	0	1	0	0	1	1	5.5
ARTN27	1	0.5	1	1	1	0	0	1	0	1	5.5
ARTN4	1	0.5	0.5	1	1	0	0.5	0.5	0.5	1	5.5
ARTN34	1	0.5	1	1	1	0	0	0	0.5	1	5
ARTN35	1	0.5	0	1	1	0.5	0	1	0	1	5
ARTN25	1	0.5	0.5	1	0	0	0.5	0.5	1	1	5
ARTN9	1	0.5	0.5	1	1	0	0.5	0	0.5	1	5
ARTN6	1	0	1	0.5	1	0.5	0	0.5	0.5	1	5
ARTN31	1	0.5	0	1	0	0	0.5	0	1	1	4

References

1. Dewangan, S.; Rao, R.S.; Yadav, P.S. Dimensionally Reduction based Machine Learning Approaches for Code smells Detection. In Proceedings of the 2022 International Conference on Intelligent Controller and Computing for Smart Power (ICICCSP), Hyderabad, India, 21–23 July 2022; pp. 1–4. [CrossRef]
2. Yadav, P.S.; Dewangan, S.; Rao, R.S. Extraction of Prediction Rules of Code Smell using Decision Tree Algorithm. In Proceedings of the International Conference on Internet of Everything, Microwave Engineering, Communication and Networks (IEMECON), Jaipur, India, 1–2 December 2021; pp. 1–5. [CrossRef]

3. Mhawish, M.Y.; Gupta, M. Predicting Code Smells and Analysis of Predictions: Using Machine Learning Techniques and Software Metrics. *J. Comput. Sci. Technol.* **2020**, *35*, 1428–1445. [CrossRef]
4. Dewangan, S.; Rao, R.S. Method-Level Code Smells Detection Using Machine Learning Models. *Lect. Notes Netw. Syst.* **2023**, *725*, 77–86. [CrossRef]
5. Yadav, P.S.; Rao, R.S. Feature reduction techniques based code smell prediction. *I-Manag. J. Softw. Eng.* **2022**, *17*, 6–11. [CrossRef]
6. Dewangan, S.; Rao, R.S. Code Smell Detection Using Classification Approaches. *Lect. Notes Netw. Syst.* **2022**, *431*, 257–266. [CrossRef]
7. Di Nucci, D.; Palomba, F.; Tamburri, D.A.; Serebrenik, A.; De Lucia, A. Detecting code smells using machine learning techniques: Are we there yet? In Proceedings of the International Conference on Software Analysis, Evolution and Reengineering (SANER), Campobasso, Italy, 20–23 March 2018; pp. 612–621. [CrossRef]
8. Guggulothu, T.; Moiz, S.A. Detection of Shotgun Surgery and Message Chain Code Smells using Machine Learning Techniques. *Int. J. Rough Sets Data Anal.* **2019**, *6*, 34–50. [CrossRef]
9. Iqbal, A.; Aftab, S.; Ullah, I.; Bashir, M.S.; Saeed, M.A. A Feature Selection based Ensemble Classification Framework for Software Defect Prediction. *Int. J. Mod. Educ. Comput. Sci.* **2019**, *11*, 54–64. [CrossRef]
10. Pecorelli, F.; Palomba, F.; Di Nucci, D.; De Lucia, A. Comparing heuristic and machine learning approaches for metric-based code smell detection. In Proceedings of the International Conference on Program Comprehension, Montreal, QC, Canada, 25–26 May 2019; pp. 93–104. [CrossRef]
11. Caram, F.L.; Rodrigues, B.R.D.O.; Campanelli, A.S.; Parreiras, F.S. Machine Learning Techniques for Code Smells Detection: A Systematic Mapping Study. *Int. J. Softw. Eng. Knowl. Eng.* **2019**, *29*, 285–316. [CrossRef]
12. Kaur, A.; Dhiman, G. A review on search-based tools and techniques to identify bad code smells in object-oriented systems. *Adv. Intell. Syst. Comput.* **2019**, *741*, 909–921. [CrossRef]
13. Azeem, M.I.; Palomba, F.; Shi, L.; Wang, Q. Machine learning techniques for code smell detection: A systematic literature review and meta-analysis. *Inf. Softw. Technol.* **2019**, *108*, 115–138. [CrossRef]
14. Kaur, A.; Jain, S.; Goel, S.; Dhiman, G. A Review on Machine-learning Based Code Smell Detection Techniques in Object-oriented Software System(s). *Recent Adv. Electr. Electron. Eng.* **2020**, *14*, 290–303. [CrossRef]
15. dos Reis, J.P.; Abreu, F.B.E.; Carneiro, G.D.F.; Anslow, C. Code Smells Detection and Visualization: A Systematic Literature Review. *Arch. Comput. Methods Eng.* **2022**, *29*, 47–94. [CrossRef]
16. Al-Shaaby, A.; Aljamaan, H.; Alshayeb, M. Bad Smell Detection Using Machine Learning Techniques: A Systematic Literature Review. *Arab. J. Sci. Eng.* **2020**, *45*, 2341–2369. [CrossRef]
17. Singh, S.; Kaur, S. A systematic literature review: Refactoring for disclosing code smells in object oriented software. *Ain Shams Eng. J.* **2018**, *9*, 2129–2151. [CrossRef]
18. Sobrinho, E.V.D.P.; De Lucia, A.; Maia, M.D.A. A Systematic Literature Review on Bad Smells-5 W's: Which, When, What, Who, Where. *IEEE Trans. Softw. Eng.* **2021**, *47*, 17–66. [CrossRef]
19. Zhang, M.; Hall, T.; Baddoo, N. Code Bad Smells: A review of current knowledge. *J. Softw. Maint. Evol. Res. Pract.* **2011**, *23*, 179–202. [CrossRef]
20. Rasool, G.; Arshad, Z. A review of code smell mining techniques. *J. Softw. Evol. Process* **2015**, *27*, 867–895. [CrossRef]
21. Fernandes, E.; Oliveira, J.; Vale, G.; Paiva, T.; Figueiredo, E. A Review-based Comparative Study of Bad Smell Detection Tools. In Proceedings of the EASE '16: 20th International Conference on Evaluation and Assessment in Software Engineering, Limerick, Ireland, 1–3 June 2016; pp. 1–12. [CrossRef]
22. Gupta, A.; Suri, B.; Misra, S. A systematic literature review: Code bad smells in java source code. *Lect. Notes Comput. Sci.* **2017**, *10408*, 665–682. [CrossRef]
23. Sharma, T.; Spinellis, D. A survey on software smells. *J. Syst. Softw.* **2018**, *138*, 158–173. [CrossRef]
24. Haque, M.S.; Carver, J.; Atkison, T. Causes, impacts, and detection approaches of code smell: A survey. In Proceedings of the ACMSE 2018 Conference, Richmond, KY, USA, 29–31 March 2018; pp. 1–8. [CrossRef]
25. Zhang, Y.; Ge, C.; Liu, H.; Zheng, K. Code smell detection based on supervised learning models: A survey. *Neurocomputing* **2024**, *565*, 127014. [CrossRef]
26. Fontana, F.A.; Mantylä, M.; Zanoni, M.; Marino, A. Comparing and experimenting machine learning techniques for code smell detection. *Empir. Softw. Eng.* **2016**, *21*, 1143–1191. [CrossRef]
27. Kaur, A.; Jain, S.; Goel, S. A Support Vector Machine Based Approach for Code Smell Detection. In Proceedings of the International Conference on Machine Learning and Data Science, Noida, India, 14–15 December 2017; pp. 9–14. [CrossRef]
28. Nizam, A.; Avar, M.Y.; Adaş, Ö.K.; Yanık, A. Detecting Code Smell with a Deep Learning System. In Proceedings of the Innovations in Intelligent Systems and Applications Conference, Sivas, Turkiye, 11–13 October 2023; pp. 1–5. [CrossRef]
29. Shah, R.N.; Mohamed, S.A.; Imran, A.; Kosar, T. CloudScent: A Model for Code Smell Analysis in Open-Source Cloud. In Proceedings of the IEEE International Conference on Cloud Computing Technology and Science (CloudCom), Naples, Italy, 4–6 December 2023; pp. 69–75. [CrossRef]
30. Draz, M.M.; Farhan, M.S.; Abdulkader, S.N.; Gafar, M.G. Code Smell Detection Using Whale Optimization Algorithm. *Comput. Mater. Contin.* **2021**, *68*, 1919–1935. [CrossRef]
31. Kitchenham, B.; Charters, S. *Guidelines for Performing Systematic Literature Reviews in Software Engineering*; Keele University: Keele, UK, 2007; Volume 2.

32. Kreimer, J. Adaptive Detection of Design Flaws. *Electron. Notes Theor. Comput. Sci.* **2005**, *141*, 117–136. [CrossRef]
33. Khomh, F.; Vaucher, S.; Guéehéeneuc, Y.G.; Sahraoui, H. A bayesian approach for the detection of code and design smells. In Proceedings of the International Conference on Quality Software, Jeju, Republic of Korea, 24–25 August 2009; pp. 305–314. [CrossRef]
34. Vaucher, S.; Khomh, F.; Moha, N.; Guéhéneuc, Y.G. Tracking design smells: Lessons from a study of God classes. In Proceedings of the Working Conference on Reverse Engineering, Lille, France, 13–16 October 2009; pp. 145–154. [CrossRef]
35. Oliveto, R.; Khomh, F.; Antoniol, G.; Guéhéneuc, Y.G. Numerical signatures of antipatterns: An approach based on B-Splines. In Proceedings of the European Conference on Software Maintenance and Reengineering, Madrid, Spain, 15–18 March 2010; pp. 248–251. [CrossRef]
36. Hassaine, S.; Khomh, F.; Guéhéneucy, Y.G.; Hamel, S. IDS: An immune-inspired approach for the detection of software design smells. In Proceedings of the 2010 Seventh International Conference on the Quality of Information and Communications Technology, Porto, Portugal, 29 September–2 October 2010; pp. 343–348. [CrossRef]
37. Bryton, S.; Abreu, F.B.E.; Monteiro, M. Reducing subjectivity in code smells detection: Experimenting with the Long Method. In Proceedings of the 2010 Seventh International Conference on the Quality of Information and Communications Technology, Porto, Portugal, 29 September–2 October 2010; pp. 337–342. [CrossRef]
38. Maneerat, N.; Muenchaisri, P. Bad-smell prediction from software design model using machine learning techniques. In Proceedings of the International Joint Conference on Computer Science and Software Engineering, Nakhonpathom, Thailand, 11–13 May 2011; pp. 331–336. [CrossRef]
39. Khomh, F.; Vaucher, S.; Guéhéneuc, Y.G.; Sahraoui, H. BDTEX: A GQM-based Bayesian approach for the detection of antipatterns. *J. Syst. Softw.* **2010**, *84*, 559–572. [CrossRef]
40. Danphitsanuphan, P.; Suwantada, T. Code smell detecting tool and code smell-structure bug relationship. In Proceedings of the Spring World Congress on Engineering and Technology, Xi'an, China, 27–30 May 2012; pp. 1–5. [CrossRef]
41. Wang, X.; Dang, Y.; Zhang, L.; Zhang, D.; Lan, E.; Mei, H. Can I clone this piece of code here? In Proceedings of the IEEE/ACM International Conference on Automated Software Engineering, Essen, Germany, 3–7 September 2012; pp. 170–179. [CrossRef]
42. Maiga, A.; Ali, N.; Bhattacharya, N.; Sabané, A.; Guéhéneuc, Y.G.; Antoniol, G.; Aimeur, E. Support vector machines for anti-pattern detection. In Proceedings of the IEEE/ACM International Conference on Automated Software Engineering, Essen, Germany, 3–7 September 2012; pp. 278–281. [CrossRef]
43. Maiga, A.; Ali, N.; Bhattacharya, N.; Sabané, A.; Guéhéneuc, Y.G.; Aimeur, E. SMURF: A SVM-based incremental anti-pattern detection approach. In Proceedings of the Working Conference on Reverse Engineering, Kingston, ON, Canada, 15–18 October 2012; pp. 466–475. [CrossRef]
44. Palomba, F.; Bavota, G.; Di Penta, M.; Oliveto, R.; De Lucia, A.; Poshyvanyk, D. Detecting bad smells in source code using change history information. In Proceedings of the IEEE/ACM International Conference on Automated Software Engineering, Silicon Valley, CA, USA, 11–15 November 2013; pp. 268–278. [CrossRef]
45. Palomba, F.; Bavota, G.; Di Penta, M.; Oliveto, R.; Poshyvanyk, D.; De Lucia, A. Mining version histories for detecting code smells. *IEEE Trans. Softw. Eng.* **2015**, *41*, 462–489. [CrossRef]
46. Fontana, F.A.; Zanoni, M.; Marino, A.; Mäntylä, M.V. Code smell detection: Towards a machine learning-based approach. In Proceedings of the IEEE International Conference on Software Maintenance, Eindhoven, The Netherlands, 22–28 September 2013; pp. 396–399. [CrossRef]
47. Fu, S.; Shen, B. Code Bad Smell Detection through Evolutionary Data Mining. In Proceedings of the International Symposium on Empirical Software Engineering and Measurement, Beijing, China, 22–23 October 2015; pp. 1–9. [CrossRef]
48. Amorim, L.; Costa, E.; Antunes, N.; Fonseca, B.; Ribeiro, M. Experience report: Evaluating the effectiveness of decision trees for detecting code smells. In Proceedings of the International Symposium on Software Reliability Engineering, Gaithersbury, MD, USA, 2–5 November 2015; pp. 261–269. [CrossRef]
49. Yang, J.; Hotta, K.; Higo, Y.; Igaki, H.; Kusumoto, S. Classification model for code clones based on machine learning. *Empir. Softw. Eng.* **2015**, *20*, 1095–1125. [CrossRef]
50. Palomba, F.; Panichella, A.; De Lucia, A.; Oliveto, R.; Zaidman, A. A textual-based technique for Smell Detection. In Proceedings of the IEEE International Conference on Program Comprehension, Austin, TX, USA, 16–17 May 2016; pp. 1–10. [CrossRef]
51. White, M.; Tufano, M.; Vendome, C.; Poshyvanyk, D. Deep learning code fragments for code clone detection. In Proceedings of the IEEE/ACM International Conference on Automated Software Engineering (ASE), Singapore, 3–7 September 2016; pp. 87–98.
52. Aras, M.T.; Selcuk, Y.E. Metric and rule based automated detection of antipatterns in object-oriented software systems. In Proceedings of the International Conference on Computer Science and Information Technology, Amman, Jordan, 13–14 July 2016; pp. 1–6. [CrossRef]
53. Tarwani, S.; Chug, A. Predicting maintainability of open source software using Gene Expression Programming and bad smells. In Proceedings of the International Conference on Reliability, Infocom Technologies and Optimization (ICRITO), Noida, India, 7–9 September 2016; pp. 452–459. [CrossRef]
54. Hozano, M.; Antunes, N.; Fonseca, B.; Costa, E. Evaluating the accuracy of machine learning algorithms on detecting code smells for different developers. In Proceedings of the International Conference on Enterprise Information Systems, Porto, Portugal, 26–29 April 2017; Volume 2, pp. 474–482. [CrossRef]

55. Fontana, F.A.; Zanoni, M. Code smell severity classification using machine learning techniques. *Knowl. Based Syst.* **2017**, *128*, 43–58. [CrossRef]
56. Kim, D.K. Finding Bad Code Smells with Neural Network Models. *Int. J. Electr. Comput. Eng. (IJECE)* **2017**, *7*, 3613–3621. [CrossRef]
57. Kaur, K.; Jain, S. Evaluation of machine learning approaches for change-proneness prediction using code smells. *Adv. Intell. Syst. Comput.* **2017**, *515*, 561–572. [CrossRef]
58. Jesudoss, A.; Maneesha, S.; Durga, T.L.N. Identification of code smell using machine learning. In Proceedings of the International Conference on Intelligent Computing and Control Systems, Madurai, India, 15–17 May 2019; pp. 54–58. [CrossRef]
59. Mhawish, M.Y.; Gupta, M. Generating Code-Smell Prediction Rules Using Decision Tree Algorithm and Software Metrics. *Int. J. Comput. Sci. Eng.* **2019**, *7*, 41–48. [CrossRef]
60. Gupta, H.; Kumar, L.; Neti, L.B.M. An empirical framework for code smell prediction using extreme learning machine. In Proceedings of the Annual Information Technology, Electromechanical Engineering and Microelectronics Conference, Jaipur, India, 13–15 March 2019; pp. 189–195. [CrossRef]
61. Kiyak, E.O.; Birant, D.; Birant, K.U. Comparison of Multi-Label Classification Algorithms for Code Smell Detection. In Proceedings of the International Symposium on Multidisciplinary Studies and Innovative Technologies (ISMSIT), Ankara, Turkey, 11–13 October 2019; pp. 1–6. [CrossRef]
62. Guggulothu, T.; Moiz, S.A. Code smell detection using multi-label classification approach. *Softw. Qual. J.* **2020**, *28*, 1063–1086. [CrossRef]
63. Kaur, I.; Kaur, A. A Novel Four-Way Approach Designed with Ensemble Feature Selection for Code Smell Detection. *IEEE Access* **2021**, *9*, 8695–8707. [CrossRef]
64. Gupta, H.; Kulkarni, T.G.; Kumar, L.; Neti, L.B.M.; Krishna, A. An Empirical Study on Predictability of Software Code Smell Using Deep Learning Models. *Lect. Notes Netw. Syst.* **2021**, *226*, 120–132. [CrossRef]
65. Dewangan, S.; Rao, R.S.; Mishra, A.; Gupta, M. A novel approach for code smell detection: An empirical study. *IEEE Access* **2021**, *9*, 162869–162883. [CrossRef]
66. dos Reis, J.P.; Abreu, F.B.E.; Carneiro, G.D.F. Crowdsmelling: A preliminary study on using collective knowledge in code smells detection. *Empir. Softw. Eng.* **2022**, *27*, 69. [CrossRef]

MDPI AG
Grosspeteranlage 5
4052 Basel
Switzerland
Tel.: +41 61 683 77 34

Applied Sciences Editorial Office
E-mail: applsci@mdpi.com
www.mdpi.com/journal/applsci

www.ingramcontent.com/pod-product-compliance
Lightning Source LLC
Chambersburg PA
CBHW040802250926
51850CB00007BA/1061
9783725877218